Nonverbal Communication

Nonverbal Communication

Forms and Functions

Peter A. Andersen
San Diego State University

MAYFIELD PUBLISHING COMPANY
Mountain View, California
London • Toronto

*To my wonderful colleagues with whom the mysteries of nonverbal
communication were revealed:*

Jan Andersen
Larry Barker
David Buller
Judee Burgoon
Joe Capella
John Garrison
Laura Guerrero
Mark Knapp
Jim McCroskey

and to Jan and Kirsten with whom I experience nonverbal communication each day.

Library of Congress Cataloging-in-Publication Data
Andersen, Peter A.
    Nonverbal communication : forms and functions / Peter A. Andersen.
        p.   cm.
    Includes bibliographical references and index.
    ISBN 1-55934-726-0
    1. Nonverbal communication (Psychology).   2. Interpersonal
communication.   I. Title.
    BF637.N66A53   1998
    153.6'9—dc21   98-36051
                                                                CIP

Manufactured in the United States of America
    2 3 4 5 6 7 8 9 QSR QSR 06 05 04 03

Mayfield Publishing Company
1280 Villa Street
Mountain View, CA 94041

Sponsoring editor, Holly J. Allen; production editor, Julianna Scott Fein; manuscript editor,
Andrea McCarrick; art director, Jeanne M. Schreiber; text designer, Leslie Thomas Fitch; cover
designer, Linda Robertson; art editor, Amy Folden; illustrators, Natalie Hill and Cartographics;
manufacturing manager, Randy Hurst. The text was set in 11/13 Minion Roman by G&S
Typesetters, Inc., and printed on acid-free 45# Highland Plus by Malloy Lithographing, Inc.

Contents

Preface

As the twentieth century draws to a close, we find ourselves in the midst of a communication revolution. Telecommunication connects us in a global community, transportation gives us instant access to friends and colleagues, and an exponential increase in research has provided us with valuable insights regarding interpersonal communication and personal relationships. It has been my privilege to be a part of this revolution as a communication researcher and teacher. Although my interests range from the global impact of telecommunication to the subtleties of intimate relationships, nonverbal communication has been the heart of my scholarly and teaching interests over the past twenty-seven years. My primary motivation for writing this book is to share with students my enthusiasm for and knowledge of this vital and interesting subject.

Research Orientation

Nonverbal Communication: Forms and Functions is based on the best and most current theory and research in the field of nonverbal communication. However, it is not a handbook of nonverbal behavior. The literature is too extensive to cover every study in an undergraduate text. The primary goal of this book is to make the huge body of research and theory on nonverbal communication accessible to undergraduates.

Conceptual Organization

Most nonverbal communication texts are organized by the codes of nonverbal communication. This book, however, takes a more intellectually sound and exciting approach; it is organized conceptually around the major functions, purposes, and uses of nonverbal communication. Although attention to the codes of nonverbal communication is necessary to orient the student to this field and its terminology, I adhere to the belief that a conceptual and functional orientation is most engaging, useful, and intellectually rich. The book is organized into three parts with a total of twelve chapters.

Part 1, "The Fundamental Forces of Nonverbal Communication," contains five chapters that introduce and orient students to the field of nonverbal communication. Chapter 1, "Nonverbal Communication and Language," provides the student with a unique, research-based definition of nonverbal communication that is based on the human brain and the structure of message codes. This chapter also outlines nineteen fundamental differences between nonverbal and verbal communication. Chapter 2, "The Body Codes of Nonverbal Communication," introduces the student to the primary ways we communicate: through our physical appearance, body motion (kinesics), eye behavior (oculesics), spatial behavior (proxemics), and touch (haptics). Chapter 3, "The Contextual Codes of Nonverbal Communication," outlines the contexts for all communication and serves as a bridge to the discussion of nonverbal functions; this chapter examines communication environments, chronemics, olfactics, and vocalics. Although culture as an aspect of nonverbal communication is emphasized throughout the book, Chapter 4, "Cultural Cues," provides a foundational understanding of culture and emphasizes the ways in which nonverbal communication is used to convey and maintain culture. The chapter reviews briefly how different cultures employ the codes of nonverbal communication, and it focuses on six dimensions of culture that underlie all differences in nonverbal communication. Chapter 5, "Gender, Sex, and Nonverbal Communication," examines the similarities and differences between male and female nonverbal communication by exploring both biological and cultural differences.

Part 2, "Affective Exchanges: Feelings and Nonverbal Communication," contains four chapters that focus on this fundamental and often ignored macrofunction of human communication, the exchange of emotion, for which nonverbal communication is primarily responsible. Chapter 6, "The Nonverbal Communication of Emotion," (1) introduces the student to the biological and cultural origins of emotion and its expression, (2) examines the face, voice, and body—nonverbal channels of emotional expression—(3) reviews the communication of fifteen emotions (happiness, sadness, fear, surprise, anger, disgust, contempt, pride, shame, embarrassment, guilt, love, jealousy, warmth, and sexual desire), and (4) discusses how emotions are a primary source and outcome of nonverbal communication. Chapter 7, "Communication and Stress," outlines the critical role arousal plays in nonverbal communication and provides an overview of the nonverbal aspects of three forms of communication avoidance: communication anxiety, social anxiety, and touch avoidance. Chapter 8, "Immediacy and Nonverbal Communication," focuses on the interpersonal communication of warmth, closeness, and involvement through the various body codes of nonverbal communication. Chapter 9, "Nonverbal Communication in Intimate Relationships," focuses on nonverbal communication in close relationships by examining the nature of intimacy, introducing cognitive-valence theory—a model of intimacy development—and discussing the dialectics of intimate relationships in the context of nonverbal communication.

Part 3, "Implicit Influence: Nonverbal Cues of Persuasion, Deception, and Power," comprises three chapters that focus on the second major macrofunction of human communication—influence. Chapter 10, "Persuasive Posturing," (1) reviews the often ignored nonverbal aspects of persuasion through an examination of the codes of nonverbal influence, (2) outlines the prominent theories of nonverbal persuasion, and (3) explores how we sell ourselves and the role of nonverbal communication in impression formation. Chapter 11, "Concealing and Revealing," gives an overview of the explosion of research on nonverbal communication. This chapter examines nonverbal deception cues and their inconsistency, individual differences in deception cues, contextual factors, an emerging theory of nonverbal deception cues, and the detection of deception. Chapter 12, "Positions of Power," reviews the codes of nonverbal communication in the context of one of the most central functions of nonverbal communication—the establishment of hierarchy, status, and power.

Other Features

Nonverbal Communication: Forms and Functions has additional features that set it apart from other nonverbal communication textbooks. First, in addition to its emphasis on theory and research, this book provides strategies for students to improve their nonverbal communication. Many textbooks present a disembodied view of research and fail to offer advice on how the student can make changes that will improve her or his skill, sensitivity, or self-presentation. Accordingly, research-based advice is provided on such topics as coping with stress, caring for infants, increasing cultural sensitivity, and establishing intimacy.

Second, the book introduces and advocates such values as improving interpersonal relationships, creating and protecting the environment in which communication occurs, respecting culture and gender in the context of significant differences, and keeping an open mind to new perspectives without losing objectivity about the research findings.

Third, this book offers balanced theoretical positions to illuminate controversies in the social scientific literature. For instance, when considering the origins of nonverbal communication, gender differences, or emotional expression, the text encompasses both biological and cultural perspectives. Similarly, when reviewing culture or gender, the text notes both similarities and differences.

Fourth, each chapter begins with a real story or quote from literature or science to engage the reader. To facilitate comprehension, each chapter ends with a summary of the main points.

Acknowledgments

A number of people made this book possible. I especially would like to thank the ever patient editor of this book, Holly Allen of Mayfield Publishing, whose insistence on quality made this a far better book through numerous revisions. I would like to thank John Daly and Jan Andersen for urging me to write this book in the first place. Thanks to the following reviewers who provided detailed, critical reviews throughout the process of writing this book: John O. Greene, Purdue University; Laura K. Guerrero, Arizona State University; Stanley E. Jones, University of Colorado; Felecia F. Jordan, Florida State University; Sandra M. Ketrow, University of Rhode Island; Valerie Manusov, University of Washington; George B. Ray, Cleveland State University; and Chris Segrin, University of Kansas.

Thanks also to Marie Reynolds, who typed early drafts of the manuscript, and to a host of undergraduate and graduate research assistants who read and reviewed early drafts of the manuscript and gave outstanding feedback from the most important vantage point, that of the student: Molly Boler, Kim Church, Darien Eberle, Shawn Ginwright, Carolyn Gowdy, Victoria Howitt, Matt Johnson, Matt Middlebrook, Sydney Mason, Madge Peverill, Suzie Schuebel, Matt Stevens, Allison Strong, Shira Titen, and Leah Wyman.

1

Nonverbal Communication and Language

Distinctions and Connections

Human beings are talkative creatures. This is particularly true in America, where silence is seldom golden and people feel an obligation to chat continuously. Imagine a party or a date during which nobody talked! Years ago I invited my nonverbal communication class to spend a day at my home in complete silence. Neither sign language nor written messages were permitted. At first, maintaining silence was impossible; it then became merely difficult and eventually possible, but barely so. Humans are nature's linguistic creatures, constantly talking and writing. Even the latest communication technologies favor written and spoken communication. The telephone, internet, fax machine, voice mail, and answering machines are all primarily designed to transmit the "word."

Our verbal, language-using nature obscures an important fact: Much, perhaps most, of our communication doesn't rely on language at all! Although estimates vary, most communication researchers would agree that nonverbal communication is as important as verbal communication. In fact, most researchers believe that nonverbal communication is considerably more important. For example, research on interpersonal attraction suggests that 93 percent of the meaning or impact is communicated nonverbally (Mehrabian & Ferris, 1967; Mehrabian & Wiener, 1967). Scholars have justifiably criticized Mehrabian's methods (see Burgoon, Buller, & Woodall, 1996), but few challenge the basic concept: Nonverbal communication is an extraordinarily powerful form of communication. Birdwhistell, one of the founders of the field of nonverbal communication, estimates that "no more than 30 to 35 percent of the social meaning of a conversation or interaction is carried by words"(1970, p. 158), leaving 65 to 70 percent of the meaning to be carried by the nonverbal channel. A better estimate of the relative importance of nonverbal communication comes from a statistical summary of studies by Philpot (1983), who reports that no more than

1

35 percent of conversational meaning comes from verbal communication. Philpot also reports that nonverbal communication is a particularly potent message in impression formation, emotional expression, and relational communication.

Of course, the exact percentage of meaning carried by nonverbal communication isn't the issue. The important issue is that numerous studies show that all the various aspects of nonverbal communication—body movements, interpersonal distance, touch, facial expressions, and all the other components of nonverbal communication—separately or collectively, are *very* important. Nonverbal communication occurs beside language as a vital part of the communication process. Moreover, although it is an interesting academic exercise to deconstruct the relative impact of these two types of communication, verbal and nonverbal communication co-occur in almost every communication situation. Verbal communication and nonverbal communication, like respiration and circulation, exist side by side as two human processes that are part of the same system.

Nonverbal communication, as described in this book, includes all communication other than language. Language is a uniquely human form of communication that uses arbitrary symbols to convey meaning. These symbols consist of spoken or written words, arbitrary signs, computer symbols, mathematical symbols, or any other sign arbitrarily and definitionally related to its referent. Although some animals such as bees and monkeys do communicate using arbitrary codes, most animal communication is intrinsic and analogic. By contrast, humans in all cultures use language (Brown, 1991).

Nonverbal communication exists *beside language,* yet it is not language. It is present whenever we talk, but it is not talk. Although communication typically employs both nonverbal communication and language interactively, each method of communication derives from a different cognitive system, functions differently, and employs different codes. In this chapter we will examine definitions of nonverbal communication and explore the many differences between verbal and nonverbal communication.

Defining Nonverbal Communication

Differences That Make a Difference

Scholars have encountered several problems in defining nonverbal communication. One problem is that some definitions of communication exclude numerous forms of behavior, particularly nonverbal behavior, from consideration as forms of communication. Second, some scholars have failed to develop sound criteria for determining if a given act is nonverbal, resulting in long lists of potential nonverbal behaviors without any underlying reason for their inclusion on the list. Third, many behaviors are hybrids of nonverbal and verbal cues that make categorization difficult. Fourth, the degree to which a particular message is nonverbal is not always black and white. There is a gray area between verbal and nonverbal communication that sparks legitimate disagreement among researchers. Finally, because verbal communication developed from nonverbal communication, some communication that was once nonverbal and analogic is becoming verbal and digital.

The approach taken in this book is to provide a definition of nonverbal communication behaviors that is based on rigorous criteria for designating a particular action as nonverbal. In all, nineteen unique attributes of nonverbal communication are listed in this chapter, but for now, let's consider a definition based on three primary characteristics: Nonverbal messages include all communication that is *analogic, nonlinguistic,* and typically *governed by the right brain hemisphere* (Andersen, Garrison, & Andersen, 1975, 1979). "Analogic, nonlinguistic, and right hemispheric are all ways of describing an underlying nonverbal coding schema that unites a variety of communication behavior into one system" (Andersen et al., 1979, p. 83). This definition is consistent with Wilden's (1980) position:

> In human communication all non-conventionalized "gesture language," posture, facial expression, inflection, sequence, rhythm, cadence and indeed the CONTEXT within which human communication takes place is a type of analog or iconic communication in which the signal or sign has a necessary relation to what it "re-presents," whereas all denotative, linguistic communication is arbitrary and digital. (p. 163)

Gudykunst, Ting-Toomey, and Chua (1988) offer a conceptually based definition consistent with the definition employed in this book: "While verbal communication is a digital communication process, nonverbal communication is a multilayered, multimodal, multidimensional, analogic process" (p. 118).

Similarly, this book's definition is consistent with the traditional position taken by Watzlawick, Beavin, and Jackson (1967): Analogic communication "is virtually all nonverbal communication" (p. 62). This definition of nonverbal communication is almost identical to Buck's (1984, 1988) "spontaneous" communication system, which is biologically shared, nonvoluntary, right-hemispheric, and nonpropositional. Although this definition departs radically from other conceptualizations of nonverbal communication, to paraphrase Bateson (1972), it is a difference that makes a difference. Purely nonverbal messages are analogic in nature.

Analogic Message Codes: The Basis of Nonverbal Communication

Because analogic codes are the basis for nonverbal communication, it is important to understand the structure of these codes. First, analogic messages have a direct, nonarbitrary, intrinsic relationship to the thing they represent (Andersen, 1986; Watzlawick et al., 1967; Wilden, 1972). Such messages look or sound like what they refer to or represent. A pointed finger directs a person in an obvious direction. Usually, eye contact signals availability for communication. Analogic messages often are an abbreviated action: a clenched fist is an abbreviated punch, and a pat on the back is an abbreviated hug. Even these abbreviated actions directly signify meaning. These meanings are explained by the direct-effects model (see Chapter 8 for more about this model) or what Burgoon, Coker, and Coker (1986) call the social-meaning model of nonverbal communication.

Digital communication, by contrast, indirectly communicates information via arbitrary codes such as language. For example, any word can stand for cat, the English word *cat*, the Spanish word *gato*, or even a made-up word, say, *freem*. Most of you have never heard of the word *freem*, but since I have arbitrarily (for no good reason) chosen it to stand for cats, you will probably picture a cat when you read the word *freem* from this point on. Burgoon (1985b) explains that in digital coding systems,

> the connection between these semantic elements, or symbols, and their referent is arbitrary; there is no necessary or natural connection between the choice of sounds or letters and the thing for which they stand. Put another way, the meaning conveyed by symbols is socially defined rather than being derived from some instinctive meaning. (p. 272)

Analogic means of conveying love might include kissing, spending time together, prolonged eye contact, or smiling; whereas digital methods might entail writing or speaking a message such as "I love you."

A second quality of analogic messages is that each message can take on an infinite number of values or degrees. For example, a smile can range from a slight smirk to a broad grin. A vocal utterance can range from a whisper to a shout. Interpersonal distance can range from actually touching another person to being many feet or many miles apart. By contrast, digital codes possess just two values: present or absent, on or off, talking or silent. As such, digital messages are easy to repeat or reproduce, whereas analogic communication cannot be precisely replicated or easily relayed through several people with any degree of accuracy (Wilden, 1980).

This book takes the position that by definition, nonverbal communication is analogically coded. Digital messages are linguistic or verbal, and messages with both analogic and digital properties are probably some combination of verbal and nonverbal messages. The distinguishing feature of nonverbal messages is the analogic code not the channel. For example, gestures can be either nonverbal or verbal depending on the nature of the code (Andersen, 1991; Feyereisen, 1987; McNeill, 1979). Gestures that are used for emphasis—to show size, distance, or shape—and those that recreate bodily actions, such as pantomimes, are nonverbal. Note, however, that American Sign Language is linguistic and verbal (Poizner, Klima, & Bellugi, 1987). Likewise, the voice, which is usually associated with verbal communication, is nonverbal when it communicates analogically through grunts, screams, giggles, or vocal inflection during speech. The voice is involved in verbal communication only when it uses digital codes such as spoken words.

Table 1.1   Channels of Linguistic and Nonverbal Communication

CHANNEL	LINGUISTIC MESSAGES	NONVERBAL MESSAGES
Kinesics:		
Gestures	Emblems, American Sign Language	Adaptors, illustrators
Facial movements	Lip reading, facial emblems	Spontaneous expressions
Voice	Talk, speech, language	Paralinguistics, vocalizations
Haptics	Braille, vibratese	Pats, hugs, strokes, squeezes
Music	Musical notation	Singing, melody, pitch
Space	"Keep Out" or "Welcome" Signs	Interpersonal distance
Physical appearance	T-shirt slogans, labels	Style of dress, physical attributes, facial recognition
Objects	Emblematic shapes, flags, road signs	Shapes, environments
Media	Verbal dialog, subtitles, letters, E-mail	Pictures, video, movies

The channel of communication is not a defining characteristic of nonverbal communication; rather, it is the type of message code that makes a meaningful difference (Table 1.1).

The definition of nonverbal communication used in this book holds that purely nonverbal communication is analogic. Of course, it is rare that a message is purely verbal or purely nonverbal. Many messages fall in gray areas between these two message systems. Likewise, most communication is a combination of verbal and nonverbal communication. For some time, scholars have recognized that nonverbal communication has analogic properties (Birdwhistell, 1970; Koneya, 1977; Watzlawick et al., 1967; Wilden, 1972). Burgoon (1985b) argues that "many, (though not all) nonverbal behaviors better qualify as analogic coding. They are nonarbitrary, or natural behaviors that are continuous and infinite in form rather than discrete and finite" (p. 27). However, Burgoon, Buller, and Woodall (1996) argue that some nonverbal behaviors, such as the A-OK sign, are digital and arbitrary. Gestural emblems like the A-OK sign are primarily digital and arbitrary, and thus are usually considered a form of verbal communication, according to the perspective taken in this book (see figure 1.1; also see Andersen, 1979; Koneya, 1977). It is important to recognize that gestural emblems represent gray areas, and some scholars are more likely to label them as a form of nonverbal communication while others may think they are really a form of verbal communication conveyed through a gestural modality like sign language.

As we will learn, all messages were probably analogic at one time. Thus, an emblem like the kill sign, made by running one's first finger across the throat, is quite analogic because it looks like what it stands for. Interestingly, this same sign might be used in a television studio or by a waterskier to signal "kill"; in these cases, the sign is becoming more arbitrary and digitalized. Such signs as the peace sign and nodding the head are now almost entirely arbitrary, and the origins of their meaning are fading with time.

Burgoon, Buller, and Woodall (1996) maintain that a number of nonverbal behaviors are discrete and symbolic, such as kisses, hairstyles, or postural shifts. The position held in this book is that these behaviors exist on an analogic continuum; there are an infinite number of hairstyles or hair colors and infinite degrees of kissing, from a peck on the cheek to a deep, lengthy kiss. These behaviors should be classified as nonverbal because they are many-valued, analogic acts that are largely relational in nature. The difference that makes a difference is that nonverbal behaviors use analogic codes that are processed by analogically oriented cognitive structures, whereas verbal communication employs digital codes and is processed by digitally oriented cognitive structures.

The Nonlinguistic Nature of Nonverbal Communication

A second, defining characteristic of nonverbal communication is its nonlinguistic aspect. Almost thirty years ago, Eisenberg and Smith (1971) put it well when they stated, "The real distinction between verbal and nonverbal communicative behavior lies in the system by which action is organized. Verbal behavior is organized by language systems, whereas nonverbal behavior is not" (p. 20). Language is an arbitrary, indirect system that is symbolic. Symbols stand for other things but may bear no natural relationship to the things they represent. Nonverbal communication is a natural, direct system that is not symbolic. Nonverbal signs naturally represent the things they stand for. This idea is consistent with the position that nonverbal communication is analogic and verbal communication is linguistic (P. A. Andersen et al., 1979). Indeed, Wilden (1980) contends that "natural language is the most highly organized form of digital communication" (p. 170).

Some scholars believe that many linguistic properties appear in nonverbal codes since some nonverbal codes are discrete and semantic (Burgoon 1985b). Here again, there are definitional disagreements as to what constitutes nonverbal communication. Head nods and peace symbols, by my definition, are linguistic, verbal forms of communication even though they employ a kinesic (body language) or pictorial modality. One should not assume that behaviors are nonverbal simply because they employ the face or hands—a problem with many non-criterial definitions of nonverbal communication. The position taken in this book is that behaviors must be analogic and nonlinguistic to qualify as nonverbal communication. Indeed, it is the unique character of nonverbal communication that necessitated a new set of research and theory separate from linguistic research and theory. As Siegman and Feldstein (1987) observe:

> The concern with nonverbal communication is precisely a result of the increasing realization that there is more to communication than language. Infants communicate before they have even the rudimentary form of language and it is not unreasonable to assume that nonverbal communication predated verbal communication in the history of mankind as well. It will simply not do, therefore, to formulate a model of nonverbal communication based on verbal communication. (p. 4)

The Neurophysiological Basis of Nonverbal Communication

Perhaps the most compelling evidence of the difference between verbal and nonverbal communication comes from the field of neurophysiology, the study of the human brain and nervous system. Results of this research are summarized in an article by P. A. Andersen et al. (1979) that maintains, "Analogic, nonlinguistic, and right hemispheric are all ways of describing an underlying nonverbal coding schema that unites a variety of communication behaviors into one system" (p. 83). This nonverbal system is primarily governed by the right brain hemisphere. P. A. Andersen et al. (1975, 1979) reviewed research on brain damage, split-brain patients (individuals whose corpus callosa are severed to prevent severe epileptic seizures), stutterers, and people with no neurological disabilities, concluding that nonverbal skills, including spatial relations, interpersonal touch, body motions, perceptions of clothing and objects, environmental sounds and music, are primarily governed by the right brain hemisphere. The right hemisphere excels at configurational, nonverbal tasks, including melodic and vocalic qualities, facial expressions and recognition, and spatial perception and adjustment (Andersen, 1986; Bogen, 1977; Ogden, 1989).

Research on communication deficits of brain-damaged persons and split-brain persons is particularly useful for identifying the neurophysiological distinction in the processing of verbal and nonverbal communication (for a complete review see P. A. Andersen et al., 1979). Severe damage, such as strokes or gunshot wounds to a particular part of the brain, results in lost communication functions. When the injury is to the left brain hemisphere, patients lose the ability to speak, read, and understand language, leading researchers to conclude that the left hemisphere governs verbal and linguistic communication. In similar injuries to the right brain hemisphere, patients lose the ability to recognize familiar faces, to comprehend facial expression, to understand vocal inflections, to make sense of space and distance, and to create or understand music, leading to the conclusion that the right hemisphere governs nonverbal communication. People with split brains have their corpus callosa (the nerve fibers that connect the right and left hemispheres) severed, leaving the right and left brain hemispheres out of

Which face looks happier? (See box on page 10.)

contact with one another. Because the left visual field, left ear, and left side of the body are connected to the right brain hemisphere and the right visual field, right ear, and right side of the body are connected to the left brain hemisphere, researchers can selectively communicate with one brain hemisphere and not the other. The left visual field, the left ear, and the left hand can easily recognize objects and melodies but cannot name them since the right hemisphere has little linguistic ability. The right hand, right ear, and right visual field can identify verbal messages but have difficulty recognizing objects, faces, vocal intonation, and melody. The research is consistent from these groups of brain-damaged persons as well as from studies of normal persons, leading to the conclusion that nonverbal communication is governed by the right brain hemisphere and verbal communication by the left brain hemisphere. Test this for yourself. Examine the photographs of the three faces on page 9 and the line drawings of the two faces above. Answer the questions beneath each set of faces and then refer to the box "Nonverbal Communication and the Brain" on page 10.

In contrast to other definitions of nonverbal communication, P. A. Andersen et al. (1979) propose that certain behaviors normally labeled nonverbal are actually verbal if they employ a digital, linguistic, left-hemispheric code. Hand emblems, sign languages, lip reading, facial emblems, Braille type, musical notations, and slogans on T-shirts are forms of verbal communication because they use arbitrary symbols and are processed in the left brain hemisphere (Andersen, 1986; Poizner et al., 1987; Wheeler, 1994). Although this perspective differs from

Chimeric faces: Which
face looks most like the
top face—the middle one
or the bottom one? (See
box on page 10.)

(a)

(b)

(c)

some other definitions of nonverbal communication, it is supported by literally hundreds of neurophysiological studies (for summaries of this research see Andersen, 1986; P. A. Andersen et al., 1979; Bogen, 1977; Kimura, 1973; Murphy & Venables, 1970; Poizner et al., 1987). Moreover, evidence indicates "that there is relatively fixed [neural] architecture associated with the language module, although it is clearly spread across a number of different cortical and sub-cortical areas of the left hemisphere" (Marshall, 1984, p. 229). In other words, language is hardwired into the left hemisphere for most human beings.

This does not mean that the right hemisphere has no language ability. Stacks and Andersen (1989) summarize research that shows that although language is

Nonverbal Communication and the Brain

Chimeric faces are composites of two left halves or two right halves of a human face. Which face on page 9 do you think looked most like the top face (a) (an unretouched photograph of a person's face)? Most people select the bottom face (c), which consists of the two right halves of the person's face. The middle picture (b) is a composite face made from the two left halves of the person's face. You see the right half of a person's face in your left visual field, and the information you receive in the left visual field is processed in your right brain hemisphere. Because your right brain hemisphere is much better at processing nonverbal information, including facial recognition, you derive a disproportionate share of information from the right half of someone's face. Thus, the right-halves composite (the bottom photograph (c)) looks more like the actual face (the top photograph) than the left-halves composite (the middle photograph (b)).

For the same reason, most people think the bottom line drawing on page 8 is happier than the top face. Just as we recognize faces in our left visual field and with our right brain hemisphere, so we recognize facial expressions more strongly from a person's right side of the face, because it appears in our left visual field and is processed in our right (nonverbal) brain hemisphere.

primarily left-hemispheric, the right hemisphere has a rudimentary conception of language. Analogously, a pitcher can throw with either hand but usually can excel with only the dominant hand. So too with communication. The left hemisphere is specialized for language. Although the right hemisphere is specialized for nonverbal communication, it does have the linguistic ability of a pre-schooler.

Several criticisms have been targeted at the neurophysiological definition of nonverbal communication as being right-hemispheric. Some critics have argued that the two hemispheres are interdependent and that as such the hemispheric distinction is false. While Burgoon (1985a) maintains that "there is some hemispheric lateralization in the reception and production of verbal and nonverbal stimuli, with the left hemisphere typically more dominant for verbal signals and the right hemisphere for nonverbal ones" (p. 366), she also criticizes models that rigidly dichotomize brain function:

> However, there is growing evidence that the two hemispheres are highly interdependent in the processing of social information. The left-right distinction may therefore be more a matter of style differences, with the left showing a superiority in handling digital, symbolic, and rational stimuli and the right showing a superiority in encoding and interpreting analogic, visual gestalt, and emotional material. This means that the form in which a nonverbal signal is codified or perceived (for example, digital, iconic, analogic) may influence the manner in which it, and possibly its linguistic accompaniment, is comprehended and stored in memory. (pp. 366–367)

This is an excellent point that is consistent with current neurophysiological research. Indeed, P. A. Andersen et al. (1979) maintain that "we do not have a split brain, but a whole brain with highly specialized parts" (p. 75). One textbook suggests a change in the way we conceive of the brain.

> Some texts use *hemispheric differences* to refer to processing differences; however, we prefer *hemispheric style.* For most people, the left hemisphere of the brain is responsible for *most* of our verbal communication. This side of the brain is specialized in an abstract, logical, and analytical way which is best used in the analysis of language. The right hemisphere . . . is specialized for spatio-temporal, gestalt, emotive forms of communication for which nonverbal is best suited. (Hickson & Stacks, 1993, p. 13)

The human brain is exceedingly complex and even capable of varying its own neural structure. Research suggests that the typical pattern of brain organization separates messages into linguistic and nonlinguistic categories and processes them in the hemisphere best suited for that code and cognition.

A second criticism of the neurophysiological approach to defining nonverbal communication is that some nonverbal behaviors originate in and are controlled by the left hemisphere not the right (Burgoon, 1980; McNeill, 1979). Critics maintain that many nonverbal behaviors such as rhythmic gestures and certain paralinguistic (vocalic) features are actually processed in the left hemisphere. Although this criticism has validity, it ignores the complex relationships among pairs of communicators during interpersonal interaction. Gestures accompanying speech are mainly right-handed and left-hemispheric (Vaid, Bellugi, & Poizner, 1989). This phenomenon is explained by the fact that during face-to-face interaction, right-handed gestures are picked up in the *receiver's* left visual field and right hemisphere. The human brain evolved in such a way that important gestural information can be processed by the receiver's left visual field and nonverbal right hemisphere without interfering with the verbal, left hemisphere's decoding of talk (Jaffe, 1978; Kimura, 1973). Moreover, many gestures originate in the right brain hemisphere, particularly those that do not accompany speech (Kendon, 1983). According to Bavelas, Chovil, Coates, and Roe (1995), "interactive gestures assist the dialog itself rather than serving semantic or syntactic functions" (p. 404). In short, they are nonlinguistic and nonverbal.

As discussed previously, one type of gesture, the emblem (for example, the peace sign or hitchhiker's thumb), is usually a part of the verbal/left hemisphere system as are signs in American Sign Language. Koneya (1977) has shown that emblems are part of the verbal communication system because they are actually words that have precise dictionary meanings. Emblems, along with Morse code, semaphores, smoke signals, and sign languages, are primarily verbal, left-hemispheric communication codes. Indeed, extensive research (Poizner et al., 1987) shows that left-hemispheric injuries disrupt all sign language and emblematic communication, whereas right-hemispheric injuries have little effect on these abilities. Poizner et al. (1987) conclude their book, *What the Hands Reveal About the Brain,* by stating:

> Right hemisphere damage disrupts spatial relations but spares syntactic ones; left hemisphere damage disrupts the use of space for syntactic relations but spares its use for spatial relations. Taken together these data suggest that the left cerebral hemisphere in humans may have an innate predisposition for the central components of language independent of language modality. (p. 212)

A third alleged problem with using neurophysiological criteria to define nonverbal communication is that many perceptual phenomena do not conform to a left-brain/right-brain split. Burgoon (1985b) asserts that rhythmic patterns and free movement are received by the left hemisphere. Research has shown that rhythm is received and processed by the left hemisphere only when speech sounds are involved but in the right hemisphere when the sounds are nonverbal (P. A. Andersen et al., 1979; Kimura, 1973; Murphy & Venables, 1970). Burgoon (1985b) also argues that "the right hemisphere receives such 'speech tied' phenomena as note pitch and volume" (p. 271). This is true, but rate, pitch, and volume are nonverbal aspects of speech called vocalics (Burgoon & Saine, 1978), or paralinguistics, and are a form of nonverbal communication (P. A. Andersen et al., 1979). Buck (1984) summarizes research that shows that affective tone of voice is a right-hemispheric function. However, Buck (1988) maintains that much of nonverbal communication is processed in subcortical brain regions of both hemispheres but particularly of the right brain hemisphere.

Scholars have defined nonverbal communication in many ways. The requirement, in this text, that nonverbal behavior should be analogic, nonlinguistic, and right-hemispheric, is a narrower definition and suggests that a number of previously labeled nonverbal behaviors are actually verbal. These verbal behaviors include emblematic road signs, lip movements, some gestures such as emblems, musical notation, sign language, and Braille writing. However, some behaviors that at one time were labeled verbal would be considered nonverbal according to this definition. These nonverbal behaviors include some types of speech, such as greetings and curses, most phatic (emotionalized or ritualized) communication, singing, and of course vocalizations and paralinguistics (Table 1.1). Unlike the other definitions reviewed in the following section, this text's definition is based on properties of the message code itself, not on the channel or modality in which it occurs. It is irrelevant whether language is encoded with the voice, the hands, or the word processor—it is still language. Variation in the message code is the *difference that makes a difference* and the definitive criterion of nonverbal communication used in this book.

Other Definitions of Nonverbal Communication

No disciplinary consensus has formed around a single definition of nonverbal communication. Thus, it is important to examine other definitions so that you the reader can understand and appreciate other approaches and develop your own definition.

Five groups of definitions have been offered by communication scholars. The most common definition considers all communication behavior other than words to be nonverbal communication (Burgoon & Saine, 1978; Eisenberg & Smith, 1971; Harrison, 1974; Knapp, 1972; Mehrabian, 1972; Rosenfeld & Civikly, 1976). The fact that no recent texts primarily employ this definition (not even by the authors just cited) suggests that this definition may be losing favor. This definition classifies communication based on superficial criteria—the absence or presence of words—rather than on the distinction of message codes (for detailed criticisms see P. A. Andersen et al., 1975; Knapp & Hall, 1997; Noller, 1984; Richmond, McCroskey, & Payne, 1987). Words are but one class of rhetorical or symbolic messages; they are typically verbal but do not always fall in the verbal/linguistic domain. Words themselves have a number of nonverbal, paralinguistic aspects. Swearing, cursing, grunting, and singing, as you will learn, are produced orally but are really nonverbal forms of communication.

A second common approach that rarely appears in the literature today is to list various behaviors that allegedly constitute nonverbal communication (Barker & Collins, 1970; Benson & Frandsen, 1976; Leathers, 1976). The drawback to this approach is that it provides no underlying criteria for what behaviors actually belong on the list (P. A. Andersen et al., 1975).

A third approach defines nonverbal communication according to the sender orientation (Motley, 1990, 1991). This approach advocates that only intentional, symbolic behaviors should be considered communication. The problem is, most nonverbal communication behaviors are in fact spontaneous, biologically based, and nonsymbolic (Andersen, 1991; Cappella, 1991). Indeed, the sender-orientation definition of communication would exclude most of the behaviors described in this book. An even more serious problem with this approach is that many, perhaps most, messages are sent without intentional, deliberate encoding. Finally, it has been shown that senders, receivers, and even researchers cannot determine intent! We have no idea if a smile, for example, is symptomatic of a private feeling, a spontaneous communication behavior, or an intentional, symbolic act. As Bavelas (1990) has clearly stated regarding intentionality, "It is amazing to think how long we have let ourselves be dominated by a concept that its proponents admit they cannot adequately define or measure" (p. 595).

A fourth approach that continues to receive attention is that of Wiener, Devoe, Rubinow, and Geller (1972), who attempt to distinguish between nonverbal behavior and nonverbal communication. They define nonverbal communication as consisting of arbitrarily coded, intentional, and symbolic actions. Moreover, these behaviors must exist in verbal contexts. This is certainly a restrictive definition that would exclude most nonverbal behavior described in this book. Indeed, this definition would limit the study of communication to arbitrary, digital, linguistic forms of communication, which are defined in this book as verbal! Some researchers have criticized Wiener et al. (1972) for their inappropriate use of a verbal model to define nonverbal communication (P. A. Andersen et al., 1979; Ellyson & Dovidio, 1985; Siegman & Feldstein, 1978). Others have criticized this type of definition because it is very difficult to determine, even by interactants, which behaviors are intentional (Burgoon, 1985a; Harper et al., 1978). Certainly this definition is too restrictive for our purpose and, in fact, may actually exclude all nonverbal behavior from the realm of communication.

A less restrictive definition of nonverbal communication based on message orientation is provided by Burgoon and her associates (Burgoon, 1980, 1985a; Burgoon, Buller, & Woodall, 1996). Her definition is widely known and used by many scholars. According to this perspective, nonverbal communication is limited to behaviors that "are typically sent with intent, are used with regularity among members of a social community, are typically interpreted as intentional, and have consensually recognizable interpretations" (Burgoon, Buller, & Woodall, 1996, p. 13). "The message orientation, with its focus on the code rather than encoders and decoders, rules out idiosyncratic mannerisms, behaviors that do not occur with any regularity, actions or attributes that are merely informative . . . and activities that do not regularly evoke the same interpretations across members of the social system engaging in them" (Burgoon, 1980, p. 180).

Burgoon's message orientation is based on the premise that the nonverbal system is an intentional system, derivative of language and containing some of the same basic elements as linguistic codes. Several problems devolve from this definition: (1) The requirement that nonverbal communication consist of typically intentionally sent actions eliminates most nonverbal actions from the realm of communication, including proxemic behaviors—an area in which Burgoon herself conducted research (see Burgoon & Jones, 1976; Burgoon & Aho, 1982)—which are typically unintentional unconscious acts. (2) The requirement that no idiosyncratic behaviors be considered communication would rule out special codes or acts used by subcultures, as well as secret handshakes, expressions, or tokens used by intimate dyads (two-person groups) with special meaning only to that dyad. Clearly, our position is that nonverbal communication can be common to entire cultures or the entire human race or specific to a single dyad. (3) The message orientation is inherently ambiguous because individuals or researchers disagree about what is typically intentional, regularly used, and what behaviors have consistently recognizable interpretations. The requirement that nonverbal communication behaviors be typically sent with intent or typically received with intent is virtually impossible to determine. Indeed, in criticizing another perspective Burgoon (1985a) maintains, "One difficulty with this perspective is that it is very easy to deny intentionality for much of what goes on nonverbally. . . . The question then becomes who arbitrates what was intentional and what was not—the source, an 'objective' observer or who?" (p. 348).

A number of researchers take the position that the receiver determines if communication has occurred. Buck (1984) maintains that "behavior can be defined as communicative to the extent that it reduces uncertainty in the behavior of another" (p. 4). Buck argues that "many of the most interesting findings in the field of nonverbal communication involve influences via such spontaneous behaviors" (p. 5). Malandro, Barker, and Barker (1989) take a similar position that "nonverbal communication will be defined as the process by which nonverbal behaviors are used, either singly or in combination with verbal behaviors, in the exchange and interpretation of messages within a given situation or context" (p. 5). Similarly, Richmond and McCroskey (1995) summarize the receiver-based definition when they write "nonverbal behavior becomes nonverbal communication if another person interprets the behavior as a message and assigns meaning to it" (p. 5).

This receiver-based definition has received criticism. For example, Burgoon, Buller, & Woodall (1989) maintain, "The main objection to this perspective is that it is too broad. . . . It permits treating as communication such involuntary and idiosyncratic behaviors as allergic sneezing and frequent blinking" (p. 16). However, under some circumstances, receivers might obtain meaning from these bizarre actions and treat them as messages. The position taken in this book is clear. *If a receiver obtains meaning from another's action, then communication has occurred. If this action is nonlinguistic and analogic, then nonverbal communication has occurred.*

The final and broadest position defines all behavior as communication (Wilden, 1972). Barker and Collins (1970) even argue that "nonverbal communication is much broader than nonverbal behavior. A room devoid of behaving, living things communicates atmosphere and function. Static clothing communicates the personality of the wearer" (p. 344). These broad definitions have been criticized widely. For example, Burgoon (1985a) argues that to treat all nonverbal behavior as communication "is the least productive, if for no other reason than a pragmatic one. It makes the task of discovering general principles of communication nearly impossible if every facet of human behavior must be accounted for" (p. 348). Certainly, many scholars agree with the position taken in this book that receivers must assign meaning to a particular behavior before it can be called communication.

Differences between Verbal and Nonverbal Communication

What differences exist between verbal and nonverbal communication? Although verbal and nonverbal communication are both parts of human communication and frequently occur simultaneously, they are based on different systems, each with a number of unique properties that are important for the student of communication to understand. Three distinctions between verbal and nonverbal communication have already been introduced:

Principle 1 · Nonverbal communication is an analogic code; verbal communication is a digital code.

Table 1.2   Differences between Verbal and Nonverbal Communication Systems

	VERBAL COMMUNICATION IS:	NONVERBAL COMMUNICATION IS:
Fundamental Differences	1. Digital	1. Analogic
	2. Linguistic	2. Nonlinguistic
	3. Left-hemispheric	3. Right-hemispheric
Origins	4. Primarily culturally based	4. Primarily biologically based
	5. Phylogenetically recent	5. Phylogenetically ancient
	6. Developmentally secondary	6. Developmentally primary
	7. Culturally based system	7. Relatively universal system cross-culturally
Codes	8. Highly notational	8. Iconic
	9. Discontinuous/intermittent	9. Continuous
	10. Unitized	10. Nonunitized
Channel	11. Single-channeled	11. Multichanneled
	12. Awkwardly redundant	12. Simultaneously redundant
Cognition	13. Encoded/decoded discretely	13. Encoded/decoded as a gestalt
	14. Analytic	14. Syncretic
	15. Symbolic	15. Spontaneous
	16. Relatively manipulated	16. Relatively honest
Functional Distinctions	17. Used to convey precise information	17. Used to convey global meanings
	18. Logical and cognitive	18. Affective and emotional
	19. Content-oriented	19. Relational

Principle 2 · Nonverbal communication is nonlinguistic; verbal communication is a language system based on arbitrary meaning.

Principle 3 · Nonverbal communication is processed primarily in the right brain hemisphere, verbal communication is processed primarily in the left brain hemisphere.

In the following section, we will examine sixteen additional distinctions between verbal and nonverbal communication (Table 1.2).

The Origin of Communication

Without much doubt, verbal and nonverbal communication did not evolve at the same time in the species, nor are they acquired simultaneously by individual communicators. This fact is underscored by evidence that verbal and nonverbal communication originated from different systems, which leads us to the next set of differences, based on biology.

THE BIOLOGICAL BASIS OF NONVERBAL COMMUNICATION

Principle 4 · Nonverbal communication is primarily biologically based, whereas verbal communication is primarily culturally based. Most nonverbal code systems are biologically programmed. For example, Ekman and associates (Ekman & Friesen, 1975; Ekman, Friesen, & Ellsworth, 1972) identify a set of basic facial expressions that show little or no cultural variation around the world. Buck (1982, 1984, 1988) demonstrates that the spontaneous, right-hemispheric system is founded on a biologically based set of signals. By contrast, although the capacity for language is innate, verbal and symbolic communication is based on a socially developed, socially learned, culturally shared communication system. This is why some nonverbal communication is universal and pancultural, whereas no verbal codes have been discovered that are universal. Cappella (1991a) shows that the process of stimulus regulation and emotional responsiveness are biological, automated forms of nonverbal interaction. This is not to say that cultural differences are nonexistent in nonverbal communication. Indeed, all cultures communicate at different distances, use different amounts of touch, and gesture somewhat differently, to mention but a few examples. (Chapter 4 includes a detailed discussion of how nonverbal communication displays culture.)

THE PHYLOGENETIC PRIMACY OF NONVERBAL COMMUNICATION

Principle 5 · Nonverbal communication is an earlier genetic development than verbal communication. Scholars who study nonverbal processes now generally agree that nonverbal communication evolved long before verbal communication in the human species (Andersen, 1986; Bateson, 1972; Burgoon, Buller, & Woodall, 1996; Watzlawick et al., 1967). Animals are adept nonverbal communicators, suggesting to some people that nonverbal is an intellectually inferior, lower-level type of communication. But this is not the case. Animals have evolved amazing nonverbal communication systems that entail heat sensors, sonar, great visual acuity, and powerful olfactory sensing. Although the evolution of verbal language has caused nonverbal systems to decay in the human species—for example, our olfactory sense is only 1 percent as powerful as a dog's sense of smell—some forms of nonverbal communication have continued to develop right beside language. As Bateson (1972) maintains:

> The kinesics of men [and women] have become richer and more complex, and paralanguage has blossomed side by side with the evolution of verbal language. Both kinesics and paralanguage have been elaborated into complex forms of art, music, ballet, poetry, and the like, and even in everyday life, the intricacies of human kinesic communication, facial expression, and vocal intonation far exceed anything any other animal is known to produce. The logician's dream

that men should communicate only by unambiguous digital signals has not come true and is not likely to. (p. 412)

The evolutionary primacy of nonverbal communication suggests that we are biologically programmed to attend first to nonverbal signals and to give them greater weight in communication. This appears to be true particularly in times of danger or stress, when we revert to the older nonverbal system. As we will see, nonverbal communication has more personal validity than the more recent, more abstract verbal system (Watzlawick et al., 1967).

THE DEVELOPMENTAL PRIMACY OF NONVERBAL COMMUNICATION

Principle 6 · Nonverbal communication precedes verbal communication in each individual. Long before babies utter their first word or understand the words of others, they can send and receive nonverbal messages. Newborn infants can send and receive basic haptic (tactile), vocalic, kinesic, and olfactory messages (Andersen, Andersen, & Landgraf, 1985; Camras, 1982; Stern, 1980). Burgoon, Buller, & Woodall (1996) maintain that the early importance of nonverbal modes of expression at the crucial and dependent developmental stages from birth into early childhood may contribute to our continued reliance on nonverbal communication systems throughout life. Burgoon (1985a) summarizes considerable evidence of the developmental and phylogenetic primacy of nonverbal communication and concludes, "Given that these behaviors largely precede the acquisition of language, their evolutionary and ontogenetic primacy should make them particularly potent communication vehicles" (p. 356).

THE CROSS-CULTURAL SIMILARITY OF NONVERBAL COMMUNICATION

Principle 7 · Nonverbal communication displays considerable cross-cultural similarities; verbal communication does not. A number of nonverbal actions show substantial cross-cultural similarity. This suggests a biological basis for nonverbal communication, although parallel cultural developmental patterns may account for some of the similarities. In an interesting set of experiments, Ekman and his associates showed pictures of facial expressions to people from different cultures around the world (Ekman & Friesen, 1975). In culture after culture, viewers labeled each facial expression similarly. The facial expression of basic emotions including fear, disgust, anger, sadness, happiness, and surprise showed striking cross-cultural consistency. Eibl-Eibesfeldt (1979) summarizes his own research, which demonstrated that children who are blind from birth exhibit the same expressions of smiling, laughing, crying, fear, and anger as do sighted children, suggesting a biological origin of facial expression.

Some hand gestures also appear to have universal cross-cultural meanings, such as the fist, a sign of anger and aggression, and the open palm, a sign of peace or greeting in most cultures. Frick (1985) reports that prosodic (rhythmic) aspects of the voice are virtually identical in every culture: "There is little evidence for either personal idiosyncrasies or cultural differences in the prosodic communication of emotion" (p. 414).

The cross-cultural similarity of many nonverbal behaviors can significantly aid intercultural communication (although, as we will learn, cultural differences in nonverbal communication can be substantial; see Chapter 4). Smiling, patting one's stomach, frowning, laughing, shrugging, and pointing are messages that can easily communicate when two interactants share no common language. Burgoon (1985a) concludes, "Because of their ability to bridge cultural differences, such nonverbal behaviors have a communicative power lacking from culture-bound verbal languages" (p. 352).

The Distinctive Coding of Verbal and Nonverbal Communication

One of the most basic and important differences between verbal and nonverbal communication is the way they are coded. As we discussed earlier, verbal codes are linguistic symbol systems, with each word bearing an arbitrary relationship to its referent. Nonverbal codes are direct, analogic, sometimes abbreviated signs that have an intrinsic relationship to their referent. Three other properties of nonverbal codes—iconicity, continuousness, and nonunitization—distinguish these codes from the verbal communication system.

ICONICITY

Principle 8 · Nonverbal codes are iconic; verbal codes are notational. Many nonverbal messages are iconic; that is, they directly resemble the object or event they represent (Andersen, Garrison, & Andersen, 1979; Bateson, 1972). Statues, paintings, pantomimes, photographs, and facial expressions are examples of iconic codes because they directly resemble their referent. These codes are processed in the parts of the right brain hemisphere that are specialized for visual, nonverbal codes (P. A. Andersen et al., 1979; Marshall, 1984). According to Bateson (1972), most iconic messages are sent unconsciously and involuntarily. The graphic quality of iconic gestures and behaviors creates vivid, attention-getting messages that are missing from verbal communication (Burgoon, 1985a). Iconic signals tend to be easily interpreted by virtually all receivers cross-culturally because of their intrinsic meaning. Iconic communication is a principal mode of communication in animals and humans. As Wilden (1980) contends, "All non-linguistic communication through the senses, between person and person or person and world, with the single exception of conventionalized signals, involves analog and iconic communication" (p. 163). Writing, numbers, computer language, and Morse code are highly notational systems and part of the verbal domain. Computer icons, a form of nonverbal communication, are used rather than words because they directly resemble the function for which they stand.

CONTINUOUSNESS

Principle 9 · Nonverbal communication is continuous; verbal communication is discontinuous. Purely nonverbal and analogic communication codes are continuous and cannot be turned off (P. A. Andersen, 1984; Eisenberg & Smith, 1971; Richmond et al., 1987). Words come and go and start and stop, but nonverbal and

A person can try to maintain a blank facial expression, like this girl in the picture, but in reality, there are no blank facial expressions. Nonverbal communication is continuous, and the face is always sending messages. What message does this face send?

analogic messages are sent continuously. This is consistent with the receiver perspective explained earlier in this chapter. Nonverbal messages are continuously available to receivers; nonverbal communication begins when receivers assign meaning to these behaviors. Analogic systems cannot be shut off and have no form of negation, whereas digital systems introduce gaps into continuums (Wilden, 1980). It is for these reasons that one cannot choose not to communicate nonverbally (see Andersen, 1991).

There are no blank facial expressions. Attempts to create a blank expression are perceived by receivers as anger, sadness, or withdrawal. The face is continuously sending messages as long as another individual is present to receive them. Likewise, one cannot choose to stand a nondistance from another. The individual is always relatively near to or far from others and communicating through this proxemic system. Similarly, gestures cannot be shut off. Even folded or completely still hands send messages of composure or relaxation. Analogic systems, including nonverbal communication, represent the smallest differences that form a continuum along which all behaviors fall. Some scholars dispute the continuous nature of individual nonverbal behaviors. Richmond et al. (1987) contend, "Individual nonverbal messages indeed do stop. Gestures begin and end. Eye contact begins and ends" (p. 3). But this argument misses the point. Although a particular gesture may have a beginning and an end, the gestural system is continuous.

Nongestures have the potential to signal relaxation or boredom. Similarly, eye contact can begin or end, but the oculesic (visual) channel is continuously sending messages. Little or no eye contact signals boredom, rudeness, introversion, disinterest, and a variety of other messages. Even if you accept the fact that particular nonverbal messages can be discontinuous, most scholars concede that as a "package" of simultaneous messages, nonverbal communication is continuous (Richmond et al., 1987).

NONUNITIZATION

Principle 10 · Nonverbal communication has no basic units; verbal communication is unitized. Whether verbal communication is spoken, signed, written, or computer-processed, the basic unit is the word or the morpheme (the smallest linguistic unit that carries meaning). If a verbal or linguistic message contains less than a morpheme, it has no meaning. Not so with nonverbal communication. Because nonverbal communication is continuous and nonunitized, the smallest segment of nonverbal behavior is potentially meaningful. A picture of a face taken at $\frac{1}{400}$ of a second is still a face and contains a meaningful expression at that point in time. The face in a snapshot is not as meaningful as a videotaped face or a live face because its continuousness is frozen and changes in expression cannot be captured by a single photograph. Nevertheless, any small slice of nonverbal communication may be meaningful because it does not require a complete morphemic unit, as does verbal communication. In her recent summary of nonverbal self-presentation, DePaulo (1992) concludes, "It is impossible to regulate nonverbal behavior in such a way that no expression is conveyed. Thus, with regard to its attributional implications, nonverbal behavior is irrepressible" (p. 234). The nonunitized quality of nonverbal communication is why nonverbal analysis and research must abandon the linguistic model that was pioneered by Birdwhistell (1970). He used a linguistic model to study kinesics and established the kine as the basic unit of behavior. Language, however, is a poor model for nonverbal communication, and as such, Birdwhistell's linguistic model has led to no recent nonverbal research. "Unfortunately, kinesic communication is analogic and contains no basic unit of meaning" (P. A. Andersen et al., 1979, p. 85).

Channel Distinctions

A wink, a nod, a comment, a gesture all communicate through different channels. In this section, we will explore how nonverbal communication is multichanneled, inherently redundant, and viewed as a gestalt. Verbal communication is single-channeled, awkwardly redundant, and processed as a discrete unit of meaning.

MULTICHANNELIZATION

Principle 11 · Nonverbal communication is multichanneled; verbal communication is single-channeled. Virtually all nonverbal scholars agree about the multichanneled nature of nonverbal communication (P. A. Andersen, 1984; Burgoon, 1985a;

LaFrance & Mayo, 1978). Most messages contain information in multiple nonverbal channels. For example, extreme excitement can be conveyed verbally with an expression such as, "Wow, I'm excited!" Such excitement may also be accompanied by a multiple set of nonverbal messages including giggles, wide eyes, smiles, clapping hands, running, open postures, jumping up and down, rapid movements, hands covering the mouth, an open mouth, expressive gestures, hugs, and loud or fast vocal utterances, to name only a few possibilities.

Consistent multichanneled messages communicate sincerity, honesty, and believability because each channel provides additional weight to the overall message. Also, it is hard to lie in ten channels, whereas verbal lies are relatively easy to achieve. These are some of the reasons that nonverbal communication is believed over verbal communication. However, this same multichanneled system has the capacity to send simultaneously contradictory messages such as approach and avoidance, ecstasy and guilt, joy and sorrow, or love and hate. Burgoon (1985a) maintains that these multimodal nonverbal messages give both encoders and decoders rich arrays of cues to send or to observe. Such multichanneled messages can both increase precision and increase ambiguity.

SIMULTANEOUS REDUNDANCY

Principle 12 · Nonverbal communication is inherently redundant; verbal communication requires repetition for redundancy. One of the basic principles of information theory (the major theory of information flow in communication) is that repetition and redundancy increase accuracy. Redundancy increases accuracy. Yes, redundancy increases accuracy. But verbal repetitiveness is fatiguing, nagging, and boring even though it increases accuracy. Verbal communication is poorly suited to redundancy because it is a single-channeled type of communication.

Cherry (1966) maintains that if a message "has zero redundancy, then any errors in transmission and reception owing to disturbance or noise will cause the receiver to make an uncorrectable and unidentifiable mistake" (p. 186). Redundancy increases accuracy, (I know you're tired of reading that) because noise, poor reception, and inattention can prevent accurate communication. Redundant messages enhance the probability that one or more will be received, creating communication. As Bateson (1972) demonstrates, redundancy increases the signal/noise ratio and promotes communication.

Nonverbal communication is a highly redundant system. A person who is retreating, cowering, whimpering, hunched over, with a fearful facial expression is redundantly signaling fearfulness. Nonverbal messages often send simultaneous, multichanneled, consistent messages that are hard for even the most imperceptive receiver to miss. Therefore, nonverbal communication is a highly efficient system. Nonverbal communication can also signal relational messages between interactants. If someone always walks the other way, avoids eye contact, turns away, hides his or her face in your presence, negative relational messages are being clearly communicated. Bateson (1972) suggests that "human communication which increases redundancy in relationships between persons is still preponderantly iconic and is achieved by means of kinesics, paralinguistics, intention movements, actions, and the like" (p. 423). In short, nonverbal communication enables communication to overcome noise and define relationships with others.

Cognitive Differences

How do people mentally process and make sense of verbal and nonverbal messages? Research shows that the cognitive, or mental, processing of verbal and nonverbal communication is quite different. We have already reviewed research showing that verbal communication and nonverbal communication are processed in distinct neural structures, the left and right brain hemispheres, respectively. But several other important differences exist in the way these two types of messages are processed.

NONVERBAL GESTALTS

Principle 13 · Nonverbal messages are processed as a gestalt; verbal messages are processed discretely. Gestalt processing means that we make sense of an interdependent whole rather than isolated parts. This is the way nonverbal communication is encoded and decoded, as a whole. It is likely that multichanneled gestalt impressions are the basis of human intuition. Conversely, single-channeled, discrete verbal messages are the basis of logic.

Nonverbal behavior is decoded as a gestalt. Typically, we do not concentrate solely on, say, a person's feet or vocal pitch to detect nervousness or happiness. We take in the whole picture. Research shows that messages of nonverbal immediacy or warmth are processed as a gestalt. According to Andersen (1985), "It is quite clear that receivers do not count individual behaviors when judging the warmth or immediacy of interactants. Some sort of gestalt impression of immediacy is doubtlessly how receivers operate in real interactions" (p. 12). In a study by Gutsell and Andersen (1980), receivers were shown a videotaped lecture by a person who smiled either a lot, a little, or not at all. Receivers perceived that the person who smiled a lot touched the viewers more, gestured more, and stood closer to the viewers, even though he was actually in a completely still position with his hands out of view. Why did this occur? Receivers look for gestalt patterns in a communicator's behavior. If they receive information in only one or two channels, they *infer* that the other channels are congruent. This demonstrates the gestalt nature of nonverbal processing. Likewise, it is almost impossible not to encode nonverbal messages as a gestalt. Try to express affection with your body and face but not your hands or voice. It is very hard to accomplish.

SYNCRETIC PROCESSING

Principle 14 · Nonverbal messages are processed syncretically; verbal messages are processed analytically. Syncretic cognition is a kind of thinking that takes in the whole picture. It is broad rather than deep and involves synthesis rather than analysis. This is consistent with the broad, synthetic nature of right-hemispheric, nonverbal processes and the gestalt nature of nonverbal communication. Tucker (1981) demonstrates that the right hemisphere is associated with imaginal, holistic, syncretic cognition. Buck (1982, 1988) maintains that nonverbal, right-hemispheric processes are associated with syncretic cognition that is sensitive to simultaneous, holistic information as opposed to sequential, verbal stimuli. By contrast, analytic processes, including verbal processes, are logical, sequential, and involve in-depth examination of a single idea or message. Logical analysis involves sequential reasoning through verbal premises to a rational conclusion.

The left hemisphere seems to be specialized for dealing with things in sequence, such as causal relations or logical problems. The logical, sequential nature of verbal, linguistic, and mathematical processes predisposes the brain to process these types of information in the part of the brain best suited for such tasks—the left hemisphere (P. A. Andersen et al., 1979, p. 75).

So, two distinct types of cognitive processes coexist and cooperate during mental activity. Each is specialized for processing a particular aspect of a message.

SPONTANEOUS ENCODING

Principle 15 · Nonverbal messages are spontaneous, whereas verbal systems are symbolic. Nonverbal actions are not symbolic. Most are signs or signals that are spontaneously produced. Burgoon (1985b) describes this quality well:

> A final special property of nonverbal coding is its spontaneity, actual and perceived. Just as reception of nonverbal behavior is rapid and direct, so may its encoding be relatively uncontrolled and quick, especially for those behaviors that have intrinsically derived meaning. A byproduct is the popular belief that nonverbal behaviors are more spontaneous and thus more "truthful" than verbal expressions. (p. 279)

Buck (1984, 1988) has described the spontaneous communication system in detail. Spontaneous communication is not symbolic because the referent is not arbitrary or socially determined. Spontaneous communication is made up mainly of signs that have a natural intrinsic relationship to their referent. Similarly, spontaneous communication is an automatic or reflexive response, is nonpropositional, and is related to the right hemisphere (Buck, 1984). According to research by Palmer and Simmons (1995), "nonverbal behaviors may be selected and enacted as a result of cognitive processing that occurs below the level of consciousness" (p. 131).

Symbolic communication, perhaps unique to humans and the province of the left hemisphere, is verbal and linguistic. Buck (1984, 1988) has shown that symbolic communication is socially shared and learned, has arbitrary relationships to referents, and is processed in the left brain hemisphere. As Andersen (1991) concludes, "Symbolic messages have arbitrary relationships with their referents and are the creations of human beings in specific cultural contexts. Spontaneous messages have a natural, biological relationship with their referents" (p. 317).

AUTHENTICITY

Principle 16 · Nonverbal communication is perceived to be more genuine and is more likely to be believed than is verbal communication. A final cognitive quality of nonverbal communication is its greater believability. Numerous studies show that people rely more on nonverbal communication than on verbal communication for social meaning, although the relative contribution varies from study to study (Amabile & Kabat, 1982; Archer & Akert, 1977; Hegstrom, 1979; Mehrabian & Wiener, 1967; Philpot, 1983). Indeed, Philpot's (1983) meta-analysis of twenty-three studies on the relative communicative contribution of verbal and nonverbal channels demonstrates that slightly over 30 percent of the variance in meaning is attributable to verbal communication, with the remainder being attributable to nonverbal communication or an interaction among the verbal and nonverbal. Philpot (1983) reports that "the most fascinating finding of this meta-analysis is a consistent lack of a strong interaction between the verbal and nonverbal channels. Forty-five measures of these interactions are available in the literature. Only two of these interactions account for more than twenty percent of the variance" (p. 42). Evidently, most receivers process verbal and nonverbal communication separately and seldom use both together to make judgments.

Why do people believe the nonverbal channel more than the verbal channel, especially when the two conflict? First, because nonverbal communication is more spontaneous and less intentional than verbal communication, it is intuitively interpreted as more genuine. Sayings such as "The eyes are the window of the soul" show the extent to which nonverbal communication is believed to show one's "true feelings." Second, because the nonverbal system was an earlier, more basic genetic system, nonverbal perceptions may be neurophysiologically more powerful and basic. After all, virtually all communication among animals proceeds through nonverbal channels and language is a fairly recent evolutionary development. Third, because nonverbal communication is present and active in interaction with newborns, humans learn to place stock in nonverbal communication long before verbal communication is interpretable. Finally, the multi-channeled nature of nonverbal communication may give it more power as an individual seeks confirmation through redundant cues. As Bateson (1972) states, "It is understandable that an early (in an evolutionary sense) method of creating redundancy would be the use of iconic part-for-whole coding" (p. 420).

Adults trust nonverbal communication more than spoken communication, especially when the channels conflict. Burgoon (1985a) summarizes: "Adult reliance on nonverbal cues is greatest when the verbal and nonverbal messages conflict. . . . Congruency among channels just makes the verbal and nonverbal coding systems more equal in their contribution to meaning" (p. 347). Evidently, people put considerably more faith in the nonverbal message when the two channels conflict as a means of guarding against verbal deception (see Chapter 11).

The pattern with children is somewhat different. Obviously, infants are entirely reliant on nonverbal communication because they cannot yet send or comprehend linguistic messages. However, interpersonal research clearly shows that once language develops, children rely primarily on *verbal* cues rather than on *nonverbal* ones (for summaries of this research see Burgoon, 1985a; Knapp, 1978). The onset of language provides such a powerful tool for children that for years they take comments literally, relying almost exclusively on verbal communication. This is why young children have difficulty with sarcastic messages, in which the nonverbal message (for example, tone of voice, facial expression) undercuts the verbal message. Blanck and Rosenthal's (1982) summary of research suggests that children are most reliant on verbal cues, less reliant on vocal cues, and much less reliant on visual cues and tend to take verbal communication literally in the case of sarcastic messages. Andersen, Andersen, Murphy, and Wendt-Wasco (1985) report that only 14 percent of kindergartners could understand a teacher's sarcasm as compared with 39 percent of third-graders, 52 percent of sixth-graders, 55 percent of ninth-graders, and 66 percent of twelfth-graders. Indeed, grade level explained almost 30 percent of the variance in understanding sarcasm. Similarly, television research shows that young children do pretty well with verbal information but have relatively more difficulty with nonverbal communication (Hoffner, Cantor, & Thorson, 1988). Together, these findings suggest that during preschool and the early elementary school years, children are primarily tuned in to verbal communication and steadily increase their ability to integrate nonverbal communication. By adulthood, nonverbal communication is the primary channel of communication.

Functional Distinctions

During interaction, we use our two major communication systems in different ways. The nonverbal system is more globally meaningful, basic, emotional, affective, and essential in all forms of communication regarding our relationships with others. Verbal communication is more precise, contains more information, and is logical and content-oriented.

THE INHERENT MEANINGFULNESS OF NONVERBAL COMMUNICATION

Principle 17 · Nonverbal codes are more useful for global meanings and attributions; verbal communication is more useful for precise and factual information. The old saying "A picture is worth a thousand words" has been supported by communication research and theory. Global meanings regarding the situation, the relationship, the environment, or another person's state are gleaned more readily through nonverbal communication. Burgoon (1985a) concludes, "Verbal cues are more important for factual, abstract, and persuasive communications, whereas nonverbal cues are more important for relational, attributional, affective, and attitudinal messages" (p. 347). A highly technical lecture on research or theory must use verbal communication to convey abstract information. But understanding a new situation or the psychological state of a friend will be more meaningful if it is based on nonverbal observations. Wilden (1972) claims that nonverbal and analogic communication "is pregnant with meaning whereas the digital domain of signification is relatively barren" (p. 58).

What happens when we must translate nonverbal cognitions to verbal codes or verbal cognitions to nonverbal codes? Watzlawick et al. (1967) claim that there can "be no translation from the digital to analogic modes without great loss of information, but the opposite is also extraordinarily difficult: to *talk about* relationships requires translation from the analogic into the digital mode of communication" (p. 66). Wilden (1972, 1980) maintains that it is virtually impossible to translate the rich meanings of nonverbal and analogic messages into a digital or verbal form without great loss of meaning. Similarly, translation from the digital/verbal into an analogic/nonverbal message usually involves a great loss of information and precision.

THE AFFECTIVE PRIMACY OF NONVERBAL COMMUNICATION

Principle 18 · Nonverbal messages are most useful for affective and emotional information; verbal messages are most useful for logical and cognitive information. To figure out a puzzle or to pass along detailed plans, verbal communication is clearly superior. Nonverbal communication lacks the precision and syntax to deal with these precise and logical issues. However, when the information involves affect, danger, emotion, or feelings, the nonverbal realm is superior. This may have been an evolutionary development. Before the emergence of language, nonverbal communication was used to communicate fear, anger, love, or other emotion. Even after language evolved, nonverbal expression provided fast feedback as to a person's emotional state and served as a survival advantage.

Recent research suggests that emotions are more than private experiences. Typically emotions are communicated through various forms of overt, direct nonverbal behaviors (for a summary see Andersen & Guerrero, 1998b). Burgoon suggests that the power and directness of nonverbal signals are due to their capacity for direct stimulation while circumventing the cognitive system entirely. Moreover, Zajonc (1984) has summarized considerable evidence which suggests that thinking and feeling are independent, that preferences need no inferences. He has also shown that emotional and nonverbal messages are processed faster than cognitive responses and operate on different neurophysiological and biochemical systems. This is why thinking too much about your romance or your tennis game may be counterproductive; these activities do not usually require considerable thinking, nor do they benefit from too much thinking. Evidence suggests that distinct brain modules may mediate the processes (Stacks &

Andersen, 1989). In short, thoughts are much more likely to be part of the logical/verbal world, and feelings are more likely to be part of the emotional/nonverbal world.

THE RELATIONAL PRIMACY OF NONVERBAL COMMUNICATION

Principle 19 · Nonverbal messages are the primary vehicle for relational communication; verbal messages are the primary vehicle for content communication. Using written or spoken words, try to describe a romantic relationship that has lasted months or years. It is nearly impossible to do without leaving out much of the detail. Watzlawick et al. (1967) maintain that digital language lacks the meaning and semantics to communicate about relationships. Nonverbal, or analogic, communication is well equipped for conveying such relational content. Relationships are primarily a function of shared time and space, of meaningful movements and glances, of touch and smell. All relationships along romantic, status, power, relaxation, or friendship dimensions are best conveyed nonverbally. Bateson (1972) maintains:

> When boy says to girl, "I love you" he is using words to convey that which is more convincingly conveyed by his tone of voice and his movements; and the girl, if she has any sense, will pay more attention to those accompanying signs than to words. (p. 412)

Duck (1988) supports the notion that eye contact, smiling, and other nonverbal cues best communicate liking. The development of most relationships proceeds by these nonverbal, analogic means. As Eliza Doolittle said to Henry Higgins in *My Fair Lady,* "Don't talk at all, show me. When we sit together in the middle of the night, don't talk at all, just hold me tight. Anyone who's ever been in love can tell you that, this is no time for a chat."

The Complementary Relationship between Verbal and Nonverbal Communication

This chapter has focused on differences between verbal and nonverbal communication. However, these two systems work *beside* one another and share many characteristics. Both nonverbal communication and verbal communication complement one another in most cases. They are both governed by cultural rules and by laws of nature. Both verbal communication and nonverbal communication are influenced by culture and designed to perform many of the functions described in this book: to display culture and gender, to send emotion, to signal arousal and anxiety, to send messages of warmth, intimacy and immediacy, to persuade, to deceive, and to dominate. Although this book focuses on the role played by nonverbal communication in the service of these functions, always remember that most things are accomplished through the complementary interplay of verbal and nonverbal communication.

Summary

Although humans are talkative creatures, nonverbal communication may play a more important role than verbal communication in human interaction. The relative proportion of verbal versus nonverbal communication isn't very important; the important point is that nonverbal communication is a crucial, and often ignored, part of the communication process. Moreover, nonverbal communication coexists beside language and virtually always accompanies language.

This book defines nonverbal messages as all communication that is analogic, nonlinguistic, and governed by the right brain hemisphere. Other differences also distinguish verbal from nonverbal communication. Compared to verbal communication, nonverbal communication is a more basic, biologically based system, more widespread in living things, and an earlier development, both in the history of the species and each individual human.

Verbal communication and nonverbal communication represent different code systems. Nonverbal codes are analogic, iconic, continuously available, and nonunitized. Verbal codes are digital, notational, discontinuous, and unitized into words and morphemes. Verbal and nonverbal communication differ in channel capacity. Nonverbal communication is multichanneled, in both production and reception, and is simultaneously redundant. These properties may account for the relatively large impact of nonverbal messages in human communication.

Cognitively, nonverbal communication typically is encoded and decoded simultaneously and as a gestalt. It is processed holistically and syncretically. Verbal communication is encoded and decoded symbolically, intentionally, discretely, and analytically. As such, nonverbal communication is perceived as being more believable than verbal communication.

Finally, nonverbal communication and verbal communication perform different functions. Nonverbal communication is more meaningful and is the primary vehicle of interpersonal and relational communication. Verbal communication is more precise and information-laden and is the language of logic as well as the primary carrier of content-oriented communication. Paradoxically, although nonverbal and verbal systems are extraordinarily different in form and function, they necessarily coexist, co-occur, and collaborate in the process of human communication.

2

The Body Codes of
Nonverbal Communication

THE HUMAN BODY captivates us. It is hard to think of an activity in which the human body is not the center of attention. People are evaluated by how their bodies look. Sexual attraction is based in large part on bodily appearance. Sports consist of battling bodies. Television, movies, and magazines, in particular, are dominated by images of the human body. These images of the body analogically communicate without language to form powerful impressions (see Chapter 1). As Morris (1985) observes in his book, *Bodywatching:*

> Nothing fascinates us quite as much as the human body. Whether we realize it or not, we are all obsessed with physical appearances. Even when we are engaged in a lively conversation and seem to be engrossed in purely verbal communication, we remain ardent body watchers. By the time we are adults we are all highly sensitive to the tiniest changes in expression, gesture, posture, and bodily adornment of our companions. We acquire this sensitivity in a rough and ready fashion, through intuition rather than analysis. If we took the trouble to make a more analytic study of body appearances we could become even more sensitized to them, and could avoid some of the pitfalls into which our intuition sometimes leads us. (p. 7)

This chapter provides an introduction to the body as a communication medium. Across the millennia, the body has provided humans, and other animals, with the primary vehicle for communication. Whether conscious or unconscious, intentional or unintentional, symptomatic, spontaneous, or symbolic, human communication is transmitted through a set of meaningful codes that observers make sense of and interpret (Andersen, 1991; Motley, 1990, 1991). Codes form the basis of nonverbal communication. In later chapters you will learn how the body performs many important communication functions, but first, this chapter will explore five codes of the body: *physical appearance; kinesics,* or body movement; *oculesics,* or eye behavior; *proxemics,* or interpersonal spatial behavior; and *haptics,* or tactile communication.

Along with language, these nonverbal codes of the body provide the substance of human communication. Understanding these basic forms or codes of nonverbal communication behavior is essential to understanding communication. You may be surprised how much you already know about nonverbal communication; however, a thorough understanding of these nonverbal codes can make you far more effective in understanding and sending messages in everyday interaction.

Physical Appearance

It is said that a person has only one opportunity to make a first impression. It has also been shown that our physical persona has a major impact on other people's initial impressions of us. Our sex, clothing style, race, age, ethnicity, stature, body type, and mood all reveal our physical persona. Right or wrong, receivers of this initial physical information make attributions about our attractiveness, competence, moral character, personality, social status, and warmth and friendliness. (For more on this topic see Chapter 10.) Of course, these judgments are often based on stereotypes, and stereotypes can be wrong. But stereotyping others is an inevitable human process, a shortcut to evaluate other people before more information is available. Uncertainty-reduction theory suggests that during initial acquaintance, we are highly motivated to increase our certainty and familiarity with a person during interaction (Berger & Calabrese, 1975), and we use every possible cue that provides information about that person. Because physical appearance cues are so obvious, they serve as the primary source of information during initial interaction to reduce uncertainty.

Imagine a recent college graduate trying to get a job in a corporation or government agency. How would a potential employer evaluate a physically fit, attractive, appropriately dressed, well-groomed applicant compared to an overweight, unattractive, sloppily dressed, unkempt applicant? It would be no contest. Many of us would register only positive judgments about the first applicant's motivation, intelligence, character, and reliability. Of course, appearances can be deceiving, but that fact is almost beside the point. A communication perspective recognizes that subjective impressions by receivers are all that really matter. As Jackson Browne sings, "It's who you look like, not who you are." A series of television commercials featuring tennis star Andre Agassi make the same point: "Image is everything."

In our postmodern world, our self is embedded in a set of artifacts and body images that say "who we are." Critics justifiably worry about a world in which substance has been replaced by image, in which essence has yielded to illusion.

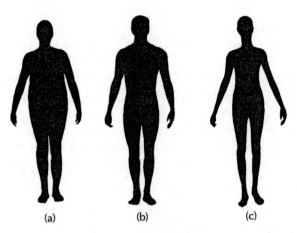

The (a) endomorph,
(b) mesomorph, and
(c) ectomorph.

(a)   (b)   (c)

The fact is that we have moved through the looking glass into a world where reality is loosely tied to outcome and perception rules supreme. The popularity of bodybuilding and fitness, fashionable clothes, makeup, designer labels, and such status symbols as homes and cars is more tied to their communication potential and image-creation value than to the intrinsic worth of fitness, fashion, or fanciness.

As a student of communication, you might find these observations obvious. You may think that everyone dresses to communicate, that image is value. Surprisingly, many choices made by people have little to do with the symbolic value of appearance. Years ago, Aiken (1963) revealed that clothing choices are made for a variety of reasons other than image, including economy, conformity, and comfort. Morris (1977) suggests that, historically, clothing has also performed the functions of modesty and protection. Moreover, Andersen (1992b) contends that clothing is situationally appropriate, because clothing enhances one's positive qualities, conceals one's negative qualities, and makes a personal statement consistent with one's desired image.

Similarly, the shape of one's body sends an important message to other interactants. Sheldon (1940) originally classified people into three general body types: *endomorphs* are rounded, soft, heavy people; *mesomorphs* are angular, muscular, athletic people; and *ectomorphs* are linear, thin, underweight people. In fact, various combinations and degrees of body types are possible, so that most people don't fit neatly into a single category, yet research has shown that discrimination exists against some body types, particularly endomorphs, who are often perceived as lazy, sloppy, slow, jolly, stupid, and unattractive (Andersen & Singleton, 1978; Spiegel & Machotka, 1974; Wells & Siegel, 1961). These stereotypes have persisted for decades and are true not only for adults but for children (Portnoy & Gardner, 1980) and even elderly adults (Portnoy, 1993). Ectomorphs, particularly male ectomorphs, are perceived as nervous, frail, weak, and sickly but also studious and intelligent (Andersen & Singleton, 1978). Female ectomorphs share some of these

Body Type Survey

PURPOSE: To demonstrate how body type affects behavior and communication.

DIRECTIONS: Fill the three blanks following each statement with one of the twelve words listed below each statement. Although an exact word to fit you may not be in the list, select words that seem to fit most closely.

1. I feel most of the time _____, _____, and _____.

calm	relaxed	complacent
anxious	confident	reticent
cheerful	tense	energetic
contented	impetuous	self-conscious

2. When I study or work, I seem to be _____, _____, and _____.

efficient	sluggish	precise
enthusiastic	competitive	determined
reflective	leisurely	thoughtful
placid	meticulous	cooperative

3. Socially, I am _____, _____, and _____.

outgoing	considerate	argumentative
affable	awkward	shy
tolerant	affected	talkative
gentle-tempered	soft-tempered	hot-tempered

4. I am rather _____, _____, and _____.

active	forgiving	sympathetic
warm	courageous	serious
domineering	suspicious	soft-hearted
introspective	cool	enterprising

5. Other people consider me rather _____, _____, and _____.

generous	optimistic	sensitive
adventurous	affectionate	kind
withdrawn	reckless	cautious
dominant	detached	dependent

(continued)

6. Underline one word out of three in each of the following lines that most closely describes the way you are:

   (a) assertive, relaxed, tense
   (b) hot-tempered, cool, warm
   (c) withdrawn, sociable, active
   (d) confident, tactful, kind
   (e) dependent, dominant, detached
   (f) enterprising, affable, anxious

   SOURCE: Cortés and Gatti, F. M. (1965).

stereotypes but are perceived much more positively than males. Research has shown that female ectomorphs are more shy and fearful about communication. Additionally, the desire of many people, particularly women, to be thin, despite more robust, genetic predispositions and bone structure, has led in recent years to potentially life-threatening eating disorders such as anorexia and bulimia. Mesomorphs are the most positively perceived group because they are perceived as strong, forceful, and healthy and are frequently chosen as leaders. However, mesomorphs may be attributed negative qualities such as vanity and still must cope with the dumb jock stereotype. (For fun, complete the Body Type Survey that appears on page 33.)

Height, particularly for men, is perceived as a positive quality. Tall men are more likely to be hired, offered higher starting salaries, and given more prominent positions (Henley, 1977). Similarly, considerable data suggest that attractive people are perceived much more positively (Berscheid & Walster, 1978) and even afforded a "halo effect"—that is, people transfer their positive evaluations of a person's appearance to aspects of her or his personality. Good-looking people are perceived as more talented, kinder, smarter, more credible, and honest (Adams, 1977; Berscheid & Walster, 1978).

In sum, characteristics such as dress, attractiveness, height, body shape, race, and hairstyle are physical traits (Andersen, 1987) that form stereotypes. Some validity exists for such stereotypes particularly since they can become self-fulfilling prophecies. For example, treating an attractive child as though he or she is more intelligent may eventually produce a more intelligent child, a result that is consistent with other people's expectations (see Rosenthal & Jacobson, 1968). Of course, initial impressions based on physical cues are often erroneous. The wise communicator observes numerous verbal and nonverbal behaviors instead of relying solely on first impressions. Over time, the power of physical appearance attenuates, yielding to personal and relational cues that determine the eventual course of the interpersonal relationship.

Kinesics

Our body is capable of sending hundreds, if not thousands, of messages. The study of communication through body movement is called kinesics, which includes the study of facial expressions, gestures, the interactive synchrony of body movements, and sometimes eye behavior. Most kinesic behavior is analogic and nonlinguistic, when gestures stand for words, as in the case of emblems or sign languages. These are cases when so-called body language really is a language. (See Chapter 1 for a discussion of analogic and nonlinguistic communication.)

Facial Expressions

Perhaps the richest source of emotional information is the face. The face conveys dozens of emotions to other people. Research by Ekman and his associates has convincingly established a basic set of at least six facial expressions that are innate, universal, and carry the same basic meaning throughout the world (Ekman & Friesen, 1975; Ekman, Friesen, & Ellsworth, 1972). As Crosby, Stills, and Nash have sung (probably without the benefit of Ekman's research), "If you smile at me I will understand, for that is something everybody, everywhere does in the same language." Research on children blind from birth by Eibl-Eibesfeldt (1972, 1979) reveals that these children employ very similar facial expressions to those of sighted children, suggesting that basic expressions are not learned but are part of an innate system of communication. Ekman and others have shown that at least six basic facial expressions are pancultural and universal: happiness, sadness, fear, anger, disgust, and surprise. Evidence shows that especially the first four of these facial expressions (happiness, sadness, fear, and anger) are easily identifiable across cultures (for a summary see Guerrero, Andersen, & Trost, 1998). There are, however, subtle cultural differences in the facial expression of some emotions, which we will explore in Chapters 4 and 6.

That facial expressions are most likely to be deployed during interaction demonstrates their communicative function. Indeed, distinct and recognizable facial expressions are fairly uncommon when a person is all alone. In an imaginative series of experiments, Kraut and Johnson (1979) studied the emotional reactions of bowlers and hockey fans. Hidden cameras demonstrated that when the bowlers got strikes, they exhibited little or no expression while facing the pins. When they turned to their friends, however, their faces lit up with smiles and excitement. Similarly, the hockey fans in this study were relatively poker-faced after their team scored a goal, but when they looked at their friends a second or two later, they showed extreme facial happiness. Likewise, research by Fridlund (1991) shows that smiling is primarily a function of other people's presence and not internal emotional states. Indeed, the more involved people are with another person, the more they smile.

Although basic facial expressions are primarily innate, their expression begins to be controlled and managed by cultural display rules as the individual matures. Infants and young children do little to monitor and manage their emotional displays, yet as they mature, they learn that manifesting certain emotions at specific times is situationally or socially inappropriate. They also learn that exaggerating or pretending to feel certain emotions can be functional in certain contexts. During the preschool and early school years, children learn how and when to suppress and manage facial affect. (For more on the expression of emotion see Chapter 6.) Management of facial affect is accomplished through the use of the following five display rules (Andersen, Andersen, & Landgraf, 1985; Ekman, 1978; Shennum & Bugental, 1982):

Simulation: showing feelings when you have no feelings.

Intensification: giving the appearance of more feelings than you actually have.

Neutralization or inhibition: giving the appearance of having no feeling when you really have a feeling.

Deintensification, or miniaturization: giving the appearance of having less feelings than you actually have.

Masking: covering a feeling with an expression of a feeling you are not experiencing.

Although these five display rules are initially employed during the preschool and early school years, they are not typically mastered until much later in life, if at all (for a summary see Guerrero et al., 1998). Most of the research has found that inhibition and deintensification increase as children develop. Interestingly, becoming an adult requires manifesting fewer outward emotions, particularly for men. Unfortunately, failing to express emotions is shown to cause an increase in detrimental physiological reactions, stress, and disease (Buck, 1979).

Gestures

Humans have uniquely dexterous and expressive hands. Not surprisingly, the hands are used extensively for communication. Ekman and Friesen (1969b) divide hand gestures into three broad categories: *adaptors,* touching behaviors that reveal internal states such as anxiety or nervousness; *emblems,* gestures with explicit meaning and dictionary definitions; and *illustrators,* nonverbal gestures that accompany speech.

There are three types of adaptors: *self-adaptors, object adaptors,* and *other adaptors* (sometimes called alter adaptors) (Ekman & Friesen, 1969b). Self-adaptors, or self-touching behaviors, such as scratching an itch, wringing one's hands, or pushing a strand of hair from one's eyes, are used to comfort oneself, cover or protect oneself, preen or groom one's body, send sexual signals, and alleviate nervousness (Morris, 1977). Object adaptors are nervous behaviors that involve the manipulation of objects such as cigarettes, drinks, wedding rings, and watches. These adaptors can also signal boredom. Other adaptors involve adjusting or grooming others. These behaviors are common among all primates, including humans. Parents are particularly likely to use other adaptors such as hair grooming, lint removal, or buttoning a child's coat.

Emblems, like spoken words, have specific, recognized meaning within a culture. Called speech-independent gestures by some researchers (Knapp & Hall, 1997; Morris, 1977), emblems such as the hitchhiking sign, the A-OK sign, the upraised middle finger, and the peace sign have explicit verbal meanings within a given culture. Although classified as nonverbal communication by some researchers (Burgoon, Buller, & Woodall, 1996; Ekman, 1976; Knapp & Hall, 1997), as discussed in Chapter 1, other researchers claim that emblems are linguistic, verbal forms of communication that take the form of gestures rather than spoken or written words (Andersen, Garrison, & Andersen, 1979; Koneya, 1977; McNeill, 1985).

The most common type of gestures are illustrators, arm and hand movements that accompany the flow of speech but usually cannot stand alone. Ekman and Friesen (1972) identified eight kinds of gestures commonly used during speech. *Batons* are gestures that are used to emphasize a particular word or phrase. Watch the batons used by public speakers, particularly political candidates, such as chopping or punching gestures that coincide with the words they accent in their speech. *Ideographs* are gestures that sketch or trace the path of an idea or relationship. An economist may show the decline of unemployment by drawing an imaginary graph in the air. A communication professor may say "As anxiety increases, performance decreases" while raising one hand and lowering the other. *Pointers,* or deictic movements, point to an object, place, or event. For example, a parent may say "Clean up your room" while pointing in the direction of the room, or a teacher may point when calling on a student in class. *Spatials* are movements that depict size or distance relations. A fisherman spreading his arms to show the size of his fish or a basketball coach gesturing by rapidly pushing her hands apart while saying "Spread the defense" are examples of spatials. *Rhythmic movements* are gestures that depict the rhythm, pacing, or timing of an event. For example, a person speaking about the chronology of events in a murder case may gesture to indicate when each event took place; similarly, a band leader may signal the tempo of a song with rhythmic gestures. *Kinetographics* are movements that depict bodily actions or a nonhuman physical action. Examples would include a surfer demonstrating how to keep one's balance when riding a particularly large wave or an eyewitness imitating the motions of the involved parties at a crime scene. *Pictographs* are movements that draw a picture of the referent in the air. The classic example is a man tracing the hourglass shape of a woman's body in the air. Likewise, if the previously mentioned surfer gesturally described the height and shape of a wave, she or he would be using a pictograph. A person indicating the physical topography of a region by sketching in the air

In every culture, people use gestures. Pointing is an example of an illustrator,
a type of gesture, or nonverbal hand movement, that accompanies speech.

would also be employing a pictograph. Finally, the eighth type of illustrators are
emblematic movements, which employ a gestural emblem that is synonymous
with a statement. Saying "You're dead" while symbolically slitting one's own
throat, extending one's middle finger while saying "Up yours," or making a circular motion next to one's head while saying "He's crazy" are examples of emblematic movements. Moreover, Ekman and Friesen (1972) correctly point out
that these eight kinds of illustrators are not mutually exclusive but can occur
simultaneously or fit into several categories.

Gestures are both innate and learned. They are used in all cultures, tend to
be tied to speech processes, and are usually automatic. Gestures are so habitual
that communicators continue to gesture while talking on the telephone, even
though they are invisible to their interaction partner. Speech and thought may be
facilitated by gestures, which explains their close association with speech and their
left-hemispheric origin in the brain. Some experts even believe that speech and
gesture evolved simultaneously as primary means of linguistic communication
(Jaffe, 1987; Jaffe & Anderson, 1979).

Interactional Synchrony

One of the most intriguing aspects of kinesic behavior is how two individuals
move almost as one as they interact. This phenomenon, called body synchrony,

matching, postural echoes, reciprocity, or body congruence, has been observed by many scholars, although these are not equivalent terms (see Burgoon, Dillman, & Stern, 1993). Communication is like a dance in which partners engage in complex actions without stepping on one another's literal or metaphorical toes. Our rhetoric reveals that we are intuitively aware of such rhythms. When we're out of rhythm with someone we speak of being "on a different wavelength," being "out of sync," having "bad vibes," and "being rubbed the wrong way." Positive interactions are described as being "in tune," "clicking," and "hitting it off together." Scheflen (1972) has shown that interactants often assume parallel postures and move synchronously, particularly when they're in rapport with one another. Condon and Ogston (1966) showed that people in rapport move together at up to forty-eight beats per second! Teachers often note that entire classes can be congruent and synchronous, indicating the students are in tune with one another or the teacher (Thompson, 1973). Even when very large groups of people congregate, synchronous action often takes place. Imagine, for example, church members sitting, standing, and kneeling together at certain times during a service or football fans doing the wave in a stadium or clapping in sync to a "Deeee-Fense" chant. Although synchrony research has been criticized on methodological grounds (McDowell, McDowell, & Hyendahl, 1980; Cappella, 1981), more recent research shows that synchronized interactions are evaluated more positively (Warner et al., 1987). Burgoon et al. (1993) recommend the term *matching* to refer to behavioral similarity among partners, regardless of the intentionality of partner influence.

Bavelas and her colleagues have also examined a similar communication phenomenon called motor mimicry. This occurs when, for example, a ball is thrown at your unsuspecting friend and *you* duck! If both your friend and the ball are visually accessible, you are likely to duck in the direction that your friend should duck to avoid getting hit by the ball. This behavior constitutes a clear communication message intended to influence the partner's movements. Motor mimicry is a unique communication behavior designed to influence another's actions through nonverbal behavior (Bavelas, Black, Lemery, & Mullett, 1986; Bavelas, Black, Chovil, Lemery, & Mullett, 1988).

Synchrony, reciprocity, and matching are behaviors that provide positive vibrations and interdependent rhythms among communicators. Our ability to synchronize our interactions with other people may be a fundamental way we develop close interpersonal relationships.

Oculesics

During interaction, people focus their attention on the face and eyes of the other person. This is partly due to the fact that the face and eyes are highly expressive, sending myriad messages during interaction. It is also due to the fact that we perceive other people to be "located" just behind their eyes as opposed to other parts of the body. The eyes attend carefully to other communicators because vision, in addition to sound, is one of two primary channels through which humans receive nonverbal messages. But the eyes do more than receive messages; they send messages. While some scholars classify eye behavior as part of kinesics, oculesics is the term others use to label the study of how the eyes send messages. Because there is so much research on oculesics, it is treated as a separate area. Oculesics involves the study of the many nonlinguistic behaviors and messages sent by the eyes, including eye contact, pupil dilation, and eye movement.

Eye Contact

The most important aspect of oculesics is eye contact. Note that there is a subtle difference between eye contact and gazing. Eye contact occurs when *both* people look into one another's eyes; gazing occurs anytime one person looks at another. Interpersonal communication typically requires a considerable amount of eye contact. In fact, conversing without eye contact is perceived in many cultures as rude, disinterested, inattentive, shy, and/or deceptive. Eye contact is an invitation to communicate and an important immediacy cue, a sign of warmth and involvement (see Chapters 8 and 9 for more on this). People attribute many personal qualities to another person based on eye contact, hence the terms *shifty eyes, evil eyes, bedroom eyes, all eyes,* and *sad eyes.* You can *give someone the eye, see eye to eye,* or *take an eye for an eye*—all metaphors that illustrate the centrality of the eyes in interpersonal relationships.

Eye contact performs at least eight functions. According to Kendon (1967), eye behavior (1) regulates interaction by providing turn-taking signals and eliciting or suppressing communication; (2) monitors interaction by receiving numerous messages from one's interaction partner; (3) signals cognitive activity, because eye contact is broken during complex information processing; and (4) expresses involvement, because interest and connection are communicated by looking. Other functions of eye contact are (5) intimidation through the use of prolonged stares and negative facial expressions (Exline, Ellyson, & Long, 1975; see also Chapter 5), (6) flirtation (Silver & Spitzberg, 1992), (7) attentiveness (Fehr & Exline, 1987), and (8) immediacy (Andersen, 1985, see also Chapter 8).

Pupil Dilation

A subtle but important eye behavior that affects interpersonal relationships is pupil dilation. The science of pupilometrics has discovered that individuals' pupils dilate when they experience arousal, positive affect, or attraction for another person (for a review see Andersen, Todd-Mancillas, & DiClemente, 1980; Hess, 1975; or Hess & Petrovich, 1987). For example, research shows that heterosexual males experience more pupil dilation when viewing photographs of women than of men, but homosexual males experience more pupil dilation when viewing

The smile is a universal expression of happiness that transcends culture and age. Smiles occur often during interpersonal interaction and tend to be reciprocal, as illustrated by this grandmother and child.

photographs of men (Hess, Seltzer, & Schlien, 1965). Such research has been used extensively in the advertising and marketing industries to test consumer preferences.

Even more surprisingly, research has discovered that pupil dilation is unconsciously perceived during interaction and results in increased attraction (Andersen et al., 1980; Hess, 1975). That is to say that if your romantic partner's pupils are dilated, your attraction to your partner may be heightened. Doubtlessly, this is part of the reason why moonlight, candlelight, and soft light from a fireplace increase romantic attraction.

Several studies have suggested that although the effect of pupil dilation on attraction is statistically significant, the effects are fairly small. Despite some methodological shortcomings of the study, Hensley (1991) reports that pupil dilation has a significant effect on attraction although the difference constitutes less than one point on a ten-point scale. Andersen et al. (1980) conducted a more detailed analysis by using a multi-item, multidimensional measure of attraction. They report that pupil dilation has a significant effect on social attraction and physical attraction but not on task attraction (the degree to which a person enjoys working on a task with another person).

This same study reports that the size of these effects is small, accounting for only 2 to 3 percent of a person's judgments of physical attraction. Nevertheless, *every* study conducted to date has revealed a statistically significant effect for pupil dilation. And, of course, the cumulative effect of various subtle nonverbal cues can have a large effect on interpersonal attraction.

Perhaps the most remarkable study in this series was conducted by Hess and Goodwin (1974), who showed participants two photographs of a mother holding her baby. Both photographs were identical in all respects except that in one photograph the eyes were retouched; thus, in one photograph the mother's pupils were dilated and in the other constricted. Participants were asked, "Which mother loves her baby more?" Students unanimously chose the mother with dilated eyes! However, few could explain why. Most misattributed the source of their impressions by saying, "Her face is more pleasant," "She's holding her baby closer," or "She has a warmer smile." Pupil dilation is one of several subtle, unconscious nonverbal cues that can repel or attract us to other individuals. This is another example of how nonverbal communication is not only analogic and nonlinguistic but also at times unconsciously communicated.

Eye Movements

Eye movements can mean many things. A solid body of research suggests that lateral eye movements (LEMs) to the left are associated with nonverbal thinking and the right brain hemisphere (as described in Chapter 1). Rightward LEMs are associated with verbal, linguistic, and left-hemispheric activity (Bakan, 1971; Bakan & Strayer, 1973; Gur & Gur, 1977). Other studies, however, have failed to consistently replicate these studies (Ehrlichman, Weiner, & Baker, 1974; Ehrlichman & Weinberger, 1978). Researchers who subscribe to an approach called neurolinguistic programming (NLP) have a similar perspective (Bandler & Grinder, 1979), that is, that certain eye movements are associated with certain kinds of thought. As Knapp and Hall (1997) maintain, the scientific community has generally been skeptical of the NLP approach. At present, research suggests a tendency, particularly for males (Bakan, 1971), to look left when employing right-hemispheric visual or spatial thoughts and to look right when using left-hemispheric, linguistic cognitions.

Proxemics

The study of communication through interpersonal space and distance is called proxemics. Space is a powerful metaphor for interpersonal relationships. In relational rhetoric, we say "I feel closer to her than ever before," or "He seems so distant," or "They just need a little space in their relationship." Scholars have examined several areas of human spatial behavior, including territoriality, crowding and density, and personal space.

Territoriality

If someone sat at "your desk" or parked in "your parking space," you might be upset or at least wonder why this person failed to regard it as yours. The study of territoriality isn't limited to humans. Animals of all types occupy and maintain territory to defend themselves, protect their young, and conserve their food supply. Humans occupy and defend territory for much the same reasons. Indeed, the Fourth Amendment to the U.S. Constitution affirms "the right of the people to be secure in their persons, houses, papers, and effects" as a fundamental cornerstone of the Bill of Rights.

To defend our territory we employ an elaborate series of defensive signals. Some employ verbal warnings such as "no trespassing," "no soliciting," or "beware of dog" signs designed to discourage intruders. Others defend their territory with barriers such as gates, fences, walls, doors, and locks. These barriers are sometimes referred to as *boundary markers*. People even defend temporary space, such as library tables, classroom desks, stadium or theatre seats, and lunch tables. Research suggests that people rarely use verbal communication to defend temporary space (Sommer, 1967a, 1969); instead, they use physical objects as "markers" (see Becker, 1973), such as leaving coats on theatre seats, blankets on bleachers at football games, and books, purses, or backpacks on classroom seats or cafeteria tables. These types of markers are sometimes referred to as *central markers* because they are placed in a central location within the territory. Markers must appear to intentionally designate territory. Several of my own unreported experiments have found that a full cup or can of soda can reserve a space in a university cafeteria for over an hour but that a half-full cup rarely works longer than ten minutes, probably because it is perceived as someone's garbage rather than a territorial marker. Tenure, the length of time a person occupies a place, also helps lay claim to territory. Students who regularly occupy the same table in the cafeteria or library often get upset when someone sits at "their table." Although I don't assign seats in my classes, students are quick to establish their territory and return to it day after day. If an unperceptive student occupies "another's" seat, the affected student often appears angry, upset, or disoriented as he or she searches for a new seat. Territory becomes a status symbol and is defended against intrusion, as in the case of Archie Bunker's famous favorite chair. In a more serious vein, even the homeless claim territorial rights under bridge overpasses and on steam vents. Gang members defend their territories against intruders, and invasion of gang territory can result in violence (see Chapter 12 for more on these issues).

Crowding and Density

When lots of people occupy our environment, we may feel crowded due to our subjective feelings of having our space invaded. Density is an objective measure of the number of people per square foot or square mile. Generally, perceptions of crowding are related to the density of a space, but not always. People from some environments such as parts of Asia or urban areas throughout the world may not feel as crowded as their American or rural counterparts under similar density levels. Moreover, attendees of such events as rock concerts, the Rose Parade, and the Super Bowl expect and even desire high density levels without experiencing the negative feelings associated with crowding.

Aiello (1976) examined children in four-person groups at various grade levels in a small room (4 × 21 feet) and a large room (10 × 12 feet). At all grade levels, students characterized the small room as more crowded, less comfortable, and more negative than the large room. Aiello, Epstein, and Karlin (1975) studied identical dormitory rooms occupied by either two or three residents. Students in the three-person rooms felt more crowded and less satisfied than those in the two-person rooms. Moreover, physiological stress tests (measuring chemicals in the urine that indicate stress) showed increased stress levels for the students in the more- versus less-dense rooms. The results, however, did not show a disadvantage in work productivity in the socially dense environments.

Research has shown that crowding can result in social pathology and criminal behavior. Galle and Gove's (1979) studies of juvenile delinquency in Chicago revealed that density explains significant increases in delinquency independent of other factors such as poverty or education. In a study by Dean, Pugh, and Gunderson (1975), military personnel in high-density settings had more accidents than those living in less-dense settings.

Calhoun (1962) showed that crowding in rat populations produces miscarriage, violence, homosexuality, and eating disorders. Do such behavioral changes occur in human populations? Although behavioral changes are not as extreme in humans, the tentative answer is yes (see Baum, Davis, & Valins, 1979; Sadalla, 1978).

Personal Space

Wherever we go, whatever we do, we are surrounded by an invisible bubble called our personal space. The bubble in North America has a radius of about 3 feet and is slightly egg-shaped, being larger in front. The bubble is invisible but is recognized as an interpersonal and psychological reality. When individuals penetrate this invisible bubble, reactions are generally negative. The exceptions, of course, are friends, lovers, and family members, who have much freer access to us.

Hall (1968) maintains that in North America there are four zones of interaction that indicate the type of relationship that exists between interactants. The closest zone, *intimate distance,* extends from bodily contact out to about 18 inches. Typically, the only people allowed within this zone are intimate friends and family members. An exception to this rule are small children, who have yet to learn about personal space boundaries; whether relations or not, small children are free to penetrate adults' personal space zone and often climb or crawl right over adults.

The distance at which most of our interactions occur, *casual/personal distance,* extends from about $1\frac{1}{2}$ feet to 4 feet from one's body. This distance, not coincidentally at about an arm's length, makes touch difficult and defines interactions that occur in this zone as relatively nonintimate. Andersen and Sull (1985) have also shown that people with an aversion to touch maintain even greater distances that are "out of touch" with potential interactants.

The third zone of interaction is *social-consulting distance,* which extends from about 4 to 8 feet. Business people, salespersons, and professors typically use social space to convey an aura of professionalism and avoid creating feelings of spatial invasion or the impression of an intimate relationship. Social-consulting distance also occurs between most people during group interaction or business meetings.

The final zone, *public distance,* extends from about 8 feet and beyond and is reserved for the president and other high-ranking officials, public speakers, celebrities, and executives. The secret service gets noticeably agitated when the president wades into a crowd to shake hands, because the protective buffer of the public interaction zone is eliminated, creating a security problem. Public speakers maintain public distances not only to signify their role as the center of attention, but to create better visual access for their audience. Celebrities gain status and protection from distancing the public, yet like executives and elected officials, they risk "losing contact" with their audiences, organizations, and constituencies with too much distance. Executive privacy, although advantageous in many respects, can result in loneliness, social isolation, and poor information flow (Andersen & Bowman, 1990; Kanter, 1979; Mehrabian, 1976).

When personal space is invaded, an interactant will seek to restore a comfortable, relationally appropriate distance through a variety of means, including retreats, changes in body orientation, reductions in immediacy, and the use of body buffers. A number of studies have shown that interactants will retreat and depart if invaded by a stranger (Russo, 1967; Sommer, 1969), particularly if the stranger is male. Similarly, people orient themselves away from an invading stranger, literally giving her or him the cold shoulder rather than a sensitive front loaded with multisensory inputs. Invasions of space also result in compensatory responses in other channels such as reductions in eye contact (Andersen, 1985; Burgoon & Jones, 1976). These compensatory reductions in immediacy (more on this in Chapters 8 and 9) are an attempt to reduce the overall intimacy of an encounter. Finally, invaded interactants will use body buffers such as boxes, purses, briefcases, or even folded arms to protect vital body parts and ward off spatial invaders. Buffers and other compensatory responses are almost always nonverbal, analogic behaviors. Rarely do people resort to language to defend their territory.

Of course, the closest interpersonal distance is no distance, or actual touch. Tactile communication, or haptics, a highly intimate personal code, is examined next.

Haptics

The incredible power of touch is obvious to people the world over. The embrace of a close friend, the stroke of a lover's hand, the firm handshake of a business associate, the warm hug of a family member in a time of bereavement communicate with an intensity that other forms of communication lack. Perhaps no mode of human interaction has the same potential to communicate love, warmth, and intimacy as actual body contact. Touch also has the potential to repel and even injure. Today, the news is full of stories of child abuse, sexual harassment, and domestic violence, situations in which touch was used destructively.

The extraordinary, yet subtle, power of touch was illustrated by a study conducted in a college library by Fisher, Rytting, and Heslin (1976). College librarians inconspicuously touched or did not touch students as they returned their library card. After students exited the library, they were asked to complete a survey regarding the library and the librarians. Students, particularly females, evaluated the library and staff more positively when they were in the touch rather than the no-touch group. Similarly, in a bogus ESP experiment in which researchers were actually observing the effects of touch, participants (college women) in the touch (as opposed to the no-touch) group found their experimental partner more responsive, likable, and attractive and indicated they would like to have the same partner again (Boderman, Freed, & Kinnucan, 1972).

Touch can have influential and persuasive effects as well (see Chapter 10 for a more detailed discussion). Willis and Hamm (1980) reported that people were more willing to sign a petition when they were touched by the circulator. Research has also shown that waitresses receive bigger tips when they touch patrons (Crusco & Wetzel, 1984), that psychologists who touch patients obtain greater compliance (Patterson, Powell, & Lenihan, 1986), and that shoppers purchase more when they are appropriately touched (Smith, Gier, & Willis, 1982). One experiment showed that complete strangers are more willing to comply when touch is employed; in this experiment, strangers who found dimes in phone booths were likely to return the coins to their owners (that is, the experimenters) when the request was accompanied by touch than when the request was unaccompanied by touch (Kleinke, 1977).

Numerous studies indicate that touch is beneficial to infant and child development and even necessary for life itself. Infants confined to orphanages who were not touched regularly are often maladjusted, quiet, and unable to learn, gain weight, or mature normally (Frank, 1957; Montagu, 1971/1978; Morris, 1971; Shevrin & Toussieng, 1965). In an experimental study in which premature babies were assigned to either a touch or no-touch group, the touched babies gained 21 percent more weight and were discharged five days earlier than nontouched babies (Scafidi, Field, Schanberg, & Bauer, 1990).

Types of Touch

Of course, not all kinds of touch are created equal or employed for the same purpose. Heslin (1974) separates touch into five major categories based on function, usage, and intensity. The least-intense touch is *functional-professional* (or instrumental) touch, which occurs between physicians and patients, physical therapists and clients, tailors and customers, coaches and athletes, and barbers and customers. Although this kind of touch is done in a professional and businesslike manner, it actually has therapeutic and interpersonal implications. Of course, the types of touch as well as the zones of the body touched are quite limited.

The *social-polite* function of touch occurs in initial-acquaintance situations, business relationships, and formal occasions. The classic example of social-polite touch is the handshake. Of course, too weak or too powerful a handshake can start a relationship off poorly, so the relational implications of these initial touches should not be underemphasized. Social-polite touch conveys recognition of the equality and humanity of the other person and signals inclusion and respect.

The *friendship-warmth* function of touch is simultaneously the most important and the most ambiguous. Because it is less formalized than social-polite touch, the type and amount of touch is negotiated relationally between partners. Too much touch or touch that is too intimate conveys love or sexual interest, whereas too little touch may suggest coldness and unfriendliness and arrest the chance for relational escalation. In private situations, friendly touches have an even greater potential for being perceived as sexual, particularly by males who perceive more sexual connotations with touch (Fromme et al., 1986; Hatfield, 1984; Stier & Hall, 1984).

The *love-intimacy* function of touch is increasingly personal, intimate, and unique. This touch is so special that it can be exchanged only by a few people, such as very good friends, close family members, lovers, and spouses, and it is unique to each particular person. When you lay your hand on another person's cheek, hold hands, or engage in a full frontal embrace, you are conveying intimacy. Typically, this type of touch is nonsexual, although in some relationships, such as romances or marriages, it may blend with sexual touch. High levels of immediacy (discussed in Chapter 8) are conveyed by this type of touch, resulting in increased psychological closeness and warmth.

Sexually arousing touch is the most personal and intimate form of touch. Often reserved for one special person or limited to only a few persons for most people, sexual touch is the most stimulating and the most anxiety-arousing type of touch. Key to this type of touch is mutual consent, a high level of attraction, and a desire to stimulate and be stimulated by one's partner. It has become increasingly common over the past several decades for most sexually active individuals to practice serial monogamy—a relationship that is sexually exclusive until it ends, whereupon the individuals move on to new sexually exclusive relationships (Rathus, Nevid, & Fichner-Rathus, 1993; Sorensen, 1973).

Touch Avoidance

Individuals differ dramatically in the degree to which they like or dislike touch (see Chapter 7 for more on this topic). Touch avoidance (Andersen & Leibowitz, 1978) is the degree to which an individual likes and approaches touch or dislikes and avoids it. Touch avoiders of opposite-sex touch tend to be female and same-sex touch avoiders tend to be male (Andersen, Andersen, & Lustig, 1987). In a related study, Andersen and Sull (1985) interviewed undergraduates regarding their television-viewing preferences. Upon arriving at the interview, students were asked to pick up a folding chair and set it up near the interviewer. Students scoring high on a previously administered touch-avoidance measure set up their chairs twice as far away from the interviewer as students scoring low on the measure. Touch avoiders stay "out of touch" through larger interpersonal distances and tend to manifest less touch and less overall intimacy (Andersen et al., 1987; Andersen & Leibowitz, 1978; Guerrero & Andersen, 1991). Similarly, touch avoiders are less open, less expressive, somewhat lower in self-esteem, and more religious. Moreover, touch avoiders judge people who touch them less favorably than do touch approachers (Sorensen, 1979).

Touch and Relationships

Field research by Guerrero and Andersen (1991) reveals that opposite-sex touch is most likely to occur at the intermediate stages of a relationship, when people are going steady or are engaged. By contrast, at both the initial stages of acquaintance and among married people, touch is dramatically lower. To collect this data, couples were unobtrusively observed while they waited in lines at theatres and amusement parks. After the amount and location of touch were recorded, the couples were approached and the partners were asked to separately complete a series of questions that included items about their relationship. Of course, these findings are limited to public touch, which was observed by the experimental assistants.

More recently, however, Emmers and Dindia (1995) conducted a questionnaire study designed to measure the amount of touch in private situations. Interestingly, the pattern was very similar to the Guerrero and Andersen study, with most private touch occurring during the serious dating and the engagement stages and slightly less touch occurring in the married stage. Research conducted in a field setting, namely an international airport, confirms the two previously discussed studies (McDaniel & Andersen, 1998). Travelers from thirty-seven countries employed the most touch if they were close friends or lovers and less touch if they were initial acquaintances or married couples.

One other recent study has found that partners' public touch is highly correlated (Guerrero & Andersen, 1994). This research indicates that in a public setting, if one person touches her or his partner, the other partner is pretty certain to match the touch level. This pattern holds true regardless of an individual's personality or touch-avoidance level; moreover, it strengthens across more intimate relationship stages. Marital touch, or lack thereof, is almost completely matched between partners. Taken together, these studies reveal that the highest level of tactile matching occurs in long-term, committed relationships such as marriages, whereas the highest frequency of touch occurs in intimate relationships at intermediate or escalating levels of acquaintance.

Touch Taboos

Because touch is such an intimate behavior, much of it is prohibited. Jones (1994) discusses seven forbidden forms of touch in the United States. First, strangers should avoid touch unless they are being introduced or giving aid. Nonfunctional touch by strangers is perceived as excessively intimate and creates negative attributions. Second, hurtful touches should be avoided at all times, even accidental touches. When they occur, an apology is surely required. Third, one should avoid startling another person with touch. For example, some people sneak up behind friends to startle them as a joke, but the friends rarely think it's funny. Fourth, interrupting touches should be avoided. Kissing your wife or husband during a phone call, hugging a child in the middle of his or her homework, or fondling your lover in the middle of a favorite television show are more annoying than affectionate forms of touch. Fifth, one should avoid moving people out of the way with touch alone. People who do this are perceived as rude or pushy. Placing a hand on someone's back while saying "excuse me" as you move through a crowded party is much more acceptable. Even hurrying a child through a door can be perceived as an aggressive violation. Sixth, playful aggression should seem more playful than aggressive. Family members who wrestle should keep this in mind. If someone is in pain or injured, the horseplay has gone too far. Mock strangleholds and armlocks can also be very scary. Nobody should get hurt physically or psychologically during playful aggression. Seventh, critical statements should not be accompanied by negative touch. Such a "double whammy" is unsupportive and unnecessarily aggressive. Finally, I must add that people should refrain from any touch that the receiver dislikes, rebuffs, or asks to be stopped. Remember, *No means no.* Respect people's right not to be touched.

Summary

The human body is fascinating in its ability to communicate without language. During initial acquaintance, the most salient code of nonverbal communication is physical appearance. Right or wrong, other people judge your physical appearance and then make attributions about your social attractiveness, intelligence, motivation, social habits, health, and character based on your appearance. Although these attributions may be incorrect, they are what people believe to be true, and frequently that is all that really matters. Research that examines different body types has found that endomorphs, who are heavy and round, are perceived most negatively within the American culture. Mesomorphs, who are strong and muscular, are most positively perceived, followed by ectomorphs, who are thin, linear people. Tall people, especially tall men, are perceived more positively and tend to hold higher status positions. Appearance can result in stereotypes, which sometimes become self-fulfilling prophecies.

Bodies in motion emit expressions, gestures, and synchronous movements that are examined by researchers studying kinesics. Research has shown that a set of basic facial expressions are universal and cross-cultural. Facial expressions are more than private muscular reactions. Facial expressions of distinct emotions mainly occur in social situations when other people are looking. As we develop and mature, we are less likely to show facial expressions than we did as young children. We learn display rules that simulate, intensify, inhibit, miniaturize, and mask our feelings.

Gestures are both innate and learned. They come in many forms, including emblems, or signs with dictionary definitions; adaptors, or self- or other-touching behaviors; and illustrators, gestures that accompany speech. Like partners at a dance, communicators match, or synchronize, their movement. People who are in rapport or who are attracted to each other are "in sync" or "on the same wavelength." One form of synchrony is motor mimicry, kinesic action designed to be imitated by one's partner.

Oculesics is the study of eye behavior, including eye contact, pupil dilation, and eye movements. Eye contact, the most important aspect of oculesics, is an invitation to communication that signals immediacy and warmth, expresses involvement, sends flirtatious messages, regulates interaction, and monitors communication. Under certain circumstances, eye contact can send intimidating messages. Pupil dilation occurs in dim light and when people experience arousal, positive affect, or attraction. More importantly, people with dilated pupils are perceived as warmer and more attractive, even though pupil dilation is perceived at low levels of awareness. Lateral eye movements are associated with cognition in the opposite brain hemisphere and can even stimulate thought.

Proxemics, the study of communication through interpersonal space and distance, is subdivided into territoriality, crowding and density, and personal space. Territoriality deals with fixed space that individuals own or occupy. Territory is reserved more often nonverbally than verbally through markers and tenure. Crowding is a subjective feeling that a space is overpopulated. Crowding has been shown to result in discomfort, stress, and even violence. Personal space, an invisible bubble that surrounds the body, is divided into four zones. Intimate distance extends from tactile contact to 18 inches and is generally reserved for children and people with whom we share very close relationships. Casual/personal distance, which extends from $1\frac{1}{2}$ to 4 feet, is where most of our daily interactions occur. Social-consulting distance, which extends from 4 to 8 feet, is used for many business relationships. Finally, public distance, reserved for high-ranking officials, public speakers, celebrities, and executives, extends from about 8 feet and beyond. When personal space is invaded, individuals attempt to restore a comfortable distance through retreat, reductions in immediacy, and the use of body buffers.

Haptics, or tactile communication, is the most intimate of the nonverbal codes. It has the power to comfort, arouse, or repel. Touch can produce compliance, create intimacy, and is necessary for healthy child development. The functions of touch include functional-professional, social-polite, friendship-warmth, love-intimacy, and sexually arousing. Touch avoidance is the degree to which an individual likes and approaches touch or dislikes and avoids touch. Touch avoiders maintain greater interpersonal distances, manifest less touch, and engage in fewer intimacy behaviors. Touch peaks in romantic relationships at the intermediate stages. Public touch is highly reciprocal; most people touch their romantic partners about the same amount as their partners touch them. Many forms of touch are taboo, so when a person says "Don't touch," you should respect his or her right not to be touched.

Scoring Your Body Type Survey

DIRECTIONS: Locate the words you selected to fill in the blanks on the survey. Give yourself one point for each word you selected from the endomorphy column; one point for each word from the mesomorphy column; and so on. Total your points for each column. These relative totals should reflect your own body type. Do they? How much do they differ from your perception of yourself?

Endomorphy	Mesomorphy	Ectomorphy
affable	active	anxious
affected	adventurous	awkward
affectionate	argumentative	cautious
calm	assertive	considerate
complacent	cheerful	cool
contented	competitive	detached
cooperative	confident	gentle-tempered
dependent	courageous	introspective
forgiving	determined	meticulous
generous	dominant	precise
kind	domineering	reflective
leisurely	efficient	reticent
placid	energetic	self-conscious
relaxed	enterprising	sensitive
sluggish	enthusiastic	serious
sociable	hot-tempered	shy
soft-hearted	impetuous	suspicious
soft-tempered	optimistic	tactful
sympathetic	outgoing	tense
tolerant	reckless	thoughtful
warm	talkative	withdrawn

SOURCE: Cortés and Gatti (1965).

3

The Contextual Codes of Nonverbal Communication

The sun was hot as I walked with my parents to the car. I climbed in the backseat, folding Father's uniform jacket across my lap. Father set his heavy bag under my feet and then got in beside Mother. I clutched the bright daffodils Father had bought for Mother, their fragrance mixing with the odors of tobacco and rubbing alcohol from my father's coat. I wondered to myself if they would last the twenty-mile drive home.

My knees bumped against the front seat, and I realized I had never sat in the back of this car before. I had always sat next to Mother, where Father now sat. And my legs were too long to fit comfortably. Now that Father was home, I would have to get used to being crowded.

As we drove past the warehouses that lined the river, I noticed that Mother's hands trembled on the steering wheel. Father had never seen her drive, and I knew she wanted to impress him. He didn't seem to notice.

The cool air riffled my hair and brushed my hot cheeks. I leaned my head against the side of the car. Mother and Father were talking, but the wind in my ears made it hard to hear more than a few words. I heard Mother say "Paul" several times and knew she was talking about the day we had heard he was dead. I remembered the sound she had made as she read the telegram and the look on my grandfather's face when he came back to the house from the shed where he had chopped wood for an hour after the telegraph came.

THIS PASSAGE FROM Margaret Rostkowski's (1986) children's novel *After the Dancing Days* describes the return of a girl's father after World War I. The rich nonverbal contexts—the sunlight, the uniform, the smells, the seating arrangements, the passing scenery, her mother's driving, the wind in her ears, and many other nonverbal cues—set the stage for the story. Similarly, nonverbal cues set the stage for understanding all communication.

In Chapter 2, we explored the nonverbal codes of the body. In this chapter, we will examine another type of codes used to send multichanneled nonverbal messages. Contextual codes include macroenvironments, microenvironments, chronemics, olfactics, and vocalics. Like the body codes of nonverbal communication, contextual codes are analogic, nonlinguistic, and multichanneled. Body and contextual codes are also multifunctional and can communicate meaning in the absence of verbal communication. Although body codes provide some context for other nonverbal and verbal messages of communication, the *primary* function of contextual codes is to provide the context for all communication. As discussed in Chapters 1 and 2, it is important to remember that nonverbal communication codes combined with verbal communication are packaged together to form an entire message, and communication messages are sent and received packages, or gestalts.

Context is vital for human understanding. "It has become axiomatic that any human action cannot be successfully interpreted outside of its context. The term 'out of context' has become synonymous with meaningless or misleading" (Andersen, 1989, p. 27). According to Bateson (1972), nonverbal communication provides the context, or frame, for other behaviors.

So much of what is considered "inappropriate" is communication that is out of context: making a sexual proposition to an employee, proposing to an already married person, laughing at a funeral, interrupting another person mid-sentence, arriving late for a special ceremony, or giving a person a compliment in a sarcastic voice. The reason you wait for your turn to talk, put on deodorant, or clean your apartment for guests involves a sensitivity to the contexts of communication. Writing about competent communication, Spitzberg and Cupach (1989) state, "Flexibility involves the adaptation of actions to the physical, social, or relational context . . . competence judgments are intrinsically contextual" (p. 22). Adaptability means adjusting to environmental factors such as heat, noise, group size, climate, and culture. Accordingly, our discussion begins here with the environments in which communication takes place.

Macroenvironments

> After a while one notices something different about otherwise familiar objects: Colors are deeper, metals are shinier, the air is cleaner, and the brilliant California sun seems to jump from every surface. Before long everyday scenes begin to look like technicolor scenes. If London fog can make the English "moody and introspective," what must the California sun do to the Californians? (Hale & Eisen, 1968, p. xiii)

California isn't Illinois. In Southern California, where I live, the sun does affect people, their lifestyle, and their communication. Sitting here in California and reflecting on my youth in Illinois, the differences are extreme. Everything in the Midwest is more subdued and less extreme than in California. Poet Dave Etter (Davis, 1992) of Illinois writes:

> Here in . . . Illinois
> I'm living in the middle,
> standing on the courthouse lawn
> in the middle of town
> in the middle of my life
> a self-confessed middle brow
> a member of the middle class
> and of course Middle Western
> the middle, you see, the middle
> believing in the middle way.

The larger environmental context, called macroenvironments, affects every interaction in numerous ways. For years, scholars have reported that the climate of a region exerts considerable impact on communicative behavior. It was Hippocrates who noted:

> I hold that Asia (Minor) differs widely from Europe in the nature of all its inhabitants and all its vegetation . . . the one region is less wild than the other, the character of the inhabitants is milder and more gentle. The cause of this is the temperate climate, because it lies toward the east midway between the risings of the sun, further away than is Europe from the cold. (Biswas, 1984, p. 6)

In his seminal book on climate, Ward (1918) reported that in Aristotle's day, climate (*klima*) referred to the inclination of the earth toward the sun, commonly called latitude. Klima, according to Ward, is highly correlated with development. Ward maintains that in both the United States and Europe, northerners are more serious, industrious, enterprising, pessimistic, and mature, whereas southerners are more cheerful, genial, impulsive, generous, easygoing, and lazy.

Thomas Jefferson described southerners as being much more "fiery, voluptuary, indolent, unsteady, zealous for their own liberties but trampling on those of others, generous and candid" than northerners (O'Brien, 1979, p. 3). The great philosopher and social observer of the early 1800s, Alexis de Tocqueville reported, "The American of the South is fond of grandeur, luxury, and renown, of gaiety, pleasure and above all, of idleness; nothing obliges him to exert himself in order to subsist" (1945, p. 411).

In his classic study of civilization, Huntington (1945) reported that mid-latitudes produce the highest efficiency and productivity, whereas high and low latitudes produce reduced efficiency due to their extremes in temperature. In a major study of world economics, John Kenneth Galbraith (1951) noted that a climatic belt several thousand miles wide, encircling the earth at the equator, contains countries with the lowest living standards, least development, and shortest life spans.

More recently in a study of college students at forty U.S. universities, Andersen, Lustig, and Andersen (1990) report that across all of the United States, "southern culture is characterized by communication that is more dramatic and stimulating but more socially isolated and communication apprehensive than northern culture" (p. 305). Quite likely, the results are explained by both environmental determinism and conscious choice. Environment certainly exerts a huge influence on behavior, affecting mood and emotion (see Thorson & Kasworm, 1984; Whybrow, 1984) through the neuroendocrine system (for a summary see Andersen et al., 1990). In recent years, seasonal affective disorder (appropriately abbreviated SAD) has been recognized as a major source of depression in northern latitudes and is often treated with light therapy. SAD is common in such places as Seattle, which has one of the highest percentages of mostly cloudy days, but uncommon in such places as Tucson, which has one of the highest percentages of sunny days.

Of course, people frequently choose their environments. Someone who is prone to SAD may choose to live in Arizona rather than in Washington State. Someone who enjoys snow skiing and snowboarding might live in Colorado, whereas someone who enjoys sailing and snorkeling might live in South Florida. My wife and I, who grew up in Illinois but live in San Diego, California, often say, only half-jokingly, that we were always Californians inside just waiting to come out. Others shun the West Coast and Southwest in favor of places that have distinct changes of season, complete with white Christmases and April showers. Some people like big, exciting cities; others prefer safe and cozy small towns. Thus, many individuals make voluntary migrations based on their own needs and preferences. Sometimes, large groups of people even migrate to the same place. The movement of Mormons and Christians to Utah, of intellectuals and artists to New York City, of outdoorsmen to Montana and Alaska, and of certain musical groups to the Pacific Northwest provides an additional explanation for the link between climate and communication.

Microenvironments

Microenvironments are smaller, local arenas constructed by people, such as buildings, rooms, parks, gardens, and patios. Microenvironments are communicative in two ways. First, they may actually communicate analogic messages. A neat house is more inviting to guests than a trashed one; and it directly communicates a message to guests. Second, microenvironments provide the context for all other types of nonverbal and verbal communication that take place within that environment. Considerable research has shown that such microenvironmental factors as temperature, color, lighting, and sound (1) affect communication by providing context and (2) constitute nonverbal messages in and of themselves.

Communication scholars and environmental psychologists are understandably aware of the important role of microenvironment in communication, but

Casinos are "unreal" environments specifically designed to make adults alter their normal behavior so that they will stay up all night and squander their money.

others are not. For example, when I was a communication doctoral student, a well-known political science professor asked me why students in his seminar never talked. I replied that for starters, he had them in a traditional, front-facing, classroom environment. When he switched to a circular seminar table, sure enough, classroom interaction picked up considerably. Sometime later, a lawyer for whom I was consulting asked me why her clients didn't open up to her and frequently failed to return after their first visit. She posed this question in a dingy, poorly lit office, from behind huge piles of lawbooks and files cluttering her desk; indeed, throughout most of our interaction I could hardly see her. Her practice improved dramatically after heeding my suggestion that she clear her desk, put the books on the shelf, and make eye contact with her clients! What was common sense for a communication major was a divine revelation for these otherwise bright professionals.

Microenvironments are designed to produce certain reactions in communicators. The bright lights, loud music, uncomfortable seats, and minimal service of a fast-food restaurant nonverbally say, "Eat and quickly make room for the next customer." The soft lights, soothing music, comfortable seats, and attentive service of a fine restaurant say, "Stay a while, relax, enjoy, spend money."

Malandro and Barker (1983) use Las Vegas as an example of a microenvironment that arouses customers and creates the emotional state of a king or queen entering a castle. Through the creation of an "unreal" environment, otherwise normal adults are encouraged to squander their money, stay up most of the night, and go to bizarre shows. Hunter Thompson (1971) describes the bizarre environment of the Circus-Circus Casino:

> The ground floor is full of gambling tables like all the other casinos . . . but the place is about four stories high, in the style of a circus tent, and all manner of strange County-fair/Polish Carnival madness is going on up in this space. Right above the gambling tables Forty Flying Carazito Brothers are doing a high-wire trapeze act along with four muzzled Wolverines and the Six Nymphet Sisters from San Diego . . . so you're down on the main floor playing blackjack, and the stakes are getting high when suddenly you look up, and there right smack above your head is a half-naked fourteen-year-old girl being chased through the air by a snarling wolverine. (p. 46)

Of course, virtual reality machines, otherworldly pirate journeys, water parks, and lobby zoos are a few other elements that add to the bizarre nature of the Las Vegas environment.

Sociopetal/Sociofugal Environments

Certain microenvironments have the effect of facilitating communication. *Sociopetal* environments (Sommer, 1967b) bring people together and stimulate interaction. By contrast, *sociofugal* environments inhibit communication and keep people apart. Sociopetal arrangements tend to be low in noise, have high levels of privacy, contain few barriers, and permit communicators to see one another and face each other directly. A semicircle of chairs by a fireplace, a hot tub, and a quiet table for two at a nice restaurant are examples of sociopetal environments. Although it can be stimulating, a crowded party with loud music is sociofugal because it makes communication difficult. In a series of interesting experiments, Mehrabian (1976) found that a straight-line bar is a sociofugal environment except at the corners, where patrons can face each other and converse more easily. Circular and zigzag bars provide more face-to-face positioning, facilitate eye contact, and enhance communication.

The typical American living room with furniture lining the walls is actually a sociofugal environment because interactants are beyond the normal 3-to-4-foot interaction range. Groups of chairs in a nook or surrounding a fireplace are far more sociopetal because they provide optimal interaction distances, feel warmer and cozier, and exclude distractions and uninvited people. Similarly, a couch is a fairly sociofugal environmental fixture when it is occupied by three or four people; eye contact among the group is virtually impossible. The maximum sociopetal seating capacity of a sofa is two; both occupants can converse as well as maximize many various forms of nonverbal communication.

Seating Arrangements

Whether in churches or homes, bars or schools, seating arrangements have a major impact on the quality and quantity of communication. In classrooms,

Leaders typically occupy the high-interaction positions in a group. Based on their seating positions at the table, who is most likely the leader at this meeting?

interaction is facilitated by arrangements that promote interaction. Hence, the typical seminar is conducted around an oblong or circular table. In one study in which students were given the opportunity to assemble chairs in a classroom to facilitate interaction, they chose a U-shaped configuration (Heston & Garner, 1972). Research has shown that such horseshoe-shaped classroom arrangements actually do facilitate interaction because every student has an equivalent position. In the traditional, front-facing classroom, students in the front and center are in much better communication positions, and they interact more (Hurt, Scott, & McCroskey, 1978; Rosenfeld & Civikly, 1976).

A whole group of studies shows that leaders select high-interaction positions, usually the head of a table (Heckel, 1973; LaFrance & Mayo, 1978; Sommer, 1967a). These positions have more visibility and are correlated with increased interaction (Ward, 1968). According to one study, persons who occupied focal positions were more likely to be selected as jury foremen (Strodtbeck & Hook, 1961; see Chapter 12 for more about positions of power).

Temperature

Indoor temperature also influences communication. Harner's (1973) summary of research concludes that students show significant decreases in reading speed and comprehension when the room temperature rises above 77 degrees. Todd-

Mancillas (1982) recommends that classroom temperatures be kept between 66 and 72 degrees to maintain optimal classroom performance. He also recommends that a "serious effort should be made to provide air conditioning in the class-room, especially during summer months" (p. 85). Similarly, Griffitt (1970) has noted that individuals' interpersonal attraction to other students decreases as temperatures and humidity become excessive.

Color

The color of an environment also exerts a substantial impact on our behavior. I knew a couple who attributed their frequent fights and sleeplessness to their orange bedroom. In Table 3.1, Burgoon and Saine (1978) provide a guide to moods and meanings associated with color. Sure enough, orange creates unpleasant, exciting, and disturbed moods. Bedrooms and studies, where relaxation and concentration are emphasized, should be white, light blue, or light green.

In his summary of research on color in the classroom, Todd-Mancillas (1982) concludes that bright, warm colors facilitate learning and improve affect in elementary school classrooms. This summary concludes that even children's IQ scores can be enhanced by learning environments that are attractive and colorful. Color affects consumer behavior as well. Malandro and Barker (1983) assert that sugar doesn't sell well in green packages, probably because consumers want mostly white packages that remind them of purity and sugar itself. Beauty aids in brown jars fail to sell well because brown is not perceived by consumers as a clean or beautiful color. Safety, too, is affected by color. White and orange cars are safest in summer months due to their high visibility, but green cars, which blend in with the foliage, are quite dangerous. Conversely, in snow, green cars are quite safe and highly visible but white cars are dangerous.

Lighting

Earlier in this chapter, we discussed the importance of sunlight to mood and mental health. Light has other important effects in communication environments as well. Dim, low lights create environments conducive to relaxation, intimacy, and romance. Bright lights have positive effects in work environments because they are stimulating. Indeed, experiments have shown that well-lit environments increase talk (Gergen, Gergen, & Barton, 1973).

In classroom environments, lighting should be bright and full-spectrum (nonfluorescent) for optimal performance. Fluorescent lighting has been shown to produce fatigue, inattention, hyperactivity, and decreased classroom performance (for a full summary see Todd-Mancillas, 1982).

Sound

Environmental sounds permeate our daily life. Sounds made by people, vehicles, appliances, televisions, radios, and so on are everywhere in our urban, mechanical,

Table 3.1   The Moods and Meanings Associated with Color in the Environment (Burgoon & Saine, 1978).

COLOR	MOODS	SYMBOLIC MEANINGS
Red	Hot, affectionate, angry, defiant, contrary, hostile, full of vitality, excitement, love	Happiness, lust, intimacy, love, restlessness, agitation, royalty, rage, sin, blood
Blue	Cool, pleasant, leisurely, distant, infinite, secure, transcendent, calm, tender	Dignity, sadness, tenderness, truth
Yellow	Unpleasant, exciting, hostile, cheerful, joyful, jovial	Superficial glamor, sun, light, wisdom, masculinity, royalty (in China), age (in Greece), prostitution (in Italy), famine (in Egypt)
Orange	Unpleasant, exciting, disturbed, distressed, upset, defiant, contrary, hostile, stimulating	Sun, fruitfulness, harvest, thoughtfulness
Purple	Depressed, sad, dignified, stately	Wisdom, victory, pomp, wealth, humility, tragedy
Green	Cool, pleasant, leisurely, in control	Security, peace, jealousy, hate, aggressiveness, calm
Black	Sad, intense, anxious, fearful, despondent, dejected, melancholy, unhappy	Darkness, power, mastery, protection, decay, mystery, wisdom, death, atonement
Brown	Sad, not tender, despondent, dejected, melancholy, unhappy, neutral	Melancholy, protection, autumn, decay, humility, atonement
White	Joyful, light, neutral, cold	Solemnity, purity, chastity, femininity, humility, joy, light, innocence, fidelity, cowardice

mediated world. Silence is such an uncommon condition for most people that when they camp or visit a rural area, they are shocked, even disturbed, by the silence.

A number of studies have shown that background music, particularly instrumental music, has numerous beneficial effects in a variety of business settings. Muzak, a company that specializes in producing background music for use in stores, restaurants, and offices, has been a multimillion-dollar industry for decades, serving millions of clients. Selections are carefully tailored to each business environment. The music is played intermittently to prevent workers or customers from becoming bored or fatigued. Research has shown that Muzak improves work performance and concentration, lessens tension, reduces absenteeism, and increases consumer spending (Rosenfeld & Civikly, 1976).

Schools also can utilize background music effectively. In his review of research on music in the school environment, Todd-Mancillas (1982) concluded that music can reduce boredom, improve social interaction, heighten pleasant feelings, and improve work performance in students from elementary school through college. It has also been successfully used in reinforcing positive classroom behavior.

By definition, noise is unwanted sound that either interferes with hearing desirable sounds or produces irritation. It can also cause hearing loss and disrupt concentration. White noise is sound—such as that produced by a clothes dryer or lawnmower—that drowns out other noise. Sometimes white noise has been shown to improve work performance, but many employees actually find it an additional source of irritation (Malandro & Barker, 1983).

Quiet elementary school environments are essential for good student performance particularly for kids from disadvantaged environments (Heft, 1979; Todd-Mancillas, 1982). Quiet environments are less important for older students; however, sudden loud noises are very disruptive to all students' concentration and should be minimized. Schools should have sufficient soundproofing to minimize distractions from outside environments and other classrooms.

Environmental Efficacy

It is very important that we not underestimate the effect our environment has on our personal welfare and interpersonal interaction. This is certainly true for internal environments, which residents, managers, school administrators, teachers, business people, and government officials can create into pleasant, attractive environments that improve interpersonal relations and facilitate social interaction.

Similarly, our external environment can benefit from our help too. Students need to learn that every bag of garbage we contribute to a landfill, every time we travel by car rather than by bicycle or by foot, and every light we turn on has negative environmental consequences. Fortunately, this message is being spread in schools, where teachers are including environmental education in their curricula and through such wonderful books as *50 Simple Things Kids Can Do To Save The Earth* (Earthworks Group, 1990), which are widely available and replete with excellent ideas. Indeed, *50 Simple Things* suggests diffusion strategies in an entire section entitled "Spreading the Word" and prefigurative strategies in a chapter entitled "Teach Your Parents Well." Al Gore (1992) includes as a primary strategic goal of his global Marshall Plan "the establishment of a cooperative plan for educating the world's citizens about our global environment" (p. 306). Communication specialists have an important role to play in designing optimal, objective, nonpropagandistic strategies that will create a generation of citizens capable of making critical choices in their daily lives about the planetary ecosystem.

It is also essential for urban dwellers, who increasingly live indoors and stay connected via cyberspace and mediated communication, to reexperience outdoor environments. A consciousness of the global environment is enhanced by understanding our natural context, through outdoor experiences and rituals. As Gore (1992) describes it, our detachment and alienation take many forms:

> Something was lost along the way, because the amount of attention necessary for this mental work detracted from the attention we paid to the context of communication. . . . The more information we consumed the more our mental lives were dominated by direct experience with information representing the world rather than direct experience of the world itself. . . . It is interesting to note that similarity between the crisis in our relationship to information and our crisis in our relationship to the natural world. (pp. 199–200)

Increasingly, we as human beings have become estranged from our natural environment, forgetting that we are part of it not masters over it. Andersen (1993b) contends: "This estrangement has caused a collective amnesia about the natural world. Gone is the smell of conifer or chaparral, the feel of sunshine or rain, the struggle and pleasure of walking in mud or snow. Our world is a world of indirect experience and our knowledge of the planet is sophisticated but incomplete, accurate but remote" (p. 17). It is because of this estrangement from the natural world that a central feature of the Sierra Club, America's largest environmental group, is the outing—excursions into the natural world, backpacking, hiking, mountaineering, rafting, and camping. The organization's philosophy holds that one cannot really know the natural world without firsthand experience.

We must all be more conscious of environmental destruction and foster communication that protects habitats and species that have no voice or power over decisions to develop, destroy, or protect. We need to do this not only for all other living things but to ensure our own survival and the survival of our children as well.

Likewise, companies, schools, hospitals, architects, and city planners have an obligation to create microenvironments that facilitate interpersonal communication and enhance the human spirit. If, indeed, environments can communicate, what is communicated by a dirty, dilapidated ghetto and a messy, poorly maintained school versus a rehabilitated and renovated neighborhood and a clean, inviting school that facilitates interaction? The many microenvironments throughout the world that lack any sense of aesthetics and inhibit quality communication stand as visual testimonials of the ignorance people often have regarding the importance of the environment in our everyday communication.

Chronemics

Chronemics is the study of the way we structure time and the meanings we attach to time during interpersonal interaction. In the United States, time is viewed as a commodity that can be manipulated. Think for a moment about the phrase "Let's spend some time together." This sort of rhetoric suggests that time is a tangible resource, a bank account that can be "budgeted." In the United States, parents and teachers frequently implore us to "budget" our time. Most Americans also try to "save" time. Actually, time irrevocably moves on, yet we persist in the illusion that time can be saved. What we really mean is that we hurry through unpleasant activities such as commuting and housekeeping so that we can get to the activities we really enjoy such as recreating, socializing, or relaxing. But we must be careful with our "commodified" time because recreating and relaxing may be perceived as "wasting" time. And of course, time marches on, so we must "capture the moment." Psychologically and rhetorically, most Americans treat time like their most prized possession or like money itself: something to be earned, saved, spent, and treasured. As we will learn in Chapter 4, other cultures have no such conception of time. Indeed, each culture or subculture has its own sense of time, which is part of the reason each culture "dances to a different drummer" and vibes between cultures are sometimes characterized by friction.

Waiting Time

Not surprisingly, cultures that "commodify" time also value being prompt. Burgoon, Buller, and Woodall (1996) argue that "being on time for a business appointment most often means literally arriving at the appointed time. Arriving more than 5 minutes late is a violation of this rule and often requires an apology" (p. 129). However, such a rule is not the case in many parts of the world, including Latin America, where individuals may wait an hour or even a day for a business appointment. For some high-status individuals, such as doctors or executives, making people wait reinforces the individual's status. Insel and Lindgren (1978) maintain that "another psychological dimension to the distress of waiting is the effect of subordination. One who is in the position to cause another to wait has power over him. To be kept waiting implies that one's own time is less valuable than that of the one who imposes the wait" (p. 105). Chronically late subordinates are particularly reviled and can actually put their evaluations and positions at risk.

Spending Time

Spending time with another person is a powerful nonverbal cue that communicates warmth, friendliness, understanding, and love. In this day and age, although many parents tell their children they love them, they proceed to spend time on dozens of activities while spending little time with their children. Not surprisingly, many of these children feel unloved despite their parents' words. In a major study of nonverbal warmth and immediacy, Andersen, Andersen, & Jensen (1979) reported that spending time with someone was a major component of immediacy and psychological closeness. Burgoon and Aho (1982) report that because of the premium placed on time in our culture, the amount of time an individual spends in conversation indicates her or his interest in the other person. In a recent study, Stelzner and Egland (1995) found that among dozens of nonverbal behaviors, spending time with someone was the leading predictor of both relational satisfaction and relational understanding.

Talk Time

Conversational time, or talk time, has an important effect on how we are perceived. We can all think of a date or an acquaintance that wouldn't let us get a word in edgewise or a group member who totally dominated the conversation. Such people are perceived as rude, bossy, self-centered, and dominant. Similarly, a person who never speaks is perceived as shy, disinterested, and uninvolved. Persons who talk a little more (but not a lot more) than their share are perceived as more competent, confident, interested, influential, and credible (for summaries see Harper, Wiens, & Matarazzo, 1978; Hayes & Metzger, 1972; see also Chapters 10 and 12). A good rule of thumb is to talk your share or a bit more (for example, 50 percent plus in a dyad, or 20 percent plus in a five-person group).

Body Speed

Humans vary greatly in body speed, a characteristic that communicates much about people. Individuals who move slowly are labeled *hypokinetic,* and those who move rapidly are termed *hyperkinetic* (Barker, Cegala, Kibler, & Wahlers, 1979). A number of factors produce slow or fast body speeds. Metabolic differences are certainly important. Hyperkinetic people are most likely to be found in the North rather than in the South, in developed rather than in undeveloped countries, and in cities rather than in rural areas. Barker et al. (1979) outline the problem when these different individuals work with one another:

> Hypokinetic group members and hyperkinetic group members potentially are annoying to each other. For example, you may have wondered how a particular person could talk so fast (or so slowly). However both a rapidly moving group member and a more slowly moving group member may be frustrated if they must work on a task together.... In extreme cases the two individuals cannot work together. Therefore, you should keep individual differences in movements in mind as group members are assigned to different tasks. (p. 192)

Similarly, some people have much longer *response latency,* the time it takes to respond to another person's statement or question. A longer response latency is not necessarily a sign of stupidity but a difference in style. Some people are more thoughtful, while others respond rapidly and spontaneously. Deceptive communicators also have longer response latencies (see Chapter 11). Interestingly, even in deception, longer response latencies and hesitations are not always perceived negatively. Burgoon, Buller, and Guerrero (1995) found that hesitancy is actually positively associated with believability when other nonverbal cues (such as expressiveness) are positive. They argue that in some cases hesitancy may be interpreted as signaling thoughtfulness rather than a lack of knowledge.

Research has also shown that fast talkers slow down when interacting with slow talkers and slow talkers speed up when talking with fast talkers. These processes are called convergence, or communication accommodation (Street & Giles, 1982). Research has shown that speakers who converge to others' rates are more attractive and persuasive (Buller & Aune, 1988a).

Speaking rate has a major effect on first impressions. Generally, faster speakers are perceived as more credible, intelligent, and competent (Buller & Aune, 1988a; Street & Brady, 1982) but less honest and trustworthy than slower speakers (Burgoon, 1978).

Other Types of Time

Time has many meanings and dimensions. E. T. Hall (1984) classifies time into eight categories, each having its own social rules and interpersonal meanings. The first of these categories, *biological time*, deals with the rhythms of living things. Fiddler crabs are tuned in to tidal cycles; deciduous trees, to the rhythms of the seasons. Similarly, we humans have circadian (daily) rhythms of sleeping and wakefulness and monthly rhythms of menstruation and activity. Disruption of our biorhythms, as in the case of jet lag, throws off our cycles and may result in negative physical, psychological, and interpersonal consequences.

Personal time is the way individuals experience time in different contexts and cultures. Personal time is subjective. For example, the last six miles of a marathon or the final days of a visit from a boring relative may seem to drag. By contrast, a vacation in Hawaii or a student's summer break usually seems to fly by. In addition, people have different orientations toward time. Those with future-time orientations are not likely to want to spend as much time looking at old photographs and letters as those with past-time orientations.

Physical time has to do with fixed geophysical cycles such as seasons or days. Ancient peoples erected observatories such as Stonehenge in England and medicine wheels in the American West to track the passage of the seasons, probably for religious, migratory, or agricultural reasons. As discussed earlier, seasonal patterns related to sunlight have been shown to affect human cycles of sociability, activity, alcohol use, and psychological well-being (for a summary see Andersen, Lustig, & Andersen, 1990). Seasonal affective disorder has been shown to result in depression and even suicide during long winters in high latitudes (Thorson & Kasworm, 1984).

Metaphysical time includes many paranormal phenomena—such as presci-ence, astral projection, and the recall of former lives—in which people claim to transcend time and space. Although such abilities are met with skepticism by scientists, they are very real to millions of people who report experiencing para-normal phenomena.

Sync time occurs when interaction partners are in rhythm. In our previous discussion of kinesics, we discussed the phenomenon of interactional synchrony, an important aspect of sync time. The African American expression "She's right on time," the whole notion of being "in sync," and the concept of "smooth" interaction all refer to the fundamental synchronization that is so vital to human interaction.

Microtime is the time frame used by a particular culture. According to E. T. Hall (1984), polychronic people maintain flexible schedules (or no set schedule at all), move in rhythm to nature, and do several things at once. Monochronic people (like northern Europeans and Americans) schedule one thing at a time, live by the clock, and believe they can conserve and spend time.

Sacred time, or mythic time, is imaginary, rooted in legend, and difficult for most Americans to comprehend. When Native Americans participate in tribal ceremonies, they cease to exist in ordinary, mundane time. Being really "into" an activity such as reading an engrossing book, watching a movie, or playing a sport may be as close as most Americans get to sacred time. Meditation and prayer are additional activities that can put people into a sacred time frame.

Profane time, or mundane time, consists of the seconds, minutes, hours, weeks, years, decades, centuries, and millennia to which we are so wedded. These time frames are only partly physical. The week, for example, has little or no geophysical counterpart, but each day seems quite different in industrial so-cieties where people: say "thank goodness it's Friday," get through the Wednesday "hump day," and bemoan "Monday malaise."

Metatime is the intellectual study and discussion of time by philosophers, scholars, historians, and futurists. Metatime consists of abstractions and con-structs of time. Einstein's theories, for example, suggest that contrary to our per-sonal experience, time need not run forward. Concepts such as time warps are also part of the scientific study of metatime.

In communication, timing is everything. Chronemic cues manage the most subtle interactions, create lasting interpersonal perceptions, and facilitate or in-hibit interaction. Time not only provides a context for other messages, it often is *the message.*

Olfactics

An important but much neglected aspect of nonverbal communication is olfac-tics, the study of nonverbal communication through scent and smell. Although smell is overlooked by most researchers in psychology and communication, its importance is not lost on the American public who spend billions of dollars annually on scent. Americans daily use perfume, cologne, aftershave, and deodorant. Commercials urge us to suppress and replace the odors of our underarms, mouths, hair, genitals, feet, and bodies. Any orifice or surface seems to be fair game for Madison Avenue messages, which have made Americans the most heavily and artificially scented society in the world. According to Doty (1974), smells are meaningful on a single evaluative continuum, good to bad. Americans are rarely neutral about smell; body odors, in particular, carry strong negative connotations. This may be due to the ancient origins of our sense of smell, including its positive effect in mating and its functionality in helping us avoid spoiled, rotten, or contaminated substances, particularly food.

One of the most interesting aspects of olfaction research is the consistent finding that smells are memory triggers, producing instant associations with past events. Meerloo (1971) suggests that many smells are nostalgic connections to previously subconscious memories of places, relationships, and activities. In their comprehensive review of olfaction, Richardson and Zucco (1989) conclude that "odors have the extraordinary ability to remind us of a sometimes far distant past. These memories are often characterized by strong emotive connotation" (p. 352).

It is my experience that vivid memories can be evoked by a variety of smells: my childhood room, the smell of perfume worn by an old girlfriend, lilacs in the spring, and even the smell of an old coffee factory near my boyhood home. I'm amazed by the number of people who have nostalgic memories of even toxic smells. After a camping trip, two friends of mine smelled the toxic smoke of steel mills at the edge of their hometown and were overcome by pleasant, nostalgic memories. Research supports these subjective experiences. Richardson and Zucco's (1989) review suggests that autobiographic memories are more likely to be evoked by smell than by either visual or verbal cues.

In the most extensive smell survey to date, Gilbert and Wysocki (1987) surveyed 1.5 million worldwide *National Geographic* readers and concluded:

> We found that the stronger the odor, the more likely it was to bring to mind a vivid memory. And just as women found all odors stronger, they also reported more memories than men for every odor but gas. Are foul odors as likely to evoke a memory as a pleasant one? They are. As it turned out, extremely pleasant and extremely unpleasant odors were both *more likely* to evoke memories than odors with a so-so rating. . . . A Coloradan wrote, "One of my favorite smells is cow manure. Yes! It brings back memories of me on my aunt's farm in Southern Ohio. The vacations I spent there were the happiest of my childhood, and any farm smell evokes wonderful memories." (p. 524)

Smell can certainly stimulate recall, but can it also be a form of nonverbal communication? The answer seems to be yes. In a summary of research on odor, Engen (1987) concludes, "Odor perception is characterized by adaptability and a relatively concrete but open-ended nonverbal coding system" (p. 501). Similarly Elliot and Jensen (1979) conclude, "The evidence presented in this discussion suggests that humans possess a significant potential for the utilization of the olfactory communication channel, however current usage appears to be considerably below this potential" (p. 16). Certainly, the writers of nonverbal communication books who include a chapter on olfaction believe it is nonverbal communication (DeVito & Hecht, 1990; Knapp & Hall, 1992; Malandro & Barker, 1983; Richmond, McCroskey, & Payne, 1987), and American communicators, who so carefully apply their daily combination of perfumes, aftershaves, and deodorants, are clearly believers in the power of olfactory communication.

In many animals, including primates, olfaction is a primary means of communicating sexual attraction. Accumulating evidence suggests that odor plays a role in sexual communication for humans as well. Many female animals prepare to mate when presented with a male sexual hormone or pheromone (external chemical messenger). Female hogs will assume a mating position when smelling boar taint (a swine pheromone; Angier, 1995). Interestingly, boar taint is considered a pleasant smell by human females but a foul smell by human males (Doty, 1974). Women, but not men, are capable of smelling testosterone acetate, a derivative of the male sex hormone (Vollmer & Gordon, 1975). Research also has shown that human females are more sensitive to smell during ovulation than during menstruation and less sensitive to smell during pregnancy, suggesting some role for smell in the human reproductive process (Doty, Snyder, Huggins, & Lowery, 1981; Gilbert & Wysocki, 1987; Richardson & Zucco, 1989). Henkin's research, reported by Richmond, McCroskey, and Payne (1987), shows that 25 percent of people who have smell disorders lose interest in sex. Finally, one substance, exaltolide, which is used as a perfume base, may be a human sexual pheromone (Engen, 1973). Smell probably played a much greater role in sexual attraction in our ancestral past than it does today. Moreover, compared with touch or vision, smell is a distinctly inferior form of sexual communication.

The word *pheromone* was coined in 1959 from the Greek *pherein* ("to carry") and *hormon* ("to stimulate or excite"; Malandro & Barker, 1983). Pheromones, unlike hormones, are external chemical messengers and may play several other roles in human communication. One such role is the *smell signature,* a unique smell carried by each individual person. Dogs have no difficulty distinguishing between the unique smell of individuals except in the case of identical twins, who smell the same to dogs (Davis, 1973; Kloek, 1961). Increasing evidence suggests that humans each carry a smell signature. Some individuals, such as the legendary Helen Keller, supposedly are able to identify friends and visitors by their unique smell (Weiner, 1966). Several research summaries report studies in which infants recognize the smell of their mother's breast but not that of a stranger (Knapp & Hall, 1997; Malandro & Barker, 1983).

Other evidence also indicates that our pheromones may influence other people. Several studies of women in group-living situations suggest that, over time, women coordinate their menstrual cycles, which are attributed to pheromonal cues (McClintock, 1971; Burton, 1976). Menstrual synchronization provides strong evidence for the interpersonal effects of pheromones. In fact, every time I discuss this phenomenon in a nonverbal communication class, several sorority women are quick to share that this has happened in their sorority houses.

Unfortunately, many people suffer from an inability to smell, a syndrome known as smell blindness, or amnosia. All of us may experience temporary or partial amnosia, such as during a severe cold.

Smell sensitivity varies greatly. Some individuals are highly sensitive to certain smells, and others are virtually unaware of them. Remember, if another person detects a strong smell but you do not, it may be that you are completely impervious to that smell. In the previously mentioned *National Geographic* study of smell, nearly two-thirds of the worldwide respondents reported a period of virtually complete smell loss, and smokers displayed reduced sensitivity to most smells (Gilbert & Wysocki, 1987). Over 25 percent of participants in this study failed to detect the smell of sweat or of musk. Additional research shows that when people are exposed to a certain smell (particularly if it is negative) for an extended period of time, they adapt by losing their ability to detect that particular smell (Knapp & Hall, 1997).

Interestingly, a number of studies indicate that women are more sensitive to smell than men. It is unclear if these are biological differences, if women are socialized to be more smell sensitive, or some combination. In a study by Cain (1990), women significantly outperformed men in identifying a variety of smells in test tubes; however, men in this study avoided a total shutout by more accurately identifying bourbon, Brut aftershave, Crayola crayons, horseradish, rubbing alcohol, soap, and Vicks Vaporub. This supports dozens of research studies (see summaries by Elliot and Jensen, 1979; Gilbert and Wysocki, 1987; Richardson & Zucco, 1989).

Vocalics

Human speech is the main vehicle by which verbal and linguistic communication is transmitted. But spoken communication also carries other messages that are nonverbal in nature. Vocal qualities such as pitch, rhythm, tempo, resonance, control, and accent lend meaning to the spoken word. The study of these nonverbal elements of the voice is called vocalics, or paralinguistics. Additionally, the study of vocalics examines other purely nonverbal characteristics such as laughing, screaming, inhaling or exhaling, sighing, yawning, and crying, as well as vocal segregates such as "uh-huh," "uh-uh," "ah," and "um" (Trager, 1958) and singing (Andersen, Garrison, & Andersen, 1979). Similar to the smell signature discussed in the previous section, *vocal signature* is as unique to each individual as a fingerprint. No two voices are exactly alike (Burgoon, Buller, & Woodall, 1996). Each has its distinct combination of pitch, volume, resonance, and other vocal qualities.

Among all of the contextual codes, vocalics may be the most important because it provides the context for everything we say. Indeed, Jaffe (1987) suggests that the human brain evolved in such a way that the left hemisphere deals with content while the right hemisphere deals with the emotional quality available through nonverbal cues such as vocalics. He asks, "If the left brains of both speaker and listener are saturated by the linguistic processing of the conversation, do their right brains remain available for the kinesic and paralinguistic phenomena that calibrate the emotional quality of a conversation? Intriguing support for such speculation has been provided" (p. 29).

Moreover, vocalics modifies everything that is said verbally. Vocalics, along with the kinesic cues described in Chapter 2, contextualize every utterance. This was recognized early by one of the fathers of nonverbal communication, Ray Birdwhistell (1970), who examined parakinesic and paralinguistic cues:

> These cross-referencing signals amplify, emphasize, or modify the formal constructions, and/or make statements about the *context* of the message situation. In the latter instance, they help to define the context of the interaction by identifying the actor or his audience, and furthermore, they usually convey information about the larger context in which the interaction takes place. (p. 117)

Vocalic cues are essential to the interpretation of spoken information. In my nonverbal communication class, we conduct an exercise in which we see how many ways we can say "yes." Depending on one's tone of voice, the word *yes* can signal agreement, affirmation, reluctance, hostility, confusion, intimacy, boredom, seduction, affection, impatience, and a host of other messages. The class is generally able to find over twenty-five independent meanings associated with the various pronunciations of the word *yes*. As this exercise illustrates, the meaning of a word has less to do with its content than with the way it is spoken.

Like other forms of nonverbal communication, vocalics exists beside language and interacts with language. Researchers have established six primary ways that nonverbal communication, and vocalics in particular, contextualizes and influences verbal communication (Ekman, 1965). First, nonverbal cues serve a *repetition*, or redundancy, function. Vocalic cues, such as an enthusiastic tone of voice, combined with the kinesic cue of nodding, repeat and reinforce the word *yes* to signal affirmation or positivity. Because repetition increases accuracy, one's nonverbal communication should repeat verbal communication to increase accuracy and clarify a message. *Complementarity*, or modification, is the second function of vocalics. Nonverbal messages may elaborate or modify verbal messages. Telling a child not to do something in a loud or angry voice complements but also strengthens a verbal message. Complementarity is similar to the repetition function when considering vocalic cues. The difference between the two is clearer when kinesics are added to the picture. For example, if a child asks if she can have a piece of candy right before dinner, the mother might shake her head (repetition) while saying no, and she might say no in a stern manner (complementarity). The third function, *accenting,* or emphasizing, involves using vocalics to stress a certain part of a verbal message. The most important word in a sentence is often accented (such as italicized words in written communication) by saying the word more loudly, carefully, or slowly. Imagine a parent saying, "Please don't fall down that hillside." By accenting a particular word, such as *please* or *that,* the meaning of the sentence, as well as the emotion conveyed, changes. *Substitution,* or replacement, is the fourth vocalic function. Sometimes nonverbal or vocalic information can replace verbal communication entirely. Vocalic expressions such as "uh-huh" replace the words "I understand what you're saying." Yawns can substitute for verbal expressions of boredom, and laughs can replace appreciative or derisive comments. In the example of the child asking for a piece of candy, if the mother shakes her head without verbalizing "no," substitution, rather than complementarity, has occurred. *Regulation,* the fifth function of vocalics, entails the use of nonverbal cues that regulate or control verbal communication. Filler pauses such as "ah" or "um" and audible inhalations of air at the end of a sentence may prevent another speaker from interjecting or interrupting. Likewise, silent pauses or exhalations of air signal to other speakers that it's their turn. The final function of vocalics is *contradiction,* which occurs when a person's vocalic messages contradict what the person says verbally. If a person says "I'll go to the dance" in a bored or lackadaisical tone of voice, the nonverbal message may be stronger than the verbal one. (See Chapter 1 for a detailed discussion on contradictory cues.)

One frequently misunderstood vocalic cue is sarcasm, a message which is often conveyed by overaccenting a verbal statement. For example, overstating "Oh great" when the opposing team scores a touchdown is understood to mean just the opposite. Several studies (Andersen, Andersen, Murphy, & Wendt-Wasco, 1985; Blanck & Rosenthal, 1982) suggest that young children have great difficulty detecting sarcasm, resulting in confusion about what a sarcastic speaker really means. Likewise, people with very low intelligence or little education may take sarcastic messages literally. Occasionally, it is difficult for anyone to tell if a message is meant to be sarcastic or serious. This is particularly true if the receiver does not know the sender's personality.

Finally, nonverbal messages associated with the voice may create very distinct impressions of the individual communicator. Attractive, influential voices are more resonant and calm, less monotonous, lower-pitched (especially for males), less regionally accented, less nasal, less shrill, and more relaxed (Addington, 1968; Pearce, 1971; Zuckerman & Driver, 1989; Zuckerman, Hodgins, & Miyake, 1990). Midwestern voices tend to be the most accent-free, which is why many toll-free phone lines originate from Nebraska and employ Nebraska operators. Nasality in particular seems to be a quality that elicits numerous perceptions of negative characteristics.

Summary

Like the body codes of nonverbal communication, the contextual codes provide the rich, analogic, multichanneled messages of human communication. Although contextual codes perform many functions, such as creating intimacy and persuasive influence, their primary function is to provide context for all of the other nonverbal and verbal messages we communicate.

Macroenvironments, the large environmental contexts that set the stage and provide the background for our many communicative actions, include landforms, climate, sunlight, and geographic regions. Macroenvironments greatly influence how people in that environment will communicate. Through voluntary migration, some people actively seek macroenvironments that facilitate the types of communication and relationships they value.

Microenvironments are smaller, local human contexts that both have impact on other messages and are messages in and of themselves. Certain environments are sociopetal, that is, they faciliate interaction; others are sociofugal, that is, they inhibit communication. Seating arrangements in homes, schools, bars, or churches directly affect the types of communication that will occur. Room temperature and color, lighting, and sound provide the context for certain types of communication; at the same time, such characteristics can virtually preclude other kinds of communication. It is important not to underestimate the significance of environments. We should all be active agents in creating communicative, pleasant, and sustainable macroenvironments and microenvironments.

Chronemics, the study of how we structure and use time, has become even more important as we enter the time-pressed twenty-first century. In America, time is a commodity that we believe can be wasted, saved, spent, and even treasured. An aspect of chronemics is waiting time, which sends messages of interest, politeness, status, and responsibility. Spending time with another person is a powerful relational message and is associated with love and closeness. Talk time is extremely important in nonverbal communication; too much talk or too little talk can be perceived negatively. One's speech rate also affects receivers' comprehension and interpersonal perceptions. Some dimensions of time include biological time, personal time, physical time, metaphysical time, sync time, microtime, sacred time, profane time, and metatime. In communication, timing is everything because it contextualizes most, if not every, communication behavior.

Olfactics is a largely neglected area of nonverbal communication that examines smell. Americans annually spend billions of dollars on products to suppress and replace body odors. Natural body odors are taboo in most situations. Smells also create nostalgia and trigger old, sometimes hidden memories. Moreover, smell plays some role in human sexual attraction, although less so than it does in other mammals. Humans have individual smell signatures that play a role in interpersonal communication, particularly for infants. Pheromones, external chemical messengers, also have interpersonal effects in communication.

Finally, vocalics, or paralinguistics, is the study of nonverbal elements of the voice—such as pitch, rhythm, tempo, resonance, control, and accent—that modify and contextualize every verbal utterance. Vocalics also comprises such nonverbal vocal behaviors as laughing, screaming, and crying. Vocalics can repeat, complement, modify, accent, replace, regulate, and contradict verbal communication. Vocal qualities, such as pitch and volume, are powerful elicitors of personality judgments.

This chapter completes our discussion of the codes of nonverbal communication and introduces the first function of nonverbal communication: providing context for other communication. Throughout the rest of the book, we will examine the other functions performed by nonverbal communication: communicating our culture and gender in a diverse world; communicating affect and emotion; sending and suppressing signals of stress, anxiety, and arousal; expressing messages of immediacy, involvement, and intimacy; influencing others by persuading and gaining compliance; concealing and revealing deception; and establishing power, control, and status relationships.

4
Cultural Cues
Nonverbal Communication in a Diverse World

A MERICA HAS ALWAYS been one of the most culturally diverse nations on earth. As Garreau (1981) maintains in his book *The Nine Nations of North America,* "It is no surprise that the second most commonly asked question after 'What's your name?' is 'Where are you from?'" (p. xvi). Although some Americans grow up in ethnically homogeneous communities, most of us live and work in communities that are ethnically and culturally diverse. Look around your classroom or your workplace. Chances are there are people who grew up in many regions of the United States, as well as people from different ethnic and racial backgrounds than your own. Intolerance and prejudice against various ethnic groups has been a problem throughout much of U.S. history, yet diversity has served as one of our nation's greatest strengths. Americans have benefited from the rich mix of traditions, foods, music, and technology contributed over the years by people of many backgrounds.

Americans are the most mobile people on earth. According to Dinnerstein and Reimers (1975), "Never before—and in no other country—have as many varied ethnic groups congregated and amalgamated as they have in the United States" (p. 1). Moreover, once immigrants settle in America, they and their families frequently move to new states and regions. More than 20 percent of Americans move annually (Fielding, 1974), and this has been true for centuries (Lewis, 1972; Zelinsky, 1973). One of the biggest communication challenges you will face is effectively interacting with people from different cultural backgrounds than your own. Indeed, without ever leaving the United States, you are likely to communicate with people from dozens of different ethnic and cultural traditions. Lustig and Koester (1993) conclude:

> On this, the threshold of the twenty-first century, competence in intercultural communication is an absolute necessity. In both your private and public lives,

in all of your personal and professional endeavors, it is imperative that you learn to communicate with people whose cultural heritages make them vastly different from yourself. (p. xv)

Furthermore, people are traveling today in record numbers, and international trade is at an all-time high (Brown, Kane, & Roodman, 1994). Never before have so many people from so many cultures had so much contact with one another. Language differences constitute a major barrier to effective intercultural communication, yet they are just the tip of the iceberg. Nonverbal behaviors are both biological (for discussions on the biological basis of nonverbal communication see Chapters 1, 5, and 7) and cultural in origin. Because cultural differences exist in each channel of nonverbal behavior and because nonverbal behaviors are multichanneled, the chance for intercultural misunderstandings in nonverbal communication is substantial.

Culture is mainly an implicit, spontaneous, nonverbal phenomenon. Most aspects of one's culture are learned through observation and imitation rather than through explicit verbal instruction or expression. The primary level of culture is communicated implicitly, without awareness, by primarily nonverbal means (Andersen, 1986, 1988; E. T. Hall, 1984; Sapir, 1928). For example, cultural customs such as how to wait in line, what foods to eat, how to treat one's elders, and how to greet other people are communicated nonverbally from adults to children, often with no verbal instruction. In fact, *one of the most basic and obvious functions of nonverbal communication is to communicate one's culture.* People cling tenaciously to cultural, religious, and ethnic customs and are unwilling to give up important aspects of their culture, including language, dress, gestures, tactile behaviors, and the many other aspects of nonverbal behavior that you will read about in this chapter. Indeed, culture is such a powerful force that throughout history people have gone to war to preserve cultural customs and behaviors.

Until people communicate interculturally, they are unaware of most of their own nonverbal behaviors, because these behaviors are enacted mindlessly, spontaneously, and unconsciously (Andersen, 1986; Burgoon, 1985a; Samovar & Porter, 1985; see also Chapter 1). Indeed, Edward Sapir stated many years ago, "We respond to gestures with an extreme alertness and, one might almost say, in accordance with an elaborate and secret code that is written nowhere, known to none and understood by all" (1928, p. 556). In fact, "culture is so basic, learned at such a tender age, and so taken-for-granted, that it is often confused with human nature itself" (Andersen, 1997, p. 224). Because we are not usually aware of our own nonverbal behavior, which we take for granted, we have great difficulty understanding or learning the nonverbal behavior of another culture. Frequently, people feel uncomfortable in other cultures because they intuitively think "something isn't right." "Because nonverbal behaviors are rarely conscious phenomena, it may be difficult for us to know exactly why they [people from other cultures] are feeling uncomfortable" (Gudykunst & Kim, 1992, p. 172).

In this chapter, we will focus on six conceptual differences among cultures that provide a theoretical explanation for *why* cultures differ in their nonverbal communication. Indeed, a multitude of nonverbal differences exist between cultures, and detailing these myriad differences would be impossible and somewhat trivial. To begin, we will briefly explore intercultural interactions in terms of the nonverbal codes that were discussed in Chapters 2 and 3. Following that, we will examine in detail the six cultural dimensions that help explain differences in nonverbal communication across cultures.

Cultural Differences in Nonverbal Communication Codes

Chronemics

According to Edward Hall, the founder of the intercultural communication field, "time talks. It speaks more plainly than words" (1959, p. 15). In the following extract, Hall (1959) describes an American diplomat in a Latin country arriving for an appointment to see a cabinet minister of the government:

> Arriving a little before the hour (an American respect pattern), he waited. The hour came and passed;—five minutes—ten minutes—fifteen minutes. At this point he suggested to the secretary that perhaps the minister did not know he was waiting in the outer office . . . thirty minutes—forty-five minutes (the insult period)! He jumped up and told the secretary that he had been "cooling his heels in an outer office for forty-five minutes and he was damned sick and tired" of this type of treatment. The message was relayed to the minister who said, in effect, "Let him cool his heels." The attaché's stay in the country was not a happy one. The principal source of misunderstanding lay in the fact that in the country in question the five-minute delay interval was not significant. Forty-five minutes, on the other hand, instead of being at the tail end of the waiting scale, was just at the beginning." (p. 18)

Cultures dance to different drummers. Chronemics is probably the most-discussed and best-researched nonverbal code in the intercultural literature (Bruneau, 1979; Burgoon, Buller, & Woodall, 1996; Gudykunst & Kim, 1992; Hall, 1959, 1976, 1984). Although each culture is unique in its use of time, Hall (1984) maintains that the big cultural gulf is between monochronic, or M-time, cultures and polychronic, or P-time, cultures. M-time cultures, including countries in northern Europe or with northern European roots (for example, England, Germany, Finland, Norway, Sweden, Canada, and the United States), believe in doing one thing at a time. P-time cultures have little regard for artificial schedules and stress informality, people-centeredness, multiple simultaneous activities, and the importance of context.

Some years ago on a trip to some remote island in the Bahamas (a P-time culture), I (being from an M-time culture) was surprised to discover that life in the islands totally stops when it rains. Until the rain stopped, the ground crew at the airport would not unload our airplane, nor would gas station attendants pump gas. We American college students who were visiting the island on our short one-week spring break were outraged by this behavior. But our anger was useless, for we were up against a cultural (P-time) custom of the Caribbean people. As this story illustrates, the time frames of cultures vary so substantially that if only chronemic differences existed, intercultural misunderstandings would still be considerable. As described in Chapter 3, people in the United States view time as a commodity that can be wasted, spent, saved, and used wisely. Of course, many cultures have no concept of time as being segmented into arbitrary units (seconds, minutes, hours, weeks, months, and so on). In many third world cultures, life moves to the rhythms of nature: the day, the weather, the tides, and such. Things are experienced polychronically and simultaneously. By contrast, in Western cultures time is modularized, and events are scheduled sequentially not simultaneously. It is thus very important to remember when interacting with people from different cultures that the beat of their life may be to a totally different drummer. As an American visiting a third world culture, it would be safe to assume that all your assumptions about time are false.

Proxemics

Research on proxemics has shown that cultures differ substantially in their use of interpersonal space, in their regard for territory, and in the meanings they assign to proxemic behavior (Burgoon, Buller, & Woodall, 1996; Gudykunst & Kim, 1992; Hall, 1959, 1976; Malandro & Barker, 1983; Scheflen, 1974; see Chapter 2 for more on proxemic behavior). For example, according to Lustig and Koester (1993), people from colder climates typically maintain larger interpersonal distances when they communicate, whereas those from warmer climates prefer closer interpersonal distances (p. 196).

One Saturday night in Mexico City several years ago, I rode in a subway train with several other Americans. As thousands of people boarded the train and the crush became intense, the Americans showed signs of pain and claustrophobia, yet the Mexicans remained blasé, though somewhat amused by our discomfort. It is common for Americans to perceive Mexicans as rude and Arabs as pushy because they maintain close personal-space boundaries and expect and employ closer interpersonal distances than do Americans. Conversely, Arabs and Mexicans may perceive Americans as aloof and unfriendly because of cultural differences in proxemic behavior.

Kinesics

Considerable intercultural differences have been observed in all aspects of people's kinesic behavior, including facial expressions, body movements, gestures, and conversational regulators (Burgoon, Buller, & Woodall, 1989; Gudykunst &

Kim, 1992; Hall, 1976; Jensen, 1985; Samovar, Porter, & Jain, 1981; Scheflen, 1974). For example, the A-OK sign, which is formed by making a circle with the thumb and index finger, is familiar to all Americans. When Richard Nixon visited Venezuela as the U.S. vice president in 1956 and gave two A-OK signs to a crowd of demonstrators in Caracas, a huge riot erupted. Nixon was later informed that the A-OK sign actually had a different meaning in Venezuela, similar to an upraised middle finger in America. In Italy, China, and Colombia good-bye is signaled by moving the palm and fingers back and forth toward one's body, a gesture that means "come here" in the United States (Jandt, 1995). These differences in emblems—wordlike gestures with explicit meanings—really constitute a different language as people travel from culture to culture.

Northern Europeans and northeast Asians engage in much more restrained nonverbal displays than, for example, Africans, southern Europeans, or Mexicans. Gestures and movements differ dramatically in meaning, extensiveness, and intensity. Americans and northern Europeans seem "square" and unexpressive to most Italians and Egyptians. Conversely, the gestural behavior of people from the Mediterranean seems almost undignified and overly emotional to most Americans.

Haptics

Research has confirmed that interpersonal patterns of tactile communication, or haptics, show considerable intercultural variation (Andersen & Leibowitz, 1978; Malandro & Barker, 1983; Prosser, 1978; Samovar, Porter, & Jain, 1981). Recent studies reveal differences in international and intercultural touch in amount, location, type of touch and whether it is manifested in public or private (Jones, 1994; McDaniel & Andersen, 1998).

Touch behavior represents a major source of diversity among couples from different cultures. During a recent data-collection session at an international airport, a colleague and I observed incredibly diverse tactile behaviors between people of many cultural backgrounds (see McDaniel & Andersen, 1998). A family leaving for Tonga formed a circle, wove their arms around each others' backs, and prayed and chanted together. A tearful man returning to Bosnia repeatedly tried to leave his sobbing wife; each time he turned back to her, they would grip each other by the fingertips and exchange a passionate, tearful kiss and a powerful embrace. Two Korean couples departed without any touch, despite the prolonged separation that lay ahead of them.

Physical Appearance

Physical appearance, the most salient nonverbal code during initial encounters, is crucial because many intercultural encounters are based on stereotypes and superficial physical cues. Certainly, what is "beautiful" varies greatly from culture

Clothing communicates culture. This man is wearing traditional clothing appropriate to his culture and climate.

to culture, particularly in terms of clothing, artifacts, body ornamentation, body type, and body shape (see Burgoon, Buller, & Woodall, 1996; Hatfield & Sprecher, 1986; Samovar, Porter, & Jain, 1981). There is some cross-cultural similarity in what constitutes an attractive face, but little else is similar. Ubangi women insert pieces of wood into their mouths to create lips up to ten inches in diameter. In China during much of this century, women often had their feet bound and deformed, which prevented walking outside the home. This culturally imposed deformity was considered a very desirable trait in China, although most Americans would consider such a tradition grotesque and perhaps evil. The amount of body and facial hair that is desirable also varies greatly from culture to culture. American advertisers have been quite successful in convincing women that hair on their legs or underarms is unsightly, and they have been somewhat successful in convincing men, particularly in the business world, that facial hair is unprofessional.

White shirts and ties have become the universal attire of the international business culture, transcending local cultural dress. Judging by their clothing alone, it would be difficult to determine what culture these businessmen are from.

By contrast, European women are much less likely than American women to remove the hair from their legs and underarms, and businessmen in the Middle East are much more likely to have mustaches or beards than American businessmen. And although T-shirts, blue jeans, business suits, and basketball shoes are now internationally accepted attire, many cultures still observe local dress customs. Recently, during the previously mentioned field study at an international airport, I witnessed Tongans in multicultural ceremonial gowns, Sikhs in white turbans, Hasidic Jews in blue yarmulkes, and Africans in white dashikis—alongside Californians in running shorts and halter tops.

Oculesics

Oculesics, the study of messages sent by the eyes, through eye contact, blinks, eye movements, and pupil dilation, has received only marginal attention by intercultural communication scholars (Gudykunst & Kim, 1992; Jensen, 1985; Samovar, Porter, & Jain, 1981). Because eye contact has been called an "invitation to communicate," its cross-cultural variation is an important communication topic, yet most books on intercultural communication fail to cite any research on this important topic.

Several years ago I served as an instructor for a university-wide orientation for teaching assistants. Among the participants were two young women from France who were in America for the first time. These very attractive young women expressed their disappointment to the class that during their brief stay they had received no attention at all from American men. "They don't even look at us," one complained. "Are American men gay?" queried the other. These women were used to the eye behavior of men in France, where staring at a woman's body is quite acceptable and, in certain contexts, even flattering. Such staring would be considered rude in America, where men take fleeting glances at a woman's body and try not to get caught looking.

Vocalics

Vocalics, or paralinguistics—the tones, pitches, and other nonverbal elements of the voice—has received relatively little attention in intercultural communication research (Gudykunst & Kim, 1992; LaBarre, 1985; Rich, 1974; Scheflen, 1972; Samovar, Porter, & Jain, 1981). The sounds of the human voice vary greatly from culture to culture. For example, to speakers of other languages, German speakers seem dominant and angry. Americans often erroneously perceive Saudi Arabians to be excited or angry due to their intonation patterns (Lustig & Koester, 1993). Despite the linguistic similarity between the Scandinavian languages Swedish and Danish, the differences in pronunciation cause Swedes to joke that "Danes don't speak, they just make animal sounds!" Italians and Mexicans complain that the tones of English are unromantic and difficult to use to communicate intimacy.

Music and singing, universal forms of nonverbal communication, have been almost completely overlooked in intercultural research, except for one excellent study (Lomax, 1968) that identified several groups of worldwide cultures through differences and similarities in their folk sounds. Lomax's research is so thorough that migration and diffusion patterns among cultures can be studied by examining his data.

Accents are one aspect of vocalics that has been widely researched (for a summary see Giles & Street, 1994). Research has shown that regional, ethnic, and blue-collar accents are preferred by members of one's own group but thought of as signs of low intelligence, low education, low status, and low success by the dominant, or "mainstream," culture. This research on vocalic stereotyping has been conducted in a number of countries, with similar patterns emerging regardless of the country.

Olfactics

Olfactic differences among cultures have not been widely studied. Reports of chemical and olfactic communication are given only cursory treatment in contemporary intercultural textbooks because of the limited research on this topic (see Gudykunst & Kim, 1992; Jandt, 1995; Lustig & Koester, 1993). One thing we do know is that North Americans are arguably the most uptight culture on earth about smell. To them, no body odor is a good body odor. Not so in other places. In the Middle East communication is so much more intense than in Europe and in the United States and Canada. According to Hall (1966b), in Arab cultures, "Not only is the sheer noise level much higher, but the piercing look of the eyes, the touch of the hands, and the mutual bathing in the warm, moist breath represents stepped-up sensory inputs to a level Europeans find unbearably intense" (p. 158). The feel and smell of another's breath, considered obnoxious and offensive by Americans and Canadians, is an intimacy cue in the Middle East, much like eye contact and nodding in the United States.

Locating and Defining Culture

The word *culture* is frequently used in a variety of ways. To avoid confusion, culture is defined in this book as "the enduring influence of the social world on one's behavior, including interpersonal communication behavior" (Andersen, 1997, p. 246). Culture, along with the social situation and the individual's personal traits and internal state, is one of the four primary antecedents of interpersonal behavior (Andersen, 1987, 1997; Figure 4.1). Culture is a learned set of shared perceptions about belief, values, and needs that affects the behaviors of relatively large groups of people (Lustig & Koester, 1993). Culture exerts a considerable force on individual behavior through what Geertz (1973) calls "control mechanisms—plans, recipes, rules, instructions (what computer engineers call 'programs')—for the governing of behavior" (p. 44). Culture has persuasive effects on members who live in its sphere, although not all people are affected uniformly. Culture is usually an intergenerational phenomenon, because the family and the community inculcate in children the views, rules, norms, and folkways of their culture. "Culture can be behaviorally observed by contrasting intragroup homogeneity with intergroup heterogeneity" (Andersen, Lustig, & Andersen, 1986, p. 11).

Culture is often confused with personal traits because both are enduring influences on a person's nonverbal behavior (Andersen, 1987, 1997). Personal traits, however, derive from multiple sources (Andersen, 1987), including genetics, environmental influences, and individual consciousness, as well as culture. Culture is also sometimes confused with the situation because both are part of one's social environment. Culture, however, is an enduring phenomenon, whereas each situation is a transient experience with an observable beginning and end. Culture, along with genetics, is the most enduring, powerful, and invisible shaper of our communication behavior.

Location of influence

	Social environment	Internal forces
Enduring phenomena	Culture	Traits
Transient phenomena	Situation	State

Time frame (labels on left: Enduring phenomena / Transient phenomena)

FIGURE 4.1 Sources of influence on interpersonal behavior.

Dimensions of Culture

Each culture manifests thousands of nonverbal behavioral differences—some small and subtle, some large and obvious—that distinguish it from every other culture. Because there are hundreds of different cultures on earth, the list of these differences is almost an endless one. Fortunately, there is a way to organize these differences into meaningful dimensions or groups. Researchers have identified a set of six dimensions that may explain *why* cultures differ in their nonverbal behavior (Andersen, 1988; Hecht, Andersen, & Ribeau, 1989; Hofstede, 1982). Arguably, most cultural variations in nonverbal behavior, including those discussed in the first part of this chapter, are the result of these fundamental dimensions.

Immediacy Orientation

Immediacy behaviors are defined as actions that simultaneously communicate warmth, closeness, and availability for communication and signal approach rather than avoidance and closeness rather than distance (see Chapter 8 for more on nonverbal immediacy). Cultures that display considerable interpersonal closeness or immediacy have been labeled contact cultures; people in these cultures stand closer to each other, touch more (Hall, 1966b), and are generally more expressive than are people in noncontact cultures, who tend to stand farther apart, touch less, and manifest less nonverbal expressiveness. Patterson (1983) maintains:

> These habitual patterns of relating to the world permeate all aspects of everyday life, but their effects on social behavior define the manner in which people relate to one another. In the case of contact cultures, this general tendency is manifested in closer approaches so that tactile and olfactory information may be gained easily. (p. 145)

Cultures also differ in the degree of sensory stimulation they prefer. Contact cultures create immediacy by increasing sensory input, whereas noncontact cultures prefer less sensory involvement.

FIGURE 4.2 Immediacy orientations of selected countries and regions.

Although much has been written about contact and noncontact cultures, only a handful of studies have examined the immediacy dimension of culture. As shown in Figure 4.2, research indicates that contact cultures include Indonesia, most Arab countries (including those in northern Africa), as well as countries in the Mediterranean region (including France, Greece, Italy, Portugal, and Spain), the Middle East, eastern Europe (including Russia), and virtually all of Latin America (including Mexico; Condon and Yousef, 1983; Hecht, Andersen, & Ribeau, 1989; Jones, 1994; Jones & Remland, 1982; Mehrabian, 1971a; Patterson, 1983; Samovar, Porter, & Jain, 1981; Scheflen, 1972). Australians are moderate in their cultural-contact level. Noncontact cultures include most of northern Europe (including Norway, Sweden, Finland, Germany, and Great Britain), Anglo-Americans (the predominant culture of the United States), as well as virtually every Asian country (including Myanmar—formerly Burma—China, Hong Kong, Japan, South Korea, the Philippines, Taiwan, Thailand, and Vietnam; Andersen, Andersen, & Lustig, 1987; Heslin & Alper, 1983; Jones, 1994; Jones & Remland, 1982; McDaniel & Andersen, 1995; Mehrabian, 1971a; Patterson, 1983; Samovar, Porter, & Jain, 1981; Scheflen, 1972).

Although, in general, the Japanese touch very little and strive to maintain their personal space, extreme crowding during rush hour in Tokyo is quite common and accepted as normal by urban commuters.

Two recent studies (McDaniel & Andersen, 1998; Remland, Jones, & Brickman, 1991) suggest that residents of the United States, Canada, and Great Britain may actually fall under the contact category. According to this research, these cultures engage in considerable touch and maintain relatively close interpersonal distances. These studies question Hall's (1966b) research and suggest that his original designation of some cultures—such as Europe and North America (excluding Mexico)—as noncontact cultures was an oversimplification. One explanation for these conflicting findings is that younger people—that is, those born after World War II—in England and the United States exhibit much higher contact and more nonverbally expressive behaviors than their parents and grandparents. Members of the baby-boomer generation and generations that followed have grown up in a culture permeated by international and intercultural media, intercultural contact, mediated sports celebrations replete with physical contact, rock and roll, and a counterculture ideologically predisposed to contact. Try giving a hug or a high five to a person over 55 (with the exception of family members) and see if I'm right. A person in his or her 20s—that is, a member of a contact culture—is much more likely to respond to your high five. It may not be that Hall's findings about Europe and North America were wrong; instead, they may have simply failed to detect the dramatic culture change that was simultaneously occurring in our globally mediated world.

Contact cultures tend to be located in the Middle East, the Mediterranean region, and in lower latitudes near the equator. Research has identified several factors—including energy level, climate, sunlight, and metabolism—that may explain such latitudinal variations (Andersen, Lustig, & Andersen, 1990). Evidently, cultures in cooler climates tend to be more task-oriented and interpersonally "cool," whereas cultures in warmer climates tend to be more interpersonally oriented and interpersonally "warm." Even within the United States, more-immediate cultures tend to be located in the warmer latitudes. Andersen, Lustig, & Andersen (1990) report a .31 correlation between latitude and touch avoidance among American university students. These data suggest that students attending universities located in the sun belt are more touch-oriented and thus constitute contact cultures or subcultures. Furthermore, research suggests that African Americans tend to be warmer, more expressive, and more immediate than European Americans (Lustig & Koester, 1993).

Recently, Pennebaker, Rime, and Sproul (1994) found a correlation between latitude and expressiveness *within* dozens of countries. Their studies show that northerners are less expressive in Belgium, Croatia, France, Germany, Italy, Japan, Serbia, Spain, Switzerland, and the United States than are southerners in these countries; in fact, a difference in expressiveness has been found to exist across the entire northern hemisphere. Pennebaker et al. (1994) conclude:

> Logically, climate must profoundly affect social processes. People living in cold climates devote more time to dressing, to providing warmth, to planning ahead for food provisions during the winter months. . . . In warm climates, people are more likely to see, hear, and interact with neighbors year round. Emotional expressiveness, then, would be more of a requirement. (pp. 15–16)

Similarly, Andersen, Lustig, and Andersen (1990) conclude:

> In Northern latitudes societies must be more structured, more ordered, more constrained, and more organized if the individuals are to survive harsh weather forces. . . . In contrast, southern latitudes may attract or produce a culture characterized by social extravagance and flamboyance that has no strong inclination to constrain or order their world. (p. 307)

McDaniel and Andersen's (1998) data on public touch suggest the biggest cultural difference in immediacy is between Asians, who rarely touch in public, and people from virtually every other culture, all of whom manifest higher degrees of public touching. These findings are consistent with other research that suggests that China and Japan are distinctly nontouch cultures (Barnland, 1978; Jones, 1994). Research by Klopf and Thompson (1991) reveals that Japanese students reported themselves to be significantly less immediate than either Finnish or American students. This provides additional evidence that Asia is a low-immediacy, noncontact region and that northern Europe and North America—excluding Mexico—may be higher-immediacy regions than previously believed,

The United States is the most individualistic culture on earth. Despite traffic jams and air pollution, individualistic Americans typically commute one person to a car.

though not as highly immediate as cultures located in Latin America, the Mediterranean, or the Middle East.

Little other research has been conducted on the differences in immediacy and contact between Asia and the rest of the world. Why is Asia such a low-immediacy culture? McDaniel and Andersen (1995) speculate that Confucianism, with its emphasis on self-control, respect, decorum, and proper behavior, may restrain the expressiveness of cultures under its influence. Perhaps the Asian emphasis on collectivism (discussed in the following section) is a primary force that emphasizes respect of others at the expense of individual expressiveness.

To summarize the cultural differences in immediacy: in general, northern countries, northern parts of individual countries, traditional cultures, and Asian countries are the least immediate and expressive; southern regions, modern countries, and non-Asian cultures are the most expressive and immediate. Obviously, these findings are painted with a fairly broad brush and must await a more detailed cultural portrait.

Individualism Versus Collectivism

Perhaps the most fundamental dimensions along which cultures differ is their degree to which the core values of a culture center on individualism versus col-

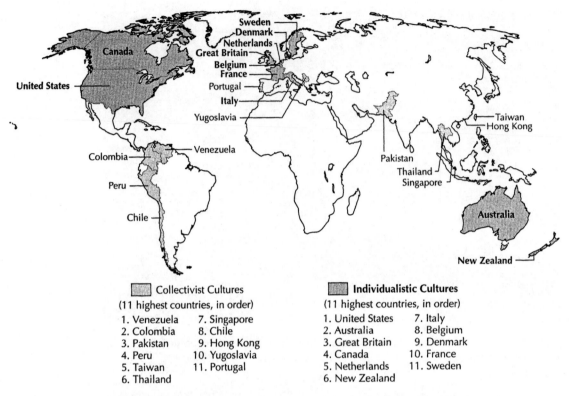

FIGURE 4.3   Individualistic versus collectivist rankings of selected countries (Hofstede, 1982).

lectivism. This dimension explains the ways in which people live (for example, alone, in families, in villages or tribes, see Hofstede, 1982), their values, and how they communicate, including how they communicate nonverbally. Individualistic cultures value space, privacy, emotional expression, and personal choice of nonverbal behavior. Collectivist cultures value contact, togetherness, and restrained individual expression of emotion, particularly the expression of negative emotion. Collectivists engage in nonverbal behaviors that benefit the group.

In his landmark study of forty noncommunist countries, Hofstede (1982) reports that the nine most individualistic nations are (in order) the United States, Australia, Great Britain, Canada, the Netherlands, New Zealand, Italy, Belgium, and Denmark—all of which are Western, developed cultures with predominantly European roots (Figure 4.3). The nine most collectivist nations are (in order) Venezuela, Colombia, Pakistan, Peru, Taiwan, Thailand, Singapore, Chile, and Hong Kong—all Asian or South American cultures. Similarly, Sitaram and Codgell (1976) reported individuality to be of primary importance in Western cultures, of secondary importance in African cultures, and of lesser importance in Eastern and Muslim cultures.

Individualism is one of the fundamental dimensions that distinguish cultures, particularly Eastern cultures from Western cultures. "There is little doubt that Western culture is individualistic, so people rely on personal judgments. Eastern cultures emphasize harmony among people, between people and nature, and value collective judgments" (Hecht, Andersen, & Ribeau, 1989, p. 170). Tomkins (1984) argues that an individual's psychological makeup is the result of this cultural dimension. He states, "Human beings, in Western Civilization, have tended toward self-celebration, positive or negative. In Oriental thought another alternative is represented, that of harmony between man and nature" (p. 182). According to Lustig and Koester (1993), individualism is characterized by the key words "*independence, privacy, self,* and the all-important *I*" (p. 144). By contrast, collectivist cultures emphasize *we* and a sense of connection and belonging. According to Jandt (1995), the Japanese concept of *amea* best typifies collectivist cultures. *Amea* is characterized by nurturing concern, dependence on others, and a wish to be loved and cared for unconditionally.

For better or worse, Americans are individualists. According to the U.S. census of 1990, the most common American household consisted of one person and the second most common household comprised two people. Americans see individualism as a blessing and have elevated it to the status of a national religion (Andersen, 1988). From the early days of the American republic, individualism has been celebrated. In his writings about America in the 1830s, the French philosopher Alexis de Tocqueville (1835/1945) noted:

> Individualism is a mature and calm feeling, which disposes each member of the community to sever himself from the mass of his fellows and to draw apart with his family and friends, so that he has thus formed a little circle of his own, . . . he willingly leaves society at large to itself (p. 104).

The best and the worst of American culture is attributable to individualism. Proponents of individualism have argued that it is the basis of liberty, democracy, freedom, and economic incentive and that it serves as a protection against tyranny. Conversely, individualism has been blamed for our alienation from one another, loneliness, selfishness, crime, and narcissism. Indeed, Hall (1976) has claimed that as an extreme individualist, "Western man has created chaos by denying that part of his self that integrates while enshrining the parts that fragment experience" (p. 9).

Although the United States is the most individualistic country on earth (Andersen, 1988; Hofstede, 1982; Prosser, 1978), regions of the United States vary in their degree of individualism. Elazar (1972) has shown that the central Midwest and mid-Atlantic regions are the most individualistic political culture, whereas the Southeast is the most traditionalistic and least individualistic. Remember, however, that these findings are all relative; by world standards, even Mississippi is an individualistic culture. Bellah, Madsen, Sullivan, Swidler, & Tipton (1985) stated:

> Individualism lies at the very core of American culture. . . . Anything that
> would violate our right to think for ourselves, judge for ourselves, make our
> own decisions, live our lives as we see fit, is not only morally wrong, it is sacri-
> legious. (p. 142)

Just as geographical regions of the United States differ in their degree of individualism, so too do various ethnic groups. African Americans, for example, emphasize individualism, whereas Mexican Americans emphasize group and relational
solidarity (Hecht, Andersen, & Ribeau, 1989). Indeed, extreme individualism
makes it difficult for most Americans to interact with and understand people
from other cultures. As Condon and Yousef (1983) stated, "The fusion of individualism and equality is so valued and so basic that many Americans find it most
difficult to relate to contrasting values in other cultures where interdependence
greatly determines a person's sense of self" (p. 65).

Whether a culture is individualistic or collectivist affects the nonverbal behavior of that culture in every way. First, people from individualistic cultures are
more remote proxemically. Collectivist cultures are interdependent, and as a result, people work, play, live, and sleep in close proximity to each other. Hofstede
(1982) cites research that suggests that as hunters and gatherers, people lived apart
in individualistic, nuclear families. As agricultural societies developed, the interdependent extended family began living in close proximity in large family or
tribal units. Urban-industrial societies later returned to the norm of individualism, nuclear families, and lack of proximity to one's neighbors, friends, and
coworkers.

Kinesic behavior tends to be more synchronized in collectivist cultures.
Where families work collectively, movements, schedules, and actions need to be
highly coordinated (Argyle, 1975a). In developed, urban cultures, family members
often "do their own thing," coming and going, working and playing, eating and
sleeping, all on different schedules. People in individualistic cultures also smile
more than in normatively, or collectively, oriented cultures, according to Tomkins (1984). This is probably due to the fact that individualists are responsible for
their relationships and their own happiness, whereas collectively oriented people
regard compliance with norms as a primary value and personal or interpersonal
happiness as a secondary value (Andersen, 1988). Matsumoto (1991) contends
that "collective cultures will foster emotional displays of their members that
maintain and facilitate group cohesion, harmony, or cooperation, to a greater
degree than individualistic cultures" (p. 132). Similarly, Lustig and Koester (1993)
maintain that "people from individualistic cultures are more likely than those
from collectivist cultures to use confrontational strategies when dealing with interpersonal problems; those with a collectivist orientation are likely to use avoidance, third-party intermediaries, or other face-saving techniques" (p. 147). People
in collectivist cultures may suppress both positive and negative emotional displays that are contrary to the mood of the group, because maintaining the group's

cohesion is a primary value (Andersen, 1988). Bond (1993) reports that the Chinese culture is lower in frequency, intensity, and duration of emotional expression. Bond contends that "the expression of emotion is carefully regulated out of a concern for its capacity to disrupt group harmony and status hierarchies" (p. 245).

People in individualistic cultures are encouraged to express emotions nonverbally, especially in their face and voice, because individual freedom is a paramount value. Research suggests that people in individualistic cultures are nonverbally affiliative. Intuitively, the reason for this is not obvious, because individualism doesn't require affiliation. However, as Hofstede (1982) explains:

> In less individualistic countries where traditional social ties, like those with extended family members, continue to exist, people have less of a need to make specific friendships. One's friends are predetermined by the social relationships into which one is born. In the more individualistic countries, however, affective relationships are not socially predetermined but must be acquired by each individual personally. (p. 163)

In individualistic countries, affiliation, dating, flirting, small talk, smiling, and initial acquaintance are more important than in collectivist countries, where the social network is more fixed and less reliant on individual initiative. Bellah et al. (1985) maintain that over the centuries, the individualistic and mobile nature of U.S. society has enabled people to meet more easily and maintain more open communication; at the same time, however, it has caused their relationships to be more casual and transient.

Finally, in an impressive study of dozens of cultures, Lomax (1968) found that song and dance styles of a country were related to its level of social cohesion and collectivism. Collectivist cultures exhibit higher cohesiveness in their singing styles and more synchrony in their dance styles (Lomax, 1968). It isn't surprising that rock dancing, which emphasizes separateness and "doing your own thing," evolved in such individualistic cultures as England and the United States. Americans' style of dancing may serve as a metaphor for the whole U.S. culture, which emphasizes individuality more than any other country in the world (Andersen, 1988).

Gender Orientation

The gender orientation of culture has a huge impact on many aspects of communication, including nonverbal behavior. Although gender is a biologically determined trait—each of us is born as a male or female—it is also regulated by the gender rules of each culture. In most cultures, males are socialized into so-called masculine roles, which emphasize qualities such as power and dominance, and females are socialized into traditionally feminine roles, which emphasize qualities such as nurturance and compassion. Gender roles regulate (1) the types of expressions permitted by each sex, (2) occupational status, (3) nonverbal aspects of power, (4) the ability to interact with strangers or acquaintances of the opposite sex, and (5) all aspects of interpersonal relationships between men and women. "While numerous studies have focused on gender as an individual characteristic, gender has been neglected as a cultural dimension" (Hecht, Andersen, & Ribeau, 1989, p. 171).

As conceptualized here, gender orientation refers to the degree of masculinity or femininity exhibited by a culture. In rigidly masculine cultures, positive traits typically include strength, assertiveness, competitiveness, and ambitiousness; less valued are typically feminine traits such as affection, compassion, nurturance, and emotionality (Bem, 1974; Hofstede, 1982). Masculine cultures also regard power and materialism as important values (Gudykunst & Kim, 1992; Hofstede, 1982). People in masculine cultures believe in ostentatious manliness (Lustig & Koester, 1993). Masculine Latino countries such as Mexico and Venezuela emphasize machismo, or macho male characteristics. Similarly, masculine Germanic countries such as Austria, Germany, and Switzerland value "manly" men—as satirically depicted in the classic "Hans and Frans" routine on *Saturday Night Live,* in which Hans and Frans are "all pumped up," not "little girlie guys."

By contrast, feminine (also called androgynous) cultures emphasize nurturance, compassion, and quality of life (Hofstede, 1982). These cultures have more flexible sex roles and allow both men and women to express more diverse, less stereotyped sex-role behaviors. Not surprisingly, women have more rights and privileges in feminine cultures.

Hofstede (1982) has measured the degree to which a culture endorses masculine or feminine goals. The masculinity of a culture is negatively correlated with a high percentage of women in technical and professional jobs and positively correlated with segregation of sexes in higher education (Hofstede, 1982).

The countries with the nine highest masculinity index scores, according to Hofstede (1982), are (in order) Japan, Austria, Venezuela, Italy, Switzerland, Mexico, Ireland, Great Britain, and Germany (Figure 4.4). The majority of the countries in this list are located in western and central Europe and the Caribbean region. The nine countries with the highest feminine scores are (in order) Sweden, Norway, the Netherlands, Denmark, Yugoslavia, Finland, Chile, Portugal, and Thailand—a good percentage of these countries being located in northern Europe. Compared to low-masculinity countries, high-masculinity countries have fewer women in the labor force, have only recently afforded voting privileges to women, and are least likely to consider wife rape a crime (Seager & Olson, 1986).

Why don't most South American cultures manifest stronger masculine orientations and the Latin pattern of machismo? Hofstede (1982) suggests that machismo is more prevalent in the Caribbean-bordering countries than in the remainder of South America. In fact, South America, as compared to Central America, has a much higher percentage of working women, much higher school attendance by girls, and more women in higher education (Seager & Olson, 1986).

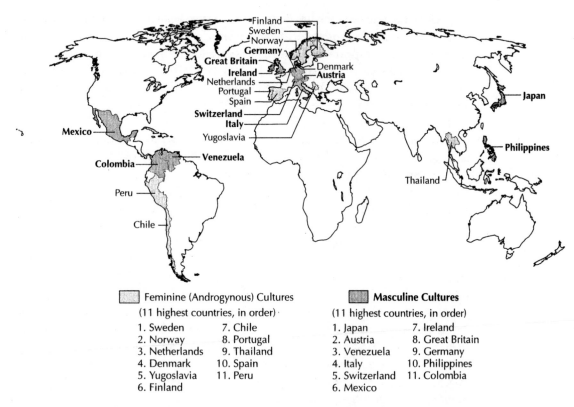

FIGURE 4.4   Gender orientations of selected countries (Hofstede, 1982).

Furthermore, Brazil—the largest country in South America—manifests considerable Portuguese influence in its language and culture. Because Portugal tends to be feminine in its gender orientations, its values may still be evident in contemporary Brazilian behavior.

Research suggests that androgynous patterns of behavior (that are both feminine and masculine) result in higher levels of self-esteem, social competence, success, and intellectual development for both males and females (Andersen, 1988) and may even lead to greater physical health, because both masculine strength and fitness and feminine expressiveness and nurturance are associated with good health. Is it a coincidence that the more androgynous (feminine) countries are associated with longer life expectancies? Perhaps not. Nonverbal styles that allow both men and women alike to express both masculine traits (such as dominance and strength) and feminine attributes (such as warmth and emotionality) are likely to contribute to physical and emotional well-being. Buck (1984) has demonstrated that many males may harm their health by internalizing emotions rather than externalizing them, as women usually do. Internalized emotions that aren't expressed result in more stress and higher blood pressure. Interestingly, more-masculine countries show higher levels of stress (Hofstede, 1982).

Considerable research has demonstrated significant nonverbal vocalic differences between egalitarian and nonegalitarian countries. Countries where women are economically important and where sexual standards for women are permissive show more relaxed vocal patterns than less-egalitarian countries (Lomax, 1968). Moreover, these egalitarian countries show less tension between the sexes, more vocal solidarity and coordination in their songs, and more synchrony in their overall movement (Lomax, 1968).

In feminine countries, as compared to masculine countries, same-sex touch is more common. Masculine cultures tend to have a more rigid and unaccepting view toward same-sex touch, particularly among males. Feminine countries have more permissive attitudes about sexual behavior, particularly for women (Hofstede, 1982). Indeed, many of the most feminine countries, such as Denmark and the Netherlands, are criticized by people of other nationalities for their liberal attitudes and laws regarding sexual behavior.

It is important to note that, according to Hofstede (1982), the United States tends to be a masculine country, although it is not among the very most masculine. Intercultural communicators should keep in mind that other countries may be either more or less sexually egalitarian than the United States. Because most countries are more feminine than the United States (that is, they are more nurturing and compassionate), Americans of both sexes frequently seem dominant, loud, aggressive, and competitive by world standards, conveying the image of the "ugly American." Likewise, Americans' attitude toward women may seem sexist in extremely feminine cultures such as Scandinavia.

Power-Distance Orientation

A fourth basic dimension of intercultural communication is power distance. Power distance—the degree to which power, prestige, and wealth are unequally distributed in a culture—has been measured in a number of cultures using Hofstede's (1982) Power Distance Index (PDI). In cultures with high PDI scores, power, wealth, and influence are concentrated in the hands of a few rather than being more equally distributed throughout the population. Condon and Yousef (1983) distinguish among three cultural patterns: democratic, authority-centered, and authoritarian. The PDI is highly correlated (.80) with authoritarianism (Hofstede, 1982).

According to Hofstede (1982), the highest-PDI countries are (in order) the Philippines, Mexico, Venezuela, India, Yugoslavia, Singapore, Brazil, France, Hong Kong, and Colombia (Figure 4.5). This list is dominated by countries located in the low latitudes of Asia and the Americas. Gudykunst and Kim (1992) report that both African and Asian cultures usually establish hierarchical relationships. Asian students are expected to be modest and deferent nonverbally in the presence of their instructors. Likewise, the Vietnamese consider teachers and employers to be their mentors and will not question orders. The nine lowest PDI countries are (in order) Austria, Israel, Denmark, New Zealand, Ireland, Sweden,

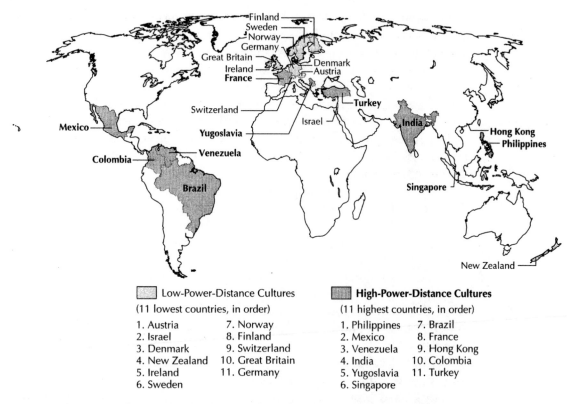

Low-Power-Distance Cultures
(11 lowest countries, in order)

1. Austria	7. Norway
2. Israel	8. Finland
3. Denmark	9. Switzerland
4. New Zealand	10. Great Britain
5. Ireland	11. Germany
6. Sweden	

High-Power-Distance Cultures
(11 highest countries, in order)

1. Philippines	7. Brazil
2. Mexico	8. France
3. Venezuela	9. Hong Kong
4. India	10. Colombia
5. Yugoslavia	11. Turkey
6. Singapore	

FIGURE 4.5   Power-distance orientations of selected countries (Hofstede, 1982).

Norway, Finland, and Switzerland (Hofstede, 1982). Most of the countries in this list are middle-class, developed democracies located at high latitudes.

A primary determiner of power distance is weather and climate (for a discussion of these macroenvironmental nonverbal factors see Chapter 3). Hofstede (1982) claims that latitude and climate are major forces that shape a culture. He maintains that the key intervening variable is climate. For example, in colder climates, technology is needed for survival. This produces a chain of events in which people come to rely on each other rather than on authority figures. Education, teamwork, and individual initiative are necessary to survive in harsh, variable climates, as are creative solutions to problems and changing conditions, rather than simple obedience to authority. The result is that most low-PDI cultures are found in high latitudes and harsh climates; in fact, Hofstede (1982) reports a .65 correlation between PDI and latitude! In a study conducted at forty U.S. universities, Andersen, Lustig, and Andersen (1990) reported a −.47 correlation between latitude and intolerance for ambiguity and a −.45 correlation between latitude and authoritarianism. This suggests that residents of the northern United States are less authoritarian and more tolerant of ambiguity than those in the southern United States. Northern U.S. cultures, like their international counterparts, may have to be less autocratic and more cooperative to ensure collaboration and survival in harsher climates.

The United States scores slightly lower than the median on the PDI, indicating lesser status differentials than many countries but more inequality than many others. Cultures differ in terms of how status in acquired. In many countries, such as India, one's status is historically ascribed according to class. In the United States, however, power and status are typically achieved through monetary success and manifested by conspicuous material displays of materialism (Andersen & Bowman, 1990).

The population of a country or a culture may be another predictor of power distance. Generally, larger cultures score higher on the PDI (Lustig & Koester, 1993). As the size of any group increases, it becomes unwieldy and difficult to manage informally. This is even true of larger classrooms, larger governments, and larger organizations. In larger aggregations, informal relationships must yield to formal rules, bureaucracies, and hierarchical relationships. For cultures with large populations to function effectively, social and political hierarchies must be created, causing the power-distance factor to increase. The fact that most low-power-distance countries are small, well-managed democracies is probably not coincidental.

Power distance affects the nonverbal behavior of a culture. In high-PDI cultures such as India, with its rigid caste system, interaction among the classes is severely limited. More than 20 percent of India's population are identified as "untouchables"; these individuals languish at the bottom of India's five-caste system (Chinoy, 1967). Any contact with untouchables by members of other castes is strictly forbidden and considered "polluting." Certainly, tactile communication between castes is greatly curtailed in Indian culture. High-PDI countries with less rigid stratification than India may still prohibit free interclass dating, marriage, and contact—opportunities that are taken for granted in low-PDI countries. Low-PDI countries are much more likely to permit nonverbal communication of all types, including liberal interpersonal association, close interpersonal distances, and greater tactile contact and visual exchanges.

Civilizations with large power discrepancies produce different kinesic behavior. High-PDI cultures foster and encourage emotions that underscore status differences. In high-PDI cultures, people are expected to show only positive emotions to others with high status and to display negative emotions to others with low status (Matsumoto, 1991; Porter & Samovar, 1998). According to Andersen and Bowman (1990), the bodily tension of subordinates is more obvious in power-discrepant relationships. Similarly, Andersen and Bowman (1990) report that in power-discrepant circumstances, subordinates smile more in an effort to appease superiors and appear polite. The ever present smiles on many Asians' faces constitute a culturally inculcated behavior of appeasing superiors and smoothing social relations; this nonverbal behavior is in keeping with a high-PDI cultural profile.

Vocalic, or paralinguistic, cues also vary according to the power-distance dimension of a given culture. Citizens of low-PDI cultures are generally less aware that vocal loudness may be offensive to others. American vocal tones are often perceived as noisy, exaggerated, and childlike (Condon & Yousef, 1983). Lomax (1968) has shown that in countries where political authority is highly centralized, singing voices are tighter and the voice box is more closed; by contrast, more permissive societies produce more relaxed, open, and clear sounds.

Uncertainty Orientation

People in all cultures face change, unpredictability, and uncertainty. Uncertainty orientation is a cultural predisposition toward risk and ambiguity (Hecht, Andersen, & Ribeau, 1989). Cultures with high uncertainty avoidance dislike ambiguity and uncertainty and believe that certain rules and beliefs will reduce uncertainty; at the individual level, this predisposition is often called tolerance or intolerance for ambiguity (Martin & Westie, 1959). People with an intolerance for ambiguity or with high levels of uncertainty avoidance want clear, black-and-white answers, fear change, and dread the future. People with a high tolerance for ambiguity and with low levels of uncertainty avoidance are more tolerant, accept ambiguous answers, see many shades of gray, and embrace future change. Hofstede (1982) demonstrates that a country's uncertainty avoidance is highly correlated with a high incidence of neuroticism and anxiety in its population. High uncertainty avoidance is negatively correlated with risk-taking and positively correlated with fear of failure.

Countries vary greatly in their tolerance for uncertainty. In some cultures, freedom leads to uncertainty, which leads to stress and anxiety. Hofstede (1982) maintains that intolerance of ambiguity and dogmatism are primarily a function of the uncertainty-avoidance dimension rather than the power-distance dimension. According to Hofstede (1982), the nine countries with the highest levels of uncertainty avoidance are (in order) Greece, Portugal, Belgium, Japan, Yugoslavia, Peru, Argentina, Chile, and France (Figure 4.6); this list is dominated by southern European and South American countries. The nine countries with the highest levels of uncertainty tolerance are (in order) Singapore, Denmark, Sweden, Hong Kong, Ireland, Great Britain, India, the Philippines, and the United States; this list is dominated by northern European and Southeast Asian cultures. Hofstede (1982) also reports that Catholic countries are high in uncertainty avoidance, whereas Protestant, Hindu, and Buddhist countries tend to be more accepting of uncertainty; Eastern religions and Protestantism tend to be less "absolute" than Catholicism. Andersen, Lustig, and Andersen (1990) report that intolerance for ambiguity is much higher in the southern United States than in the north; this tendency reflects the international pattern of tolerance at higher latitudes.

Fewer studies have examined the uncertainty dimension of nonverbal behavior than the other dimensions of culture. However, some research has shown

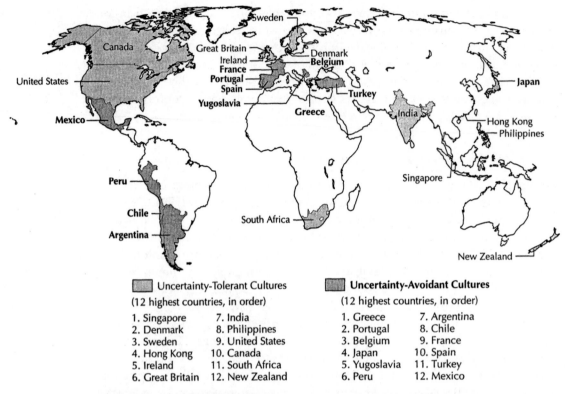

Uncertainty-Tolerant Cultures
(12 highest countries, in order)

1. Singapore	7. India
2. Denmark	8. Philippines
3. Sweden	9. United States
4. Hong Kong	10. Canada
5. Ireland	11. South Africa
6. Great Britain	12. New Zealand

Uncertainty-Avoidant Cultures
(12 highest countries, in order)

1. Greece	7. Argentina
2. Portugal	8. Chile
3. Belgium	9. France
4. Japan	10. Spain
5. Yugoslavia	11. Turkey
6. Peru	12. Mexico

FIGURE 4.6   Uncertainty orientations of selected countries (Hofstede, 1982).

that emotional displays are associated with uncertainty avoidance. Hofstede (1982) maintains that uncertainty-avoidant countries tend to display emotions more than do uncertainty-tolerant countries. Furthermore, he reports that uncertainty-avoidant countries are less tolerant in their attitudes toward young people and their emotional displays. According to Gudykunst and Kim (1992), when consensus or uniformity breaks down in high-uncertainty-avoidant countries, people become upset and show their emotions more than do residents of uncertainty-tolerant countries, who are more likely to tolerate change or nonconformity. Residents of high-uncertainty-avoidant cultures, such as Greece or France, are most likely to experience and exhibit stress and anxiety cues (Hofstede, 1982; see Chapter 7 for a complete discussion of these behaviors).

Certainly, disagreement and nonconformity are not appreciated in high-uncertainty-avoidant countries. Moreover, such cultures seem to prefer verbal behavior over nonverbal behavior. Indeed, Hofstede (1982) reports that in high-uncertainty-avoidant countries, rituals are created to provide "pseudocertainty," or the illusion of certainty. Such cultures place great importance on memos and reports and structured information collection and dissemination procedures—all with the intent of creating the illusion, if not the reality, of certainty.

Similarly, nonverbal behavior is more likely to be codified and rule-governed in high-uncertainty-avoidant countries. This means that kinesic and proxemic behaviors, for example, follow a strict set of rules and rituals. Such a profile seems to fit a high-uncertainty-avoidant country like Japan but remains to be tested and is somewhat speculative. Hofstede (1982) found that high-uncertainty-avoidant nations report more stylized and ritualized behavior, so we should expect nonverbal behavior to be more proscribed in these cultures. When communicating with people from a high-uncertainty-avoidant country such as Japan or France, Americans may come across as excessively unconventional and lacking in manners; at the same time, Americans may view their Japanese or French counterparts as too controlled and rigid (Lustig & Koester, 1993).

High Context Versus Low Context

Context is the final important dimension of intercultural communication. Context provides situational or environmental cues that frame any communication and influence its meaning (see Chapter 3 for more about the contextual codes of nonverbal communication). E. T. Hall (1976, 1984) has described high- and low-context cultures in considerable detail. "A high context (HC) communication or message is one in which most of the information is either in the physical context or internalized in the person, while very little is in the coded, explicit, transmitted parts of the message" (Hall, 1976, p. 91). Lifelong friends often use high-context, or implicit, messages that are nearly impossible for an outsider to understand. The situation itself, a smile, or a glance provides implicit meaning that does not need to be articulated. "In a high-context culture, much more is taken for granted and assumed to be shared, and consequently the overwhelming preponderance of messages are coded in such a way that they don't have to be explicitly and verbally transmitted" (Lustig & Koester, 1993, p. 133). In high-context situations or cultures, information is gleaned from the environment, the context, the situation, and from nonverbal cues that give the message meaning in the absence of explicit verbal utterance.

Low-context messages are just the opposite of high-context messages; most of the information is provided in the explicit code (Hall, 1976). Low-context messages must be elaborated, clearly communicated, and highly specific. Unlike personal relationships, which tend to utilize high-context message systems, institutions such as courts of law and formal systems such as mathematics and computer language require explicit, low-context message systems (E. T. Hall, 1984).

In a high-context country, the power structure is well known, and people behave with great deference toward their superiors. By contrast, in a low-context culture, people are oblivious to the power structure until they are told who is powerful and who is not. In a high-context culture, a negative facial expression or lack of enthusiasm may signal the cancellation of a business deal, whereas written notification would be required in the same case in a low-context culture.

Low-Context Cultures
(8 lowest countries, in order)

1. Germany	5. Norway
2. Switzerland	6. Finland
3. United States	7. Denmark
4. Sweden	8. Canada

High-Context Cultures
(8 highest countries, in order)

1. China	5. Native Americans
2. Japan	6. African Americans
3. South Korea	7. Mexican Americans
4. Taiwan	8. Latinos

FIGURE 4.7   High-context versus low-context rankings of selected countries and groups.

Cultures vary considerably in the degree of context used in communication. As shown in Figure 4.7, the lowest-context cultures are Germany, Switzerland, the United States, Sweden, Norway, Finland, Denmark, and Canada (Hall, 1976, 1984; Gudykunst & Kim, 1992). These cultures are preoccupied with specifics, details, literalness, and precise time schedules at the expense of context. They utilize behavior systems built around Aristotelian logic and linear thinking (E. T. Hall, 1984). These cultures also tend to be pathologically verbal, that is, they may miss subtle cues from other people or from the environment that are more meaningful than words (see Chapter 1 for more on the differences between verbal and nonverbal communication). Countries that exhibit characteristics of both high-context and low-context message systems include France, Great Britain, and Italy (Gudykunst & Kim, 1992); these countries are somewhat less explicit than far-northern European and Scandinavian cultures.

The highest-context cultures are found in Asia. China, Japan, South Korea, and Taiwan are extremely high-context cultures (Elliot, Scott, Jensen, & McDonough, 1982; Gudykunst & Kim, 1992; E. T. Hall, 1976, 1984). Native Americans, African Americans, Mexican Americans, and Latinos are also fairly high-context groups (Lustig & Koester, 1993). Usually, *language* implies an explicit message system, but the Chinese language is unique in that it is an implicit, high-context system. To use a Chinese dictionary, one must understand thousands of characters, which change meaning when used in varying combinations with other characters. Perhaps the best example of high-context communication is the Japanese tea ceremony, in which every behavior of both the host and the guests is carefully prescribed. The tea "ceremony is a highly scripted and ritualized experience that is almost incomprehensible to those who have not been trained to understand the meanings of even the most subtle behaviors" (Lustig & Koester, 1993, p. 132). According to Jandt (1995), in the tea ceremony "nothing is spoken; all meanings are in context. A typical response from a low-context observer is 'hurry up and drink your tea'" (p. 203).

Asian cultures are so reliant on context partly because they have been highly influenced by Buddhism, which places a high value on silence, lack of emotional expression, and the unspoken, nonverbal parts of communication (Burgoon, Buller, & Woodall, 1989; McDaniel & Andersen, 1998). Americans frequently complain that the Japanese never "get to the point," yet they fail to recognize that high-context cultures rely on the context and setting and let the point evolve (E. T. Hall, 1984). In a recent study of airport departures, McDaniel and Andersen (1998) found Asians to be the least tactile of any cultural group on earth. The influences of Confucianism and Buddhism and the value placed on context rather than on emotional expression probably explain this finding. Native American cultures with ancestral migratory roots in East Asia are remarkably similar to contemporary Asian cultures in several ways, especially in their use of high-context communication (E. T. Hall, 1984).

Before meeting with a small group of native Americans on their reservation near my home in Southern California, I instructed my Anglo-American friends to sit silently and not make a lot of idle small talk. Complying with my instructions, my friends and I sat in a circle under a pepper tree and listened to the wind and the birds before the meeting commenced. From our perspective, considerable time passed (probably only about five minutes). The Native Americans subsequently welcomed us back to the reservation for other ceremonies, projects, and meetings. By observing their high-context rules for communication, we had gained their trust.

Not surprisingly, most Latin American cultures, a fusion of Iberian (Portuguese-Spanish) and Native American traditions, are also high-context cultures. Eastern Mediterranean (including Greece and Turkey) and Arab cultures tend to fall under the high-context category as well.

Obviously, communication is quite different in high- and low-context cultures. First, explicit forms of communication such as verbal codes are more prevalent in low-context cultures such as the United States and northern Europe. Research by Ting-Toomey (1991) shows that U.S. respondents are more likely to express love overtly and explicitly through verbal communication than are French or Japanese respondents. These findings are consistent with low-context communication patterns. People from low-context cultures are often perceived as excessively talkative, belaboring of the obvious, and redundant. People from high-context cultures may be perceived as nondisclosive, wasteful of time, sneaky, and mysterious. Second, high-context cultures do not value verbal communication as highly as low-context cultures. Elliot et al. (1982) found that more-verbal people were perceived as more attractive by people in the United States (a low-context culture), but that less-verbal people were perceived as more attractive in Korea (a high-context culture). Third, high-context cultures are more likely to tune into and utilize nonverbal communication. Low-context cultures, particularly men in low-context cultures, fail to perceive as much nonverbal communication as members of high-context cultures. Nonverbal communication provides the context for all communication (Watzlawick, Beavin, & Jackson, 1967; see also Chapter 3), but people from high-context cultures are particularly affected by these contextual cues. Thus, facial expressions, tension, movements, speed of interaction, location of interaction, and other subtle "vibes" are likely to be perceived by and have more meaning for people from high-context cultures. Finally, people in high-context cultures expect more from their interaction partners than do people in low-context cultures (Hall, 1976): people in high-context cultures expect their interaction partners to pick up on unarticulated feelings, subtle gestures, and environmental cues, which people from low-context cultures simply do not process. Unfortunately, both cultural extremes fail to recognize these basic differences in behavior, communication, and context and are quick to misattribute the causes for their behavior.

The Practical Benefits of Understanding Intercultural Communication Differences

Simply reading about these six cultural dimensions of nonverbal communication will not ensure intercultural communication competence. Combining research-based knowledge from intercultural articles and courses with actual encounters with people from other cultures is the best way to gain intercultural communication competence. International travel, even travel within the United States, provides an opportunity to gain perspective on one's own behavior and the behavior of others that will help lead to intercultural communication competence.

A full, practical understanding of the dimensions along which cultures differ, as well as knowledge of how specific communication acts differ cross-culturally, has several practical benefits. First, such knowledge will highlight and challenge assumptions about our own behavior. The structure of our own behavior is invisible and taken for granted until it is exposed and challenged through actual intercultural encounters. Indeed, Hall (1976) stated that diversity in inter-ethnic communication can be a source of strength and self-discovery.

International tourism, migration, study, and business has greatly increased intercultural encounters.

Second, this chapter should convince you that conclusions about the non-verbal communication of people from other cultures are generalizd observations, not ironclad rules. No dictionary or code of intercultural behavior exists. You cannot read people like books, not even people from your own culture. However, understanding that another person is from a masculine, collectivist, or high-context culture may help shape your perception of her or his behavior as less confusing, more interpretable, and less bizarre.

Finally, understanding intercultural communication and actually engaging in intercultural encounters are bound to reduce ethnocentrism and make strangers from other cultures seem less threatening. Fear is often based on ignorance and misunderstanding. In your future life, I guarantee that you will continue to meet and communicate with many people from other cultures than your own. Learn from these differences. Intercultural diversity is a source of joy and optimism about the number of possible ways to be human.

Summary

The diversity of U.S. culture requires that Americans understand intercultural communication in order to communicate effectively. Differences in language are only the tip of the intercultural iceberg; many of the most important cultural differences are in nonverbal communication.

The codes of nonverbal communication, discussed in Chapters 2 and 3, are used differently by people in various cultures. Chronemically, the more developed cultures, such as countries in Europe and North America, employ monochronic time, a time orientation in which one thing gets done at a time and time is treated like a commodity. People in lesser-developed countries do not structure time so rigidly; such cultures employ polychronic time, a time orientation that emphasizes informality and multiple simultaneous activities. Proxemically, people from cooler, northerly climates tend to be more distant and remote interpersonally, whereas people from tropical regions tend to prefer closer interpersonal distances. Kinesically, cultures differ as greatly in their use of emblems (gestures with verbal meanings) as in their languages. People in warmer climates use more expressive gestures and movements than do people in cooler climates. Haptic behavior varies dramatically from one culture to the next; for example, Asian cultures engage in very little touch, whereas Mediterranean cultures employ a great deal of touch in their interpersonal interactions. The physical appearance of people around the world in terms of hair, clothing, artifacts, and body decorations is extremely varied. Cultures also differ greatly in their use of oculesics. For example, many Mediterranean cultures use much more direct eye contact than do Americans or Asians. Vocalics also shows considerable cultural variation in intonation, loudness, pitch, and tone. In terms of olfactics, Americans are much more tuned in to smell than are most of the world's people.

Nonverbal differences across cultures center on six dimensions of human behavior. Cultures differ in immediacy, the degree to which nonverbal behavior communicates warmth, closeness, and availability for communications. Cultures high in immediacy—contact cultures—stand close to each other, touch more, and are generally more expressive. Cultures low in immediacy—noncontact cultures—tend to stand farther apart, touch less, and manifest less nonverbal expressiveness. Individualistic cultures value independence and privacy and manifest these values in their nonverbal behavior. Conversely, collectivist cultures value interpersonal connection and group behavior and reflect these values in their nonverbal behavior. Gender orientation is the degree to which a culture emphasizes typically masculine traits or typically feminine traits. The nonverbal behavior of a masculine culture emphasizes assertiveness, competitiveness, and ambitiousness. Cultures that are more feminine exhibit nonverbal behavior that stresses equality, nurturance, emotionality, and compassion. Cultures also differ in power distance, the degree to which wealth and prestige are equally or unequally distributed in a culture. High-power-distance cultures have more formal, hierarchical relationships and show only positive emotions to authority figures. Low-power-distance cultures exhibit nonverbal behavior that is more informal and not structured along class lines. Uncertainty orientation is a cultural predisposition toward risk and ambiguity. Uncertainty-avoidant cultures are more controlled and ritualized in their behavior but exhibit more nonverbal emotional displays when under stress. Uncertainty-tolerant cultures tend to exhibit fewer prescribed nonverbal behaviors and greater tolerance toward young people and their emotional displays. Context is the final dimension of intercultural communication. In low-context cultures, verbal communication is emphasized and nonverbal communication is more informal. In high-context cultures, nonverbal communication is highly stylized and replete with meaning.

5
Gender, Sex, and Nonverbal Communication

POPULAR BOOKS TODAY would have us believe that men and women are completely different—members of different cultures and perhaps even creatures from different planets. Likewise, traditional stereotypes often lead people to believe that men and women are cut out for completely different roles. Research has shown that these are oversimplified and erroneous views of reality. A more accurate though less sensationalistic view is offered by Dindia (1997), who claims that men are from South Dakota and women from North Dakota. To North Dakotans, those South Dakotans seem pretty strange, and vice versa. But to Texans, Californians, Floridians, or residents from any other place in the world, all Dakotans, appear to behave pretty much alike.

None of this is to deny that differences exist in the communication behaviors of men and women. Indeed, there are differences. As you will learn in this chapter, these differences—both real and perceived—are governed by a complex set of forces, including biology, culture, stereotypes, and prejudice. Four overriding principles can be used to organize the complex body of theory and research on sex differences in nonverbal communication:

1. Men and women are far more similar than they are different.
2. Some biological sex differences do exist.
3. Learned gender differences occur in every culture.
4. Men and women can consciously alter their nonverbal behavior.

Similarities between the Sexes

Men and women behave similarly in most respects: Men and women easily recognize each other's facial expressions, learn similar norms for the use of touch and space in interpersonal interaction, and maintain fairly continuous eye contact when listening but alternate between gaze and gaze aversion when speaking. Men and women both use gestures, reveal emotions on their face, hug their children, enjoy sexual intimacy in the right relational contexts, and are conscious of interpersonal meanings of time, space, smell, and appearance. The nonverbal behaviors of both men and women are synchronized to a remarkable degree during interaction. Recent research shows that men and women have very similar expectations and standards for their partner's behavior in romantic relationships (Vangelisti & Daly, 1997).

These behaviors are hardly the alien expressions of creatures from different planets. They are familiar, universal ways in which all humans communicate. The gestures, touches, and facial expressions of men and women are recognizable behaviors of Earthlings, not Martians or Venusians.

A number of recent analyses have statistically summarized hundreds of previous studies on sex and gender differences in communication (see Canary & Hause, 1993; Halberstadt & Saitta, 1987; Hall, 1985: Stier & Hall, 1984; Wilkins & Andersen, 1991). These studies have turned up significant differences between the communication behavior of men and women, but the differences are usually *tiny*. Overall, sex differences in communication are so small that men and women are about 99 percent similar and only 1 percent different. A few larger differences do exist, and we will discuss these. In this chapter, we will examine *sex differences,* the result of the biology of men and women, as well as *gender differences,* the result of cultural role socialization.

In summary, the communication of men and women is exceedingly similar. Communicatively speaking, men and women inhabit the same planet and have the ability to communicate effectively with one another.

Sex Differences: Biological Explanations

In animal species, two sexes exist for the primary purpose of reproduction. The search for sex differences in communication should always begin with the most basic biological differences: the differences in each sex's reproductive role or the differences that are a consequence of reproduction. Years ago, Birdwhistell (1970), one of the founders of the field of nonverbal communication, discussed three types of differences in the nonverbal communication behavior of men and women: (1) primary differences that relate to the production of ova or spermatozoa; (2) secondary differences that are anatomical but not directly related to reproduction, such as muscle mass, body hair, and physical size; and (3) tertiary differences that are learned patterns of social behavior.

Politics, Prejudice, and Biology

An examination of textbooks on sex, gender, and communication reveals an almost complete avoidance of biological sex differences. Often, these books ignore the topic entirely or devote a paragraph or two before dismissing biology as a meaningless source of gender behavior. Recently, I have said that books in our field are in a state of "biological denial" (Andersen, 1998). Many people fear the forthright discussion of biological differences between men and women for several political reasons.

Because of our commitment to equality, many of us in American universities have been part of a project to eradicate prejudice and to make sure that men and women are provided an equal opportunity to succeed in college and in life. This goal has been so important that some people fear that discussing biological differences between men and women will be used as a pretext for denying people (usually women) equal opportunity. A few years ago, a famous neuropsychologist was asked not to speak at the University of Illinois for this very reason:

> When Rachel Gur gave a talk to M.D.-Ph.D. students in Illinois about sex differences in brains, a group of women asked her to stop publicizing this work: they were afraid that women would lose 20 years of gains if word got out that the sexes weren't the same. (Begley, 1995, p. 51)

These concerns are understandable: biological differences have been used by many hate groups such as the Nazis and the Ku Klux Klan to justify racism and sexism, even though these differences have not shown one group of people to be any more intelligent than another. Just decades ago, women in communication were denied access to graduate school because of a perception that the woman's role in society was as homemaker and mother.

Hopefully, we are at a point in the history of the field of communication at which a real discussion of biological differences can take place. Understanding real differences makes it easier to refute bogus differences. Moreover, identifying differences does not imply the superiority or inferiority of either males or females. Additionally, most of the differences that have been discovered are extremely small. (Remember: similarities between the sexes are much more substantial than are the differences.) Finally, the recognition of differences provides the opportunity for men and women to remediate behavioral differences and enhance their skills as effective communicators.

Biological Differences between the Sexes

As stated earlier, the primary biological difference between men and women is reproductive. Men can ejaculate and impregnate, and women can menstruate, gestate, and lactate. These differences lead to other basic differences between men and women: women have proportionally wider hips, more subcutaneous fat, and larger breasts than men. Some people believe that women are more innately nurturant than men due to their role in breast feeding and caring for young children.

What about other differences? Why are men taller, more muscular, hairier, shorter-lived, more spatially aware, and seemingly more violent than women? Why are women more socially perceptive and more nurturant than men? It is likely that some of these differences are attributable to evolutionary, sex-linked variations in men and women.

Over several million years of human evolution, men and women have played different roles in maintaining the survivability of the species. Today, we share our genetic and biological heritage with ancestors who spent several million years adapting to hunting, gathering, and scavenging. Comparatively, we have spent just several thousand years as agricultural people and only a few hundred years as urban people. Our modern culture is a relative new development, but our biology dates back to before the Stone Age.

Throughout most of our history, growing old was a luxury few humans enjoyed. For hundreds of thousands of years, human life expectancy was less than 30 years (for a summary of this literature see Andersen, 1998). Even during the more recent agrarian period (when most people were subsistence farmers), life was short, brutish, and nasty (Whicker and Kronenfeld, 1986). Up until the last several generations, short life expectancy, high infant mortality, and—ultimately—the survival of the species meant that most women were pregnant throughout most of their dozen or so child-bearing years. Likewise, women were almost continuously nursing and caring for infants and toddlers. Women who failed to bear and nurse children had no genetic legacy to be passed along.

Because males were not occupied with pregnancy and nursing, they were largely responsible for hunting, gathering, scavenging, and combat. The larger, more muscular physiques of men evolved so they could be relatively more efficient hunters, gatherers, and combatants than women. Likewise, navigational and spatial skills were more essential for hunters and combatants. Men of low muscle mass, small stature, or a poor sense of space and direction were unlikely to survive long enough to father many offspring.

Of course, in contemporary society few men choose to be hunters, scavengers, or combatants, though some do. Most men work in factories, offices, classrooms, and boardrooms, where their survival skills must be adapted to modern life. Likewise, few women spend their entire adult life pregnant and mothering. Their social skills are increasingly employed in the same roles and occupations held by men, although all too frequently at lower salaries than men receive. Humans are incredibly adaptable. Women can be hunters and soldiers, and men can nurture their children and be preschool teachers. Nonetheless, some of our behavior is biological, a relic of our pre–Stone Age evolutionary heritage. Women's somewhat superior nonverbal sending and receiving ability and men's somewhat superior visuospatial abilities are vestiges of our evolutionary past.

Gender Differences: Cultural Explanations

As underscored earlier in this chapter, men and women are Earthlings and members of the same human species, yet continuing debate questions whether men and women are from the same culture (see Vangelisti & Daly, 1997; Wood, 1997a).

Whether or not men and women come from different cultures, American culture (and most others) treats men and women differently. Differential rearing, socialization, and treatment result in variations between male and female behaviors and perceptions.

Men and women are aware that gender differences exist. In a fascinating study, Briton and Hall (1995) found that men and women are quite accurate in identifying sex differences in nonverbal behavior. When asked to name behaviors they believed were generally different between men and women, men's beliefs correlated .68 with actual, observed sex differences and women's beliefs correlated .74 with actual, observed sex differences. As expected, women were more accurate in identifying differences, but the real news here is how closely our stereotypes and beliefs conform to reality. (To see how closely your stereotypes and beliefs conform to reality, complete the checklist at the end of this chapter entitled "Behaviors That Reveal.") These interesting findings do not reveal, however, which came first, the beliefs or the behaviors. On the one hand, these beliefs may simply reflect that people accurately perceived differences between men and women. On the other hand, beliefs about sex differences influence behavior and attitudes and serve as powerful socializing agents that maintain "gender-appropriate" behavior.

Without a doubt, most societies treat men and women differently. The difference in the treatment of men and women in our society is the result of many forces: exaggerations of biological differences, patriarchal sexism designed to maintain gender inequality, and unconscious socialization processes that perpetuate gender differences.

Exaggerations of Biological Differences

Sometimes cultural forces exaggerate preexisting biological differences between men and women. There are numerous ways in which women and men accentuate their biological sex. For example, women wear push-up bras and shave their legs, and men wear elevator shoes and shoulder pads. Women and men employ other nonverbal gender-role behaviors to underscore their biological differences. Men often speak in deep, loud voices, whereas women speak in soft, breathy tones to exaggerate already present sex differences in the size of the vocal cords and the pitch of the voice. Likewise, men use space more expansively than women when sitting, standing, and gesturing to accentuate their size. "Ladylike" positions—for example, women sitting with the arms and legs together—emphasize a woman's relatively smaller size.

Our society rewards us for behaving consistently with our sex roles. Feminine men are considered strange and gay, and transsexual men face harassment and even violence in a homophobic society. Gay men are called names such as *queer* and *fag* because they threaten our highly gendered definitions of what it means to be a man or a woman. Similarly, lesbians are called *dykes* and other derogatory terms because they threaten our definition of what it means to be female and also because they are unavailable to men sexually, a cardinal sin among patriarchal men.

Patriarchal and Oppressive Sexism

People in positions of power rarely seek to relinquish it. Just as slavery and racism have benefited certain powerful ethnic groups, so sexism sometimes benefits those in positions of power. Some men seek to exploit the lower status of women by requiring them to serve their needs and satisfy them sexually. The old double standard that says women should be faithful and monogamous but men can sow their wild oats is just one example of exploitative sexism.

The home is another locus of exploitation by men. In their review of research, Canary, Emmers-Sommer, and Faulkner (1997) report that the division of labor in the home still exploits women. Women work an hour or two more each day than men. Although this gap has narrowed, women are still more likely than men to be domestic servants; in other words, they tend to be limited in their movements and social networks by the requirements of home and family. Chronemically, women are more likely to accommodate to men's schedules than vice-versa. This is not to say that women never exploit men. Indeed, women exploit men for money and status, whereas men are more likely to exploit women sexually. In balance, however, women as a social class historically have been exploited by men, who have often viewed women as a resource in terms of both labor and sexuality.

Unconscious Socialization

Societal expectations about gender are very prevalent but not always particularly obvious. These unconscious expectations about what it means to be a man or a woman create gender roles that are generally consistent with biological sex differences. As Wood (1997b) contends, "To be feminine is to be attractive, deferential, unassertive, emotional, nurturing, and concerned with people and relationships" (p. 27). Women are supposed to look pretty or sexy; old, homely, or fat women are devalued in our society. By contrast, men are expected to be strong, unemotional, aggressive, brave, successful, and wealthy. Pity the poor fellow who is perceived as weak, unsuccessful, or poor, for he fails to meet society's expectations of what it means to be masculine and is thus devalued.

From the time we are infants, our gender roles are shaped. Girls are given dolls and dishes, told to be ladylike, and discouraged from roughhousing. Boys are given trucks and guns, told to take pain "like a man," and warned not to let others push them around. A boy's aspiring masculinity or a girl's evolving femininity becomes a fixed aspect of one's identity (for summaries of this research see Pearson, West, & Turner, 1995; Wood, 1997b). Parents, families, church, school, and peers all send consistent messages about "appropriate" feminine and masculine behavior. Sometimes these messages are very subtle: a smile or a nod

Socialization contributes to gender differences in communication. Girls are much more likely to be given dolls and encouraged to be "ladylike" and to participate in "feminine" activities, such as dance.

provides a silent message of approval for a particular behavior; a frown, a furrowed brow, or the lack of approval discourages another behavior. Society does not have to work actively to produce manly men and womanly women; the process is subtle yet pervasive.

Gender is continuously modeled for us. At home, mother and father model what it means to be masculine and feminine (see Wood, 1997b). At one time, this meant that boys were socialized to be breadwinners and women to be housewives, because that was the predominant gender role of the day. Increasingly, the norm has moved toward dual-career couples. These changes are slowly but surely changing the model of what constitutes male and female roles in the family.

The omnipresent mass media of television, radio, film, and popular music send powerful and quite consistent gender messages that are emulated by viewers, especially young viewers (see Pearson et al., 1995; Wood, 1997b). Gerbner's cultivation theory has shown that repeated exposure to media messages creates attitudes and behavior consistent with those messages (see Gerbner, Gross, Morgan, & Signiorelli, 1986). The images cultivated by the media usually portray men and women in traditional roles. As Wood (1997b) states:

> Media continue to present both women and men in stereotyped ways that limit our perceptions of human possibilities. Typically men are portrayed as active, adventurous, powerful, sexually aggressive, and largely uninvolved in

human relationships. . . . Female characters devote their primary energies to improving their appearances and taking care of homes and people. (p. 279)

These stereotypes, however, are changing slowly in America. At no time in U.S. history have men and women had greater opportunity to free themselves from the constraints of either biology or culture.

Sex Differences (and Similarities) in Nonverbal Behavior

Despite the overwhelming similarities between men and women, some differences do exist in our nonverbal communication, resulting from the twin forces of biology and culture. In this section, we will review these sex differences in terms of each nonverbal code. Additionally, we will look at how men and women differ in their ability to send and receive nonverbal messages, in their interpersonal perceptions and attributions, and in their relational communication.

Physical Appearance

In her book *Moving Beyond Words,* feminist Gloria Steinem (1994) recalls, "I and other women of my generation grew up believing—as many girls still do—that the most important thing about the female body is not what it does but how it looks. The power lies not within us but within the gaze of the observer" (p. 93). Without a doubt, physical attractiveness is important to both sexes. In Chapter 2, we discussed how attractive people generally have considerable advantage over unattractive people. "What's beautiful is good" is an important principle, particularly in beauty-conscious America, where image is often, unfortunately, more important to the success of a person or product than is substance (see Chapter 10 for a detailed discussion of how we sell ourselves).

Gender plays an important role in the power of physical attraction in important ways. First, research has shown that a woman's physical attractiveness is even more important to men than a man's physical attractiveness is to women (for a complete review of this literature see Feingold, 1990). Research on human mating patterns throughout the world shows that men prefer young, nubile women. Having a physically attractive mate is a sign of status for men. Of course, a man's attractiveness is also important to women, yet wealth and social status are much more important to them (Kenrick & Keefe, 1992).

Why is physical attractiveness of women so important to men? The sociobiological explanation is that youth and beauty are innately attractive to men because they are signs of health and fertility. Men are programmed unconsciously and biologically to seek mates with these qualities, which explains why men in all cultures value these characteristics. Women, on the other hand, are inclined to select men with sufficient resources to care for them, which is why women of all cultures are attracted to wealth, power, and status.

The socialization that takes place within a patriarchal male society offers another explanation for the difference between men's and women's perceptions of physical appearance. Today, although many men are not sexists, much of society still subscribes to sexist patriarchal attitudes. In keeping with the traditional patriarchal view, men like attractive, compliant women who are sex objects. Because men control the resources and the power structure, women are socialized to maintain and display their physical appearance to please men and gain access to the resources that men control. The tragic increase in life-threatening eating disorders that occur overwhelmingly in young women is, in part, a product of our culture's preoccupation with thinness and physical beauty. Of course, family communication patterns, genetic predispositions, and control issues also play a part in the heightened incidence of anorexia and bulimia; nevertheless, these diseases were unheard of in the days before beautiful, thin models dominated our mass media. Our cultural expectations cause women to be preoccupied with their own beauty and men's reactions to their appearance. Teen magazines are mostly manuals for fashion, grooming, makeup, and dieting (Wood, 1997b). In a survey of 33,000 young women, 42 percent said that losing weight would make them happier than would success at work (Wooley & Wooley, 1984). Of course, the biological and cultural explanations for sex differences in physical attraction are not mutually exclusive. It is likely that sexual and romantic attraction is affected by a combination of biological and sociocultural forces.

A second, equally disturbing finding is that the higher a woman's occupational status, the more her physical attractiveness becomes a disadvantage for her! Although receptionists and secretaries and even celebrities and newscasters are likely to profit from good looks, a woman's attractiveness actually may be a disadvantage in positions of leadership, particularly managerial positions. To paraphrase Heilman and Saruwatari (1979), beauty can be beastly; these researchers found that attractiveness was an advantage for all men but an advantage for only those women seeking low-level, nonmanagerial positions. So society creates a double bind for women by requiring them to be beautiful but precluding beautiful women from high-status positions!

Few highly attractive women have appeared on the political scene—both in the United States and worldwide (see Chapter 10 for more on physical attractiveness and selling oneself). Relatively recent research, however, paints a somewhat more optimistic picture for female political candidates. A study by Lewis and Bierly (1990) had people rate black-and-white photographs of forty-four male and female candidates serving in the House of Representatives in the late 1980s. Men were equally likely to rate male and female candidates positively, although women showed a preference for female candidates, rating them more competent than males. Although prior research had shown that attractiveness was a disadvantage for women seeking high-status positions, results of this study showed that the more attractive male and female candidates were rated as more competent. Perhaps women are escaping from the double bind that turns beauty into a positive or negative trait depending on a woman's career status. Although it is somewhat disturbing that attractiveness in general is still so highly associated with competence, it is heartening that Lewis and Bierly's (1990) data revealed little sexism: attractive men and women were rated as more competent by both men and women. Perhaps our society is ready for women who are both attractive *and* competent.

There are obvious biological differences between the physiques of men and women. In general, women are shorter, less muscular, more rounded, wider in the hips, and narrower in the waist and shoulders; they also have larger breasts, female reproductive organs, less body hair, and a lower incidence of receding hair lines. In many cultures, including our own, these biological qualities have been exaggerated to communicate gender even more clearly (Morris, 1977). Women shave their legs and armpits to amplify the fact that they have less body hair than men. In past years, women wore corsets to exaggerate their narrow waists and to enhance their breasts and bustles to increase their hip size. Men have worn shoulder pads and epaulets to give the appearance of wider shoulders, codpieces to exaggerate the size of their penis, and elevator shoes to unobtrusively add to their height.

Remember, throughout this chapter we talk about *sex,* a biological characteristic, and *gender,* a learned cultural definition of what it means to be a man or a woman. Frequently, these terms are confounded and difficult even for scholars to sort out. As we have seen in this section, biology and culture go hand in hand; men and women exaggerate biological differences to more clearly communicate their gender.

Proxemic Behavior

INTERPERSONAL DISTANCE

A number of studies have shown that in same-sex dyads, women interact at closer distances than do men (for a summary see J. A. Hall, 1984), although men are more likely than women to lean forward during interaction (Guerrero, 1997). Because women are generally smaller than men, one would expect them to interact at closer distances. But size is not the entire explanation. Even when controlling for body size, research has found that women still interact at closer distances than men. Even though women's arms are shorter than men's, women tend to interact at distances closer than an arm's length, whereas men interact with other men at more than an arm's length (Aiello, 1987). The belief that women are more interactively intimate than men may be due in part to their tendency toward closer, more intimate interaction distances.

Interestingly, when men and women interact with one another, they adopt the closer, more intimate interaction distance that women, not men, typically employ. Opposite-sex interaction is an area where women have more power than men: the power to make men interact more intimately than they typically would man to man. Indeed, women may have a unique effect on men—the ability to make men more sensitive and intimate.

Men require and are given more space than women. They tend to have larger offices and use more space when they are working, relaxing, sitting, and standing (see Aiello, 1987; see also Chapter 12). Some researchers have attributed men's greater spatial needs to their larger body sizes, but these differences seem to be based in part on power and status differences between men and women. Even as we approach the next century, women, who have made so much progress in the workplace, hold few of the very top jobs in business and politics. Because men hold the majority of very high status jobs and because with status comes greater, more remote, and more commanding space, men at the top have larger territories than most women. Likewise, sex-role socialization encourages boys to venture out and explore their environment, whereas girls are encouraged to stay closer to home.

BODY ORIENTATION

Research has also shown that women are more likely to face their interaction partner than are men (Guerrero, 1997; J. A. Hall, 1984). A more direct orientation is perceived as warmer and more immediate and may make it easier for women to receive nonverbal cues from their interaction partner.

CROWDING

Studies of crowding and density have shown a fairly consistent sex difference. Interpersonal density is an objective measure of the number of people in a given area. As the number of people in an area increase, humans often experience crowding, a negative, subjective feeling of not having enough space. Women seem to experience less negative feelings of crowding in high-density situations (Aiello, 1987). Men are more likely to react negatively to crowding and even become physically violent when crowding is excessive.

SPATIAL ABILITY

One of the larger differences between the sexes is spatial ability. Just as it is likely that women's general superiority in nonverbal receiving ability (more on this later in the chapter) is primarily a biological difference, so it is likely that men's greater ability in spatial and navigational skills is also biologically based (see Andersen, 1998; Gaulin, 1992). Gaulin (1992) concludes that among well-documented sex differences, men are clearly more adept than women at visuospatial tasks. Gaulin contends, "Such explanations can only be evolutionary. When psychological features under study are widely distributed across human societies and are also present in nonhuman mammals the argument that they are cultural epiphenomena is substantially weakened" (1992, p. 127). This male advantage appears across an impressive array of spatial tasks, including object rotation, water-pouring and water-tipping tasks, field independence, tracking tasks, and spatial memory tasks (Andersen, 1998). Although men's greater competence in some of these tasks may be due to practice, other tasks, such as the water-tipping task, are not stereotypically "male tasks." Halpern (1986) reasons, "It does not seem likely that males

Despite the substantial progress made by women in recent decades in securing equal opportunity, many of the top organizational positions are still held by men.

have more or better experience with a tipped glass of water. In fact, one could argue that females, the primary cooks and dishwashers in many homes, might have more related experience with tipped glasses of water and other liquids than males" (p. 151).

Men and women generally employ different strategies when attempting to perform spatial tasks. Men try to visualize the entire pattern. When finding their way driving or walking, most men tend to view themselves on a map of the entire terrain, whereas women tend to rely on landmarks and verbal labels (Gaulin, 1992).

As we will see later in the chapter, women's right brain hemispheres may have evolved to be particularly sensitive to interpersonal nonverbal cues, whereas men's right brain hemispheres may have evolved to specialize in nonverbal cues involving spatial perception (see Chapter 1 for more on this issue). Of course, none of this means that men are insensitive or that women can't navigate, only that each sex has some general predispositions that are likely biologically based.

Kinesic Behavior

FACIAL EXPRESSIONS

One way in which men and women clearly differ is in their use of facial expressions. Studies have shown that women are much more expressive in the face than men and reveal their emotions more accurately and more frequently than men (Brody & Hall, 1993; Broverman, Vogel, Broverman, Clarkson, & Rosenkrantz, 1972; Hall, 1978). Men believe it is important to hide or conceal their emotions, even in very close relationships (Aune & Aune, 1997).

Perhaps the biggest gender difference in facial expressions is in smiling. Women smile considerably more than men (J. A. Hall, 1984, 1998), and women are much more likely to smile when they are happy than are men (Coates & Feldman, 1996). The fact that women smile more may be an advantage because people like people who show positive emotions. Women may be more able to communicate warmth and be more persuasive because they smile more than men (see Chapter 10).

Women's ability to communicate positive emotions through their facial expressions may be due to a number of factors. If, indeed, women are more innately nurturant than men, positive facial expressions (including smiling) may have evolved as nurturing, comforting, and caregiving behaviors. Smiling, however, has many functions, so this may be only part of the story. Research has shown that smiling evolved in primates as a display of submission or appeasement, a sign of friendliness and harmlessness. Given the history of the oppression of women, smiling may have evolved as an important, naturally selected display to appease the larger, more aggressive males. Finally, research has shown that girls are rewarded for emotional expression, especially positive expressions like smiling, whereas young boys are rewarded for suppressing emotional displays. Women are more likely than men to smile in many contexts, including flirtation (McCormick & Jones, 1989).

Anger is one facial expression that men use more than women. A study by Coates and Feldman (1996) indicates that men are more likely to show their anger while they are feeling angry than are women. Whether men's higher level of anger expression is biological, cultural, or both is not certain.

GESTURES

Gender differences in gestural behavior have also been found (J. A. Hall, 1984). As with other areas of expressive behavior, women are more likely to gesture than are men, although men tend to use larger, more expansive gestures. Not all studies, however, have shown a gender difference in gestural behavior (see Kennedy & Camden, 1983), so it is likely that this gender difference may vary from context to context. Overall, Hall's (1985) comprehensive review of gender differences shows that women gesture more than men.

FOOT MOVEMENTS

Another kinesic gender difference is that men have more restless, fidgety hands and feet than women (J. A. Hall, 1984). Probably, women are socialized to suppress such cues because they are not "ladylike." Men may be more restless in confined social situations because they have a greater predisposition to action and a disinclination to quiet interaction.

Women tend to display emotions more than men.

Some studies reveal considerable gender similarity and very small differences overall in kinesic behavior. Halberstadt and Saitta (1987) searched for three gender-related kinesic signs of dominance—head tilting, body canting (leaning), and smiling—by examining 1,106 media portrayals of men and women and observing 1,257 people interacting in public places. They found virtually no differences except for a slightly higher incidence of smiling among women. They concluded, "Males' and females' nonverbal behaviors are very similar when observed in natural settings" (p. 268).

Oculesic Behavior

As we saw in Chapter 2, women are much more visually oriented than are men. Women look more at other people and attempt to make more eye contact; women are also looked at more. This is the case when they are speaking or listening and during silences and while flirting (Guerrero, 1997; J. A. Hall, 1984; McCormick & Jones, 1989; Mulac, Studley, Wiemann, & Bradac, 1987). The highest levels of eye contact occur between two conversing women, the lowest levels between two men; the level is somewhere in between for male-female interactions. The considerably higher level of oculesic activity that occurs between two women partly explains why women are more sensitive to nonverbal communication cues, particularly since so many nonverbal cues are visual.

Mulac et al. (1987) have found, however, that although female-female dyads exhibit high levels of gaze, female-male dyads (like male-male dyads) exhibit less gaze. Unlike proxemic behavior in mixed-sex dyads—in which males adopt the female interpersonal distance—gaze behavior shows that females in mixed-sex dyads accommodate to the male oculesic norm.

Several explanations have been offered for women's greater oculesic activity. Primate studies have shown that more submissive, less powerful members of a species are more visually attentive because they are wary of the stronger, more dominant animals. Given women's history of oppression by men, visual attentiveness may have evolved as both a naturally selected, genetic behavior and a learned response within oppressive cultures. Second, women's greater use of eye contact is consistent with many studies. These studies report that women learn to be more socially oriented and responsive. Finally, listeners look more than speakers during interaction, and women both listen more and listen more attentively than men.

Vocalic Behavior

One fairly basic biological difference between men and women is the pitch of the voice. After puberty, men's vocal cords thicken, producing a biological difference in pitch between men's and women's voices. Like the physical-appearance cues discussed earlier, men and women may exaggerate these sex differences according to their specific gender roles. Many men speak in low or harsh voices to exaggerate their masculinity, and many women use high-pitched, breathy voices to emphasize their femininity. Additionally, gay males may speak in a higher pitch to distinguish themselves as a gender group from straight men.

LaFrance and Mayo (1978) have shown that women are socialized to use their voices differently than men. Women use more vocal variations and often end sentences in a rising pitch, implying a qualified answer or a lack of certainty (Lakoff, 1975).

In Chapter 3 we discussed positive and negative aspects of the voice. Research has shown that men are more likely than women to lapse into negatively perceived vocal disfluencies, such as false starts, stutters, and speech interruptions (J. A. Hall, 1984). Likewise, men speak in louder voices than women.

Some studies have shown that men interrupt more than women during conversations (for two different summaries of this research, see Burgoon, Buller, & Woodall, 1996; Crawford, 1995). Men's alleged tendency to interrupt may be due to (1) their need to assert dominance, (2) the belief that women's talk is unimportant, or (3) insensitivity to others' turns at talking. Researchers, however, do not consistently find sex differences in interrupting. For example, Dindia (1987) reports no sex differences in terms of interrupting or being interrupted. Instead, in her very thorough study, she reports that both sexes are more likely to engage in cross-sex interruptions rather than same-sex interruptions.

Haptic Behavior

Contrary to common stereotypes, there is little evidence that men touch women more than women touch men. Where touch-related sex differences are found, they are very small (Guerrero & Andersen, 1994; J. A. Hall, 1984, 1996; Hall & Veccia, 1992; Major, Schmidlin, & Williams, 1990; Stier & Hall, 1984). There is, however, evidence that men initiate touch more than women in casual dating relationships and that women initiate touch more than men in marital relationships. Some evidence shows that women are the recipient of more touch from both men and women (Major et al., 1990), although more recent data suggest that this is true only in the early stages of a relationship. Overall, recent research has found cross-sex touch to be almost entirely reciprocal (Guerrero & Andersen, 1994): that is, in couples in which one person doesn't touch very much, neither does the other partner; in couples in which one person touches a lot, so does the other partner. This evidence suggests that men and women select individuals with similar touch preferences and that couples become more like each other as the relationship develops.

Despite beliefs to the contrary, there is also little evidence that touch primarily communicates power (see Chapter 12) or that males touch females more when they are in positions of power (Hall & Veccia, 1992). Touch is much more likely to be perceived and employed as an immediacy cue (see Chapter 8) than a power cue. Although touch is a behavior that mostly conveys immediacy and intimacy, it can also convey sexuality, comfort, and commitment for both males and females. One difference between the genders is that increasingly intimate touch—particularly intimate sexual touch—is more likely to be viewed as a sign of commitment by females than by males (Johnson & Edwards, 1991). As such, the potential for miscommunication increases in heterosexual relationships as tactile behavior escalates. During flirtation, women are more likely than men to use brief touches, whereas men are more likely than women to employ intimate touching.

A number of studies have shown that female-female touch is much more prevalent than male-male touch (Andersen & Leibowitz, 1978; Major et al., 1990; see Chapter 7). These findings are also consistent with research on touch attitudes. Studies show that men have more positive attitudes towards opposite-sex touch than do women. Conversely, women have more positive attitudes towards same-sex touch than do men, although these differences appear to be more pronounced in the United States than in other countries (Andersen, Andersen, &

Lustig, 1987; Andersen & Leibowitz, 1978; Larsen & LeRoux, 1984; Willis & Rawdon, 1994; see Chapter 7). Another take on these findings implies that both men and women are reluctant to touch men, a tendency that may lead to feelings of tactile deprivation among males.

Regarding self-touching behaviors, research shows that women are more likely to touch themselves than are men (J. A. Hall, 1984). Because self-touching behaviors are perceived as sensual or sexual by many observers, it could be that these cues are courtship or flirtation behaviors that call attention to a woman's body (McCormick & Jones, 1989; Morris, 1977). However, self-touching behavior is also associated with anxiety and subordination, which given women's traditionally lower social status, may provide an alternative explanation for women's self-touching patterns.

Nonverbal Receiving Ability

Numerous studies have shown that women throughout the world are more accurate, sensitive receivers of nonverbal communication than are men (J. A. Hall, 1979, 1984, 1998; Keeley-Dyerson, Burgoon, & Bailey, 1991; Rosenthal, Hall, Dimatteo, Rogers, & Archer, 1979). Research by Rosenthal and DePaulo (1979) shows a consistent female advantage in nonverbal receiving ability across eleven diverse nations. Hall (1979) also found that this female advantage was stable across the decades in which the study was conducted. Likewise, research suggests that these differences emerge early in life. Studies have found that 1- to 3-day-old girls tend to cry more than boys in response to another infant's cries but not to other sounds (Rosenthal et al., 1979).

Although it is probable that these differences are the result of both learned skills and biological differences, it is likely that receiving ability primarily represents a biological difference between men and women. Recent research in the field of genetics (Skuse, James, Bishop, & Coppin, 1997) suggests that the women's skill may be inherited through the X chromosome that women receive from their father! Women missing their father's X chromosome are socially inept and communicatively insensitive. Boys, of course, have only one X chromosome, and it comes from their mother. Unfortunately, the mother's X chromosome is not the one on which social skill is carried. This is not to say that sex differences of this type cannot be remediated. In the context of a laboratory experiment on nonverbal decoding, Keeley-Dyerson et al. (1991) reported that men's decoding ability improved after several trials, suggesting to the experimenters that there exists "the possibility that with practice, men can improve their decoding ability" (p. 601). This finding comports with research by Rosenthal et al. (1979) who found that some of the best decoders were students—men and women—who had completed a single course in nonverbal communication!

Several other explanations for women's superior nonverbal receiving ability have been offered: the gender explanation, the oppression hypothesis, and the social-rules perspective. The gender explanation says that differences in non-verbal receiving ability are due to a person's psychological gender rather than a person's biological sex. This does not seem to be the case, however. In her meta-analysis of eleven studies that correlated masculinity and femininity scores with nonverbal receiving ability, Hall (1979) concluded, "Overall the correlations be-tween masculinity and femininity measured on unipolar scales with nonverbal decoding ability were small and nonsignificant" (p. 52). In short, nonverbal re-ceiving ability is associated with being female but not with being feminine.

The oppression hypothesis posits that because of their low status and op-pressed state, women must be more sensitive to nonverbal cues to ensure their survival. However, the data do not seem to support this hypothesis either. Hall (1978) reveals one flaw of the oppression hypothesis by showing that there is no age effect for the female advantage in nonverbal sensitivity: "That young girls should be better judges of nonverbal communication than young boys is incon-sistent with this hypothesis, unless one seriously believes that young girls as well as women are oppressed in our society" (p. 354).

Other, more direct evidence casts further doubt on the oppression hy-pothesis. Hall (1979) has shown that women with more egalitarian attitudes are *more*, not less, sensitive to nonverbal communication. Similarly, she reports that women who subscribe to traditional sex roles have lower nonverbal receiving scores than less traditional women. Likewise, recent research by Hall and Hal-berstadt (1994) has found that less subordinate women are better decoders of nonverbal communication than more subordinate women. They conclude, "Al-though the subordination hypothesis has frequently been cited as an explanation for women's greater decoding skill compared to men, our results reveal serious difficulties for any simple version of this hypothesis" (p. 163).

Some scholars support the oppression, or subordination, hypothesis and offer methodological and conceptual criticisms of Hall's work (see LaFrance & Henley, 1997). Although the oppression hypothesis has not fared well in empiri-cal tests, it should not be completely dismissed (see Hall & Halberstadt, 1997). Sex differences are complex processes and may be the result of complementary factors that enhance sex differences or competing factors that minimize sex dif-ferences.

The most plausible, nonbiological explanation for women's superior non-verbal receiving ability is the social-rules perspective (Noller, 1986). Noller provides evidence that women's decoding advantage disappears under certain circumstances: men are just as accurate as women when they know the sender. Similarly, no sex difference is generally observed in detecting deception (see Chapter 11). Noller maintains that women know the social rules for a situation better than men do, so that in situations that are rule-governed, they are more accurate decoders. In deceptive situations, however, the rules are ambiguous and often strategically manipulated, and in acquaintance situations, general rules are unnecessary because unique relational rules govern the interaction. Of course, this perspective fails to specify how women acquire these rules. It may be that women are better observers, are socialized to be more empathic, or are genetically programmed to better process such information.

While little mention is made of biological explanations in the literature, there may be sex differences that produce greater nonverbal sensitivity in women. Hall (1978) concludes:

> Another kind of explanation, in its simplest form, would hold that females are wired from birth to be especially sensitive to nonverbal cues or especially quick learners of such cues. This would make evolutionary sense, because nonverbal sensitivity on a mother's part might enable her to detect distress in her youngsters or threatening signals from other adults, thus enhancing the survival chances of her offspring. (p. 854)

Andersen (1998) suggests that three mechanisms could produce sex-linked differences in nonverbal receiving ability: brain lateralization, chromosomal differences, and hormonal differences. Which, if any, of these mechanisms can explain sex differences in nonverbal receiving ability is a subject for future research.

Among the many advantages women have in nonverbal receiving ability is their greater skill at recognizing faces (J. A. Hall, 1984). It is unclear whether this is mainly an innate difference or whether women are socialized to look more at others' faces and focus more on their appearance. Women's accuracy—but not men's accuracy—in receiving nonverbal messages is enhanced by the presence of an expressive, immediate sender (Bush & Connolly, 1984). This "nonverbal recall facilitation effect" may help explain why interactions among women are often highly involved, animated, and satisfying.

Nonverbal Sending Ability

As is the case with nonverbal receiving ability, women are better, more accurate senders of nonverbal messages than men (Buck, Miller, & Caul, 1974; J. A. Hall, 1984). Research has shown that women are generally more expressive than men (Buck, 1984). This is particularly true for positive emotional messages (Noller, 1986), conveyed not only through facial expressions but also through other nonverbal channels as well, such as through vocal inflection, gestures, and attire. As discussed earlier, women are much more likely than men to smile across a wide variety of situations (Hall, 1984). Women are also more likely than men to encode virtually every facial expression except for anger (Guerrero & Reiter, 1998). In general, women's nonverbal sending ability is an advantage because it allows others, particularly friends and family, to read the sender's mood. Sometimes, however, being poker-faced is beneficial, putting men at an advantage in various circumstances, such as during a business negotiation or during a confrontation with an adversary. Of course, how men and women send nonverbal messages is a function of maturation; as children and adolescents mature, they learn display rules and gradually reduce their sending of unmonitored nonverbal messages (Andersen, Andersen, & Mayton, 1985; see Chapter 11).

Nonverbal Perceptions and Attributions

In the opening chapter of her book *Gendered Relationships,* Julia Wood (1996) recalls a conversation with her 4-year-old niece:

> When I asked her who she was she immediately replied, "I'm a girl." Only after declaring her sex did she proceed to describe her likes and dislikes, family and so forth. In Western society, gender is fundamental to social life and to individuals' identities, roles and options. The influence of gender is evident in everything from social policies and laws to intimate interaction. (p. 3)

Our sex and gender roles affect our perceptions in many ways. As males and females, we perceive the world in different ways. Moreover, we are taught to view our own behavior and behavioral options through the lens of gender.

For years, it has been noted in the literature on communication and gender that boys and girls are taught to view their own potential in different ways. Boys have been taught to develop a view of themselves that features independence, assertiveness, and a virtually unlimited choice of potential occupations. Girls have traditionally been taught to view themselves as being dependent on family and on men, being submissive, and having a narrower range of potential occupational choices. Although women today have greater choices and more independence than at any time in history, they still are socialized into narrower and more conventional roles than are men.

Another difference between men and women has to do with their perceptions regarding sexuality. Research has shown that men are much more likely to see sexual intent in the behavior of other people. Men are more likely than women to view closer interpersonal distances, eye contact, increased touch, and a variety of other warmth and friendship cues as more sexual in intent (Abbey & Melby, 1986; Major & Heslin, 1982; Metts & Spitzberg, 1996). For instance, men are much more likely than women to attribute sexual intent to a smile. In fact, men probably overattribute sexuality to situations that have no sexual intent, whereas women are likely to underattribute sexuality to situations that have sexual intent.

Differences in the perception of sexual intent in nonverbal behavior may help explain some common misunderstandings and behaviors. Because men overattribute sexuality to the behavior of female friends, they often suffer disappointment when a woman's warm nonverbal behavior is just a manifestation of friendliness, not sexual intent. Indeed, recent research has shown that socially incompetent men may engage in sexual coercion or assault when their expectations about receiving sex are not met (Spitzberg, in press).

It is difficult to know if these discrepant attributions about sexuality in everyday interaction represent biological or cultural differences between males and females. Sociobiologists contend that because frequent mating has greater biological value for males than for females, men are biologically programmed to see many nonverbal communication behaviors as sexual. Advocates of the different-cultures perspective argue that our society raises men and women to fulfill different roles; that is, society treats men and women as if they were members of different cultures (see Wood, 1997a). These different socialization and enculturation processes result in genders with different orientations, expectations, and worldviews.

Perceptual differences between men and women also occur in organizational settings. In a study by Eagly, Makhijani, and Klonsky (1992), men and women were asked to evaluate female and male managers. The managers were instructed to display either typically feminine or typically masculine leadership styles. The evaluators—particularly male evaluators—rated female managers more negatively than male managers when the leadership was carried out in a typically masculine style (that is, an autocratic or directive style). This sort of finding reveals that female managers may be in a bind due to these sexist views: they must either limit their repertoire of behaviors to traditionally feminine leadership styles or risk negative evaluation. Of course, females should not be evaluated on different or more stringent criteria than are males.

Relational Communication

A central function (perhaps *the* primary function) of nonverbal communication is the establishment of close interpersonal relationships with others (see Chapter 9). Research shows that males and females are likely to establish somewhat different relationships with people of the same sex. Most of this research has suggested that women establish closer relationships with other women than men do with other men (see Wood & Inman, 1993). These findings may be due in part to two differences discussed earlier: women are emotionally more expressive than men, particularly in communicating positive emotions; and women are more likely to accurately perceive emotions in other people. Thus, the highest exchange of warm emotional communication typically occurs in interactions between women. This suggests that women may develop closer, more intimate relationships than men.

Recently, a new perspective has emerged that suggests that part of this difference is actually a bias in favor of the way women express intimacy (Bate, 1988; Wood & Inman, 1993). Whereas women express intimacy through physical expression, nonverbal warmth, and emotional expression, men convey intimacy through shared activities and experiences (Duck, 1988). For men, intimacy may be more likely to occur between teammates during a sports event or between friends going for a run or taking a fishing trip. Helping one another out or partying and drinking together may be more masculine ways of communicating closeness. This suggests that from a man's perspective, there is no distinction between emotionally expressive communication and task communication; sharing a task or activity *is* expressive communication. In fact, when men and boys express intimacy, it may look more like aggression than affection. Males may punch each other in the arm, give each other high fives, or play fight as expressions of affection.

Always remember, however, that men and women are more similar in their intimacy needs than different. Although men tend to express intimacy in terms of shared activity more than women do, both men and women find disclosure and emotional expression more important than activity sharing. As Wood and Inman (1993) note, men and women both value friendship, seek intimacy, and desire warm, close, validating, and satisfying connections. As is so often the case in the "sex differences" research, the similarities between men and women outnumber the differences.

Remediation of Sexism

In the late sixties and early seventies, women formed consciousness-raising groups to try to understand the powerful but often hidden sexism that permeates our culture. Today, men's and women's groups still attempt to uncover and rectify hidden sexism that may limit our potential as human beings.

A number of successful measures are being taken to defeat the negative effects of sexual stereotyping. Many couples are actively practicing role sharing. At one time, few women worked outside the home as either primary or secondary breadwinners. Today, the vast majority of women are in the workforce, many with excellent careers as businesswomen and professionals. At the same time, men are realizing that child rearing and even homemaking are fulfilling functions missed by many men who rarely spend much time with their family or in their home. Moreover, recent advances in telecommuting have made it possible for both men and women to integrate family, home, and work.

Another imperative change facing our society is freeing women from the nightmare of sexual assault. Statistics reveal the horrifying fact that every woman has a one-in-three chance of being the victim of sexual assault in her lifetime (Ullman & Knight, 1992). Moreover, virtually all women live with the fear of sexual assault and often limit their activity as a result. Limitations on women's proxemic and chronemic freedoms may be the ultimate form of sexism. In the past decades, women have taken a number of proactive measures to stop this sexual terrorism. Women have insisted on the prosecution of sexual predators, armed themselves, taken self-defense classes, and organized rallies to "take back the night."

Several studies have shown that conscious alterations in a woman's nonverbal behavior can reduce the chance of becoming the victim of an attack or sexual assault. Several studies report that rape victims often signal their vulnerability to rapists through the use of submissive nonverbal behaviors and revealing clothing (Edmonds & Cahoon, 1986; Grayson & Stein, 1981; Richards, Rollerson, & Phillips, 1992). A study by Murzynski and Degelman (1996) found that students and police officers perceived that women with either longer or shorter strides, more lateral weight shifts, more one-sided limb movements, and more lifted-foot movements were more vulnerable to rape. Research that surveyed convicted felons found that they use a number of nonverbal cues to identify potential assault victims. The felon's most likely victim is a female who is wearing fancy clothing or visible jewelry, appears intoxicated, looks physically weak, takes short steps, and does not swing her arms. Similarly, looking worried, looking away, and avoiding stares were associated with victimization (Mezzakappa & Andersen, 1996). A knowledge of these subtle nonverbal behaviors may offer protection for women and men against the horror of assault.

Summary

Men and women are not from different planets. Although some sex differences in nonverbal communication do exist, men and women are far more similar than they are different. Furthermore, these relatively small differences are due to both biology and learned, cultural differences. Men and women can be active agents in changing their nonverbal behavior to become more effective communicators.

Men and women are somewhat different in physical appearance. Men are larger and more muscular, have more body hair, and have male sex organs. Women have wider hips, larger breasts, more subcutaneous body fat, and female sex organs. Beyond these anatomical differences, women have been socialized to be more concerned about their physical appearance than have men. Disturbingly, women have traditionally been valued for how their bodies look, not what they can do: women's physical attractiveness is more important to men than men's physical attractiveness is to women. A second disturbing finding is that despite all this emphasis on physical beauty, the more successful a woman is occupationally, the more her physical attractiveness is a disadvantage rather than an advantage, which poses a genuine double bind for women.

Men stand farther apart from one another than do women during interaction. However, when a man and a woman interact with each other, the man adopts the interaction distance of the woman. Women are more likely to face their interaction partner directly. In general, men have better spatial and navigational skills than women; this may be a biologically based sex difference.

Women are more facially expressive than men and more attuned to the facial expressions of others. This is particularly true for smiling, which women do more frequently than men. Men are more likely to show anger in their faces. Women tend to gesture more than men, although men's gestures are more expansive that women's. Despite these differences, the kinesic behavior of men and women is highly similar.

Women look at other people more than men do and are looked at more than men are; this is true while they are speaking or listening and even during silences. Women are probably better senders and receivers of nonverbal communication because they look more and are looked at more.

Men have deeper voices than women. Both men and women tend to exaggerate these biological differences to emphasize their masculinity and femininity, respectively. Women speak more softly than men and often use vocal variations that qualify an answer and signal uncertainty. Some studies suggest that men interrupt more than women.

Men and women exhibit fewer differences in tactile behavior than once assumed, and those differences that do exist are often due to other factors such as relational stage. Men initiate more touch in the beginning stages of a romantic relationship, whereas women initiate more touch in marital relationships. Touch is more likely to signal immediacy and warmth than power when used by men or women. In opposite-sex relationships, touch is highly reciprocal; men and women touch each other about the same amount. In same-sex relationships, women touch considerably more than men, at least in American culture.

Women are better receivers of virtually every type of nonverbal behavior than are men. This heightened sensitivity to nonverbal communication by women is probably biologically based but increased by socialization.

Regardless of the origins of sex differences in nonverbal communication, biology is not destiny. Men and women can alter their abilities, attitudes, and behaviors to become more effective nonverbal communicators.

Behaviors That Reveal

DIRECTIONS: In observing people, you have probably noticed differences between males and females in terms of their gestures, body postures, and facial expressions. Identify the following nonverbal behaviors as behaviors that are predominantly performed by males, predominantly performed by females, or are performed equally by each sex. Be honest. Check the behaviors that are *actually* performed by one sex or the other, rather than behaviors you would *like* to associate with one of the sexes. Then, compare your results with your own *observations* of typically male and female behaviors.

PREDOMINANTLY PERFORMED BY MALES	PREDOMINANTLY PERFORMED BY FEMALES	PERFORMED EQUALLY BY BOTH MALES AND FEMALES	BEHAVIOR
_____	_____	_____	1. Staring
_____	_____	_____	2. Lowering one's eyes
_____	_____	_____	3. Interrupting
_____	_____	_____	4. Frowning
_____	_____	_____	5. Smiling
_____	_____	_____	6. Cocking (tilting) one's head
_____	_____	_____	7. Pointing
_____	_____	_____	8. Yielding (moving out of another person's way)
_____	_____	_____	9. Cuddling to another person's touch
_____	_____	_____	10. Averting another person's gaze
_____	_____	_____	11. Taking up a large amount of space
_____	_____	_____	12. Initiating touch

PREDOMINANTLY PERFORMED BY MALES	PREDOMINANTLY PERFORMED BY FEMALES	PERFORMED EQUALLY BY BOTH MALES AND FEMALES	BEHAVIOR
_____	_____	_____	13. Pausing during a conversation (allowing another person to interrupt)
_____	_____	_____	14. Crowding another person's space
_____	_____	_____	15. Blinking
_____	_____	_____	16. Holding one's head erect or forward (chin-up position)

6

The Nonverbal Communication of Emotion

*A*NNE *FRANK: THE Diary of a Young Girl* is an account of a young girl hiding out in a warehouse during the Nazi invasion of Holland. Anne writes to an imagined friend:

> Do you think that Daddy and Mummy would approve of my sitting and kissing a boy on the divan—a boy of seventeen and a half and a girl of just under fifteen? I really don't think they would but I must rely on myself over this. It is so quiet and peaceful to lie in his arms and to dream, it is so thrilling to feel his cheek against mine, it is so lovely to know that there is someone waiting for me. . . . I sat pressed closely against him and felt a wave of emotion come over me, tears sprang to my eyes, the left one trickled onto his dungarees. . . . Did he notice? He made no move or sign to show that he did. I wonder if he feels the same way I do? He hardly says a word. (Frank, 1952, pp. 225, 231)

As this passage illustrates, nonverbal communication and emotion are inseparable. Without speaking, two young lovers received and expressed messages conveying many emotions: love, fear, happiness, warmth. The communication of emotion is a two-way process. The nonverbal communication from the important people in our lives directly affects our deepest emotions. In return, we convey our emotions to others. Most of this emotional dialog takes place nonverbally. In everyday interaction, talking about our feelings is less common than spontaneously revealing them through nonverbal communication. It is too personal, too private, too energy consuming, and too "uncool" to verbally reveal everything we're feeling. The natural system of communicating emotion is nonlinguistic, analogic, nonverbal communication (see Chapter 1 for more on the nonlinguistic, analogic basis of nonverbal communication). As discussed in Chapter 1, nonverbal communication is primarily processed in the right brain hemisphere. Not

132

surprisingly, as Silberman and Weingartner (1986) state, "the right hemisphere is specialized for processing the emotional aspects of communication" (p. 323). Furthermore, the right hemisphere seems to have exclusive control over negative emotions.

In this chapter, we will explore the complex interrelationship between emotion and nonverbal communication. Although we will examine each emotion separately, in reality, feelings are complex combinations of many emotions. Anne Frank felt love, guilt, arousal, excitement, sadness, and anxiety almost simultaneously. Rarely do we experience one emotion in isolation; rather, our feelings are complex arrays of mixed emotions.

Our discussion will begin with an examination of the genetic and cultural origins of emotions and emotional control. Next, we'll look at the three primary channels of emotional expression—the face, the voice, and the body—and then review fifteen separate emotions and their expression. Finally, we'll examine three principles that govern the inextricable relationship between emotional and nonverbal communication.

The Fundamental Characteristics of Emotion

A precise definition of *emotion* is somewhat elusive. Six fundamental characteristics comprise every human emotion. First, emotions involve subjective experiences or feelings. We know when we are experiencing an emotion because we feel happy, angry, ashamed, guilty, or one of many other emotions. Second, emotions are inherently valenced affectively; that is, they always produce positive or negative feelings (see Chapter 9 for more on this topic). There are no neutral emotions; all emotions involve pleasure or displeasure in response to stimuli (Guerrero, Andersen, & Trost, 1998). Third, emotions involve physiological arousal and other physical reactions. Emotions can be monitored via changes in one's heart rate, respiration, electrical conductivity of the skin, brain temperature, and a host of other physiological functions. Fourth, most emotions interrupt our thoughts, intrude on our cognitions, and require appraisals of the emotion and our reactions to it. People weigh the significance of an emotion cognitively; they judge whether it is desirable or undesirable, acceptable or unacceptable, controllable or uncontrollable, and so forth (Frijda, Kuipers, & ter Schure, 1989). Fifth, emotions are expressed behaviorally (Andersen & Guerrero, 1998b). In virtually all cases, emotions produce intentional or unintentional changes in our behavior that result in the transmission of our emotional state to other people. Finally, emotions are adaptive in that they are innate reactions to stimuli that motivate the organism to adapt to the situation or the environment (Burgoon, Buller, & Woodall, 1996). Emotions motivate us to flee, fight, mate, express remorse, grieve, and to enact dozens of other necessary and usually beneficial human responses. If we as human beings were not biologically programmed to experience emotions, to act upon these feelings, and to share them with others, our ability to survive would be impaired—which brings us to the genetic and biological origins of emotional communication.

The Genetic Origins of Emotional Communication

Emotions are internal control mechanisms, but they are much more than that. Emotions evolved as universal communication systems that promote the individual and group survival of human beings. Research has revealed a high degree of similarity in the expression of emotions across virtually all cultures (Ekman, 1993; Izard, 1992; Scherer & Wallbott, 1994), and any behavior that is highly similar across many diverse cultures is likely to be biologically based. These universal displays of emotion had survival value for our species or they would not have evolved. Humans are hardwired to express their emotions through nonverbal communication (Andersen & Guerrero, 1998b; Dillard, 1998). As DePaulo (1992) states, "There may be automatic links between the elicitation of an emotion for nonverbal but not for verbal behavior" (p. 205).

Throughout the ages, the expression and recognition of emotions have provided the human species with a unique survival advantage. Emotional communication allows us to understand the moods and emotional states of other people and to adjust our behavior accordingly. When people communicate their anger, we can avoid them and thus avert potentially dangerous—and even deadly—conflicts. People who express warm, happy emotions show they are available as friends, partners, or mates (see Chapter 9 for more on nonverbal communication in intimate relationships). People who express shame or guilt have a greater chance of being reassimilated into the group rather than being isolated, ostracized, or even killed.

Emotional recognition is a spontaneous, genetic, nonsymbolic, nonlinguistic process that is one of the most basic functions of nonverbal communication (Andersen, Garrison, & Andersen, 1979; Buck, 1984). In short, emotional communication permits most people to adjust to the behavior of others to ensure that cooperative rather than conflictual relationships are the norm. Most humans are remarkably successful in harmoniously adjusting to their social group and culture. This brings us to the next foundation of emotional expression—socialization and culture.

Socialization, Culture, and Emotional Expression

In every culture, children learn the appropriate expressions of emotions through a process called socialization. Throughout the world, infants and very young children differ little in how, when, and where they express their emotions. As children mature, each culture shapes and teaches children the rules for emotional expression. All children are great imitators, and as they grow up they imitate the behaviors modeled by their parents, siblings, and friends (Andersen & Guerrero, 1998b; Saarni, 1993). Today, a major agent for the socialization of emotional expression is the media, particularly television and film (Wilson & Smith, 1998). Of course, this is why many parents are concerned about the content of television, film, and even the internet, because children are apt to imitate even mediated behaviors, particularly those they view frequently.

Parents covertly and overtly shape the emotional behavior of their children. For example, mothers frequently gesture or whisper to their children to be quiet, to cheer up, or to stop making faces. Sometimes these are overt verbal instructions such as "Wipe that smile off your face," "Be a man, don't cry," or "That's not a very ladylike way to act!" In America, children—particularly girls—are punished for negative emotions such as anger (Guerrero & Reiter, 1998; Lemerise & Dodge, 1993). Fear and sadness are also discouraged, but most often for boys. These numerous processes of socialization modify the nonverbal expression of emotions through the use of display rules.

Display Rules

The socialization of emotional communication produces culturally based display rules (see Chapter 11 for more on display rules relating to interpersonal deception). These learned display rules govern the appropriate expression or suppression of various emotional communication displays (Andersen, Andersen, & Landgraf, 1985; Ekman and Friesen, 1975; Saarni, 1993). For example, exaggerated anger displays may be appropriate on a football field but not in the classroom. Public displays of affection may be considered inappropriate and "tacky," but the same affectionate displays might be appropriate and desirable in private. Humans control the expression of emotion by employing the following five display rules.

SIMULATION

Simulation occurs when we feel a need to show emotions we are not feeling (Andersen, Andersen, & Landgraf, 1985; Shennum & Bugental, 1982). We may smile when receiving a gift even before opening it so as not to hurt the giver's feelings. We may feign surprise at a surprise party that we knew about in advance. And we may laugh at a boss's joke, even if it wasn't funny, to be polite. Children learn these behaviors early. For example, toddlers cry to get attention even when they are not hurt.

INTENSIFICATION

Under certain circumstances, we need to show stronger feelings than we are experiencing internally, a process called intensification, or maximization (Andersen, Andersen, & Landgraf, 1985; Saarni, 1985). Unlike simulation, intensification involves experiencing a milder form of the emotion than one communicates.

Examples of intensification would be crying at the funeral of an uncle you neither knew very well nor liked or acting warmly and affectionately toward your boyfriend or girlfriend even though you're physically and emotionally exhausted at the end of a hard day.

MINIATURIZATION

The opposite of intensification is miniaturization, also known as minimization or deintensification (Andersen, Andersen, & Landgraf, 1985; Saarni, 1993). Miniaturization is one of the primary products of socialization. As children develop and mature, they gradually decrease their show of emotion (Andersen, Andersen, & Mayton, 1985). Children as young as two years old use miniaturization (Saarni, 1993). Examples of miniaturization in children include frowning rather than throwing a temper tantrum and showing less fear than they are actually experiencing. Teens may smile faintly at a really funny joke or express less overt affection for a date they really like in order to "play it cool." Adults may show only mild surprise even though they are intensely surprised over the news of a friend's divorce, or they may show only mild pride to appear humble when receiving an award of which they are very proud.

INHIBITION

Sometimes people attempt to show no emotion even though they are truly experiencing an emotion, a process called inhibition, or neutralization (Andersen, Andersen, & Landgraf, 1985; Ekman, 1978). Examples include hiding your attraction to someone else when your boyfriend or girlfriend is present, holding back tears when you are really upset and ready to cry, and keeping a straight face when you think something is really funny. Inhibition is also evident during deception, when guilt, shame, duping, delight, anxiety, and other emotions are concealed to avoid detection (Buller & Burgoon, 1998; O'Hair & Cody, 1994; see also Chapter 11 for more on deception). Similarly, suspicious receivers of deceptive messages use inhibition to avoid tipping off the sender (Buller & Burgoon, 1998).

MASKING

Sometimes people show a completely different emotion than they are feeling, a process called masking, or substitution (Ekman, 1978; Saarni, 1993). Masking appears later in the developmental cycle than other display rules because it requires considerable communication skill to show a totally different emotion than one is experiencing (Saarni, 1993). Showing disappointment instead of glee over the straight flush you've been dealt when playing poker or feigning sadness over an enemy's misfortune are examples of masking. During deception, masking is a vital skill when substituting joy for guilt or calmness for anxiety (Buller & Burgoon, 1998; O'Hair & Cody, 1994).

Biological evolution and cultural socialization both play important roles in the communication of emotion. In the following sections, we will take a close look at the channels of emotional expression as well as the individual emotions and how they are communicated.

Nonverbal Channels of Emotion

The Face

For many people the communication of emotion is virtually synonymous with facial expressions (Planalp, 1998). Such a view is not particularly naive, because the face is the primary location of emotional communication. We are most likely to look at another person's face during social interaction to quickly assess her or his emotional state. Does that person's face convey messages of affection, anger, fear, sadness, or joy? Ekman and Friesen (1975) have found six basic facial expressions that are cross-culturally and universally identifiable: anger, surprise, disgust, fear, happiness, and sadness. In his taxonomy, Izard (1977) includes Ekman's six basic expressions but argues for four additional basic emotions—contempt, shame, shyness, and guilt—each with its own unique facial display. The cross-cultural recognizability of these basic emotions suggests their innate, nonverbal, right-hemispheric origins (see Chapter 1).

Facial expressions are spontaneously communicated to others without conscious thought or linguistic representation. Of course, as we discussed previously, we clever humans can simulate facial expressions for feelings we don't have. Indeed, a primary form of strategic deception behavior involves managing facial displays. Deception researchers have found that smiling and other pleasant facial expressions are often used to conceal deceit; positive facial expressions are more commonly used by deceivers than by truth-tellers (Buller & Burgoon, 1998; see Chapter 11). Most people, however, are unable to continuously control their facial expression and frequently leak their emotions for others to read.

The Voice

Everyone who has used a telephone knows that the voice conveys many emotions; even when vocalic cues are the only available nonverbal behavior, we can still accurately identify other people's emotions. In fact, research shows that our accuracy in detecting emotions through vocal cues is generally as good as or better than our accuracy in identifying emotions through facial expressions (Kappas, Hess, & Scherer, 1991; Planalp, 1998). Research has shown that harsh tones of voice usually elicit crying in young infants (Magai & McFadden, 1995), suggesting that emotional communication by voice is a hardwired, innate behavior.

Research by Scherer and Wallbott (1994) has shown a cross-cultural similarity in the vocal expression of several emotions. Joy, for instance, is accompanied by higher pitch, more vocal variation, and, of course, laughing. Anger is expressed by yelling, screaming, shouting, and considerable vocal variation. An entire profile of vocalic behaviors characterizes depression, including slower, quieter, halting speech, lower pitch, more vocal interruptions or hesitations (such as *ah* or *um*), and a more monotonous tone of voice (Segrin, 1998). Sadness is often expressed by crying or weeping, although it sometimes is expressed through silence. Interestingly, four emotions—fear, disgust, shame, and silence—are all communicated primarily through silence (Scherer & Wallbott, 1994). This illustrates the power of emotion not only to promote communication but also to inhibit or interrupt it (Guerrero, Andersen, & Trost, 1998).

Research by Planalp and her associates (1998; Planalp, DeFrancisco, & Rutherford, 1996) has shown that vocal cues are the most recognizable sign of emotions, as reported by their subjects. Loudness and speed of talking were the most commonly reported vocal cues that indicated an emotion was being expressed. Interestingly, unlike vocal cues, direct verbal cues were reported to be very uncommon in interpersonal interaction (for example, "Boy, I'm angry.").

Our voice is extremely crucial in helping to comfort a person who is upset. Recent research by Burleson and Goldsmith (1998) shows that people are most successful in comforting an upset person when they provide emotional support, affection, and concern. An important aspect of comforting is helping the upset individual to express herself or himself by asking leading questions and providing encouragement vocally with nonverbal backchannel cues (such as *uh-huh* and *mm-hmm*) that both legitimize the person's feelings and encourage verbal expression.

The Body

Like the face and the voice, the body is also quite capable of expressing emotions. Planalp (1998) reports that people can easily interpret a person's emotional state from cues such as "being physically energetic, bouncy, jumping up and down, clenching hands or fists, making threatening movements, holding the body rigidly, shuffling, or having a slumped, droopy posture, dancing around, and using hand emblems" (p. 34). Some bodily shapes and movements seem to convey innate meanings. Round shapes, patterns, and movements of all types—including the eyes, breasts, face, and smooth gestures—communicate warmth. Even newborn babies find rounded objects pleasant, suggesting that this is an instinctive preference. Angular or diagonal movements and bodily shapes, such as angry frowns and tense muscles, tend to convey threat (Aronoff, Woike, & Hyman, 1992).

Research has revealed that certain postures can convey attitudes, although the communication of specific emotions through posture has not really been thoroughly investigated. Studies by Bull (1987) have revealed that folded arms typically convey disagreement, whereas crossing one's legs is associated with positive affective interpretations such as friendliness and relaxation.

Immediacy cues (which we will discuss in detail in Chapter 8) such as happy facial expressions, enthusiastic gestures, closer interpersonal distances, and friendly touches are powerful indicators of warmth (see Andersen & Guerrero, 1998a). Such cues have been shown to increase affection, intimacy, and attention in both interpersonal and classroom interactions and contagiously affect the emotional states of others.

A number of physiological behaviors convey emotional states: blushing may convey shame or embarrassment; trembling often communicates fear or anxiety; penile erections and vaginal secretions may indicate sexual desire; heavy breathing can reveal sexual arousal or physical exertion; sweating often signals nervousness; and fidgeting may communicate anticipation or anxiety. No exact correspondence has been established between these behaviors and singular emotions, so caution should be exercised in interpreting such cues; many of these behaviors can convey more than one emotional state. For instance, although crying usually communicates sadness, in some social settings it can communicate sentimentality or even joy, such as crying at weddings or upon reuniting with old friends.

The Human Emotions

Happiness

Happiness is one of the most positive human emotions. Every researcher includes happiness on their list of basic human emotions. Overwhelmingly, when people are asked to list words that fit into the category "emotion," *happiness* and *joy* are among the most frequently mentioned words (Fehr & Russell, 1984; Shaver, Schwartz, Kirson, & O'Connor, 1987). Some researchers have chosen to examine the emotion joy (Izard, 1977; Scherer & Wallbott, 1994), but both the conceptualization and expression of joy are virtually identical with happiness. Happiness is so important to Americans that the Declaration of Independence guarantees "the pursuit of happiness" as "inalienable." Happiness is the only emotion given the status of a human right.

Among facial expressions, happiness is one of the most basic and most universally recognized emotions. Ekman and Friesen (1975) have found that people worldwide are able to recognize and name the facial expression of happiness. This facial expression, called smiling, involves a widening and upturning of the lips and mouth. It also involves raising the cheek muscles and squinting the eyes at the corners, producing smile lines at the corners of the mouth and eyes that may be either temporarily or more permanently etched on the face of a person who smiles frequently. Everyone smiles—babies, teenagers, and adults—because smiling is an innate part of our biological heritage (Konner, 1987). Babies attract caregivers, potential victims appease attackers, and young adults attract mates with the most pleasant of facial expressions, the smile.

Happiness, a universal facial expression, is characterized by widened and upturned lips, raised cheeks, and characteristic upturned smile lines at the corners of the eyes.

Aside from smiling, happiness produces other changes in a person's nonverbal behavior, including increased vocal pitch, intensity, and rate, a more melodious tone of voice, a lighter walking style, closer interpersonal distances, and increased laughing (Planalp, 1998; Scherer & Wallbott, 1994). Happy people are also more likely to touch more, to hug their friends and family, and to refrain from violent behavior (Andersen & Guerrero, 1998b; Shaver et al., 1987).

Happy expressions rarely occur when a person is alone; instead, they are reserved for social occasions, when they can be shared with other people (Kraut & Johnson, 1979; Rime, Mesquita, Philipott, & Boca, 1991). It is difficult to think of a really joyous or happy moment that was not shared with significant others. Sharing happiness may have provided the human species with a survival advantage: people tend not to be dangerous when they are displaying positive emotions. In fact, among all primates, including humans, smiling is a primary display of appeasement and submission, designed to calm and build positive relationships with other members of the species (Van Hoofe, 1972). Conversely, positive relationships with friends, colleagues, and family are the major source of one's own happiness (Andersen & Guerrero, 1998b; Taraban, Hendrick, & Hendrick, 1998).

Sadness

Sadness, like its opposite happiness, is a basic emotion (Fehr & Russell, 1984; Shaver et al., 1987). Depression, a similar emotion, is characterized primarily by a chronic, sad affect, melancholy feelings, and a host of other symptoms (Russell, 1989; Segrin, 1998). Grief, another melancholic emotion, is a special form of sadness involving the loss of a loved one through death or separation. Sadness is experienced as a loss of an object or person closely associated with one's identity in which there is typically no blame for the loss (Burleson & Goldsmith, 1998) and no way to reverse the loss aside from accepting it. If blame is involved, typically the emotion becomes anger (blame of another) or guilt and shame (blame of oneself).

Sadness is displayed nonverbally in several ways. The sad face, easily drawn by any schoolchild, includes a downturned mouth and downturned eyes. The facial expression of sadness is easily recognized by people of virtually every culture, suggesting its universality (Ekman & Friesen, 1975; Scherer & Wallbott, 1994). Behavioral indications of sadness include a slumping posture, frowning, moping, a lowered head, prolonged silences, withdrawal, social isolation, talking in a monotone, lower vocal volume, decreased smiling, reduced eye contact, and, in more extreme cases, crying, sobbing, and throwing oneself on the ground (Guerrero et al., 1998; Magai & McFadden, 1995; Segrin, 1998).

Sad people look pitiful, and the main function of expressed sadness may be to elicit support and comforting (Planalp, 1998). Comforting involves verbal and nonverbal communication that alleviates distress, such as sadness, in another person (Burleson & Goldsmith, 1998). Offering nonverbal or verbal solace to a sad person is probably the most effective comforting behavior.

Sadness is an interpersonal emotion in another way: the main cause of sadness is relationship loss (Andersen & Guerrero, 1998b; Shaver et al., 1987). Similarly, depression is almost always associated with social isolation, little interpersonal intimacy, and a lack of social support, although these factors are probably both the cause and the effect of depression (McCann & Lalonde, 1993: Segrin, 1998).

Fear

A considerable amount of research has been conducted on the experience, effects, and expression of fear. Fear is a transitory, negative emotion characterized by avoidance of painful or dangerous stimuli (Gaines et al., 1998). Everyone experiences fear. Studies show that when asked to list basic emotions, virtually all respondents include fear on their list (Fehr & Russell, 1984; Shaver et al., 1987). Fear is probably essential for survival because it activates the human body to

Sadness, another universal facial expression, is characterized by a downturned mouth and lowered brows. Other signs of sadness include a slumping posture, immobility, and social withdrawal.

respond to impending danger. The expression of fear also serves as an instant warning to other members of one's social group, enabling them to take the necessary actions. So both the experience and expression of fear have survival benefits for individuals, for group members, and for their future offspring.

Fear typically occurs in the presence of an external threat, but phobic or paranoid states can also produce feelings of fear. At one time in the history of the human species, fear was primarily induced by nature in the form of large predators and severe storms, for example. Fear today, however, is often socially induced, resulting from interpersonal stimuli, such as a threatening teacher, a scary movie, and anxiety-producing social situations (Andersen & Guerrero, 1998b; Wilson & Smith, 1998), as well as close calls on the freeway (see Chapter 7 for more on arousal, anxiety, and nonverbal communication). Moreover, parents, doctors, politicians, police officers, and advertisers use fear appeals to persuade us to eat less fat, practice safe sex, and wear seatbelts (see Witte, 1998).

Worldwide, the expression of fear is characterized by raised eyebrows, wide eyes, and a stretching of the lips.

Fear is usually accompanied by an increased heart rate, muscular tension, changes in breathing patterns, perspiration, trembling, increased skin conductivity, and cold extremities (Scherer & Wallbott, 1994). In human beings, fear produces a very recognizable facial expression in addition to other behaviors. The expression of fear is characterized by raised eyebrows and a narrowing of the eyes to an almost triangular shape. The upper eyelids are raised, the lower eyelids are tightened, and the lips and mouth are stretched horizontally to reveal the lower teeth (Dillard, 1994; Ekman & Friesen, 1975). Fear is often manifested through various forms of defensive avoidance, including outright flight, cowering, protecting the body, covering the face, and hiding.

Numerous studies have shown that both the experience and expression of fear is cross-culturally universal (Ekman & Friesen, 1975; Scherer & Wallbott, 1994), suggesting that fear is an innate, unlearned expression. Of course, like all emotional expression, when we reveal or conceal fear is governed by culture.

One of the briefest facial expressions, surprise is characterized across cultures by a rapid opening of the eyes, raised eyebrows, open mouth, and dropped jaw.

Surprise

Most nonverbal communication researchers have included surprise on their lists of basic emotions (Darwin, 1872/1904). Surprise is one of Ekman's (1972) six basic emotions, and it also appeared on Tomkins' (1962) and Izard's (1977) lists of basic emotions (for a summary see Guerrero et al., 1998). More recently, Shaver, Wu, and Schwartz (1992) have suggested that because surprise doesn't always produce the same feelings, it may not be a basic emotion. Unlike other emotions, surprise can be negative (for example, getting an unexpected, bad grade on a test) or positive (for example, getting an unexpected pay raise). According to this view, surprise is not a pure emotion but a fuzzy one that may be part of many emotions. Most researchers, however, consider surprise a basic emotion.

Surprise is the most transient of human emotions (Ervin & Martin, 1986). By definition, one cannot be continuously surprised. Research has shown also that surprise is the most fleeting facial expression. The facial expression of surprise is universally recognized, though not viewed initially as either positive or negative (Ekman, 1972; Ekman & Friesen, 1975). The facial expression of surprise involves a rapid opening of the eyes and a raising of the eyebrows, such that the sclera, the area above the iris, is exposed. The mouth opens rapidly, the jaw drops, and the teeth are slightly parted. Often, an expression of surprise changes quickly to another emotion such as fear, joy, excitement, embarrassment, or anger. This change occurs once the person has had a second or so to process the source of the surprise and to react to it.

Anger

Anger is an intense feeling of displeasure that usually results from being injured, harmed, or mistreated by another person. In a study examining anger, respondents were asked to describe their experience of anger. In 95 percent of their accounts, respondents reported having been harmed illegitimately as the source of their anger (Canary, Spitzberg, & Semic, 1998). Anger's manifestations are often aggression or revengeful displeasure. Although anger can occur outside of interpersonal interaction, it is usually the result of a troubling interpersonal circumstance (Andersen & Guerrero, 1998b) and most often the result of interpersonal communication (Canary et al., 1998; Guerrero, 1994). The most common causes of anger are physical or verbal attacks, thoughtless, inconsiderate, and rude behavior, the frustration of one's goals by another, threats to one's identity, and relationship threats such as unfaithfulness and disloyalty.

Anger has a unique facial expression: knit and lowered brows, a direct stare, narrowed eyes, and a tense jaw, with the mouth often open and the teeth exposed. Like the other basic facial expressions, this behavior is universally and cross-culturally recognized, indicating its biological origins. Anger also incurs changes in the voice. Vocalic behavior is louder, harsher, and often deeper in pitch. Anger behaviors may also include breaking things, slamming doors, stomping one's feet, making threatening gestures, clenching one's fists, staring at someone in a hostile fashion, "getting in someone's face," giving someone the "silent treatment," and walking out on someone (Andersen & Guerrero, 1998b; Canary et al., 1998; Guerrero, 1994; Shaver et al., 1987). Research has consistently shown that anger displays occur most often during social interaction rather than when one is alone (Canary et al., 1998; Shaver et al., 1987).

Researchers believe that the expression of anger evolved as a way to warn other individuals of—and thus avert—an impending attack (Andersen & Guerrero, 1998b; Darwin, 1872/1904; Planalp, 1998). Today, as in years past, attacks without warning have the potential of resulting in death or injury to one of the combatants. But warnings through the expression of anger result in symbolic combat, aggression displays, or flight by one or both parties. According to this evolutionary perspective, individuals who express emotions like anger have a better chance of avoiding potentially life-threatening combat and have a greater likelihood of passing their genes on to the next generation.

Anger is a unique, universal facial expression characterized by knit and lowered brows, a direct stare, and a tense jaw, with the teeth often exposed.

Disgust

In the distant past, humans originally experienced disgust when they encountered a foul taste or smell. Today, although we are still disgusted by some tastes and smells, we experience disgust in new contexts; disgust now also applies to people, groups, situations, and interactions. Disgust is deeply ingrained and prewired in human nature. According to numerous theorists and researchers, disgust is a basic emotion (Darwin, 1872/1904; Ekman, 1972; Izard, 1977; Tomkins, 1963).

In interpersonal communication, feelings of disgust are reserved for individuals with extremely obnoxious personal qualities. Disgust is closely associated with rejection and leads to interpersonal avoidance (Gaines et al., 1998). Like disgusting smells or tastes, disgusting people are discarded and avoided.

The facial expression of disgust is well known to everyone, even preschoolers: the eyes are nearly shut, the nose is wrinkled, and the mouth is turned down; in extreme disgust, the tongue protrudes outward and downward. In the 1980s, a cartoon version of this facial expression was portrayed in the form of "Mr. Yuck,"

The universal facial expression of disgust is characterized by a downturned mouth, nearly closed eyes, and a wrinkled nose. In extreme disgust, sometimes the tongue is extended.

a widely recognized icon featured on containers of toxic household substances. Research has demonstrated that disgust is a universal facial expression (Ekman, 1972; Porter & Samovar, 1998), produced and recognized in all cultures.

Contempt

Scholars have debated whether or not contempt is an independent emotion or a blend of other emotions. Izard (1977) includes contempt among his primary emotions, yet some scholars have suggested it is a secondary emotion, a blending of anger and disgust (Plutchik, 1980). In their early work, Ekman, Friesen, and Ellsworth (1972) classified contempt as a variety of disgust; in their later work, however, Ekman & Friesen (1986) argue, like Izard, that contempt is a free-standing emotion. In his circumplex model, Plutchik (1980) classifies contempt as the opposite of submission.

According to some researchers, contempt does produce a recognizable facial expression: a blank expression accompanied by a tightened, curled lip (Ekman & Friesen, 1986). Other researchers (Russell, 1991) have failed to support the existence of a contempt expression. Gaines et al. (1998) conclude that there is no consensus regarding the existence of a distinct contempt expression. Pittam and Scherer (1993) have identified a vocal profile of shame but admit that the contempt profile is mostly undifferentiated arousal.

Pride

Pride is often overlooked by researchers as a human emotion, despite its inclusion as one of the "seven deadly sins" (Andersen & Guerrero, 1998b). Pride isn't entirely negative but really a mixture of good and evil. On the negative side, too much pride can make someone seem arrogant and boastful; excessively proud people are warned that "pride comes before a fall." Research suggests that for some individuals, pride is a barrier to seeking social support or help with one's problems (Barbee, Rowatt, & Cunningham, 1998). However, too little pride can be injurious to one's self-esteem. On the positive side, pride can be a very constructive reaction to the compliments and approval of others and to socially valued accomplishments (for more on this topic see Andersen & Guerrero, 1998b). According to Gaines et al. (1998), pride is a subset of a cluster of "delight" emotions. Pride, a highly interpersonal emotion, has been characterized as one of the most "social" emotions (Barrett, 1995). Pride is typically dependent on a social audience (Greenwood, 1994). Under the rare instances of private pride, an audience is usually imagined.

Although little research has been done on pride, some studies have identified nonverbal behaviors that are associated with the experience of pride: proud individuals stand taller, make themselves larger, and exhibit signs of strength (Andersen & Guerrero, 1998b). Proud individuals display their body to others, smile broadly, and produce celebratory gestures such as the high-five sign (Mascolo & Fischer, 1995). Like adults, children display their pride nonverbally with broad smiles, increased eye contact, and conspicuous kinesic displays designed to attract attention from others.

Shame

Shame is an intensely negative feeling that one is inferior to others and has lost the respect of others due to one's own immoral behavior or incompetence (Andersen & Guerrero, 1998b). Shame typically involves global negative feelings about oneself rather than about one's particular actions. Shamed individuals experience a substantial loss of face and feel unworthy of the respect or love of others. Shame involves an overall loss of self-esteem and is accompanied by persistent feelings of worthlessness (Lewis, 1995). According to many theorists and researchers, shame is a basic emotion (Darwin, 1872/1904; Izard, 1977; Tomkins, 1962), although others would classify it as a secondary emotion or an emotional blend (Ekman, 1982). Shame is usually accompanied by other emotions, including dejection, sadness, depression, helplessness, and sometimes anger (Ferguson & Stegge, 1995).

Shame does not occur in solitude. It is always the product of one's perceived transgressions against others and their negative interpersonal reactions. Shame, like its cousins embarrassment and guilt, is a so-called self-conscious emotion because it frequently fosters moral behavior and inhibits transgressions against others (Tangney, 1995). Self-conscious emotions evolved to protect the group against the immoral or injurious behavior of an individual. Were there no guilt, embarrassment, or shame, people would be emotionally unrestrained in behaviors that are damaging to other people and to their primary group. Throughout the ages, people who experienced distress over the impressions they made on others were more likely to survive as reproductive members of the group than those who felt disdain or disregard for other people's feelings (Miller & Leary, 1992).

Shamed individuals engage in a number of nonverbal behaviors best characterized by the desire to disappear, hide, and avoid observation by others. People who feel shame are motivated to avoid interpersonal contact and experience overwhelming feelings of pain and loss of face. Avoidance reactions include shrinking one's body (by exhaling air from the chest, for example), covering the face with one's hands, avoiding eye contact, slouching, lowering one's head, and fleeing from social contact (Andersen & Guerrero, 1998b). Some other nonavoidance reactions include blushing (although this is a more common reaction to embarrassment), self-control behaviors such as biting or licking one's lips, wrinkling one's forehead, increased facial touching, and forced, weak smiling (Keltner, 1995; Leary & Meadows, 1991; Scheff, 1995).

Embarrassment

Like shame, embarrassment is expressed through numerous nonverbal behaviors. As mentioned in Chapter 1, most nonverbal behaviors are analogic. Many of the nonverbal reactions to embarrassment, such as smiling, are analogic apologies designed to maintain face in an embarrassing situation. Other behaviors are designed to appease onlookers, avoid observation, and release tension: avoiding gaze and eye contact; covering one's mouth, eyes, or entire face; making fake, feeble, or silly smiles; laughing half-heartedly; blushing; interrupting others; lowering one's head; turning one's face or body away from others; and making moves to depart (Andersen & Guerrero, 1998b; Cupach & Metts, 1990, 1994; Keltner, 1995; Miller & Leary, 1992).

Guilt

Guilt is an interpersonal emotion. In fact, it is hard to imagine how one could experience guilt except in reference to other people. Although intrapersonal guilt does exist (for example, eating a second piece of cake when one is home alone), it usually involves an interpersonal failure (for example, appearing fat because you ate too much cake). One typically experiences guilt as the result of a perceived transgression against another person, especially when the transgression (such as sexual infidelity) occurs in the context of a close relationship (Metts, 1994;

Vangelisti & Sprague, 1998). Guilty emotions occur when a person has unjustly deceived, injured, cheated, hurt, or failed to help someone (Friedman, 1985; Vangelisti & Sprague, 1998). Guilt is most likely to occur when in the presence of other people and often works to strengthen a relationship after an offense has occurred (Baumeister, Reis, & Delaspaul, 1995). People may feel guilty that they have received too many benefits (Andersen & Guerrero, 1998b; Metts, 1994). Guilt may also occur when people mistakenly take responsibility for a transgression; even victims can experience guilt. For example, Holocaust survivors, who were themselves victims, often feel deep, crippling guilt even though they could have done nothing to prevent the deaths of other victims (for a summary of these findings see Vangelisti & Sprague, 1998).

Guilt shares some similarities with regret, shame, and embarrassment (White & Mullen, 1989) and may sometimes accompany these other emotions. Research conducted in thirty-seven countries by Scherer and Wallbott (1994) found that guilt occurs in virtually all cultures. Guilt is considered a basic, primary emotion by some researchers (Izard, 1977) because it can occur by itself. It frequently appears as one of the basic, or prototypic, emotions.

Responses to guilt are likewise highly interpersonal in nature. Guilty individuals may engage in interpersonal avoidance or seek to make up for their behavior through apologies, repairs, or promises to change their behavior. Indeed, recent conceptualizations of guilt suggest it is a phenomenon that "happens between people rather than just inside them" (Baumeister, Stillwell, & Heatherton, 1994, p. 243).

Guilt is an emotion that functions to exert social control over one person's actions in a group. Indeed, Miller and Leary (1992) suggest that social emotions such as guilt are functional because they show remorse to the injured party rather than a disregard for others. Those who act with consistent disregard for others may be ostracized, banished, or even killed. Guilty behavior, however, demonstrates a remorseful attitude that may be reassuring to other group members. Guilt also serves to prevent others from engaging in behavior that deviates too greatly from social standards (Andersen & Guerrero, 1998b). Moreover, guilt is used as a strategic behavior to manipulate or persuade or to change the behavior of another person (Vangelisti & Sprague, 1998).

Most of the literature on guilt deals with either guilt's internal experience or with many verbal responses to guilt (see Vangelisti & Sprague, 1998). Relatively little has been written about nonverbal responses to guilt. There is no single facial expression associated with guilt (Izard, 1977); however, sad or worried facial expressions, a lump in one's throat, and remorseful and sorry expressions during apologies are common reactions to guilt. Avoidance and silence are other behavioral responses to guilt across a variety of cultures (Scherer & Wallbott, 1994). Guilt often produces actions that are designed to repair the situation, redeem the guilty person, or reduce guilt, although guilty nonverbal behaviors, including reduced smiling and less pleasant tones of voice and facial expressions, may evoke suspicion in others and lead to perceptions of deception (Buller & Burgoon, 1998).

Love

Love is one of the most basic and culturally universal human emotions (Scherer & Wallbott, 1994; Taraban et al., 1998). Love is part of our emotional heritage; it is built into the fabric of our genetic structure. Love is perhaps the strongest positive emotion that a person can experience (Shaver et al., 1987; Taraban et al., 1998). Although most scholars consider love a basic or primary emotion, Plutchik (1980) maintains that it is actually a combination of two positive emotions: joy and acceptance. Shaver et al. (1987) classify love as a basic emotion closely related to adoration, affection, fondness, liking, attraction, arousal, desire, lust, and longing.

Love is typically experienced in the context of interpersonal relationships (although one could experience a love for nature or a love for God that is independent of interpersonal influence). Love creates in each of us a desire to reinforce social bonds and to establish and maintain close relationships. Love serves the social purpose of creating feelings of connectedness, and messages of love begin the process of creating close interpersonal ties. Love is an inherently interpersonal emotion because it occurs in relation to a particular other and is always associated with the desire to maintain a close relationship with another person (Andersen & Guerrero, 1998b). Love can take many forms, from familial to dyadic, from intimate to passionate (see the section "Sexual Desire" later in this chapter; for more on the many aspects of love see Sternberg, 1986; Taraban et al., 1998).

Love is such a basic emotion that we are motivated to extremes by the desire to protect and nurture loved ones. Emotional appeals to love are frequently employed in persuasive communication: tire commercials (whose message is "So much is riding on your tires") feature babies sitting in sturdy radials, and phone commercials (which implore us to "Reach out and touch someone") picture elderly relatives weeping over calls from their grandchildren (see Chapter 10 for more on nonverbal communication and persuasion).

Love is communicated in a variety of ways: through verbal expression and through various obvious and subtle nonverbal behavioral displays. Although no single facial expression of love has been identified (Fischer & Tangney, 1995), nonverbal manifestations of love include prolonged eye contact, closer interpersonal distances, increased time spent together, blushing, pupil dilation, increased smiling, and increased and prolonged touch across many areas of the body (for more about these behaviors see Andersen & Guerrero, 1998a; see Chapters 8 and 9). Couples who are falling in love, going steady, and newly married actually touch more than couples who have been married for many years (Emmers & Dindia, 1995; Guerrero & Andersen, 1991; McDaniel & Andersen, in press). As compared to secure, stable, long-term relationships, the intensity of new love relationships makes visible displays of love more essential. In relationships of all durations, touching, hugging, kissing, and caressing are vital to the communication of love. According to research on "love ways" by Marsden, Hecht, and Robers (1987), touch is especially important to the communication of love, as is smiling, making eye contact, and spending time together. One study (Egland, Stelzner, Andersen, & Spitzberg, 1997) shows that one of the most important behaviors in establishing understanding and in creating long-term relational satisfaction is spending more time together.

Nonverbal behavior, evidently, is more important in the communication of love than is verbal communication: "nonverbal behaviors are viewed as less strategic, more spontaneous, and therefore more honest than verbal behaviors" (Montgomery, 1988, p. 348). Love is expressed best through nonverbal behavior.

Jealousy

Just as love has its bright sides, so too love has its dark sides. One of love's darkest sides is jealousy, an emotion that occurs when a real or perceived rival threatens a close relationship, usually a romantic one. Jealousy likely has a genetic basis because it is a ubiquitous, cross-cultural phenomenon (Hupka, 1981; White & Mullen, 1989). Sociobiologists argue that paternity certainty and mate retention are genetically based and essential to the survival of one's genes (Buss, 1988; Daly & Wilson, 1987). Jealousy certainly has a long history; it is central to classic writing—from Homer to Shakespeare to Hawthorne, to name only a few (see Guerrero & Andersen, 1998).

Jealousy occurs in close interpersonal relationships and involves communication among members of a jealous triangle. People communicate feelings of jealousy in many ways, including through nonverbal communication. Immediately upon experiencing jealousy, people report feeling a jealousy flash—an intense, hot feeling due to sudden increases in physiological arousal. They also report feeling a blend of anger, fear, sadness (Izard, 1977), and hurt simultaneously.

But jealous communication is more than immediate feelings and reactions. In a series of studies, my colleagues and I examined jealous communication and its consequences (see Andersen, Eloy, Guerrero, & Spitzberg, 1995; Guerrero & Andersen, 1998; Guerrero, Andersen, Eloy, Jorgensen, & Spitzberg, 1995). People communicate their jealousy in many ways, including through nonverbal communication. Among the fourteen sets of communicative responses to jealousy we discovered, eight responses were entirely or partly nonverbal in nature including: (1) *negative-affect expression,* including crying, pouting, appearing hurt, and exhibiting displeasure facially; (2) *active distancing,* such as leaving the scene, storming out of a room, giving the partner cold looks, using the silent treatment, and withholding sex; (3) *avoidance/denial,* such as acting nonchalant about a rival, avoiding jealousy-inducing situations, and decreasing contact with the partner; (4) *violent communication/threats,* including threatening to hit the partner, pulling the partner away from a rival, and pushing, punching or slapping a rival; (5) *signs of possession,* such as always appearing in public with the partner, wearing rings or other "tie" signs, and holding or kissing the partner in the presence of potential rivals; (6) *surveillance/restriction,* such as spying on the partner, searching through the partner's belongings, and restricting the partner's access to rivals at parties; (7) *manipulation moves,* such as flirting with others to make the partner jealous or going out with rivals in retaliation; and (8) *violence toward objects,* such as slamming doors, breaking dishes, or throwing the partner's possessions against a wall.

How do these nonverbal behaviors, or even verbal behaviors, affect relationship satisfaction? Our results suggest that all forms of jealousy are associated with relational dissatisfaction. Moreover, all of the previously listed responses to jealousy seem to make matters worse, by reducing relational satisfaction, with one important exception: A combination of integrative verbal communication combined with negative-affect expression seems to counteract the deleterious effects of jealousy. Our results suggest that the best approach to dealing with jealous emotions is to express one's concerns and show negative emotions in a constructive way (Andersen, Eloy, Guerrero, & Spitzberg, 1995).

Warmth

In the presence of others about whom we care deeply, we experience pleasant, cozy feelings that some researchers call warmth (Andersen & Guerrero, 1998a). The emotion warmth has received sparse attention by researchers, yet it is perhaps the most social of all the emotions. Interpersonal warmth is universally experienced but goes by a variety of labels, including intimacy, closeness, bonding, attachment, involvement, confirmation, and validation, although these terms are not exact equivalents (see Chapter 9). *Warmth,* admittedly, is a vague and arbitrary term used to describe a specific emotion. Unfortunately the English language lacks a more precise word, as compared to the Danish *hugge* and the German *gemütlichkeit* (see Andersen & Guerrero, 1998a). Sternberg (1986, 1988) employs thermal metaphors to describe passion (*hot*), commitment (*cool*), and intimacy (*warm*). According to Sternberg (1988), intimacy refers to feelings of warmth that "promote closeness, bondedness, and connectedness" (p. 38).

Obviously, interpersonal warmth can occur only in the context of close relationships, although warm, contented feelings may be generated by a cozy house, feeling connected to nature and natural beauty, or reading a good book on a rainy day. Warmth, as conceptualized here, refers to the flood of good, soothing, pleasant feelings that occur when you are with a group of people or an individual about whom you care deeply.

Warmth is expressed primarily through nonverbal immediacy behaviors, which are covered extensively in Chapter 8, so only a brief mention will be made of them here. Warmth is conveyed by spending time together, maintaining closer interpersonal distances, smiling, nodding, using warm, reinforcing vocal tones, touching, interacting synchronously, and a number of other verbal and nonverbal behaviors (Andersen & Guerrero, 1998a).

Sexual Desire

In contrast to warmth, sexual arousal is passionate and hot. Whether sexual desire is an emotion is still debated among researchers. Sexual desire clearly includes arousal, the interpretation of the arousal as sexually stimulating, the activation of cognitive schemata associated with desire, and subjective feelings that seem to be distinguishable from other emotions. Certainly, sexual desire is a multifaceted experience accompanied by subjective feelings, emotions, situational responses, physiological reactions, thoughts, interpersonal interactions, and nonverbal behaviors (Metts, Sprecher, & Regan, 1998). In one study, very few sexually active college students defined sexual desire in terms of psychological arousal or sexual activity; most defined sexual desire as a motivational state, and many defined it as an emotional state or part of an emotional syndrome (Ragan & Berscheid, 1996).

Sexual desire is associated with many other emotions, including love, happiness, loneliness, jealousy, and guilt. Romantic love typically involves sexual desire as a major component. Similarly, having a partner who is sexually attractive and sexually satisfying is essential to the experience of passionate or romantic love (Sternberg, 1987). Sexual jealousy is one of the most common types of jealousy, particularly for men, and is a leading precursor of violent behavior (Guerrero & Andersen, 1998a, 1998b). Conflicts over sexual feelings and behaviors have long been recognized as a primary source of guilt (see Freud, 1930/1961; Vangelisti & Sprague, 1998). Similarly, sexual rejection is associated with feelings of hurt and even depression (Baumeister & Wotman, 1992; Vangelisti & Sprague, 1998).

Sexual desire has a number of behavioral manifestations, including obvious physiological reactions such as erection of the penis, clitoris, and nipples, genital secretions, flushed skin, increased heart rate and respiration, and various vocal behaviors (Masters & Johnson, 1966; Rathus, Nevid, & Fichner-Rathus, 1993). Of course, sexual desire does more than prompt physiological reactions. It is also a vital component of flirting, sexual behavior (including intercourse), dating, and marriage.

Some of the most interesting nonverbal behaviors occur during flirtation and courtship. Sexual desire is expressed through eye contact and a whole set of interesting courtship-readiness behaviors: preening behaviors, such as touching, combing, or flipping one's hair or smoothing one's clothing; open-palm presentations; head cocking; pelvis rolling; and postural adjustments such as standing straighter, expanding or protruding one's chest, crossing one's legs, pulling in one's stomach, and revealing more of one's body (Scheflen, 1965, 1974).

Emotion As Communication

Traditionally, emotions have been thought of as purely internal, subjective experiences. Certainly, emotions can be experienced in private, yet recent research has shown that in many ways nonverbal communication is an inherent part of the emotional experience (Andersen & Guerrero, 1998b; Dillard, 1998; Planalp, 1998; Fischer & Tangney, 1995). In this final section, we will explore three important principles that govern the relationship between emotion and nonverbal communication: (1) most emotions are the result of interpersonal nonverbal communication; (2) emotions are typically expressed through nonverbal communication; and (3) emotions are contagious.

Emotions Result from Interpersonal Nonverbal Communication

In recent years, studies have shown that a primary source of our emotional state is our interactions with others (Andersen & Guerrero, 1998b; Metha & Clark, 1994). Bowlby (1979) has shown that our most intense emotional experiences occur during the formation, maintenance, disruption, termination, or renewal of close relationships. The formation of close, new relationships involves increases in time spent together, eye contact, touch, proxemic closeness, and other forms of nonverbal communication; such experiences create joy, happiness, excitement, and warmth. The disruption of interpersonal relationships results in emotions such as jealousy, hurt, sadness, anxiety, and anger. And the loss of a relationship, which involves decreased nonverbal communication, results in grief, hurt, sadness, and depression. Even the recall of intimate touch, of spending an evening with someone close, or of the visual image of someone you love can create waves of emotion.

Emotions Are Expressed through Nonverbal Communication

As we learned earlier in this chapter, every emotion can be communicated nonverbally. But the relationship between nonverbal communication and emotion is stronger than that. The *primary* means through which emotions are expressed is nonverbal communication, and studies show that emotional expression is much more likely to occur when others are present than when we are alone (Kraut & Johnson, 1979; Planalp, 1998). Like it or not, when we are in the presence of other people, it is difficult not to reveal our emotions nonverbally. As Andersen and Guerrero (1998b) state:

> Even when the nonverbal expression of emotion is unintended, it can send
> a clear message to a receiver. Indeed, emotions so automatically generate

communicative displays that they can be problematic for the maintenance of competent self-presentations during interaction, particularly when negative emotions are unwittingly revealed. (p. 73)

Although concealing all our emotions is impossible to do, revealing our every emotion would be a sign of immaturity and incompetence. It takes great skill and years of practice to learn and deploy the display rules examined earlier. We all feel emotions we'd rather not show. We may prefer not to reveal our physical attraction for our spouse's best friend, our glee at a "perfect" coworker's misfortune, or our eagerness to sign a business deal still under negotiation. Likewise, as a receiver, detecting unintended nonverbal communication can be disadvantageous. Some emotions are better left undetected; picking up on guilty deception from a close friend, subtle sexual interest from one's boss, or hostility from a coworker can cause hard feelings and awkwardness.

Sometimes, however, the automatic expression of emotion through nonverbal communication can be advantageous to both senders and receivers. Sometimes nonverbal leakage can send messages that one might not have the courage or competence to intentionally reveal: you may communicate subtle dissatisfaction at work and prompt your boss to give you a pay raise, or you may inadvertently show romantic interest in a friend that sparks off a romantic relationship. As receivers, tuning in to subtle displays of emotion can be equally advantageous. Remember, in the main, "emotions exist so that one's affective states can be shared to ready others for parallel action, to forewarn others of individual feelings, and to create a particular affective atmosphere for communicating" (Andersen & Guerrero, 1998b, p. 73).

Emotions Are Contagious

Patterns of reciprocity or matching generally govern the communication of emotion (Andersen & Guerrero, 1998b; Burgoon, Stern, & Dillman, 1995). For example, it is easier to be happy when your relational partner is happy (Oatley & Johnson-Laird, 1987). Likewise, fear spreads quickly in a group, and depressed individuals increase the depression of those around them (Segrin, 1998). How does this take place? At least six processes may account for the contagiousness of emotions (Andersen & Guerrero, 1998b). One thing is certain, however: emotional matching is no mere coincidence.

SOCIAL REFERENCING

One explanation for the contagiousness of emotions is called social referencing (Klinnert, Campos, Sorce, Emde, & Svedja, 1983). When we try to make sense of any event (a funeral, a meeting, a party), we look to others for cues as to how we should behave and what we should feel. Cialdini (1984) discusses a similar concept called social proof, a process whereby people determine what to do and feel based on the actions of others. This process has been used to explain phenomena as diverse as mass hysteria and why it is that bystanders fail to come to the aid of an assault or rape victim. In the latter case, more than fear is at work. If someone were being assaulted while bystanders continued going about their merry way, the conclusion that most people would draw is that the situation is not too serious. In the case of mass hysteria, the observation that everyone else is experiencing fear and panic would make it seem foolish to stay calm.

CONTAGION

Research on emotional contagion has attempted to provide an explanation for a whole group of processes, including mob panic, mass euphoria, contagious laughter, group grief, and collective panic (Hatfield, Cacioppo, & Rapson, 1994). Contagion occurs in dyads as well (Magai & McFadden, 1995). Although the exact process underlying contagion are not entirely understood, the emotions sadness, fear, joy, and anxiety seem particularly susceptible to the phenomenon (Klinnert et al., 1983).

IMITATION

People of all ages, particularly children, imitate the behavior of others. Magai and McFadden (1995) maintain, "The literature on the proclivity of infants to match the facial and vocal expressions of their caregivers is now quite substantial" (p. 282). Imitation is the primary process in modeling and plays a significant role in all human learning. Although it is frequently unconscious, imitation can also be intentional. Imitation is most pronounced when the person being imitated is of high status or prestige. This process occurs in various settings. Many professors, for example, have protégés who move and act exactly like the professor. Observe children watching a football or basketball game; they will imitate the moves and behavior of their heroes from how they unsnap their helmet to how they spike a football or dunk a basketball.

MOTOR MIMICRY

One mechanism that may explain the contagiousness of emotions is motor mimicry. Bavelas and her colleagues have shown that affect or emotional sharing is a common communication behavior (Bavelas et al., 1986, 1988). In a series of imaginative laboratory experiments, Bavelas and her colleagues were able, for example, to get observers to wince when a television was placed on another person's hand and to duck when a ball was thrown at another person's head. These researchers suggest that motor mimicry is more than mere empathy; it is a powerful form of communication by an observer that conveys appropriate affect to the observed person or warns the person of a dangerous situation. In the vast majority of cases, the observer simultaneously and symmetrically mirrors the other's emotional response. Because this reaction often occurs earlier in the observer than in the person being observed, it is not mere imitation. Motor mimicry is a parallel process between two communicators that puts the interactants in highly similar emotional states. This is particularly true in light of the next process, Cappella's (1993) interpersonal facial feedback hypothesis (IFFH).

THE INTERPERSONAL FACIAL FEEDBACK HYPOTHESIS

The IFFH is based on considerable research that demonstrates that people match or mimic each other's facial expressions (see, for example, Bavelas et al., 1988; Cappella & Palmer, 1990). The IFFH is also based on the original facial feedback hypothesis, which has demonstrated that as a person's facial expression changes, so her or his mood changes in the direction of the facial expression (Buck, 1995; Izard, 1991). Cappella (1993) has shown that when people smile, they feel more affection toward their interaction partner. The IFFH contends that because people match the expressions of their partners and because facial expressions provide facial feedback that alters one's mood, the result is, ultimately, matched emotions.

CONGRUENT INTERPRETATIONS

Finally, emotions may be interpersonally contagious because both interactants interpret the other's emotions as the same as their own (Metha & Clark, 1994). Happy people think other people are happy. Sexually aroused interactants often erroneously believe that their partner is similarly aroused. Grieving people believe that others share their grief. In one study of this process, researchers had two groups—one group had exercised, the other had not—view a target person (Clark, Milberg, & Erber, 1984). The exercising group viewed the target person as having stronger emotions than the nonexercising group (for example, joy versus contentment). In short, if we are angry, we see others as angry. If we are happy, we see others as happy. These self-fulfilling expectancies may help explain why we believe we are experiencing the same emotions as others.

Summary

Nonverbal communication and emotion are inseparable. It is almost impossible not to express emotions nonverbally. The natural system of communicating emotion is analogic, nonlinguistic, nonverbal communication. The nonverbal communication of emotion is a biologically based genetic system that provides both an internal control system for each of us and a means of communicating these emotions to others. Emotions and their expression have provided humans with a survival advantage; by allowing us to adjust our behavior to the emotions of others, we can prevent dangerous and deadly conflicts, promote the well-being of the individual and group, and initiate mating relationships to ensure the survival of the species.

Emotions are socialized differently in each culture. Display rules that govern emotional expression include simulating nonexistent emotions, intensifying mild emotions, miniaturizing strong emotions, inhibiting emotions that are inappropriate to express, and masking one's felt emotion with the display of another emotion.

The primary channel of emotional expression is the face. Facial expressions show great consistency among cultures, indicating their genetic, biological origins. At least six basic expressions—anger, surprise, disgust, fear, happiness, and sadness—are recognizable across cultures. The face is not the only nonverbal channel for emotional expression. The voice and the body also carry considerable emotional information. Nonverbal communication is used to convey fifteen emotions described in this chapter: happiness, sadness, fear, surprise, anger, disgust, contempt, pride, shame, embarrassment, guilt, love, jealousy, warmth, and sexual desire.

Three important principles govern the relationship between emotion and nonverbal communication: emotions are the result of interpersonal, nonverbal communication; emotions are expressed through nonverbal communication; and emotions are contagious. Theories regarding the contagiousness of emotions include social referencing, contagion, imitation, motor mimicry, the interpersonal facial feedback hypothesis (IFFH), and congruent interpretations.

7
Communication and Stress
Nonverbal Reactions to Arousal and Anxiety

THE CONCEPT OF stress was first researched by Hans Selye (1956), who wrote:

> I believe that the mere fact of understanding the general rules about the way stress acts on the mind and body, with a few remarks about the way this has been used as a basis for one man's personal philosophy, can help others, better than fixed rules, to formulate their own solutions. . . . The study of stress has shown that complete rest is not good, either for the body as a whole, or even for any organ within the body. Stress, applied in moderation, is necessary for life. Besides, enforced inactivity may be very harmful and cause more stress than normal activity. (pp. 294, 300)

Every human being walks a tightrope between boredom and stress, between stimulation and relaxation, between maintaining privacy and avoiding loneliness. Imagine spending a few days resting alone, without friends or family. The need for stimulation and companionship would quickly return. From infancy through adulthood, we all desire human contact; too little human contact can lead to loneliness, boredom, and depression. Stern (1980) maintains that humans "from birth, will seek out stimulation and even work for it. In fact, the seeking of stimulation has now achieved the status of a drive or motivational tendency not unlike that of hunger" (p. 52). Now imagine having out-of-town guests who planned to stay for a month during a particularly hectic time of the year. Privacy would become nonexistent, and soon you would feel like hiding, fleeing, or attacking. Interpersonal overstimulation, so common in our present-day world, is one source of stress, anxiety, and apprehension.

Finding and maintaining a balance between understimulation and overstimulation is the key to personal sanity and interpersonal harmony. Each person must find her or his own mix of privacy and interpersonal interaction (for more on these relational dialectics and paradoxes see Chapter 9). Because introverts, high communication apprehensives (discussed later in this chapter), and stimulation avoiders are individuals who have much lower stimulation thresholds, they are more likely to suffer from overstimulation and stress. By contrast, sensation seekers, low communication apprehensives, and extroverts have much higher stimulation thresholds and are more likely to suffer from loneliness and boredom.

The stress of modern life is taking its toll on today's college students. According to a recent survey conducted by the UCLA Higher Education Research Institute (Weiss, 1997), the class of 2000 is more stressed than any previous college class. This survey, completed by over one quarter of a million freshmen, revealed that 29.4 percent of respondents feel "overwhelmed by all they have to do"—up from 16 percent in 1985. Much of the stress seems to be self-inflicted: a record 66.3 percent of freshmen planned to go on to graduate school, 49 percent intended to maintain at least a B average in college, and 72 percent reported being involved in volunteer work.

Arousal and Mood

Arousal is the degree to which a person is stimulated or activated. Internal signs of arousal, such as increased heart rate, brain temperature, and blood pressure, prepare the body for action. Feelings of excitement, anxiety, stress, or stimulation are also part of arousal. As we will learn in this chapter, arousal is also accompanied by behavior changes, including many nonverbal communication behaviors.

Research and theory have established a curvilinear relationship between arousal and mood (Cappella & Greene, 1982; Eysenck, 1976). As illustrated in Figure 7.1, moderate arousal is generally experienced neutrally or positively. Low arousal and the accompanying feelings of boredom, understimulation, and loneliness, tend to be unpleasant and may motivate an individual to seek higher levels of stimulation and human contact. Very high arousal or sharply increasing arousal creates fear, anxiety, and stress and is generally aversive and unpleasant.

This theory regarding the relationship between arousal and mood may help explain a diverse set of nonverbal behaviors and reactions. For example, a sexual encounter with your relational partner should result in optimal sexual arousal. But sexual dysfunction can result from understimulation that is insufficient to support sexual arousal and that may cause feelings of boredom. Similarly, sexual dysfunction can be the result of overstimulation, which may produce feelings of anxiety, unease, or fear. This theory also explains the use and abuse of many drugs and alcohol. Small doses of the substances generally produce increases in positive subjective feelings, but large doses may produce anxiety, stress, and psychosis (Eysenck, 1963). Optimal arousal can be achieved by driving fast in a car or boat, but at some point the excitement turns to fear if the speed becomes

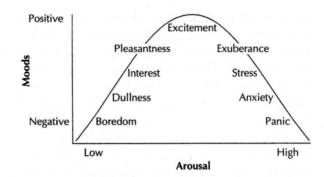

FIGURE 7.1   The relationship between arousal and mood

excessive. Achieving optimal arousal levels is critical to achieving more positive states of mind and more pleasant interpersonal relationships. The relationship between arousal and mood may also be important in explaining much of what we still do not understand about human communication.

Nonverbal Communication and Arousal

Nonverbal communication among humans leads to increases in arousal. Andersen's (1985) review of two dozen studies concludes that "the research generally supports a positive relationship between nonverbal immediacy increases and increases in arousal" (p. 15). Physiological arousal results from increased gaze and eye contact, closer interpersonal distances, more-direct body orientations, greater crowding and density, more smiling, and increased touch.

A number of models and theories attempt to explain how these nonverbal processes work in interpersonal communication, including cognitive-valence theory, explained in Chapter 9. Both cognitive-valence theory and discrepancy-arousal theory posit that moderate arousal is pleasurable but that very high arousal leads to stress and anxiety. This position has stimulated a number of efforts at theory building that have been at least moderately successful (see Andersen & Andersen, 1984; Burgoon, Stern, & Dillman, 1995). These models all recognize that nonverbal involvement produces arousal and that under some conditions, arousal fuels and promotes positive interpersonal relationships. Communication that promotes positive arousal leads to harmonious interpersonal relationships. This principle is useful in such diverse arenas as dating behavior and infant communication.

In dating behavior, negative arousal has detrimental relational effects. Most people are happy or flattered to be asked out on a date or to have another person accept their invitation to go out on a date. Dating can be fun, exciting, and even lead to long-term friendship or romance. However, when things move too fast, particularly in terms of tactile involvement, one person may get "cold feet" (an indication of negative arousal) and become an involvement reducer. The "involver" may want to spend all of her or his time with the other, become more sexually involved than the partner desires, or manifest desperate cues such as jealousy and surveillance. The "reducer" then becomes overstimulated and stressed and tries to reduce involvement. Fearing that his or her autonomy and individuality are in danger, the reducer withdraws. The involver views this withdrawal as a sign of rejection and potential breakup, which in turn leads the involvers to become more desperate and seek even more closeness. The reducer then engages in defensiveness, compensation, and withdrawal and feels reduced attraction for the involver. To the reducer, the involver may seem pathetic and desperate, and these negative attributions about the involver's mental health and seemingly insatiable need for a relationship may cause additional relational decay. These moves and countermoves illustrate how easily negative arousal can spiral within interpersonal relationships (for more on cognitive-valence theory, see Chapter 9).

Assessing another person's readiness for involvement in a close relationship is an important nonverbal skill. Too much or too little touch, too close or too remote an interpersonal distance, too much or too little eye contact fails to produce optimal, symbiotic relationships. The appropriate amount of nonverbal involvement produces the best relationships (see Chapter 9). Perceiving a partner's optimal arousal level and producing the right amount of involvement are difficult interpersonal skills to develop, yet their mastery contributes to the success of interpersonal relationships.

Optimal stimulation and involvement are important in all types of relationships. Take, for example, a parent's nonverbal interaction with a fussy infant who won't stop crying. After checking to see if the baby is wet, hungry, or pinned to the diaper, the parent may give up hope of calming his or her infant. Because stimulation is as basic a need as hunger, the fussy baby may simply be seeking contact. After all, being a baby must be pretty boring. Lying in a crib hour after hour looking at the sheets or ceiling can't be very exciting. "Just as food is needed for the body to grow, stimulation is needed to provide the brain with the 'raw materials' required for the maturation of perceptual, cognitive, and sensorimotor processes" (Stern, 1977, p. 52). So, when a baby fusses, one cause might be understimulation and a need for interpersonal contact. Many babies respond positively to playful tactile contact, exaggerated facial expressions, and games such as peekaboo. However, babies can also be overstimulated and overaroused, so bouncing a baby on one's knee or shaking a rattle in her or his face may just make matters worse. For an overstimulated infant, nonverbal behaviors such as gentle rocking or soft, firm hugs may be the necessary responses to comfort and to reduce arousal and stress.

Reading Nonverbal Arousal Cues

Unfortunately, most communicators, including most parents, are unaware of the concepts of overarousal and underarousal. Nonetheless, most parents do a pretty good job of intuitively reading an infant's nonverbal cues and responding to her or his needs. Less-skilled parents are unable to read an infant's nonverbal cues, and they often respond habitually with gentle rocking or aggressive bouncing or by simply ignoring the baby. Assessing a baby's stimulation level by reading her or his nonverbal behavior and then responding appropriately with arousal-increasing or arousal-decreasing actions may be the key to positive parent-infant relations.

Oftentimes, parents are so thankful when their baby stops crying that they seldom touch or interact with their happy baby. Unfortunately, such a response is probably misguided. First, if parents interact with their babies only when they are crying, then crying is behaviorally reinforced and more crying occurs. The infants learn that crying results in attention and stimulation. Second, parents may develop more positive relationships with their babies if they interact with them when they're happy and playful as well as when they are distressed. Third, playing with babies when they're happy reinforces happy, positive, and prosocial communication. Letting happy babies lie has intuitive merit but may be a poor strategy in the long run.

Some scholars actually believe that raising a child is a process in which the baby trains the parents how to be caregivers; indeed, the child already knows how to be a baby. This paradigm suggests that the infant may actually be more powerful and influential than her or his parents. This position is elaborated in an excellent series of articles edited by Lewis and Rosenblum (1974) on *The Effect of the Infant on Its Caregiver*. Of course, parents can be proactive in shaping their infant's behavior, as the previous discussion suggests.

Recent work has examined nonverbal indications of arousal. Some indices of arousal are emerging, although research on arousal is difficult and controversial (see the recent debate between Burgoon & LePoire, 1992; Greene & Sparks, 1992; Sparks & Greene, 1992). Unfortunately, arousal behaviors, whether they are behavioral or physiological, rarely correlate very highly among one another (Buller, Jorgensen, Andersen, & Guerrero, 1998; Sparks & Greene, 1992). Increases in negatively valenced arousal have been found to produce a number of changes in nonverbal behavior, including increased random movement, more self-touching behaviors (called self-adaptors), less immediacy, less attentiveness, reduced body coordination, more vocal tension, and less vocal warmth (Burgoon, 1994; Burgoon, Kelley, Newton, & Keeley-Dyerson, 1989; Burgoon, LePoire, Beutler, Bergan, & Engle, 1992); these studies, however, have been criticized for failing to correlate any of these indices with physiological arousal (Sparks & Greene, 1992). Alternatively, Burgoon and her associates have correlated nonverbal behavior with observers' ratings of arousal. Buller et al. (1995) observed the reactions of female/male dyads in a laboratory setting. One of the people in each dyad had been told to increase intimacy with her or his partner. Observers' ratings of the partners' positive arousal were associated with greater nonverbal immediacy and fewer self-adaptors. Reduced pulse volume—a measure of increased arousal—was associated with nonverbal immediacy and fewer self-adaptors. The search for a valid profile of arousal is difficult, but strides are being made.

For some individuals, communication is too arousing and communication anxiety develops. These people inherit and/or develop an extreme aversion to various forms of communication. The next two sections of this chapter explore the nonverbal behavior of people with two types of aversion to communication: communication anxiety and touch avoidance.

Communication Anxiety, Apprehension, and Avoidance

In the early evolution of the human species, anxiety was often a functional, beneficial reaction. When attacked by an animal or another human, an individual might have responded by fleeing, retreating, or counterattacking. Rapid increases in arousal accompanied by a faster heart rate, surges in adrenaline, and increased blood pressure motivated the individual to defend herself or himself. For hundreds of thousands of years, these reactions increased one's chance for survival. More recently, the accelerating rate of change in modern society has made anxiety a more common phenomenon. Gone are the days of solitude and boredom. Today the senses are overloaded by people, media, technology, deadlines, change, and the competing demands for one's job, family, and self. We may feel an adrenaline surge telling us to flee when we're on a crowded freeway, in the middle of a difficult exam, in an argument with our spouse, or in a tense discussion with a business client. Usually we suppress such responses, leading to greater internal pressures within the body, such as an increased heart rate and higher blood pressure (see Buck, 1984), or we avoid situations that lead to stress by cutting class, skipping meetings, or avoiding one's spouse. Avoidance, however, is not usually a viable alternative.

Today, one of the most common forms of anxiety actually results from communication. This type of anxiety has been variously labeled communication apprehension, social anxiety, or unwillingness to communicate. Recent surveys indicate that various forms of communication are the *leading* sources of anxiety for Americans today. The most severe form of such anxiety is communication apprehension, which extends across situations. Communication apprehension results in stress not only during communication but whenever an individual *thinks* about communicating (see McCroskey, 1982). Even temporary, "state" apprehension can be problematic, creating patterns of avoidance and incompetence. Communication apprehension is exceedingly common; virtually everyone experiences temporary, state communication apprehension. This trait, with its many debilitating effects, afflicts fifty million Americans and is arguably one of the most prevalent social or psychological problems in our society. Moreover, communication apprehension is at least as common in other cultures as it is in America.

Social anxiety occurs in even more situations than does communication apprehension. Anytime a person appears in public, the potential exists for social anxiety to occur. Researchers have developed a self-presentational theory to explain the widespread existence of social anxiety (see Leary & Kowalski, 1995; Schlenker & Leary, 1982). People are likely to feel some increase in social anxiety when they are observed nonverbally, particularly when they want to make a good impression (see Chapter 10 for more on self-presentation and impression maintenance). Social anxiety tends to occur more in people who are highly self-conscious, in settings where a person is conspicuous, in circumstances during which a person is being evaluated, in novel situations such as the first day of a new job or a first date, and in larger audiences of observers. High levels of social anxiety occur during adolescence; adolescents must adjust to more adult roles and expectations, cope with bodily changes and their developing sexuality, and deal with the novelty of dating and possibly holding a job. Moreover, changes in physical appearance make adolescence an awkward time (see Chapters 2, 5, and 10 for more on the importance of physical appearance as a nonverbal cue). Finally, researchers have discovered that people who are lower in social skills and who nonverbally present themselves poorly are more prone to social anxiety. Of course, this may start a negative spiral, with poor nonverbal skills leading to anxiety and anxiety undermining a person's nonverbal skills.

Research reveals that three predominant communication patterns are experienced by communicatively apprehensive (CA) or socially anxious (SA) individuals: withdrawal, reduced awareness, and tension (see Andersen & Guerrero, 1989). The following sections discuss these three patterns in detail.

The Withdrawal Response

Fear and stress are unpleasant, even painful emotions. It is natural to withdraw from, or avoid entirely, situations or activities that produce fear. The most basic responses to communication apprehension and social anxiety are escape, avoidance, and withdrawal. SAs and CAs avoid social encounters, make themselves nonverbally inaccessible,and use architecture and objects to isolate themselves (for reviews of some of this research see Leary & Kowalski, 1995; McCroskey, 1976; Ohman, 1993). Usually, avoidance is considered a dysfunctional behavior because communication is vital to functioning in today's world. Dates, interviews, service encounters (for example, a waiter taking an order or a customer checking into a hotel), meetings, classes, parties, and presentations all require communication. Many of us find that interaction is anxiety producing, which is why people report communication as the most potent stressor in today's world.

Withdrawal during interaction is a typical response to anxiety. In a study by Daly (1978), high school students high in social anxiety talked less during interviews than their less-anxious counterparts. Schlenker and Leary (1985) show that high SAs fail to participate fully in interaction, exhibit introversion or reticence, and physically or psychologically withdraw from situations. Burgoon and Koper

(1984) report that among reticents and CAs, "cues of detachment, nonaffiliation, and nonintimacy were more pronounced" (p. 615). Even in romantic relationships, social anxiety may lead to withdrawal and detachment. Guerrero (1996) found that individuals who characterize themselves as avoidant (that is, they feel uncomfortable when others get too close to them) tend to exhibit low levels of immediacy/affection, fewer forward leans, less gaze, and decreased facial pleasantness and attentiveness when interacting with their romantic partners.

A number of studies have reported that high CAs and SAs avoid eye contact and face-to-face communication (for a summary see Patterson & Ritts, 1997). Daly (1978) reports that high SAs make less eye contact and exhibit shorter periods of eye contact than less-anxious subjects. Andersen and Coussoule (1980) maintain that high CAs fail to perceive immediacy and intimacy cues because of their low levels of eye contact. In several experiments, Burgoon and Koper (1984) show that communication apprehension and reticence are negatively correlated with eye contact. Studies have also shown that experimentally induced interpersonal stress is associated with low levels of eye contact (Exline & Winters, 1965; Slane, Dragan, Crandall, & Payne, 1980). Indeed, all types of anxiety, including general trait anxiety (experienced by people who are chronically anxious) are associated with decreased eye contact (Eckman, 1978; Leary & Kowalski, 1995).

Other nonverbal avoidance behaviors are correlated with increased communication apprehension and social anxiety. Burgoon and Koper (1984) demonstrate that during interaction, communication apprehension and reticence are associated with more backward leaning, more body blocking or barrier behaviors, and more face covering. Across a series of forty geographically diverse samples, Andersen, Andersen, and Lustig (1987) report strong evidence that communication apprehension is associated with touch avoidance (a concept discussed later in this chapter). A study of the conversational behavior of high CAs shows that they exhibit more silences and longer silences than more-self-confident speakers. Not surprisingly, CAs are perceived as nonaffiliative by others (Burgoon & Koper, 1984).

Communication apprehension also affects interpersonal distancing behavior in an unusual, sometimes counterintuitive, pattern. Because high CAs seek to avoid interaction, one would predict intuitively that they would maintain greater distances, thereby reducing the chances of interaction. Some evidence supports the position that CAs are spatially remote, but other evidence indicates they are less remote.

On the one hand, several studies report that high CAs tend to select low-interaction seats on the periphery of classes, meetings, and group discussions (McCroskey & Sheahan, 1976; McCroskey & McVetta, 1978; Patterson & Ritts, 1997; Weiner, 1973). Carducci and Webber (1979) report that shy persons tend to maintain large interpersonal distances. A study by Slane et al. (1980), exploring the behavior of stress repressors and stress sensitizers, found that stress-sensitive individuals maintain greater interpersonal distances. Patterson and Edinger(1987) report several studies that found a relationship between social anxiety and distance such that subjects with higher anxiety maintained greater distances. In their recent summary of correlates of social anxiety, Patterson and Ritts (1997) report that, "reducing gaze and interacting at greater distances allow socially anxious individuals to disengage partially from social interactions yet remain in the encounters. Socially anxious individuals may totally disengage by withdrawing from social encounters or attempting to avoid them altogether" (p. 273).

On the other hand, three studies have found that high CAs actually maintain closer distances than other individuals (Cardot & Dodd, 1979; McCroskey, Richmond, & Young, 1977; Schwarzwald, Kavish, Shoham, & Waysman, 1977). Cardot and Dodd (1979) paired students in three same-sex dyadic combinations consisting of two high CAs, two low CAs, or a high CA paired with a low CA. Results showed that the high-CA dyads maintained closer distances (12 to 18 inches) than mixed-CA dyads (30 to 51 inches). Participants' apprehension level accounted for over 70 percent of the variance in interpersonal distance. Why did high CAs sit so close to one another? Cardot and Dodd (1979) report that 47 percent of the high-CA dyads—but none of the low-CA or mixed-CA dyads—spoke so softly that they were virtually inaudible through laboratory microphones. They concluded that the high-CA dyads were forced to sit close together in order to hear each other speak. A similar finding with a different explanation is offered by Schwarzwald et al. (1977), who report that in a fear-induction condition, subjects sit closer to same-sex individuals but not to opposite-sex individuals. The experimenters suggest that in a fear-provoking situation, people tend to associate and identify with "like" individuals. Perhaps the most compelling explanation is provided by McCroskey et al. (1977), who demonstrate that high-CA males preferred smaller interaction distances than low-CA males by about 6 to 9 inches. The authors explain that because eye contact invites interaction and intimacy, high CAs are more comfortable at distances that are so close as to discourage eye contact and communication.

The research on proxemic correlates of anxiety and apprehension are seemingly contradictory and certainly complex. A number of variables such as sex, task, partner type, and method interact to produce this complex pattern. In any case, the simplistic prediction that high CAs always maintain large interpersonal distances is probably incorrect. High CAs are not stupid; they cleverly use proxemics to avoid communication. Instead of maintaining normative interaction distances, they strategically employ excessively near or far distances to inhibit communication.

The avoidance behavior of high SAs is perhaps most evident in their backchannel behaviors—receiver actions that encourage senders while they are speaking. Burgoon and Koper (1984) report a series of correlations, all of which indicate that CAs and SAs display significantly less nodding, less interest, and less involvement during interaction. These behaviors, which normally increase interactants' desire for communication, are exactly the behaviors that high CAs and SAs fail to manifest.

Clearly, the evidence suggests that the nonverbal behavior of high CAs constitutes an attempt to avoid communication. But because communication is often important or required in many settings, strong approach-avoidance forces compete within these individuals. The avoidance behavior of high CAs and SAs represents the classic flight response of humans and other animals. The simplest way to avoid fear and anxiety is to withdraw. Unfortunately, social situations are rarely simple. Various avoidance responses, short of full-blown flight, may be the most effective and appropriate defense.

Reduced Awareness

A series of studies demonstrate that high CAs and SAs are oblivious to various social and environmental cues. An anxious, frightened individual in a threatening situation would profit from increased social awareness because more social information would facilitate functional adaptations and adjustments. Unfortunately, the excess anxiety experienced by CAs and SAs produces responses that actually screen out relevant social information, creating a cycle of increased confusion and anxiety.

Several studies have suggested that during interaction, CAs become self-focused and self-conscious rather than other-focused (Andersen & Coussoule, 1980; Andersen & Singleton, 1978; Daly & Stafford, 1984; Greene & Sparks, 1983; Patterson, 1995). In a study by Guerrero (1996), avoidant individuals who characterized themselves as uncomfortable with social interaction tended to be fairly inattentive when communicating with their romantic partners. Avoidant individuals also tended not to engage in forward leaning. Andersen and Singleton (1978) summarize several studies that suggest that CAs are cerebrotonic, a trait characterized by excessive self-focus, introversion, and tension. Andersen and Coussoule (1980) report the results of an experiment on the interpersonal perceptions of high CAs; the study concluded that "high CA individuals did not generally perceive significant differences between gaze conditions, even though gaze was operationalized as two extreme conditions." High CAs are preoccupied with their own internal states. Thus, as Patterson (1995) summarizes, "as cognitive resources are invested in concerns other than the immediate interaction, fewer resources are available to attend and process information about the partner" (p. 18).

Research suggests that a focus on the self rather than on others is generally viewed as an incompetent communication strategy. Indeed, Andersen (1986) suggests that extreme self-awareness and self-consciousness are detrimental to effective communication and concludes that "economy in consciousness is essential to competence in communication" (p. 97). This is particularly true for self-consciousness. Similarly, Spitzberg and Cupach (1984) contend that self-consciousness is particularly detrimental to communication competence and typically increases one's anxiety. Cappella (1985) reports that SAs are cognitively overloaded. When faced with a complex cognitive task, their performance deteriorates. He reports that anxious, cognitively overloaded people display more nervous self-touching behaviors and more hesitations and pauses than nonanxious, cognitively overloaded people. Evidence also suggests that high SAs not only are self-focused but are preoccupied with negative aspects of their performance (Ritts & Patterson, 1997). Schlenker and Leary (1985) conclude that when SAs are threatened, "their minds race with thoughts about the unreachable goal and their problems in attaining it; they become self-preoccupied and self-focused, continually re-examining their limitations" (p. 180). Research shows that SAs become preoccupied with how other people evaluate them (Smith, Ingram, & Brehm, 1983). In short, social anxiety produces a debilitating cycle of excessive self-awareness, reduced skill, and increased anxiety.

Other research suggests that a syndrome of problematic defensive reactions produces a cycle of anxiety and incompetence in high CAs (Andersen & Guerrero, 1989). Anxious individuals' lack of eye contact (described earlier) compounds their inability to receive relevant social information (Andersen & Coussoule, 1980). Their backward leans and facial covering further limit the sending and receiving of important social information. Their excessive self-focus prevents psychological attention to the other and the situation. Keeley-Dyerson, Bailey, and Burgoon (1988) confirm that experimentally induced stress reduces nonverbal decoding accuracy over time. In their study, the biggest effects occurred late in the conversations, suggesting that anxiety during interaction may be cumulatively detrimental to nonverbal decoding accuracy. Moreover, they found that the greatest decrease in decoding ability was in the vocal channel, suggesting that decreased sensitivity is a function not only of decreased eye contact but also of decreased cognitive processing.

The apprehension syndrome of increased self-focus, decreased other-focus, reduced visual monitoring, partial withdrawal from the situation, and inefficient cognitive processing of social information produces a spiral of fear, negativity, panic, incompetence, and confusion. This results in avoidance of valuable interaction and decreased performance as a communicator.

Tension

The third behavioral pattern exhibited by high CAs and SAs is increased tension. Tension has the simultaneous effects of (1) increasing anxiety through somatic feedback, (2) limiting blood flow to various parts of the body, including the brain, and (3) sending negative, confusing messages to conversational partners.

The tension felt by people experiencing communication anxiety ranges from mild excitement to sheer panic. Some evidence suggests that mild anxiety during social interaction or even public speaking may get a person "up" for the interaction, but if arousal and fear increase, any positive feelings quickly become negative. The experience of social anxiety is universally unpleasant. Indeed, Leary and Kowalski (1995) explain:

> With increasing levels of anxiety, people are able to detect physiological signs of arousal (such as heart palpitations or bodily tension) that are often unpleasant. When anxious, people sometimes experience a sinking or nauseated feeling in their stomachs, or feelings of weakness or dizziness. (p. 137)

To understand the feelings that extremely high CAs and SAs experience, imagine yourself falling off a cliff, going 90 miles per hour on skis, or being buried alive. Some people actually experience trembling, heart palpitations, or fainting when they encounter social anxiety (Leary & Kowalski, 1995).

Studies demonstrate a relational pattern between increased tension and nervous behaviors in high CAs. Burgoon, Pfau, Birk, and Manusov (1987) demonstrate that the bodies of high CAs are significantly more tense than less-apprehensive individuals. Because bodily relaxation is an immediacy cue that leads to more positive, intimate interactions (Andersen, 1985; see Chapter 8) and contributes to perceptions of increased credibility and attraction (Jensen & Andersen, 1979), tension has certain negative interpersonal consequences. Excessive tension may be perceived as a signal of emotional buildup that later may be manifested in aggressive or hostile actions (Eibl-Eibesfeldt, 1974).

Schlenker and Leary (1985) report that "high social anxiety is associated with an array of nervous responses including fidgeting, self-manipulation, perspiring, and the appearance of overall tension" (p. 178). We have all witnessed a nervous speaker who plays with a pen or strokes her or his hair. Nervous communicators repeatedly touch their hands or face. It is unclear whether CAs exhibit more self-manipulations and self-adaptors; one article reports several significant correlations between communication anxiety and self-touching (Burgoon & Koper, 1984), but two other studies fail to find such a relationship in the laboratory (Burgoon, Pfau, Birk, & Manusov, 1987; Comadena & Andersen, 1978). Nonetheless, the preponderance of evidence suggests that high CAs manifest nervousness nonverbally. Burgoon and Koper (1984) conclude that high CAs, compared to others, "tend to show more negative forms of arousal through increased bodily tension, more self-touching and more protective behaviors" (p. 618).

Several other changes in nonverbal behavior occur because of the tension experienced by SAs. One common, visible response to social anxiety is blushing, particularly the "creeping blush," which appears as splotches of red on a person's cheek, neck, or jaw (Leary & Kowalski, 1995; Patterson & Ritts, 1997). Blushing sends involuntary messages of anxiety and overarousal and, ironically, usually makes the poor, anxious blusher even more embarrassed and anxious. Tension also restricts blood flow to the extremities, often resulting in cold, clammy hands. Because handshakes are obligatory in many social situations, clammy hands send a tactile message of tension and anxiety to interaction partners. Other signs of

High-CA speakers exhibit tension through stiff body postures, sweating, shaking, and a variety of arousal cues. Unpleasant feelings, increased self-consciousness, and poor performance accompany these behaviors.

tension may include jiggling feet, rapid breathing, pale skin, disfluent speech, higher vocal pitch, and negative facial expressions (Leary & Kowalski, 1995; Mulac & Wiemann, 1984). For example, Guerrero's (1996) research suggests that SAs display more vocal tension than their more socially secure counterparts. She also shows that SAs who fear intimacy are especially likely to engage in nonfluent speech characterized by long response latencies.

There may also be a relationship between apprehension and the use of power and/or force. Aida (1993) reports that high CA couples use more unilateral, noninteractive negative power strategies in their marriages than do non-apprehensive couples. Few high CAs are dangerous to others; however, many mass murderers are described as nice, shy, quiet people who never disturbed anyone previously. It may be that for some severely disturbed individuals, their inability to communicate verbally, along with excessive tension, leads to the most destructive nonverbal response possible, murder.

Coping with Communication Apprehension and Social Anxiety

Most people who experience communication apprehension or social anxiety do a pretty good job of dealing with it. They lead relatively quiet but satisfying lives. They are less likely to get into conflicts and confrontations, and they like it that way. They seek lifestyles and occupations that offer them less social contact.

Sometimes, however, communication apprehension or social anxiety limits a person's social life, occupational growth, financial success, and relational satisfaction. What can these people do to feel more comfortable about social interaction when they desire it? Several books offer sound, research-based advice (Leary & Kowalski, 1995; Richmond & McCroskey, 1985). First, nearly everyone gets the jitters or feels nervous before a public speech, yet most of us do very well once we get underway; after a while, the butterflies begin to go away. A similar, calming progression occurs during a first date; after a few hours (and especially after a few dates), the initial nervousness is ancient history.

To overcome communication apprehension and social anxiety, there are several guidelines to follow without needing to seek professional help: (1) *Reduce self-awareness.* Avoid focusing on your performance; instead, think of the task or person at hand and "get out of yourself." Most good communicators nearly forget about themselves during an interaction because they are so focused on their audience or topic. (2) *Breathe.* Anxious individuals tend to hold their breath or engage in shallow breathing. Watch a basketball player at the free-throw line or an Olympic diver; they often take a deep breath to alleviate the jitters and make sure enough oxygen gets to the brain. (3) *Relax.* Stretching techniques reduce the physical tension that accompanies communication apprehension and social anxiety. Hatha yoga, athletic stretching, or even just reaching your arms high above your head or opening or closing your fists may help you relax. (4) *Be prepared.* Anxiety is often the result of poor preparation. Whether you are facing a job interview, presentation, or speech, being prepared can greatly reduce your anxiety.

For some people with persistent traitlike communication apprehension or social anxiety, self-help is not enough. Fortunately, several therapies have proven to be quite successful: (1) relaxation therapies, especially systematic desensitization; (2) skills training, which helps individuals develop more competence, a key to overcoming anxiety; (3) cognitive therapies, particularly cognitive restructuring, which can change negative internal dialog into positive internal dialog; and (4) role playing and practice interactions, which help individuals "rehearse" appropriate behaviors under less threatening conditions (for more about these methods see Leary & Kowalski, 1995; Richmond and McCroskey, 1985). Fortunately, some of these methods do not require expensive psychiatric treatment and may be offered through your college communication department or counseling center.

Touch Avoidance

The preceding discussion focused on verbal communication apprehension and general social anxiety, along with the nonverbal behaviors that accompany anxiety and avoidance. A similar sort of fear and negativity relates to intimate nonverbal communication, particularly touch. Researchers have examined a concept called touch avoidance, a negative attitude toward touch that also affects an individual's proxemic behavior and other types of nonverbal communication.

Few would argue that touch is a crucial part of personal and intimate relationships. For example, imagine a mother who never touched her baby or an engaged couple who never touched one another. Such relationships would be considered abnormal, even pathological. Investigators of tactile communication have equated touch with intimacy itself (Morris, 1971) and have suggested that love cannot be successfully conveyed in the absence of touch (Montagu, 1971/1978). Touch deprivation has been associated with a host of undesirable consequences, including increased mental illness in adults and both a failure to thrive and even death in infants.

Anxiety about touch or avoidance of touch undoubtedly has a negative impact on an individual's personal relationships. Numerous communication researchers have investigated how people develop attitudes toward touch, what behaviors are associated with these attitudes, and what consequences occur for those who are anxious or avoidant of touch. Jourard and Rubin (1968) were the first to examine the notion of "touchability" and touch avoidance and suggested that separate sender-receiver and opposite-sex/same-sex dimensions may exist for touchability and touch readiness. A series of investigations followed, which examined the related constructs of touch avoidance (Andersen, Andersen, & Lustig, 1987; Andersen & Leibowitz, 1978; Andersen & Sull, 1985; Guerrero & Andersen, 1991; Jones & Brown, 1996; Leibowitz & Andersen, 1976), tactile attitudes (Deethardt & Hines, 1983; Larsen & LeRoux, 1984), and touch comfort (Fromme et al., 1986, 1989). We are just beginning to understand the causes and consequences of negative attitudes toward touch. "The touch avoidance construct is not a direct index of how much a person touches or avoids being touched. Instead, it is an index of a person's affect toward touch" (Andersen, Andersen, & Lustig, 1987, p. 90). So, touch avoidance is an attitudinal measure of how much a person likes or dislikes touch.

Research consistently shows that two independent dimensions of touch attitudes exist, an opposite-sex dimension and a same-sex dimension. Separate sending and receiving dimensions have not been discovered (Andersen & Leibowitz, 1978; Fromme et al., 1986; Jones & Brown, 1996). Evidently, most people have generally similar attitudes toward both being touched and touching others.

How do negative attitudes toward touching develop? Andersen and Leibowitz (1978) report that the cultural roles people perform as a function of their sex, age, marital status, and religion are associated with their touch-avoidance levels. Older persons, married persons, and Protestants generally are more touch avoidant than others. Several studies suggest that parental attitudes toward touch are the critical determiners of their offspring's attitudes toward touch. Fromme et al. (1986) report that an individual's touch comfort is associated with perceived parental touch comfort, particularly with the comfort level of the father. Another study (Spradlin & Fromme, 1989) shows a very strong relationship between parents' and children's attitudes toward touch, accounting for 50 to 90 percent of the variance between the two sets of measures. Evidently, parental attitudes are critical determiners of children's tactile attitudes; however, other variables play a role as well. Fromme et al. (1989) demonstrate that subjects who experienced a lot of hitting while growing up had much more negative attitudes toward touch. This is consistent with the observation that child abuse is an intergenerational phenomenon.

People's self-reports of touch avoidance or touch comfort correlate with actual behavior. In one experiment, Sorensen (1979) conducted school-related interviews with volunteers who had previously filled out a touch-avoidance instrument. (A sample touch-avoidance instrument appears at the end of the chapter for you to complete and score your answers.) At the conclusion of the experiment, as the interviewees were being thanked for their participation, half were touched by the experimenter and the other half were not. Sorenson found that touch avoiders had significantly more negative attitudes toward the experimenter when touched than when not touched, but touch approachers had more positive attitudes toward an experimenter when touched than when not touched. In another laboratory study, Andersen and Sull (1985) found that touch-avoidance scores were fairly good predictors of interpersonal distance: touch avoiders chose to interact at greater distances than touch approachers. Guerrero and Andersen (1991) found that people's touch-avoidance scores correlated with their actual touch behavior. In this study, experimenters unobtrusively observed and recorded the tactile behaviors of people waiting in theatre and zoo lines. The observed people were then asked to complete a questionnaire about their perceptions of their own touch behavior. Similar experiments found that the touch-comfort test significantly predicted personal space (Fromme et al., 1986, 1989): these studies demonstrated that college students with higher touch-comfort scores were more likely to volunteer to participate in a "hugging experiment." Moreover, even among the volunteers, people with greater touch-comfort scores rated hugs more positively than those with lower touch-comfort scores.

Touch avoidance and touch comfort may actually be an index of a person's general intimacy or immediacy level. Interpersonal touch is a critical component of both intimacy and immediacy (Andersen, 1985; Thayer, 1986a; Jones, 1994; see also Chapters 8 and 9). As Andersen and Leibowitz (1978) originally argued, "The failure to utilize touch is indicative of interpersonal avoidance and lack of interpersonal closeness" (p. 90). Thayer (1986a) contends, "If intimacy is proximity, then nothing comes closer than touch, the most intimate knowledge of another. The expression to "know" someone in the biblical sense is equivalent to having been sexually intimate with them, to have known their body" (p. 12). Hall (1966a) suggests that touch and close interpersonal space are indices of intimacy because at the closest distances, one can actually grasp or hold the other person. As noted previously, several studies show that touch avoiders maintain greater interpersonal distances, literally staying out of touch and out of reach from others. Fromme et al. (1989) suggest that "touch comfort reflects a more active interpersonal style and more satisfactory social relationships in general" (p. 18).

What other factors seem to be associated with touch comfort or avoidance? Andersen and Leibowitz (1978) found that married, older, and Christian people reported relatively more negative, avoidant attitudes toward touch. Similarly, Fromme et al. (1986) reported that touch comfort was lower for older people, people of high socioeconomic status, and younger, later-born children in families. However, family size was positively related to touch comfort. Touch comfort is positively correlated with social success and happiness, life satisfaction, self-satisfaction, self-confidence, assertiveness, active problem solving, and social acceptance (Fromme et al., 1989). In short, positive tactile attitudes seem to be related to a healthy personality, successful social relations, and intimate personal relationships. Research demonstrates that touch avoidance is negatively associated with social self-confidence (Jones & Brown, 1996). In other words, people who enjoy and use touch are better adjusted and more socially confident across a wide variety of situations.

Some evidence (Fromme et al., 1986; Jones, 1994; Noller, 1978) shows that females are generally more comfortable with touch than males. However, this is probably because females have more positive attitudes toward same-sex touch than do males. Research has shown that attitudes toward same-sex and opposite-sex touch are not meaningfully associated; therefore, we will examine these two bodies of research separately.

Same-Sex Touch Avoidance

Considerable evidence suggests that males have far more negative attitudes then females toward same-sex touch. Derlega, Lewis, Harrison, Winstead, & Costanza (1989) report that in friendships, males display less tactile intimacy with males than with females and less tactile intimacy than females display with other females. Several studies conclude that males are more touch avoidant of same-sex individuals than are females, regardless of age, religion, or marital status (Andersen & Leibowitz, 1978; Silverman, Pressman, & Bartell, 1973). In an intercultural study of touch avoidance, Jones and Remland (1982) report that both Asian and American females were less averse to same-sex touch than were males from either cultural group. In a study of touch avoidance among nurses, Lower (1980) reports that male nurses had significantly more same-sex touch avoidance than female nurses. Similarly, Larsen and LeRoux (1984) show that females have more positive scores on the same-sex touching scale than do males. Fromme et al. (1986) report a series of significant correlations, all demonstrating that women are comfortable with same-sex touch, particularly in such areas as the face, buttocks, outer thighs, and knees.

Evidently same-sex touching is more threatening, anxiety provoking, and repugnant for males than it is for females. One explanation is homophobia—the fear of homosexuals or of even appearing to be homosexual (Andersen & Leibowitz, 1978).The extreme avoidance of other males by males, according to one study, is probably the result of homophobia (Derlega et al., 1989). Males may overcompensate for this fear by developing negative attitudes toward same-sex touch and by avoiding intimacy with other men. A second related explanation is that because men are more likely to associate touch with sexuality than are women (Fromme at al., 1986), men find opposite-sex touch to be socially appropriate but not same-sex touch. With the exception of roughhousing, males are quite reluctant to touch other males. This may be because observers perceive male-male touch to be sexual but make no such assumptions about female-female touch (Derlega et al., 1989). A third explanation is that many men avoid gentle, loving, or nurturant communication acts because these activities are not masculine as traditionally defined. When male-male touch does occur, it is often in the form of roughhousing or contact sports such as football, basketball, and hockey. In this way, males are permitted to touch in a manner they perceive to be sex-role appropriate.

A final explanation for men's high levels of same-sex touch avoidance may stem from the fact that in many primate species, including humans, males are more aggressive and hostile than females. Whether male aggressiveness is biologically or culturally induced is a matter of considerable debate (see Andersen, 1998). Such differences may be due to low parental involvement and reproductive advantages for aggressive males. In other words, women carry a child during pregnancy and often breast-feed the infant after birth. As such, women have a greater parental investment from a biological standpoint than men. Moreover, males may attempt to have several mates without investing much time or material resources in any mate. In his book on universals of human behavior, Brown (1991) explains:

> In mammals it is almost always the male that invests less, is larger, is more actively competitive and is prone to seek multiple mates. . . . The greater aggressiveness of males is at least partly a result of sexual selection, aggression being an effective male strategy in competition for females. (pp. 108–110)

If this evolutionary argument is valid, then males have a propensity to be combative or competitive with one another. Male-male touch then can be seen as a hostile, aggressive act, a challenge for dominant status. Even well-socialized males may be predisposed to avoid male touch.

Both men and woman with certain types of personalities are more likely to be same-sex touch avoiders. Same-sex touch avoiders of both sexes are more authoritarian and rigid (Larsen & LeRoux, 1984), suggesting more intolerant, autocratic orientations among these individuals. Similarly, same-sex touch avoiders of both sexes have more socially undesirable conceptions of femininity, suggesting less nurturance and less responsiveness among touch avoiders. Male same-sex touch avoiders have been found to possess an external locus of control, that is, they conform to others' wishes and attitudes as opposed to an internal locus of control, which is characterized by self-confidence and self-direction. This suggests that conformity to sex-role norms may be an issue with these individuals. Female same-sex touch avoiders appear lower in self-esteem and more conservative than touch approachers (Larsen & LeRoux, 1984). Same-sex touch avoiders also tend to be less androgynous than touch approachers (Crawford, 1994). People who are rigidly masculine or feminine view same-sex touch as a violation of their definition of appropriate sex roles (for more on sex and gender roles see Chapter 5).

A number of studies have reported that negative attitudes toward same-sex touch are associated with religiosity. Montagu (1971/1978) suggests that Christian religions, particularly fundamentalist Christian religions, discourage interpersonal touch. In a study by Andersen and Leibowitz (1978), Protestants were found to be more avoidant of same-sex touch than were non-Protestants. Their data show that people with no religious affiliation were the least touch avoidant. In a study by Lower (1980), Jewish nursing students were significantly less same-sex touch avoidant than their Protestant or Catholic counterparts. Larsen and LeRoux (1984) report that same-sex touch avoidance correlates with religious orthodoxy of males but not of females. This body of research suggests that religiousness, particularly for Christian religions, is associated with same-sex touch avoidance.

Some limited intercultural research suggests that Americans may be less touch avoidant than residents of Mediterranean countries, India, Pakistan, and Asia (Jones & Remland, 1982; see Chapter 4). The restrictive religious prohibitions against touch in these parts of the world may explain this cultural variation. Far Easterners are even more touch avoidant, supporting findings that Asian countries are noncontact cultures. McDaniel and Andersen (1998) report that Asians touch less than any other group.

Some light has been shed on the development of same-sex touch avoidance by Fromme et al. (1986), who find that if mothers and fathers are comfortable with same-sex touch their children reported more comfort with same-sex touch. This effect is particularly true for the father but also strong for the mother. In general, if your family is comfortable with same-sex touching, you will be too.

Opposite-Sex Touch Avoidance

Although a number of studies (J. A. Hall, 1984, 1985; Stier & Hall, 1984) have shown small or nonexistent sex differences in actual touch (observed touch behavior), other studies demonstrate that women are more reluctant about and have more negative attitudes toward opposite-sex touch than men (Guerrero & Andersen, 1991; Hall, 1985; Henley, 1977; Silverman et al., 1973). Research shows that females have significantly higher levels of opposite-sex touch avoidance than males across numerous diverse samples (Andersen & Leibowitz, 1978; Andersen, Andersen, & Lustig, 1987). Fromme et al. (1986) report that "regardless of body area or degree of acquaintance, men are more comfortable than women with opposite-sex touch" (p. 56). Andersen et al. (1987) collected samples from forty American universities and found that for thirty-nine of the forty samples, females reported more opposite-sex touch avoidance than males, with thirty-two of the forty samples showing statistically significant differences.

Why do females have more touch-avoidant attitudes toward opposite-sex touch than men? One possibility is that females' natural expressiveness and immediacy are tempered by restrictive attitudes toward touch. A corollary explanation is that opposite-sex touch is most likely to have sexual connotations. Traditionally, women have been enculturated to believe that employing "forward" touch is out-of-role and excessively aggressive. A woman in one of my classes explained this finding by saying, "I don't touch men; men don't need any encouragement." In their exhaustive study of American couples, Blumstein and Schwartz (1983) found that, regardless of marital status, males reported initiating considerably more sexual contact than females; this finding held true in reports from both males and females. Indeed, their research supports the traditional position that females exert a restraint on sexual behavior, whereas males play an initiator role. One final explanation for greater female touch avoidance of males concerns psychological sex roles. In a study by Eman, Dierks-Stewart, and Tucker (1978), androgynous and masculine individuals reported less touch avoidance than feminine or undifferentiated (neither feminine nor masculine) individuals. Evidently, individuals with more masculine psychological profiles are less touch avoidant in opposite-sex relationships, suggesting that biological sex is less important than sex-role orientation.

Lower touch-avoidance scores for opposite-sex relationships are related to a number of other attitudes and predispositions. Results suggest that touch approachers are better adjusted, have better communication relationships, and are more relaxed (Larsen & LeRoux, 1984). Evidence by Andersen et al. (1987) shows that among forty geographically diverse samples, opposite-sex touch avoidance was negatively correlated with self-esteem in thirty-eight of these samples, thirty-two of which were statistically significant. Evidently, individuals with more self-worth and self-esteem are more likely to have positive attitudes toward opposite-sex touch. A series of findings also has shown that opposite-sex touch avoiders are more communicatively apprehensive, less predisposed to verbal behavior (Andersen et al., 1987), and more reticent (Fromme et al., 1989) than other individuals. This portrait suggests that opposite-sex touch avoiders find it difficult and anxiety producing to communicate with others of the opposite sex. Touch avoiders have also been found to have less open communication styles, confirming their noncommunicative nature (Andersen et al., 1987).

One study suggests that actual touch behaviors and touch-avoidance scores are correlated in dating relationships (Guerrero & Andersen, 1994). This study found significant correlations in touch-avoidance scores between partners in both dating and married relationships, suggesting that people tend to find romantic partners with the same tactile attitudes as their own. More importantly, this study found that touch was *highly* correlated across all relational levels ($r = .88$), suggesting that individuals' own attitudes toward touch become much less important than the relationship itself. People tend to reciprocate their partner's touch level whether it is high or low. As the relationship grows, so does the reciprocity of touch. Dating couples showed highly reciprocal tactile behavior ($r = .81$); seriously dating couples showed even more tactile similarity ($r = .88$); and married couples showed almost entirely reciprocal tactile behavior ($r = .96$). Evidently, becoming a committed relational partner involves a virtual merging of intimacy levels between partners. This may be the real meaning of relational intimacy (for more on relational intimacy see Chapter 9).

Technology, Overarousal, and Stress

In our not-so-distant past, interpersonal relationships were few, limited to the social confines of the family, tribe, or village. Today, because of technological advances in communication and transportation, our circle of interpersonal interaction has expanded to include not only close friends and intimate loved ones but also innumerable acquaintances and strangers with whom we come into contact via telephones, fax machines, the internet, airplanes, and so on. We are living in what McLuhan (1964) calls a global village, a place where contact with virtually every other human being is possible. Human relationships have been devalued by their abundance, and stress is one of the most commonly used words in our vocabularies. Overarousal and anxiety are common characteristics of everyday life. Kenneth Gergen (1991) observes:

> As a result of the technological development just described, life is a swirling sea of social relations. Words thunder in by radio, television, newspaper, mail, radio, telephone, fax, wire service, electronic mail, billboards, Federal Express, and more. Waves of new faces everywhere—in town for a day, visiting for the weekend, at the Rotary lunch, at the church social—and incessantly and incandescently on television. Long weeks in a single community are unusual; a full day in a single neighborhood is becoming rare. . . . As this increase becomes extreme we reach a state of social saturation. (p. 61)

Overstimulation and overarousal are everywhere. The greatest challenge most of us face is how to live in a world of information and interpersonal overload.

A personal experience helps illustrate how overstimulation and overarousal function in people's everyday lives. I called my secretary one morning. Upon inquiring how she was, I was informed that she was drowning in a sea of papers. I empathized and replied that it is the disease of the 90s and told her how my desk was a paper disaster as well, scattered with grant proposals, student papers, memos from our director, newsletters, warnings from the campus security. But the blizzard of paper was only the tip of the iceberg, I explained. I had dozens of unanswered messages to deal with as well.

It was the first week of fall classes at San Diego State University, and as I returned to my office, I realized I hadn't checked my voice mail or E-mail. Voice mail, the high-tech version of the answering machine, permits message storage, retrieval, transfer, and, best of all, noninteracative responses—all with the touch of a button. I picked up my phone to listen to my messages with trepidation; I hadn't picked them up for eight hours, and I didn't know what to expect. The virtual voice of the cyberoperator answered my prompt, "You have 22 messages." Forty minutes later I had finished hearing all my messages. I had not responded to them, but at least I had heard them. Next, I turned to my E-mail, which contained 140 new messages. I began to process the messages, discarding the obsolete and irrelevant, making lists—one for urgent, one for nonurgent, and one for longer conversations with friends and colleagues with whom I actually wanted to chat. The goal of all this, however, was not communication; it was emptying inboxes. In the last few years, I have observed an interesting phenomenon. I get more satisfaction from discarding my mail than reading it and responding to it. And I'm an extrovert. Pity the poor sufferer of communication apprehension!

But the problem is more than information overload. The unfortunate reality of modern communication is a retreat from the sources of information themselves—colleagues, teachers, politicians, and so on, who all complain they can't "get their message across." As I observed recently at a campus taskforce meeting, we are living in an information purgatory. At work, I read my mail and messages from my secretary, browse my E-mail messages, listen to voice mail, check my fax machine, and go home. By heading home I realize I face more of the same: more mail, E-mail, voice mail, and faxes, not to mention the 88 (soon to be 500) channels of cable television to which I've been upgraded.

Demands are made on our time by other forms of communication as well. At one time, humans desired close contact with others and longed for the sight and feel of close friends. Today, the cancelled dinner party, date, or concert is as likely to bring feelings of relief as disappointment. In fact, it is only during my solitary, daily long-distance runs that I feel refuge from this communication crisis.

If we once walked a tightrope between boredom and stress, we are far less likely to stumble into boredom today. Nonverbal intimacy is becoming increasingly hard to achieve, and we are awash in a sea of relationships, most of them nonintimate and indirect. Finding special relations may be harder now than at any time in history.

The popularity of ecovacations in the wilderness, of weekends at country inns, of cross-country skiing, of solitary runs, of trips to the mountains shouldn't be surprising. One of the hot topics in communication research is privacy maintenance (see Petronio, 1993). I have written that we would do well to leave our desks, computers, and conference tables to swim in the ocean, climb a mountain, touch a glacier (Andersen, 1993b). The challenge of the next century will be to

The stress of modern society, overstimulation, and the pressure of communicating with an increasing number of people have contributed to the popularity of ecotourism and other means of "getting away from it all."

maintain close relationships while avoiding the perils of excess arousal and anxiety. This may make quiet, nonverbal forms of communication even more important in our close relationships. Quiet sharing of eye contact, space, and touch and an exchange of warm, genuine, caring smiles, may be the ultimate antidote to the stress of our fast-paced technological world.

Summary

Humans thrive on interpersonal arousal and stimulation. Too little contact with others produces loneliness and boredom. Too much contact produces stress and anxiety. For each person, an optimal level of arousal exists. Introverts become easily overstimulated and often choose to avoid contact with others. Extroverts require more stimulation and seek verbal and nonverbal interaction. For all of us, overarousal is stressful. Being able to assess and respond appropriately to another person's arousal cues is an important interpersonal skill. Overaroused people need calming; underaroused people need stimulation.

Two of the most widespread forms of anxiety are known as communication apprehension and social anxiety. For high CAs and SAs, communication is anxiety provoking and elicits the following responses: withdrawal, reduced awareness, and tension. Each of these responses is accompanied by its own distinctive array of nonverbal behaviors. High CAs and SAs withdraw from communication by talking less, avoiding other people, invading or avoiding the interaction space of others, reducing eye contact, leaning backward, and creating body barriers that impede interaction. These individuals are also so preoccupied with feelings of anxiety that they become self-focused, self-conscious, and oblivious to the nonverbal behavior of interaction partners. They experience cognitive overload and fail to process external information. This produces a spiral of additional anxiety, confusion, and incompetence. The tension felt by high CAs and SAs produces negative nonverbal behaviors that are perceived negatively by interactional partners. Their nervous movements, blushing, halting speech, and clammy hands send negative nonverbal messages to other interactants.

The most widely researched form of nonverbal anxiety and withdrawal is touch avoidance, a negative predisposition to touch that is nonverbally manifested in less touch, greater interpersonal distances, and reduced intimacy. Touch approachers tend to experience less communication anxiety, better social relationships, and better psychological adjustment. In close relationships, touch avoiders touch their partners frequently, even though they touch somewhat less than touch approachers. Touch avoiders also touch at the same level as their partners, suggesting that reciprocal touch is vital to relational intimacy and that people can often overcome anxious feelings in the context of close relationships.

Touch-Avoidance Questionnaire

DIRECTIONS: This instrument is composed of eighteen statements concerning feelings about touching other people and being touched. Please indicate the degree to which each statement applies to you by circling whether you (1) strongly agree, (2) agree, (3) are undecided, (4) disagree, or (5) strongly disagree with each statement. Although some of these statements may seem repetitious, take your time and try to be as honest as possible.

1 2 3 4 5   1. A hug from a same-sex friend is a true sign of friendship.

1 2 3 4 5   2. Opposite-sex friends enjoy it when I touch them.

1 2 3 4 5   3. I often put my arm around friends of the same sex.

1 2 3 4 5   4. When I see two people of the same sex hugging it revolts me.

1 2 3 4 5   5. I like it when members of the opposite sex touch me.

1 2 3 4 5   6. People shouldn't be so uptight about touching persons of the same sex.

1 2 3 4 5   7. I think it is vulgar when members of the opposite sex touch me.

1 2 3 4 5   8. When a member of the opposite sex touches me I find it unpleasant.

1 2 3 4 5   9. I wish I were free to show emotions by touching members of the same sex.

1 2 3 4 5   10. I'd enjoy giving a massage to an opposite-sex friend.

1 2 3 4 5   11. I enjoy kissing a person of the same sex.

1 2 3 4 5   12. I like to touch friends that are the same sex as I am.

1 2 3 4 5   13. Touching a friend of the same sex does not make me uncomfortable.

1 2 3 4 5 14. I find it enjoyable when my date and I embrace.

1 2 3 4 5 15. I enjoy getting a back rub from a member of the opposite sex.

1 2 3 4 5 16. I dislike kissing relatives of the same sex.

1 2 3 4 5 17. Intimate touching with members of the opposite sex is pleasurable.

1 2 3 4 5 18. I find it difficult to be touched by a member of my own sex.

Scoring Your Touch-Avoidance Questionnaire

1. Label each question as an A, B, X, or Y in this manner.

   Question 1=Y   10=B
            2=B   11=Y
            3=Y   12=Y
            4=X   13=Y
            5=B   14=B
            6=Y   15=B
            7=A   16=X
            8=A   17=B
            9=Y   18=X

2. Total separately your responses for all A questions, all B questions, all X questions, and all Y questions. In other words, see what number you circled to answer questions 7 and 8. Add those two numbers together and that's your A total.

3. To arrive at your touch-avoidance measure for same-sex touch (TAM1), use the following formula:

$$TAM1 = 15 + Y - X$$

   To figure out your touch-avoidance measure for opposite-sex touch (TAM2), use the following formula:

$$TAM2 = 10 + B - A$$

   Following are some experimental findings based on the use of this touch-avoidance instrument:

   The male average for same-sex touch avoidance is 26.4; the female average is 21.7.

   The male average for opposite-sex touch avoidance is 12.9; the female average is 14.9.

   The Protestant group average for touch avoidance is 15.0.

   The non-Protestant group average for touch avoidance is 12.9.

   The highest touch avoiders are married, Protestant females with an average score of 15.8.

   The lowest touch avoiders are married, non-Protestant males with an average score of 9.8.

8

Immediacy and Nonverbal Communication

IN THE NOVEL *The Bridges of Madison County,* Waller (1992) describes the initial meeting between Francesca and Robert:

> He smiled. "I'm sorry to bother you, but I'm looking for a covered bridge out this way and I can't find it. I think I'm temporarily lost. . . ." His eyes looked directly at her, and she felt something jump inside. The eyes, the voice, the face, the silver hair, the easy way he moved his body, old ways, disturbing ways, ways that draw you in. Ways that whisper to you in the final moment before sleep comes, when the barriers have fallen. Ways that rearrange the molecular space between male and female. (p. 28)

Friendly, warm, involving actions, called immediacy behaviors, are the basis of all interpersonal relationships. When combined with intense attraction, these behaviors form the basis of romantic attraction, as the passage from Waller's novel illustrates. However, even in nonromantic relationships, immediacy behaviors signal interest in communication and promote psychological closeness between interactants. Whenever we are with another person, we send messages about our feelings regarding our interaction with and our relationship to that person. There is no such thing as an affectively neutral message; every message communicates something about our emotions and about the state of our relationships.

The interpersonal exchange of nonverbal immediacy is the central function of nonverbal behavior. The term *immediacy* describes messages that signal feelings of warmth, closeness, and involvement with other people. Mehrabian (1971a) first developed the immediacy principle, which states, "People are drawn toward persons and things they like, evaluate highly and prefer" (p. 1). What communication behaviors convey these warm, positive feelings to others? Immediacy behaviors include any interpersonal behavior that performs the following four

Proxemic, haptic, and kinesic immediacy are all displayed in this historic Middle East peace-agreement meeting between Yitzhak Rabin, Bill Clinton, and Yasir Arafat.

functions (Andersen, Andersen, & Jensen, 1979; Andersen, 1985): signals availability and inclusion, communicates approach and involvement, increases sensory stimulation, and communicates warmth and positive affect.

Immediacy behaviors signal availability and inclusion. Behaviors that signal our availability for communication make others feel included in the interaction (Andersen, 1985; Burgoon & Hale, 1984). Behaviors such as eye contact, close interpersonal distance, touch, and open, direct body positions signal availability and inclusion and invite communication from others. Conversely, avoiding eye contact, distancing oneself, facing away from another person, and avoiding touch all signal exclusion and unavailability and are typical nonimmediacy behaviors.

Immediacy behaviors communicate approach and involvement. Actions that communicate physical or psychological closeness to another person are generally considered immediacy behaviors (Andersen, 1985). Burgoon and Hale (1984) suggest that involvement is an essential aspect of immediacy. Cappella (1983) and Burgoon (1994) take the position that immediacy is a part of involvement, not the reverse. Involvement has been defined as the degree to which an individual is engaged and interested in the conversation at hand. Cappella and Burgoon both maintain that involvement behaviors are not always perceived positively; how they are perceived depends on situational, relational, and individual factors. Nevertheless, although it is certainly true that involvement behaviors can take on new meanings in light of other behaviors, personal factors, or relational factors, in general, involvement behaviors are perceived positively (Andersen, 1985; Burgoon, Coker, & Coker, 1986).

Immediacy behaviors increase sensory stimulation. When someone looks or smiles at us or touches us, physiological changes occur in our body. Interpersonal gazes, close distances, direct body positions, touches, and smiles cause increases in our heart rate, brain activity, blood pressure, and bodily movements (Andersen, 1985). Because immediacy behaviors are typically multichanneled and occur in clusters, we show considerable activation and arousal when others communicate immediacy to us.

Immediacy behaviors communicate interpersonal warmth and positive affect. To a considerable degree, interpersonal intimacy, friendship, and love are communicated by immediacy behaviors. Gifford (1994) shows that receivers attribute warmth to smiles, attentiveness, reclining postures, extended hands, the absence of nervous movements, and head nods, among other behaviors. In positive relationships, immediacy is the vehicle for propelling a relationship to higher levels of intimacy, closeness, and enmeshment. Imagine yourself in a new dating relationship. You really like your partner a lot. During the evening, your date looks into your eyes, touches you appropriately on several occasions, sits very near to you, and speaks in a warm, affectionate voice. Chances are these immediacy behaviors will increase your level of closeness. Moreover, you are likely to reciprocate with your own set of immediacy behaviors, which will take the relationship to a higher level of intimacy. (More on this process will be discussed in Chapter 9.)

In less-positive or overstimulated interactions, immediacy cues carry messages of too much closeness and are perceived as threatening, stressful, anxiety provoking, suffocating, overwhelming, and even harassing. (See Chapters 7 and 9 for more on what happens when immediacy is unwanted.) Nevertheless, regardless of the reaction produced, immediacy messages, in general, are intended by the sender to convey warm, positive, and intimate feelings. The power of immediacy is illustrated in Manusov's (1991) study of interpersonal conversations. Results show that immediacy behaviors lead to more favorable evaluations of a communicator's social skills, competence, and pleasantness. Manusov reports that interactants believe immediacy behaviors to be natural, unintentional, spontaneous behaviors that signal positive feelings.

Components of Nonverbal Immediacy

Nonverbal immediacy is typically encoded and decoded as a set of redundant, interrelated behaviors. In this section, each component of nonverbal immediacy will be examined carefully for conceptual purposes. But keep in mind that this is an artificial fragmentation; immediacy behaviors are sent and received as a gestalt, a multichanneled set of nonverbal behaviors that signal availability and warmth, decrease interpersonal distance, and provide increased stimulation.

Like the other nonverbal behaviors discussed in Chapter 1, immediacy behaviors are encoded as a gestalt. For example, when you feel attraction for a person on a date, you send more than positive verbal messages; you communicate your attraction in more than one channel. You might touch your date, move closer, make eye contact, talk in warm tones, and face in your date's direction. Immediacy is typically a mindless, spontaneous expression of positive affection for another person that is encoded as a combination of cues. The following excerpt illustrates this principle:

> A few years ago, when this author was training experimental confederates to use continuous (90 percent) or averted (15 percent) gaze, an interesting and troubling experience occurred. The validations of our manipulations revealed that the confederates in the continuous gaze condition used more forward leans, more vocal enthusiasm, and more smiles. Only after considerable training were some confederates able to suppress these collateral immediacy cues. Some were unable to suppress immediacy in other channels and weren't used in the experiments. Other researchers have reported similar problems. . . . The point is that immediacy cues are encoded and decoded as a conceptual, behavioral gestalt. (Andersen, 1986, p. 13)

Human perception is rarely a direct function of the objects or events we receive through our senses. In fact, when something is missing from a sentence, a scene, or an interaction, our minds often fill in the missing information. These principles were illustrated nicely in the following immediacy experiment. In a study of televised immediacy, Janis Andersen and one of her graduate students were attempting to determine if smiling faces were perceived as happier, more credible, and more immediate than "straight" faces. The experimenters videotaped a person giving a speech twice—once with a smiling face and the other time with a straight face. Viewers were given a set of measures to complete, including the Behavioral Indicants of Immediacy scale (BII; J. F. Andersen et al., 1979). The BII contains items on smiling, as well as items on fourteen other immediacy behaviors. To the researchers' surprise, people seeing the smiling face, as opposed to the straight face, reported that the smiling person also stood closer, gestured more, touched more, and stood facing them more directly. None of these cues had been visible to the viewers! These results suggest that receivers fill in the blanks with plausible responses. When immediacy is increased in one channel, we infer that it increased in other channels as well. The principle here is that immediacy is decoded as a gestalt, not behavior by behavior. Keep this principle in mind as we now turn to the individual behaviors that contribute to this gestalt.

Oculesics

During interaction, we usually focus our attention on the eyes of the other interactant. Thus, oculesic behavior is central to both sending and receiving nonverbal messages. Indeed, most people believe that a person's conscious essence is located in or behind the eyes.

EYE CONTACT AND GAZE

One of the behaviors most central to the immediacy construct is eye contact, or mutual gaze, which occurs when two communicators both look at each other's eyes or faces. Eye contact does more than signal availability; it is an invitation to communicate. The literature on interpersonal gaze is so extensive that it is only possible to provide a brief overview of this research (for an extensive review see Fehr & Exline, 1987). Gaze, which occurs when one person looks at another, performs a number of functions, including monitoring interaction and turn-taking, dominating and threatening others, and receiving feedback. Nonetheless, its primary function is to convey immediacy (Andersen, 1985).

Eye contact typically produces positive perceptions in receivers and observers, although numerous studies reveal that very high levels of eye contact are not necessarily perceived more positively than moderate levels. In a study by Goldberg, Kiesler, and Collins (1969), people who spend more time gazing at an interviewer received higher socioemotional evaluations from the interviewer. Mehrabian (1968a, 1970, 1971b) demonstrated that increased eye contact communicates a more positive interpersonal attitude and increases affiliative behavior. Kleinke, Meeker, and Fong (1974) report that gazing couples were rated more positively by observers on all evaluative dimensions. Thayer and Schiff (1974) found that dyads who engaged in more extended or reciprocated eye contact were perceived to have more enduring relationships. Noller (1980) showed that happily married couples looked at each other frequently during the exchange of positive messages and less frequently during negative exchanges than did less-happily married couples. Beebe (1980) found increased eye contact to be associated with greater perceived dynamism, believability, and likability. One study showed that general gaze aversion communicates negative relational messages, including dissimilarity, superficiality, nonaffection, nonreceptivity, lack of trust, and nonimmediacy (Burgoon et al., 1986). A study of the nonverbal behavior of therapists found that increased eye contact improved respondents' ratings of the therapists' trustworthiness, expertness, and attractiveness, as well as increasing the likelihood that participants would revisit the therapist (Ziegler-Kratz & Marshall, 1990). In general, eye contact is perceived as positive, immediate behavior in interpersonal interaction.

A similar body of literature suggests that eye contact is used strategically to send messages of positive affect. When Mehrabian and Friar (1969) asked experimental subjects to role-play "liking" for an interactant, they substantially increased their eye contact. Similarly, when people are requested in experiments to increase their conversational involvement, they gaze more at their partner (Burgoon & Coker, 1988; Coker & Burgoon, 1987). Likewise, people spontaneously engage in more mutual gaze with friends and people they like than with strangers or people they dislike (Coutts & Schneider, 1976; Exline & Winters, 1965). Guerrero (1997) also demonstrates that people tend to gaze more at their dating partners than at their same-sex and opposite-sex friends. At the same time, however, people sometimes look less at their partner with whom they share *highly* committed and *very* intimate relationships. Dindia, Fitzpatrick, and Attridge (1989) found that people engage in less eye contact and gaze with their spouse than with opposite-sex strangers. This is similar to several findings that show that spouses touch less after they are married than when they were engaged or dating. This behavior is true for both public touch (Guerrero & Andersen, 1991) and private touch (Emmers & Dindia, 1995). Three reasons explain this decrease in eye contact and touch in long-term relationships. First, marriage is a commitment, so spouses may not need such constant reassurances as eye contact and touch, which are vital in dating relationships. Second, once people are married, other symbols of the relationships (such as wedding rings and children) serve as reminders of the partners' commitment to each other. In serious dating relationships, other "tie" signs, such as hand holding and long stares, may signal unavailability to potential rivals. Third, many married people simply take their spouse for granted. This shouldn't be the case, but with familiarity and comfort may come less excitement and immediacy.

Although eye contact is *usually* perceived as a positive nonverbal behavior and occurs most in positive relationships, this is not always the case. Eye contact can interact with other variables to intensify other meanings. Under some circumstances—such as very prolonged gaze or gaze accompanied by an angry facial expression—gaze is perceived as a threat display (Exline, Ellyson, & Long, 1975). Several studies have shown that in hostile interactions or in negative relationships, increased eye contact leads to negative affect (Scherwitz & Helmreich, 1973; Noller, 1980).

PUPIL DILATION

Pupil-dilation research, or pupilometrics, has shown that pupil dilation is both the result of positive interpersonal feelings and a subconscious immediacy cue (Hess, 1965, 1975). In one classic study, Hess and Goodwin (1974) showed people two identical pictures of a mother with her infant; in one photograph the mother's pupils were retouched to appear dilated, and in the other photograph they were retouched to appear constricted. Subjects overwhelmingly perceived that the mother with the dilated pupils loved her baby more. Interestingly, few subjects reported having detected any cues from the eyes. Many said the mother's face was warmer or that she was holding her baby more closely, although these characteristics were identical in the two photographs. This and other experiments illustrate that some immediacy cues are encoded and decoded at very low levels of awareness. In a study by Andersen, Todd-Mancillas, and DiClemente (1980), subjects were shown pairs of identical photographs of a woman—identical, that is, except for the pupils, which were retouched to be constricted in one photograph and dilated in the other—and asked to rate the woman's attractiveness. Although pupil dilation did not increase subjects' perceptions of the woman's task attractiveness (the desire to work with the woman), it did significantly increase their perceptions of her social and physical attractiveness. This suggests that immediacy cues may be more important in interpersonal relationships as opposed to role relationships. The observation that pupil dilation does not enhance task attraction suggests that this display occurs only for the benefit of relationally intimate people rather than nonintimates, such as store clerks, secretaries, or salespeople.

Proxemics

Like oculesic behavior, proxemic behaviors are primary messages of immediacy. Indeed, by definition, an immediacy behavior decreases psychological or physical distance. Several different proxemic behaviors communicate immediacy.

PHYSICAL DISTANCE

First among Argyle's (1972) five primary intimacy (or immediacy) cues is physical proximity. In many subsequent studies of immediacy, close interpersonal distances are at the core of what people perceive as immediacy (Andersen, 1979; J. F. Andersen et al., 1979).

Closer interpersonal distances typically result in more attraction, more warmth, and more immediacy. Mehrabian and Ksionsky (1970) report several studies that show closer distances of various kinds to result in more-positive interpersonal attitudes. One study found that closer residential distances elicited greater friendship and liking among dormitory residents (Priest & Sawyer, 1967). Another study found that when a speaker stood at a closer interpersonal distance, a receiver's nonverbal agreement responses increased (Kleck, 1970). This effect of proximity on attraction and immediacy is most powerful among friends and other "rewarding" people (people who we find attractive, credible, wealthy, or high in status), is less powerful among strangers, and is negative among enemies or threatening people. Morton (1977) reports that although acquaintances prefer close interpersonal distances, unacquainted people are more intimate and comfortable at intermediate distances. In a series of studies, Burgoon and her associates report more compliance and positive affect in response to rewarding people at distances closer than typical norms. By contrast, nonrewarding people are perceived more positively at normative distances (Burgoon, 1978, 1983; Burgoon & Aho, 1982; Burgoon, Manusov, Mineo, & Hale, 1985). Evidently, close interpersonal distances produce an intensification effect that makes negative interactions more negative and positive interactions more positive (Schiffenbauer & Shiavo, 1976). In a study by Stelzner and Egland (1995), closer interpersonal distance was the leading predictor of relational satisfaction. Because most of our interactions occur in the context of positive relationships (such as between friends and family), closer interpersonal distances are generally perceived as positive, immediate behaviors.

Just as proxemically close interactions generally produce positive impressions, so positive relationships produce proxemically closer interactions. Mehrabian and Friar (1969) show that communicators are most likely to interact at close distances with people they like. Guerrero (1997) also demonstrates that individuals sit closer to romantic partners than to friends. In addition, a study in which subjects were asked to increase their involvement or immediacy with another person found that subjects stood closer together than they did in uninvolved control conditions (Coker & Burgoon, 1987).

THE PHYSICAL PLANE

Immediacy is also communicated by interacting on the same level or physical plane as another person (Andersen, 1985). When people tower over us, it increases their power and our submissiveness (more about this in Chapter 12), and it makes them seem less warm and approachable and more psychologically distant. In short, it doesn't convey immediacy. Interacting on the same physical plane is particularly problematic in interactions between young children and adults who tower over them (Andersen & Andersen, 1982) and between disabled people, particularly people in wheelchairs, and nondisabled people. One way people can increase their immediacy is to sit or lean in a manner that minimizes height differences. Brown (1965) has suggested that interacting on the same plane is a manifestation of interpersonal solidarity and closeness.

BODY ORIENTATION

Whether you face someone directly, at an angle, or literally give them the "cold shoulder" (as opposed to a nice, "warm front"), your body angle sends messages of immediacy. People are interpersonally cold, unavailable, and uninvolved in side-to-side and back-to-back positions. In fact, when an interactant wants to reduce the immediacy of an encounter that is too close, he or she frequently compensates with a less direct body orientation (Patterson, 1973a, 1977). Conversely, one of the main ways people increase involvement and immediacy is to assume a more direct body orientation (Coker & Burgoon, 1987). Stelzner and Egland (1995) report that a direct body position is one of the three behaviors that best predicts relational satisfaction.

FORWARD LEANS

A number of scholars have included forward leans on their lists of nonverbal behaviors that convey immediacy (Andersen, 1985; Mehrabian, 1971a). Several studies have reported that forward leans communicate greater rapport and immediacy than upright positions or backward leans (Burgoon, Buller, Hale, & deTurck, 1984; Trout & Rosenfeld, 1980). In a study in which subjects were asked to increase involvement or immediacy, the one behavior they increased significantly was the forward lean (Coker & Burgoon, 1987). Forward leans produce closer interpersonal distances and more involvement. Interactants typically feel more warmth and friendship for people who lean forward slightly during conversations.

Haptics

Tactile communication is probably the most important intimate and involving immediacy behavior. But it can be one of the most threatening behaviors as well. Touch is threatening because it is the only immediacy behavior that can physically harm a person and because it often has sexual connotations. Reactions to touch are dependent on cultural and personal norms as well as the specific interpersonal relationship (Andersen & Leibowitz, 1978; Jourard, 1966; Thayer, 1986a; Trenholm & Petrie, 1980). Normative, appropriate touch, however, is usually perceived as a warm, immediate behavior. Certainly, a large number of scholars include touch on their lists of primary immediacy behaviors (Andersen, 1979; J. F. Andersen et al., 1979; Andersen & Leibowitz, 1978; Heslin, 1974; Heslin & Boss, 1980; Mehrabian, 1971a; Patterson, 1977).

A number of studies using a variety of methods have been conducted on tactile communication. Interestingly, regardless of the method used, the results are fairly similar. The entire body of research, based on laboratory studies, questionnaires, field studies, and diary studies, reveals that touch communicates intimacy and immediacy.

In a laboratory study by Burgoon et al. (1984), subjects viewed videotaped interactions, one in which the interactants touched and another in which they didn't touch. Subjects rated the people in the touch condition as more intimate and immediate than the interactants in the no-touch condition. Research by Burgoon, Walther, and Baesler (1992) shows that even slight touches generally result in increased credibility and attraction toward the toucher for *all* individuals and particularly for well-groomed, high-status, and expert communicators. Jones (1994) demonstrates that touch is the central behavior in human bonding and the development of close relationships.

Several studies employing self-report measures have researched attitudes toward touch. These studies show that individuals who touch are generally more self-confident, warmer people who enjoy intimacy and physical closeness (Andersen & Leibowitz, 1978; Andersen & Sull, 1985; Andersen, Andersen, & Lustig, 1987; Jones & Brown, 1996). A study by Fromme et al. (1989) reveals that a touch-comfort test could predict whether or not students would volunteer to participate in a study on hugging. Moreover, among the volunteers, subjects with higher touch-comfort scores rated hugging most positively. Finally, touch comfort is related to an active interpersonal style and the degree to which one's relationships are satisfactory.

A study by Pisano, Wall, and Foster (1986) employed a questionnaire to rate thirty-one descriptions of nonreciprocated touch in romantic relationships. Subjects rated most touch as indications of warmth or love, followed by playfulness, sexual desire, and comfort. Interestingly, all of these functions suggest that touch is typically interpreted as an immediacy behavior. Similarly, in their study of the functions of touch, Heslin and Alper (1983) classify friendship/warmth as one of the five basic meanings associated with touch.

Tactile communication is probably the most intimate and involving of any immediacy behavior.

In an extensive field study, Jones and Yarbrough (1985) had undergraduates record all their touch behaviors. The researchers then separated the meanings of touch into six categories: positive affect, playful, controlling, ritualistic, hybrid, and task-related. The study revealed that positive-affect touch is the most common of these types. Positive-affect touch includes five basic touch subtypes, which follow:

Support touches: behaviors that serve to nurture, reassure, or promise protection. This form of touch is most common in close relationships and generally involves touching, patting, or holding the other person by the hand or arm. Verbalization often accompanies support touch; for example, a person may say, "It's okay," or ask, "Are you all right?"

Appreciation touches: tactile messages of thanks that are often followed by verbalization. This form of touch is most common in close, opposite-sex relationships and mainly involves hugging or holding.

Inclusion touches: behaviors that seek to bring people together and enhance psychological closeness. This form of touch is used by close friends and sexual intimates and mainly consists of holding or pressing up against another person.

Sexual touches: behaviors that seek to express sexual interest or physical attraction mostly among people with a sexually intimate relationship.

These tactile behaviors include touching the genitals, buttocks, or a woman's chest and usually involve holding or stroking. A study (Henchy & Falk, 1995) indicates that although sexual touch is a fairly common behavior observed in both heterosexual and lesbian bars, it is significantly more common in lesbian bars.

Affectionate touches: the most common form of positive-affect touch, which sends messages of positive regard beyond mere greeting. This form of touch primarily occurs in opposite-sex relationships (and, secondarily, in same-sex relationships between females) and is often expressed in the form of kisses, hugs, caresses, tactile reinforcers, and pats.

In addition to Jones and Yarbrough's (1985) functions of touch, Afifi and Johnson (1993) suggest that some types of touch function as relationship-presentation tools. Their study, which was conducted in college bars, suggests that touch, particularly male touch, sometimes functions to publicly communicate that one's partner is taken. Of course, not all touch functions to convey positive affect or to display relational intimacy to others. Some types of touch function to display aggression, hostility, or negative responses. For example, in an observational study on children's touch, Guerrero and Ebesu (1993) found that children used two forms of negative affect touch: aggression (such as hitting and kicking) and affection withdrawal (such as pushing someone's comforting hand away). They also found that more younger children than older children used negative-affect touch, suggesting that as people mature, they use aggressive touch less frequently, presumably because they learn that such touch is socially inappropriate.

In sum, although prior research indicated that touch is a dominant behavior used (particularly by males) to manipulate and control (Henley, 1977), recent research suggests that the principal function of touch is to convey immediacy and positive affect. Recent research also disputes the belief that males engage in more opposite-sex touch than females. In fact, there is no sex difference in opposite-sex touch between males and females (Hall & Vecchia, 1992a). Jones and Yarbrough (1985) did identify a category called control touch, but this was only one of five major categories of touch. Similarly, Guerrero and Ebesu (1993) found children to display more intimate touch than controlling or aggressive touch. Moreover, they found that most of the control touch was not used in an attempt to dominate but rather to get attention (Guerrero & Ebesu, 1993), in other words to signal availability for communication.

Other studies have found little effect of touch on perceptions of dominance. One researcher (Forden, 1981) showed college students three videotapes of a conversation. In the first videotape, a male touched a female on the shoulder; in the second, a female touched a male on the shoulder; and in the third, no touch occurred. Subjects perceived the females who touched to be more dominant and the males who were touched to be more passive. Contrary to Henley's (1977) gender hypothesis, men were not perceived as more dominant when they touched. In a similar experiment by Burgoon et al. (1984), interpersonal touch increased subjects' perceptions of composure, relaxation, and informality but not dominance. Finally, in a study by Pisano et al. (1986), subjects frequently perceived touch as communicating warmth and love but rarely as expressing dominance and control. In sum, although tactile behaviors convey multiple messages, they are typically perceived as immediate or intimate behaviors rather than dominant or powerful ones.

Kinesics

Communicative movements of our face, head, body, and hands (called kinesics) have considerable impact on the perceived immediacy of interaction. At one time, *kinesics* referred to almost all nonverbal behavior; kinesics was the nonverbal counterpart to linguistics. But over the last several decades, the study of nonverbal communication has expanded to include other forms of nonverbal communication. Nonetheless, the study of kinesics, the body in motion, is central to the study of nonverbal communication and, specifically, immediacy.

SMILES

Another central immediacy cue is the smile. No expression communicates as much warmth or provides such a strong invitation to interact as does the smile. Bayes (1970) reports that the best single predictor of interpersonal warmth is frequency of smiling. In a number of investigations, smiles are classified as a crucial part of nonverbal immediacy (J. F. Andersen et al. 1979; Andersen, 1985; Mehrabian, 1971a; Patterson, 1978), intimacy (Argyle, 1972), and warmth (Reece & Whitman, 1962). Studies examining the interactions between therapists and their patients found that the more frequently the therapists smiled, the greater their patients' perceptions were of their expertise, trustworthiness, and interpersonal acceptance. The therapists' increased smiling also increased the likelihood that the patients would return to the therapist in the future (Reece & Whitman, 1962; Ziegler-Kratz & Marshall, 1990).

Several studies have also reported that smiling is a primary means of communicating interpersonal affiliation (Mehrabian, 1971b; Mehrabian & Ferris, 1967; Rosenfeld, 1966a, 1966b). In one study, a speaker lectured to classes while either smiling or not smiling. Results showed that increased smiling produced higher perceptions of immediacy and affiliation (Gutsell & Andersen, 1980). Similarly, Burgoon et al. (1984) show that the absence of smiling communicates less immediacy than smiling in dyadic interactions. When Coker and Burgoon (1987) asked participants to increase their conversational involvement, a number of immediacy behaviors increased, including smiling. Finally, smiling is a contagious immediacy cue. Several studies report that smiles are reciprocated during interaction (Kendon, 1967; Rosenfeld, 1966a, 1967).

HEAD NODS

In North America, nodding is a sign of agreement and rapport. Research shows that monkeys and apes, as well as humans, use ritualistic bowing gestures to signal submission and friendliness (Eibl-Eibesfeldt, 1974, 1979). Listeners signal warmth and agreement by nodding. Nodding is a type of backchannel behavior, or reinforcing listener response (Dittman, 1972). In studies in which subjects were asked to simulate approval seeking (Rosenfeld, 1966a, 1966b) and conversational involvement (Coker & Burgoon, 1987), subjects exhibited frequent head nods. Like smiling, nodding is contagious and tends to be reciprocated during interaction (Rosenfeld, 1966a, 1966b).

BODILY RELAXATION

When you seem relaxed during interaction, people are likely to perceive you as more available, warmer, and friendlier. Tension and stress signal nonimmediacy and are often perceived as emotional buildup that can potentially lead to an aggressive release of tension (Eibl-Eibesfeldt, 1974). In interactions between patients and therapists, patients perceived therapists' relaxed, nonaggressive behavior as a sign of warmth (Reece & Whitman, 1961). One study shows that still, relaxed hands are one type of behavior that communicates warmth (Reece & Whitman, 1962). Several major studies have found relaxation and tension reduction to be important components of nonverbal immediacy (J. F. Andersen et al., 1979; Mehrabian, 1968b). Relaxation is perceived positively during interaction. Mehrabian (1968a, 1969) finds that relaxed body positions communicate more liking than tense positions. Similarly, Jensen and Andersen (1979) report that relaxation behaviors are associated with higher credibility and attractiveness. One caveat, however, is in order: *extremely* relaxed body positions may sometimes convey boredom and detachment (such as slumping back in a chair), especially when coupled with nonimmediacy cues such as decreased eye contact. Therefore, Burgoon (1994) argues, moderately high relaxation conveys the most warmth, interest, and involvement.

GESTURES

When you gesture with your hands, others perceive you as more involved and interested in the interaction. Several studies have shown that increases in gestural activity communicate increased affiliativeness (Mehrabian, 1971b) and immediacy (J. F. Andersen et al., 1979). In studies in which subjects were asked to seek approval from or increase involvement with others, they responded with increased gesturing (Coker & Burgoon, 1987; Rosenfeld, 1966a, 1966b).

BODY SYNCHRONY

Like good dancers, good communicators act almost as one, rarely stepping on one another's toes, flowing smoothly, and emitting positive "vibes." Good communicators attune and adjust their movements to the other interactant. In a study by LaFrance and Mayo (1978), synchronous posture sharing between students and instructors increased interpersonal rapport. Several studies indicate that body congruence produces more positive affect and rapport in interactions between therapists and patients (Scheflen, 1972; Trout & Rosenfeld, 1980). In a laboratory experiment, confederates who produced congruous movements were perceived as more competent, composed, trustworthy, extroverted, and sociable than confederates who enacted incongruous movements (Woodall & Burgoon, 1981).

GAIT

A number of our interpersonal interactions occur while walking. Moreover, even in the absence of verbal interaction, how we walk communicates a considerable amount of information about us. Our gait or walking style affects an interactant's perception of immediacy. In one study, happy moods were associated with arm swinging, moderate-length strides, light-footedness, and erect posture (Montepare, Goldstein, & Clausen, 1987). It is likely that people are perceived as more approachable when they display an animated but unhurried walking style.

OPEN BODY POSITIONS

When people have their heads down, their arms folded, and their legs crossed, they convey little warmth or availability. Open body positions symbolize openness for interaction. Morris (1977) uses the term *barrier signals* to describe a set of gestures and positions that communicate defensiveness and avoidance in social situations. In children, these positions are quite obvious, such as hiding behind a mother's skirt. As adults, these barrier signals, or body buffers, become abbreviated, such as folding one's arms, crossing one's legs, adjusting one's cuffs, and covering one's face. In a study by Mehrabian (1969), females who used more open arm and leg positions were perceived by receivers to have a more positive attitude. In a study of marital communication, Beier and Sternberg (1977) report that close, well-adjusted couples used more open leg positions than couples experiencing conflict. In most cases, holding one's legs tightly together and folding one's arms communicates defensiveness and unapproachability rather than immediacy.

Vocalics

Research shows that nonverbal elements of the voice play a major role in communicating interpersonal liking (Mehrabian, 1971a; Mehrabian & Ferris, 1967) and nonverbal immediacy. In fact, one study found that vocal expressiveness is the behavior most central to immediacy (J. F. Andersen et al., 1979).

Using an electronic synthesizer to vary the pitch, amplitude, duration, and tempo of nonverbal sounds, Scherer (1979) shows that affect and emotion are primarily the result of vocal changes in pitch and tempo. Bebee's (1980) study shows that pitch variation has a major effect on liking. Similarly, Burgoon and Aho (1982) report that increased vocal fluency, pleasantness, clarity, and variety increase a speaker's credibility as well as perceptions of the speaker's sociability. Even with infants, warm, pleasant voices produce more attentiveness than unpleasant voices (Milmoe, Novey, Kagan, & Rosenthal, 1974).

BABY TALK

Certain vocalic behaviors produce very high levels of intimacy and immediacy. Perhaps the most interesting vocalic behavior is baby talk—a varied, high-pitched, imitation of children's speech used by adults when they communicate with infants and small children. Sometimes baby talk involves the use of nonsense phrases (such as "kutch-ee-kutch-ee-koo") accompanied by touch or smiles. At other times, ordinary phrases, such as "You're my little sweetie," are simply accented with baby-talk vocalics.

Interestingly, baby talk is not used only when talking to infants or children. One study has shown that baby talk is commonly used when communicating with the elderly (Caporael, 1981). Baby talk, which employs immature pronunciation and high vocal pitch, typically is perceived by the elderly as conveying affection and nurturance. But communicators must be careful: research shows that slow, loud speech may be perceived as patronizing by the elderly (Ryan, Bourhip, & Knops, 1991). Baby talk is also common among lovers during sexual foreplay, during phone conversations, and during face-to-face interactions. Shaver and Hazan (1988) suggest that in both parent-child and adult romantic relationships, baby talk is used to communicate attachment and bondedness. Ferguson (1964) shows that baby talk is used worldwide in languages as diverse as Arabic and Comanche.

BACKCHANNELING

As discussed earlier, backchannel behaviors, or reinforcing listener responses, are behaviors performed by listeners while another person is talking. These behaviors are not attempts to talk or to gain the floor, but rather they provide feedback and encouragement to the speaker, often signaling her or him to continue speaking. Frequently, such backchannel behaviors are vocalic. Utterances such as "hum" and "uh-huh" are clearly backchannel behaviors. Utterances such as "yeah" and "okay" are probably more nonverbal than verbal, although some scholars would disagree. One study found that the backchannel utterance "mm-hmm" belongs to a set of reinforcing nonverbal behaviors that actually cause an increase in the length of another's speaking turns (Matarazzo, Wins, & Saslow, 1965). A number of cultural differences exist in backchanneling and are described in Chapter 4. In sum, vocal backchanneling increases immediacy, signals that the listener is comprehending the speaker's message, and reinforces the speaker's role in a conversation. One exception, however, should be noted. When backchannel behaviors such as "mm-hmm" and "uh-huh" are used in *rapid* succession, they sometimes signal that the listener understands the point and wants the speaker to stop talking.

VOCAL SYNCHRONY

Communicators who are in rapport with one another are able to converse, back-channel, take turns talking, and laugh without interrupting each other or getting out of sync. Although synchrony involves some kinesic behaviors (discussed earlier), vocal synchrony is an essential part of establishing immediacy as well. People who like one another manifest vocal convergence (LaFrance & Mayo, 1978; Street & Giles, 1982), a similarity in pitch, rate, and accent during a conversation. Vocal convergence is a common phenomenon in which, over time, people start to communicate like one another. For example, as a boy from Illinois, I sometimes spent summer vacations in Massachusetts. My Illinois friends often told me I had picked up a New England accent over my vacation. Fast talkers slow down when talking to slow talkers, and slow talkers speed up when talking to fast talkers. Vocal convergence is a form of immediacy that brings people even closer together. A sure way to reduce warmth, rapport, and immediacy is to get out of vocal sync with another person by interrupting, talking simultaneously, or yelling when the other person is whispering.

Chronemics

The way we use time communicates a lot about our relationship with another person. In the United States, Canada, and northern Europe, time is treated like a commodity. People believe that time can be wasted, spent, saved, and invested as if it were money. A number of studies suggest that immediacy can be communicated through such chronemic cues (J. F. Andersen, 1984; Andersen & Andersen, 1982; Burgoon & Aho, 1982).

Spending time with someone is perhaps the best way to signal immediacy because it involves availability and closeness (J. F. Andersen et al., 1979). A recent study by Egland, Stelzner, Andersen, and Spitzberg (1995) reports that the immediacy behavior most associated with relational satisfaction is spending time together. As I discussed in the opening chapter, spending time with another person is a major indicator of that person's importance. Another interpersonal chronemic cue that signals immediacy is pause time, the length of time between utterances in a conversation. Pause time is an immediacy cue because it allows for interaction from one's partner and signals an other-orientation.

Punctuality is another important chronemic immediacy cue, particularly in classroom contexts (Todd-Mancillas, 1982). Students who arrive to class late are perceived as low in immediacy, inconsiderate, and incompetent. One study of secretaries by Baxter and Ward (1975) demonstrates that late arrivers were perceived as low in competence, composure, friendliness, and sociability. Friends and romantic partners who constantly arrive late or do not call at a specified time may also be evaluated negatively.

Finally, monochronistic (versus polychronistic) use of time, which involves focusing on only one thing during a particular time span, may be considered an immediacy behavior in American culture. We like others to concentrate on the conversation at hand rather than busy themselves with other tasks while they listen. For example, hearing your conversation partner typing on a computer in the background while you are talking on the phone might anger you—after all, the person you are talking to should be paying full attention to *you,* not working on something else!

Antecedents of Immediacy

What causes a person to communicate nonverbal immediacy to another person? Two of these antecedents, or causes of immediacy behaviors—culture (see Chapter 4) and interpersonal valence (see Chapter 7)—were discussed earlier in the book. Next, we focus on four other antecedents of immediacy: the relationship, individual differences, the situation, and temporary states.

The Relationship

Obviously, we are most likely to touch, gaze at, approach, and smile at individuals with whom we share positive relationships. But relationships are tricky things. For one thing, both people must have similar perceptions of the relationship if the display of immediacy behavior is to be reciprocal. For example, immediacy behaviors that are normally reserved for close friends or lovers would be inappropriate if used between business associates or relatively new acquaintances.

Most theories of relationship development maintain that as a relationship develops, communication becomes more immediate (Altman & Taylor, 1973; Berger & Calabrese, 1975; Duck, 1988; Knapp, 1984). Likewise, research shows that when two individuals increase their immediacy, observers infer that they have an extended, stable relationship (Thayer & Schiff, 1974). A body of empirical evidence suggests that across the early stages of a relationship, nonverbal communication becomes more intimate. Hays (1985) reports that hugging increases during the first three months of a relationship. Levinger (1980) shows that intimate couples touch more than strangers do when working together on projects. Gendrin and Honeycutt (1988) discovered in their experimental interactions that acquaintances smiled more at each other than did strangers. Similarly, a study by Hill, Blackman, and Crane (1982) demonstrates that married couples stood closer than did strangers during experimental interactions. None of these findings are too remarkable. Among individuals in well-acquainted or intimate relationships, nonverbal immediacy is higher than among new acquaintances.

A number of scholars question whether immediacy continues to increase linearly as people become more acquainted or have more-bonded relationships. Several scholars, however, characterize relational communication as capricious and nonlinear (Duck & Miell, 1986; Honeycutt, Cantrill, & Greene, 1989).

Various studies on touch have shown that greater immediacy is not necessarily characteristic of well-developed, stable relationships. Recall the study by Dindia et al. (1989), which showed that we gaze less at our spouses than at opposite-sex strangers. Burgoon, Buller, and Woodall (1989) report that tie signs such as holding hands, linking arms, or putting arms around one another "are more prevalent among dating and courting couples than among marrieds" (p. 318). Guerrero and Andersen's (1991) field study shows a curvilinear relationship between relational stage and touch among dating and married couples: couples who were engaged or seriously dating touched each other significantly more than did couples who had either just started dating or were married. More recently, Emmers and Dindia (1995) report a similar finding based on a questionnaire study of private, intimate touch. Couples' touch behaviors rise from the casual dating stage to the serious dating stage and then diminish slightly during marriage. Burgoon, Buller, and Woodall (1989) provide an explanation for this type of finding: "Once a relationship is well established, the need for public displays of affection is no longer necessary" (p. 318). Likewise, Patterson (1988) maintains, "It is as though relationship intimacy gives individuals some license to ignore their partner" (p. 52).

Another relational purpose for immediacy behaviors is interpersonal comforting. Comforting strategies are messages that are intended to alleviate or moderate another's distressed emotional state (Burleson & Goldsmith, 1998). Two recent studies indicate that most nonverbal comforting strategies make use of immediacy behaviors, including hugs, pats, other forms of touch, eye contact, attentiveness, sympathetic facial expressions, and close interpersonal distances (Bullis & Horn, 1995; Dolin & Booth-Butterfield, 1993). The closer we are to someone, the more likely we are to use immediacy behaviors as a form of comfort.

Evidently, nonverbal immediacy does increase as relationships develop but only up to a point. In close, stable, long-term relationships, high immediacy levels are not needed to constantly define the relationship. Very close friends, family members, and married couples, however, must be careful not to show so little immediacy as to signal distancing or deterioration of these close relationships.

Individual Differences

Individuals vary greatly in the degree to which they send immediacy messages, even in close relationships. Some individuals rarely smile, touch, stand at close interpersonal distances, or make eye contact. Others, however, regularly produce such immediacy behaviors during interaction. Why is this? Some evidence suggests that inherited biological differences are part of the explanation. Eysenck (1967, 1971) shows that extroverts seek more social interaction and adventure because they have chronically low cortical arousal levels. Introverts manifest a pattern of interaction avoidance and stimulation inhibition due to their chronically high arousal levels. The same pattern may be true for high communication apprehensives, who decrease arousal by reducing immediacy during interaction (Andersen, 1987; Andersen & Coussoule, 1980).

Another explanation for individual differences in immediacy levels is cultural background. Based on research conducted over the past four decades, certain groups—ethnic, national, and regional—have been identified as contact cultures; that is, touch and high levels of immediacy are the norm among group members (Hall, 1959, 1966a; see Chapter 4 for a detailed discussion on this dimension of culture). Contact cultures interact at close interpersonal distances, touch frequently, and are generally more demonstrative and immediate. Interestingly, most contact cultures are located in relatively warm climates at low latitudes (Andersen, 1988; Hecht, Andersen, & Ribeau, 1989). By contrast, most noncontact cultures are located in cool climates at high latitudes. Evidently, cooler climates produce interpersonally "cooler" and more task-oriented cultures. Differences between contact and noncontact groups have been found even within the United States. Those living in warmer zones of the United States report being more dramatic, more expressive, and more positive toward touch than do those living in cooler zones (Andersen, Lustig, & Andersen, 1990).

In addition to physiology and culture, individual differences in immediacy are also the result of interpersonal environments that model, reward, and punish various immediacy behaviors. Immediacy behaviors are shaped during infancy and childhood and often result in lifelong patterns of behavior. At one extreme are abused children, who may have difficulty interacting in a warm, immediate style after experiencing the trauma of abuse. In one study abused children, and abused girls in particular, exhibited less touch and greater interpersonal distances and generally had less social engagement than nonabused children (Hecht et al., 1986).

Regardless of the cause, a number of studies show that individual differences in immediacy usage prevail across interactions with different relational partners. Patterson (1973b) reports that individuals are highly stable in their use of interpersonal distance, body orientation, eye contact, and body leans regardless of their interaction partner. Crouch (1980) also reports that individuals maintain similar levels of eye contact regardless of their partner. In a study by Guerrero (1997), subjects were videotaped interacting with three different relational partners: a close same-sex friend, a close opposite-sex friend, and a romantic partner. Despite several differences due to relationship type, Guerrero found that behaviors such as smiling, vocal warmth, proxemic distancing, bodily relaxation, composure, head nods, relaxed laughter, body orientation, and conversational fluency were correlated across all three interactions. Patterson (1973b, 1978) reviewed a number of studies that also show that people maintain about the same amount of personal space across various relationships. Even children show a number of consistent nonverbal immediacy behaviors in interviews with different people, including gazes, smiles, bodily movements, facial expressions, and head nods (Feldstein, 1972; Takala, 1977). Gallaher (1992) reports that individuals are very consistent in their level of expressiveness. Over time and across interactions, people exhibit consistent individual differences in immediacy behaviors regardless of the partner with whom they are interacting.

A number of personality measures are related to immediacy behaviors. For example, extroverts stand closer to others than do introverts (Patterson, 1978), and approval seekers position themselves closer to others than do people who do not seek approval (Rosenfeld, 1965). Additionally, the tendency to be affiliative is related to using closer interpersonal distances (Mehrabian & Diamond, 1971), and both communication apprehension and touch avoidance are negatively related to close interpersonal distance (Andersen & Sull, 1985; Cardot & Dodd, 1979).

People's tactile orientations may also be a general index of immediacy. Touch avoiders, defined as people with negative attitudes toward interpersonal touch, not only engage in less touch (Guerrero & Andersen, 1991) and maintain greater conversational distances (Andersen & Sull, 1985), but they are also less predisposed toward interaction and have lower self-esteem (Andersen, Andersen, & Lustig, 1987). Conversely, Deethardt and Hines (1983) report that touch approachers are more talkative, cheerful, and optimistic and less fearful of affection. Andersen and Sull (1985) conclude that the "touch avoidance measure probably taps into an underlying trait of approach and avoidance of nonverbal communication generally" (p. 69).

Research has shown that some individuals are more predisposed to experience aversive states than others, a trait called negative affectivity (Watson & Clark, 1984). Negative affectivity encompasses trait anxiety, neuroticism, weak ego strength, repression, and general maladjustment. High-negative-affectivity individuals tend to be distressed and upset, have a negative self-concept, and manifest withdrawal and nonimmediacy in interpersonal interaction. Simply put, some people just aren't very immediate.

One final personal trait that is highly linked to immediacy is biological sex. Women in our society are generally expressive and immediate, whereas men tend to be poker-faced and withdrawn. Buck (1984) has summarized numerous studies that suggest that women are much more likely than men to send positive-affect messages as well as more accurate in sending such messages. In a study of nonverbal communication between men and women in college bars, Afifi and Johnson (1993) showed that women manifested more nonverbal affection displays than men. In particular, women smiled more and initiated more ties signs than men. These findings suggest that women tend to externalize and display their emotions, whereas men tend to internalize and hide their emotions.

The Situation

The situation is an important variable that determines whether immediacy is expressed. Formal, public, negative, or conspicuous situations inhibit the expression of immediacy. The situation has a lot to do with why people engage in certain communication behaviors (Funder & Ozer, 1983). Participants in an interaction use situational information to restrain or display immediacy behavior. Acitelli and Duck (1987) maintain that a critical variable in the expression of intimacy "is the perspective on it that is taken by the participants, particularly their judgments about the level of intimacy appropriate for a given situation or occasion" (p. 301). Andersen (1989) suggests that situationally inappropriate intimacy or immediacy behaviors are viewed negatively and decrease closeness and attraction: "When intimacy behaviors are perceived to be situationally inappropriate, the episode will be negatively valenced, whereas when intimacy behaviors are perceived to be situationally appropriate, the episode will be positively valenced" (p. 28). Obviously, certain immediacy behaviors with high intimacy value, such as affectionate or sexual touching and prolonged eye contact, are constrained in certain situations.

Temporary States

We all go through moods or temporary states that alter our communication behavior. Studies have shown that drugs, foods, amount of sleep, the quality of one's interpersonal relations, and one's self-image are among the factors that have an impact on temporary states (Andersen, 1987). Temporary states have a definite impact on immediacy or intimacy, as Acitelli and Duck (1987) describe:

> Intimacy as a process is seen to develop, fluctuate and change over time. . . .
> The very notion of process implies that there will be changes in subjects' reports about their feelings and behaviors over time. A relationship may be intimate overall, but interactions can be intimate at one moment and not intimate the next. (p. 300)

Andersen (1985) shows that others' moods are related to how much immediacy they desire: "A fight with one's boss, a headache, a raise, a heavy workload, or any number of temporary factors can cause immediacy behaviors to be valenced either more positively or more negatively" (p. 28). Badzinski (1986) concludes that moods affect the messages we send, the judgments we make about others, and the judgments others make about us such that our actions and evaluations shift in the direction of our mood. Thus, when we are in a bad mood, we are likely to be less enthusiastic and less vocally expressive and to exhibit negative facial displays. Other people also react to our bad moods. In other words, if we are in a "bad mood," we may cause our partner to reduce her or his immediacy.

The Direct-Effects Model of Immediacy

In general, immediacy behaviors produce direct, positive effects on other people. This *direct-effects model* suggests that in most circumstances, immediate interactants are perceived as warmer, friendlier, more intimate, and more attractive. Many of our interactions occur with one of two types of partner: friend or stranger. In either of these relational situations, immediacy cues usually are perceived positively (Andersen, 1985; Coutts, Schneider, & Montgomery, 1980). Research supports a similar model of nonverbal immediacy, the *social-meaning model* (Burgoon, Coker, & Coker, 1986; Burgoon & Newton, 1991). According to the social-meaning model, many nonverbal behaviors have such a clear social meaning that most interactants react in the same way across most relationships.

Support for the direct-effects and social-meaning models has been accumulating, suggesting that immediacy behaviors have strong positive meanings in social interaction. Of course, immediacy behaviors interact with personal or situational variables in some circumstances. As Andersen (1985) points out, "When approach behaviors are employed in negative or hostile relationships they will not be perceived as immediacy cues at all, but will most likely generate negative affect and compensating responses" (p. 3). So, although immediacy behaviors can produce negative effects in negative relationships, the norm is for immediacy behaviors to produce direct, positive effects across most sorts of relationships. Let's now take a look at what sorts of positive effects are most likely to occur.

Interpersonal Effects

Our most common interactions occur with acquaintances, friends, loved ones, and romantic partners. In these relationships, immediacy behaviors are the primary means by which we exchange positive feelings. Following are several types of interpersonal effects generated by immediacy behaviors.

INTERPERSONAL ATTRACTION

Studies consistently show that warm, immediate, expressive individuals are perceived as more attractive than their reserved, inexpressive counterparts. This even holds true with strangers. Sabatelli and Rubin (1986) report that nonverbal expressiveness, or the degree to which people show their feelings, correlates positively with interpersonal attraction, warmth, and likability, independent of physical attractiveness. Both unattractive and attractive communicators seem to benefit from increased expressiveness. Sabatelli and Rubin concluded, "These findings also suggest, however, that nonverbal expressiveness may in some way compensate for an absence of physical attractiveness as a factor impacting on initial interpersonal impression" (p. 132). In one study, subjects reported that their interaction partner's nonverbal immediacy behaviors, including gestures and eye contact, signaled their interactional involvement (Cegala & Sillars, 1989). In a similar study, Remland and Jones (1989) found that nonverbal involvement behaviors, particularly backchanneling, forward leans, direct body angles, and other-directed gaze, produced large increases in interactants' attraction; and this was true for all people, whether shy or outgoing. Remland and Jones conclude, "The difference between high and low levels of NVI [nonverbal involvement] was substantial enough, even in a short interview, to result in differential attributions of interpersonal regard" (p. 181). Hale, Lundy, and Mongeau (1989) report that immediacy is a leading predictor of relational intimacy, particularly for best friends.

Perhaps the most dramatic illustration of the power of immediacy on initial attraction is Fisher, Rytting, and Heslin's (1976) library study. Subjects in this experiment, particularly females, felt much more positive toward librarians who briefly touched them during the exchange of a library card then they did toward librarians who did not touch them. So, even a single immediacy cue in one channel can have positive effects on interpersonal attraction. Burgoon and Saine (1978) put it well when they described how attraction occurs among humans: "The messages used to communicate attraction and liking are a mixture of inclusion, confirmation, and affection messages" (p. 140). Interestingly, these are the primary components of nonverbal immediacy messages.

RELATIONAL MESSAGES

Once a relationship is established, immediacy behaviors continue to signal positive messages between relational partners and help them maintain their relationship and move it toward even greater levels of intimacy. Patterson (1983) reviewed a large number of studies that collectively show that interactions between friends are more immediate than between either acquaintances or strangers. He summarized by stating, "The expected pattern of higher involvement in developed relationships than in initial relationships is well supported by empirical research" (p. 91). Bell and Daly (1984) report that one of the strategies that people typically employ to get others to like them is to display nonverbal immediacy behaviors. Similarly, nonverbal immediacy behaviors, including attentiveness, eye contact, concerned vocal tones, empathic facial expressions, closer interpersonal distances, hugs, pats, and other forms of touch, are associated with interpersonal comforting (Bullis & Horn, 1995; Dolin & Booth-Butterfield, 1993). Guerrero and Andersen (1991) show that touch occurs most frequently among steadily dating or engaged couples—as compared to early-dating or married couples—suggesting that immediacy is vital in close, developing relationships. Moreover, one's comfort with another person's immediacy is important to relational growth. Fromme et al. (1989) report that touch comfort is related to the establishment of intimate relationships and is even correlated with the ability to establish satisfactory relationships of any type. Stelzner and Egland (1995) show that immediacy is highly related to relational satisfaction for friends, casual daters, serious daters, and marriage-bound relational partners. Sending and receiving immediacy messages appear to be essential to bonding and growth in all types of relationships.

SEXUAL INVOLVEMENT

Sexual interaction, including flirtation, courtship, and actual sexual encounters, is predicated on high levels of immediacy. Indeed, sexual interaction involves every immediacy behavior discussed so far; however, these behaviors are often exaggerated and convey even more intimacy. For example, in sexual interaction, touch and gaze may be prolonged and directed to more private areas. Flirtation cues occur in combinations such as prolonged gazes and smiles, or close interpersonal distance, touch, and relaxed posture.

A number of studies suggest that immediacy cues are the most potent attractors in cross-sex relationships. For example, Kahn and McGaughey (1977) report that closer interpersonal distances result in greater attraction in opposite-sex pairs but not in same-sex pairs. Johnson and Edwards (1991) show that escalating levels of sexually intimate touch are highly associated with relational commitment for both sexes, particularly for females. Patterson (1983) summarizes the research in this area: "As the intimacy of the relationship increases in romantic relationships, greater involvement is typically expressed in a variety of behaviors. However, mutual gaze and touch are particularly important in facilitating a high level of involvement" (p. 96).

Recent studies of dating and flirting have shed even more light on the role of immediacy behaviors. Condra (1988) shows that flirtation behaviors are important signals from a sociobiological standpoint; they ensure mating rituals, which ultimately lead to reproduction of the species. Condra maintains, "It is clear that nonverbal communication may play a critical, maybe even defining, role in what is considered flirtatious" (p. 4). In her study, she reports that flirting is positively correlated with the number of dates spent together and negatively correlated with sociability, shyness, and loneliness (Condra, 1988).

Several studies have carefully examined the cues that convey interest and attraction in dating among college students (Afifi & Johnson, 1993; Moore & Butler, 1989; Muehlenhard, Koralewski, Andrews, & Burdick, 1986). These studies report that most courtship or dating cues are immediacy behaviors, including eye contact, room-encompassing glances, smiling, forward leans, sideways leans, direct shoulder orientation, closer interpersonal distances, touching, smoothing another's hair, catching another's eye, humor, attentiveness, frequent nodding, and animated speech. Research shows that acceptance of sexual initiation is usually done nonverbally, whereas rejection of sexual overtures is typically done verbally (Byers & Heinlein, 1989; Cupach & Metts, 1991; Metts, Cupach, & Imahori, 1992). Sexual involvement often proceeds without much verbal communication, yet when verbal communication is used to tell a partner to stop escalating sexual involvement, it is important to ignore nonverbal cues of sexual arousal and to stop the behavior. Sexual harassment or date rape can result from ignoring these explicit verbal cues in favor of nonverbal cues that seem positive and encouraging. We should all be aware: "Stop" means stop and "no" means no.

MARITAL SATISFACTION

Obviously, immediacy is important in marital relationships, as it is in friendships and dating relationships. However, contrary to common sense, immediacy may not be *as* important in marriage as it is in somewhat less established relationships. Burgoon, Buller, and Woodall (1989) report that "tie-signs are more prevalent among dating and courting couples than among marrieds. Once a relationship is well established, the need for public displays of affection and oneness are no longer necessary" (p. 318). As noted earlier, research on touch has confirmed this tendency by showing that public touch is over twice as common among couples going steady or engaged couples than among marrieds (Guerrero & Andersen, 1991). Married couples are bound together formally and legally; their home, investments, children, history, and relationship provide tangible reminders of their closeness to each other. Less-established couples need more reassurance about their relationships, so immediacy behaviors become a primary vehicle for conveying involvement, attraction, and closeness.

Although married couples may not exhibit as much immediacy as engaged couples, several studies show that happily married couples manifest more immediacy than their less-happy counterparts. In a study by Beier and Sternberg (1977), close, well-adjusted couples sat closer together, looked at each other more, touched more frequently, and maintained more open body positions than couples experiencing disagreement. Similarly, research by Noller (1987) on marital adjustment (happiness or compatibility) shows that "the greater degree of pleasantness of the high marital adjustment subjects stands in contrast to the intense negativity in the behavior of the low marital adjustment subjects" (p. 170). Evidently, she continues, "high marital adjustment subjects leak their comfortable happy feelings in their interactions with a spouse, while low marital adjustment couples leak their unhappiness and resentment" (p. 170). Thus, although immediacy is less important in marital relationships than in some other relationship types, it is still important. Reducing immediacy too far can signal marital distress and actually threaten the marriage.

Finally, research also shows that receiving immediacy cues is as important as sending them in marital relationships. Noller (1987) found that happily married couples are more successful at decoding nonverbal communication than are unhappy couples. Particularly important to marital satisfaction is the husband's ability to both send and receive nonverbal messages. Dissatisfied wives want more nonverbal affection, appreciation, and attention; all of which are communicated as nonverbal immediacy behaviors.

Instructional Effects

Some of the most fruitful research on nonverbal immediacy has been conducted in the classroom. The primary conclusion of this research is that immediate teachers are the most effective teachers—contradicting conventional mythology that asserts that stern teachers are the most effective. Andersen & Andersen (1987) address this myth:

> Perhaps the most frequently quoted admonition to new teachers is "Don't smile until after Christmas!" Although well-intentioned, this advice is a misdirected attempt to enhance instructional effectiveness. Somehow an instructional myth has been created which suggests a trade-off between being nice and being effective in the classroom. . . . Regardless of how the myth began or is sustained, recent research in instructional effectiveness requires the destruction

of this myth. Our research and that of our colleagues clearly demonstrate that nice teachers are highly effective. This research demonstrates that contrary to much popular opinion, students respond best to "nice" teachers—to teachers who are warm, friendly, immediate, approachable, affiliative and fostering of close, professionally appropriate personal relationships. (p. 57)

In fact, the recent educational trends requiring more discipline, less fun, less personal closeness, and more homework may be counterproductive in producing educational gains. The following sections review the research on nonverbal immediacy and its positive relationship to instructional outcomes.

AFFECTIVE LEARNING

Perhaps the most basic finding of seventy years of behavioral psychology is that people are drawn to things they like and avoid things they dislike. So it is with learning. We learn to like certain kinds of material and to dislike others. This process, called affective learning, may have more to do with learning over the long term than so-called cognitive learning. Likeable schools, teachers, books, and subjects attract students and keep their interest. Moreover, high, positive affect and positive attitudes create commitment and, as we will see, produce lifelong learning.

Research suggests it is the teacher who is most responsible for affective learning. Indeed, immediacy behaviors are the primary way to promote positive student attitudes. Early studies showed that college students preferred teachers who interacted warmly with them as opposed to cool and formal teachers (Beck & Lambert, 1977; Hyman, 1968). Leeds (1950) reports that creating a friendly atmosphere is one of the two most important elements of teaching, across all grade levels. Similarly, Ryans (1960, 1964) shows that teacher warmth and friendliness are important predictors of positive student response.

In her classic study, Andersen (1979) reports that teacher immediacy was a powerful predictor of students' attitudes toward the teacher, the course, and the subject matter in general. Students with immediate teachers reported about 20 percent higher satisfaction in their attitude toward the teacher. A number of other studies have supported this finding. In a study by Plax, Kearney, McCroskey, and Richmond (1986), students of highly immediate teachers reported a 50 percent increase in liking for the course at both the high school and college levels. Immediacy is strongly related to positive affect for the course content and for the instructor in both secondary school and college classrooms. Giglio and Lustig (1987) report that in introductory college communication courses, teacher immediacy increased students' positive attitudes toward class by over 30 percent. Sanders and Wiseman (1990) have found that higher levels of teacher immediacy increased affect and positive attitudes for white, Asian, Hispanic, and African American students. Although all types of students responded positively to immediate teachers, Hispanic students had the most positive responses to instructional immediacy. In a recent study by Comstock, Rowell, and Bowers (1995), a high-immediacy condition produced more affective learning than a low-immediacy condition; students in a moderately high immediacy condition reported more motivation, more positive attitudes toward the course content, and more positive attitudes toward the teacher than did students in a low-immediacy condition (Comstock et al., 1995). Interestingly, a *very* high immediacy condition resulted in slightly less affective learning than the *moderately* high immediacy condition, suggesting that teachers can be too immediate.

Even when a lecture is televised, the more immediacy the lecturer exhibits has been shown to increase liking for a course by 22 percent (Andersen & Withrow, 1981) and to enhance students' perceptions of the teacher as likeable and trustworthy and of the course as interesting and valuable (Guerrero & Miller, 1996). These highly consistent findings show that a teacher's immediacy level is one of the main reasons why students like a class, a teacher, or a subject. Why is immediacy so highly associated with affective learning? Frymier (1994) shows that nonverbal immediacy promotes positive affect and increases student motivation, which in turn increases student learning (Frymier, 1994).

Studies have even shown that increasing immediacy in only a single nonverbal channel produces a significant improvement in student affect. In an experimental study on teacher-student conferences, teachers either touched students on the arm at the beginning and at the end of the conference or did not touch students at all. Students rated the conferences much more positively in the touch condition than in the no-touch condition; in fact, touch accounted for almost a 25 percent increase in students' conference evaluation scores (Steward & Lupfer, 1987). In a similar study, subjects were divided into two groups. In one group's meetings with a teacher, a desk was placed between the interactants; in the other group's meetings, there was no desk blocking the teacher from the student. The result was that the students in the no-desk situation rated the teacher much higher than did the students in the other group (Zweigenhaft, 1976).

Most importantly, teachers can be trained to be more immediate and, as a result, produce more positive student affect. Richmond, McCroskey, Plax, and Kearney (1986) compared teachers with immediacy training to teachers with no such training and discovered that students had more positive affect toward the teachers who had been trained to be nonverbally immediate.

BEHAVIORAL COMMITMENT

Students with more positive affect become more committed students. Studies have shown that students are more likely to become motivated, committed, longtime learners as their positive affect for a class or instruction increases. As Andersen and Andersen (1987) stated:

> Warm, affiliative teachers are likely to produce lifelong learners. Students under the tutelage of "nice" teachers are more likely to engage in continued reading and studying after the homework is done and the school year is ended. Teachers who engage in affiliative behavior motivate self-initiated work by students and create a desire for further coursework in the subject area. (p. 58)

Studies have actually shown that in classes with immediate teachers, students substantially increase their likelihood of continued reading in that area, enroll in future classes as opposed to dropping out, and engage in behaviors recommended by the teacher (Andersen, 1979; Andersen, Norton, & Nussbaum, 1981; Beck & Lambert, 1977; Comstock et al., 1995; Gorham, 1988; Richmond et al., 1986). Comstock et al. (1995) have demonstrated that—as with affective learning—*very* high immediacy is slightly less effective than moderately high immediacy in producing behavioral commitment.

PERCEIVED COGNITIVE LEARNING

Research shows that students are more likely to enjoy school and become committed students if they have immediate, affiliative teachers. But do they learn more? A series of studies has shown that students certainly believe they learn more from immediate and affiliative teachers. Over four decades ago, Harrington (1955) reported that parents believed kindergarten teachers were more effective if the teachers smiled more. A study by Powell and Harville (1990) showed that increased teacher immediacy generally improved teacher clarity or the degree to which teachers avoided ambiguous and unclear messages. This finding varied across different ethnic groups, but the effect was highly positive for white students and even more powerful for Latino and Asian American students. Similarly, Sanders and Wiseman (1990) found that perceived cognitive learning was increased by immediate teachers for white, Asian, Hispanic, and African American students. Studies show that students report they learn up to 50 percent more from immediate teachers than from nonimmediate ones (Giglio & Lustig, 1987; Gorham, 1988; Gorham & Christofel, 1988; Gorham & Azkahi, 1990; Richmond, Gorham, & McCroskey, 1987). The most important immediacy behaviors that correlate with increased perceived learning are vocal expressiveness, smiling at the class, relaxed body positions, looking at the class, and moving around the classroom (Richmond, Gorham, & McCroskey, 1987).

ACTUAL COGNITIVE LEARNING

Studies certainly show that students *think* they learn more from immediate teachers, but do they really learn more? A number of studies show that students do learn more from immediate teachers, but other studies have failed to find a statistically significant relationship. Early studies showed that some immediacy behaviors did increase student learning. For example, lecturer eye contact with students increased student comprehension (Breed, Christiansen, & Larson, 1972); speaker dynamism increased information recall by students (Coats & Smidchens, 1966); lectures accompanied by gestures improved listening comprehension (Gauger, 1952); proximity, smiling, and touch in one-on-one counseling increased learning (Kleinfeld, 1974); and positive rather than negative kinesics increased learning but only if the teacher was female (Esp, 1978). Steward and Lupfer (1987) reported a small but significant increase in examination scores for students who had received touch rather than those who had not been touched by their instructors.

Unfortunately, a number of studies using measures of immediacy have failed to find increases in short-term cognitive learning (Andersen, 1979; Andersen & Withrow, 1981; Giglio & Lustig, 1987). All of these studies used multiple-choice tests to measure short-term learning of course content. Perhaps other factors, such as study time and reading ability, wipe out the effects of teacher immediacy on objective test measures. Medley and Mitzel (1958) reported no long-term differences in intellectual growth between students who had warm teachers and those who had cold teachers.

Nevertheless, studies have shown that actual student learning may be associated with teacher immediacy. Christiansen (1960) found a positive relationship between teacher warmth and both vocabulary and arithmetic achievement in grade school children. McDowell, McDowell, Hyendahl, and Steil (1980) reported a small but significant increase in cognitive learning in high school students taught by more immediate teachers. The strongest evidence for an immediacy–cognitive-learning relationship is provided by Kelley and Gorham (1988), who report that eye contact and physical immediacy produced a nearly 20 percent increase in college students' short-term recall. Other, more recent and compelling evidence for a positive relationship between teacher immediacy and learning is provided by Comstock et al. (1995), who report that a lecturer moderately high in immediacy produced more retention of material than a low-immediacy lecturer. However, a *very* high immediacy condition resulted in less learning than the moderately high immediacy condition, suggesting that a lecturer can be *too* immediate. Still, the very high immediacy condition produced significantly more cognitive learning than the low-immediacy condition. This suggests that lecturers and teachers should strive to be highly immediate; erring in the direction of very high immediacy is still far better than erring in the direction of low immediacy.

The pattern of findings is somewhat less consistent for the immediacy–cognitive-learning relationship than for the relationship between immediacy and affective learning, behavioral commitment, and perceived learning. Nonetheless, none of the studies suggest that immediacy reduces cognitive learning, and a number of studies now show that actual cognitive learning increases in response to increased immediacy.

Institutional Effects

Institutional communication in organizations, on the job, or in customer–service-provider encounters differs somewhat from communication in interpersonal relationships. Institutional communication—which involves interactions between such people as doctor and patient, subordinate and superior, or police officer and citizen—is less spontaneous and more rule-governed. Nonetheless, research has shown that nonverbal immediacy has positive benefits even in impersonal institutional encounters. Recall the Fisher et al. (1976) study, which found that subtle touch from librarians improved students' attitudes toward librarians and the library in general. Research on immediacy in organizational communication by Koermer, Goldstein, and Fortson (1993) found that "supervisors who were communicatively immediate left subordinates with the impression that supervisors respected them, encouraged more input, valued their work, and wanted to get to know them professionally" (p. 277). Supervisors who were nonimmediate caused subordinates to feel betrayed, to feel like outcasts, and to regard work as a waste of time. As we will learn in Chapter 12, immediacy cues from supervisors and other powerful people serve as particularly effective motivators.

Druckman, Rozelle, and Baxter (1982) report a series of studies that showed that more-immediate behavior was beneficial even in police-citizen encounters. In the positive nonverbal condition, police were trained to employ relaxed postures, friendly facial expressions, head nods, and eye contact—all immediacy behaviors. The authors concluded:

> Results supported predictions that positive verbal and nonverbal encoding conditions would lead to more favorable ratings on interpersonal and job-related qualities of the police officer than would be the case for the standard presentation. In addition, nonverbal behaviors accounted for a greater proportion of the variance in the obtained ratings than did verbal behaviors. (p. 102)

In health-care settings, immediacy has several benefits. Several studies report a strong positive correlation between physician affiliativeness or immediacy and patient satisfaction (Conlee, Olvera, & Vagim, 1993; Street & Buller, 1988). Similarly, Harrigan, Oxman, and Rosenthal (1985) found that patient-doctor rapport was much higher when doctors used immediacy behaviors, including uncrossed legs, a body position directly facing the patient, symmetrical arms, and closer interpersonal distances. Even a doctor's tone of voice has been related to successful treatment of alcoholism, showing that a physician's nonverbal behavior is not trivial. Patients were likely to seek treatment if the doctor's voice was low in anger and high in anxiety or concern (Milmoe, Rosenthal, Blane, Chafetz, & Wolf, 1979). Burgoon and Saine (1978) summarized several studies that have shown psychiatrists and nurses to have the most rapport with patients when their upper bodies were in positions that mirrored their patients' upper-body positions. Similarly, Ziegler-Kratz and Marshall (1990) reported that potential clients were more likely to seek counseling from a therapist who smiled more or used more eye contact than from a less-immediate therapist. Only recently has the medical community realized the power of communication in patient satisfaction, patient compliance, and healing. Hopefully, immediacy training will become a standard part of the education of all health professionals.

Summary

One of the most central functions of nonverbal communication is the communication of immediacy. Immediacy behaviors signal availability and inclusion, communicate approach and involvement, increase sensory stimulation, and send messages of warmth and positive affect. In some, less positive relationships, immediacy behaviors are perceived as threatening and suffocating, but in most relationships they are perceived (and intended) as warm, positive behaviors that promote interpersonal closeness. Immediacy is usually a mindless, positive expression of warmth and involvement with another person, although it is sometimes displayed strategically.

We communicate immediacy primarily through a multichanneled set of nonverbal codes, including (1) oculesics, through gaze, eye contact, and even pupil dilation; (2) proxemics, by way of closer interpersonal distances, communicating on the same physical plane, orienting one's body toward one's partner, and forward leaning; (3) haptics, via various types of increased touch appropriate to one's relationship; (4) kinesics, by employing positive facial expressions, especially smiles, as well as head nods, bodily relaxation, gestures, body synchrony, a light and happy gait, and more-open body positions; (5) vocalics, by varying the pitch, amplitude, duration, and tempo of the voice, by maintaining vocal synchrony with others, and, in some relationships, by using baby talk; and (6) chronemics, by spending time with another person and being punctual.

Several factors affect the amount of immediacy expressed between interactants. (1) *The relationship:* Close, positive relationships generally produce the most immediacy, although stable, long-term relationships often require less immediacy than developing ones. (2) *Individual differences:* A number of communication predispositions or personality traits cause some people to show immediacy more overtly than others. Likewise, gender and cultural background have an impact on the amount of immediacy individuals display. (3) *The situation:* Some settings are more conducive to immediacy expression than others. (4) *Temporary states:* Moods and physical states determine the level of immediacy a person feels like expressing.

The direct-effects model holds that immediacy generally is perceived as a warm, friendly, intimate, and attractive behavior. According to the social-meaning model, a similar model of immediacy, many nonverbal behaviors, including immediacy behaviors, have such a clear social meaning that most interactants react to them the same way across most relationships. Considerable support exists for these models.

Immediacy has positive interpersonal effects including increased attraction for the person expressing immediacy, the maintenance of close relationships, sexual attraction and involvement, and improved marital satisfaction. Similarly, in the classroom, students show substantially increased affective and behavioral learning and some increase in cognitive learning from more-immediate teachers. Finally, in organizational communication, immediacy has numerous positive effects, even in impersonal encounters.

9
Nonverbal Communication in Intimate Relationships

I̶N A. A. MILNE's (1957) intimate tale of friendship, Christopher Robin asks:

> "What do you like doing best in the world, Pooh?" "Well," said Pooh, "what I like best—" and then he had to stop and think. Because although Eating Honey *was* a very good thing to do, there was a moment just before you began to eat it which was better than when you were, but he didn't know what it was called. And then he thought that being with Christopher Robin was a very good thing to do, and having Piglet near was a very friendly thing to have. (pp. 306–307)

Intimate, close relationships are as important as any aspect of one's life. In a chapter entitled "The Bright Side of Relational Communication," Andersen and Guerrero (1998a) state:

> Almost without exception, our relationships with friends and loved ones are the cornerstone of our lives and our emotional well-being. The warm feelings of an intimate conversation, a reassuring hug, seeing a close friend after a long absence, or sharing joy with one's family are experiences each of us has had. Indeed, the brightest side of life's experiences often occurs in close intimate relationships during the exchange of warm involving immediate messages. (p. 303)

It is through our relationships with friends, family, romantic partners, and spouses that we truly experience intimacy. Close, intimate relationships enhance our lives, provide satisfaction, promote health, create security, and engender some of the most positive emotions humans can experience.

The Dimensions of Intimacy

Intimacy is a broad term that references warm, involving behaviors, interactions, experiences, and relations. Other terms that suggest intimacy include *love, warmth, closeness, support, bonding, sexuality, attachment, immediacy, involvement, confirmation, validation,* and *friendship* (Andersen & Guerrero, 1998a; Praeger, 1995). But intimacy can be any or all of these. In fact, intimacy—the expression of a truly close relationship—lies at the intersection of these concepts. So, if one of these other terms helps you understand close relationships better than the term *intimacy,* go with it. *Intimacy,* however, is the central term used here to refer to close relationships because it encapsulates what it means to have a unique, high-quality relationship with another person.

Intimacy has been conceptualized as the "proverbial elephant" by Acitelli and Duck (1987), who describe intimacy researchers as a group of blind people who feel the same elephant but reach dramatically different conclusions about the shape of the beast. Intimacy is multifaceted; it entails dimensions of behavior, interaction, ideology, emotion, and relationships. Because intimacy *must* be communicated, our discussion begins with communication behaviors that convey intimacy in interpersonal interaction.

Intimacy As Communication Behavior

Intimate behaviors are typically called immediacy behaviors (Andersen, 1989, 1998); intimate behaviors signal warmth, availability for interaction, and relational closeness. In Chapter 8 we discussed how actions such as eye contact, smiling, touch, and interpersonal space communicate immediacy, so we won't repeat that discussion here. It is clear that *immediacy behaviors are the foundations by which intimate interactions and intimate relationships are created and sustained.* It is nonverbal communication in particular that creates intimacy. Andersen (1989) states:

> Nonverbal communication is the primary means of relational communication. The multichannelled nature of nonverbal communication, its spontaneity, its phylogenetic and ontogenetic primacy, and the difficulty in concealing or controlling nonverbal cues, may be reasons why it has such heavy relational impact. (p. 5)

Writing about intimacy, Montgomery (1988) states, "As sure as intimacy is the goal of this search, communication is its method. For it is through verbally and nonverbally sharing, disclosing, revealing, and expressing themselves that two people become intimate" (p. 347).

Research shows that nonverbal communication is the primary means of establishing and maintaining an intimate relationship. In their classic book,

Intimate interactions among close friends are characterized by unique nonverbal behaviors. What signs of intimacy are displayed by this group of close friends?

Watzlawick, Beavin, and Jackson (1967) show that verbal and other forms of digital communication are far less important than nonverbal communication: "Wherever relationship is the central issue of communication, we find that digital language is almost meaningless" (p. 63). In Chapter 1 we learned that nonverbal communication is at least as important as verbal communication. For relational communication, however, nonverbal communication is certainly *more* important. This is not to suggest that some forms of verbal communication, such as self-disclosure (revealing private information about oneself), are irrelevant to relational closeness and intimacy. Indeed, scholars have long recognized that self-disclosure is a key component of relational closeness and intimacy (see Hatfield, 1984). However, Montgomery's (1988) review of the relationship literature shows that "the nonverbal mode of expression appears to be more closely linked to relationship quality than the verbal mode" (p. 348).

Research indicates that certain kinds of nonverbal behavior are vital to the communication of intimacy and the establishment of relational closeness. Certainly, the immediacy behaviors discussed in Chapter 8 (including eye contact, touch, smiles, and close interpersonal distances) are essential to intimate communication and relational closeness, but immediate communication is also important in nonintimate relationships, with strangers, acquaintances, classmates, coworkers, and customers. So, although immediacy is essential to intimacy, it is not enough. Intimacy and relational closeness are communicated when immediacy behaviors are *sustained* and *prolonged*. Research by Register and Henley (1992) shows that nonverbal behavior, in general, defines intimacy but that three particular kinds of nonverbal behavior are especially important to intimacy: prolonged time spent together, lingering gazes, and sustained touch. Other research has shown that total time spent with a relational partner is a vital part of relational satisfaction in marital and dating relationships (Egland, Stelzner, Andersen, & Spitzberg, 1997). Although gaze is an important nonverbal behavior, it is prolonged gaze that signals intimacy (Patterson, 1983). It is the sustained communication of immediacy that distinguishes the intimate relationship from one that is just mildly positive or socially polite.

Similarly, sustaining immediacy across many interactions and situations seems to be essential for relational intimacy to occur. Being immediate one moment and cold and aloof the next is not a recipe for intimacy. As Miller, Cody, and McLaughlin (1994) state:

> It is very likely that high intimacy not only reflects a particular set of qualities of the relationship (emotional attachment and so on) but also reflects a greater number of shared situations; nonintimates communicate in a limited range of events while intimates experience more situations together as well as a wider range of them. (p. 183)

This, of course, does not mean that intimacy requires people to share every one of life's moments. In fact, some breathing space is necessary to help intimacy thrive and keep the relationship exciting. It does mean, however, that intimate behavior occurs across many diverse situations in which nonverbal immediacy is high.

Relational closeness and intimacy also seem to rely particularly on one nonverbal behavior, touch. As Morris (1971) notes in his classic book *Intimate Behavior*, "To be intimate means to be close, and I must make clear at the outset that I am treating this literally. In my terms, then, the act of intimacy occurs whenever two individuals come into bodily contact" (p. 9). Johnson and Edwards (1991) supported this position when they found that increasingly intimate touch was the major indicator of relational commitment. In all relationships—between parents and offspring, grandparents and grandchildren, close friends, teammates, sorority sisters, siblings, lovers, and married couples—touch is a vital part of communicating intimacy.

In summary, intimate relationships require three elements of nonverbal behavior. First, intimate relationships require high levels of nonverbal involvement and immediacy beyond that which occurs in most relationships. Second, warm, immediate nonverbal behavior must be sustained over many interactions and

Intimacy is shown in many ways: through intimate feelings, behaviors, relationships, and interactions.

situations. Finally, the most important behaviors needed to establish an intimate relationship involve physical closeness, particularly touch.

Intimacy in Interactions

Of course, one person behaving intimately does not necessarily make for an intimate interaction. In fact, when people *unilaterally* move closer, smile, maintain eye contact, and/or touch their interaction partners, they may be perceived negatively—they may seem intrusive, overbearing, harassing, or even threatening—by their partners. In general, intimate interactions move slowly, with both partners gradually manifesting more immediacy, sharing more space and time, and lowering their defenses.

As we will see later in this chapter, building a relationship involves a complex series of moves and countermoves that gradually escalate the intimacy level and slowly build a truly intimate relationship. Relationships develop through a series of well-organized interactional moves. Most scholars have recognized that all social interaction is synchronously, rhythmically, and interactionally organized (Burgoon, Stern, & Dillman, 1995; Cappella, 1981, 1991b). Burgoon et al. (1995) maintain that social interaction "entails regular *patterns* of behavior in which each interactant's behavior influences the other's behavior. The dyad rather than single individuals, and dynamic rather than static behaviors, are at the heart of synchrony" (p. 19). All interactants, especially intimate interactants, must synchronize and coordinate their communication behaviors to achieve good "vibes" and to be on the same "wavelength."

Although most of these synchronous patterns are reciprocal, some are not. Some are complementary: one person gives a back rub, and the other receives it; one person discloses, and the other listens and nods attentively. More often, though, synchronous nonverbal behaviors are reciprocal: for example, two lovers caressing one another while gazing into each other's eyes (Praeger, 1995).

One problem with conceptualizing intimacy as an interactive concept is that both parties in an interaction have unique and separate points of view (see Acitelli & Duck, 1987; Praeger, 1995). One person may find an interaction highly intimate, whereas the partner may find it only mildly intimate or not intimate at all. Partners have different cognitive schemata (social knowledge structures) for the relationship (Andersen, 1993a), and in their minds they may even have two distinct psychological relationships (Acitelli & Duck, 1987).

Although different psychological relationships and perspectives exist in all intimate interactions, it has been widely noted that males and females have different notions of intimacy (for more on gender differences and similarities see Chapter 5). Traditionally, males find intimacy in recreational and task-related activities whereas females find intimacy in sharing time with others and communicating with others verbally and nonverbally (Helgeson, Shaver, & Dyer, 1987; Monsour, 1992). Research, however, has shown more similarity than difference in males' and females' perceptions of intimacy in both same-sex and opposite-sex relationships (Monsour, 1992; Parks & Floyd, 1996). Burleson, Kunkel, Samter, and Werking (1996) found that males rated instrumental or task skills as more important than did females in close relationships, whereas females rated affective, or emotional, skills as more important than did males; however, both males and females overwhelmingly viewed affectively oriented skills as more relationally important than instrumental skills. Moreover, Burleson et al. found that "affectively oriented communication skills appear to be important for both genders in the conduct of intimacy—regardless of whether intimacy is realized in same-sex friendship or opposite-sex romances" (p. 218). Because nonverbal communication is the most important part of affective messages, nonverbal skills are a vital part of intimate interaction.

This, of course, does not mean that in any given interaction both parties will evaluate the interaction as equally intimate. Although intimacy is created in interaction, it exists in the minds of individuals. For this reason, I subscribe to the position taken by Acitelli and Duck (1987): "The question is whether intimacy is a quality of persons or interactions. Rather than decide between them, we opt for an amalgamation of the two—Intimacy can be a property of persons and interaction" (p. 298).

Intimacy As an Ideology

Throughout history, a set of beliefs have evolved that make intimacy an important value. This "ideology of intimacy" sugggests that life is incomplete without friends, mates, parents, and even children. Historically, we have been persuaded that intimate bonds and attendant feelings of intimacy are a basic need. McAdams (1988) has suggested that as individuals, we have an intimacy motive, "a recurrent preference or readiness for experiences of warm, close, communicative interchanges with others" (p. 19). Intimacy has come to be perceived as an end in itself, not as a means to an end. In recent decades, intimacy has even increased in importance! Bookstores are glutted with how-to manuals on intimate relationships; internet chat lines are used primarily for personal, intimate conversations; and card companies have institutionalized the mandatory celebration of mother's day, father's day, grandparents' day, and so on.

Of course, when basic, individual needs are not being met, such as our need for food or shelter, intimacy doesn't seem very salient (Maslow, 1968). But in today's developed world, most of our "basic" needs have been met, yet many people feel a longing for something less tangible. Loneliness, separation, alienation, stress, and uneasiness characterize our times. People are searching for meaning. Although we come in contact with more people now than ever before in the history of humankind, our relationships have not necessarily become more intimate. Some would even say that relationships today are less intimate than ever before in spite of the high value society places on intimacy.

For several decades, society has been preoccupied with this "ideology of intimacy," which is described in some detail by Sennett (1977) and extended to communication by Parks (1982). Montgomery (1988) contends that "by the late 1970's people were placing more importance on interpersonal sources of happiness like being close to their children, 'really' getting to know their friends and having meaningful relationships" (p. 347). Having met our material needs, we have begun a quest for intimacy. Sennett (1977) suggests:

> The reigning belief is that closeness between persons is a moral good. The reigning aspiration today is to develop individual personality through the experience of closeness and warmth with others. The reigning myth today is that the evils of society can all be understood as evils of impersonality, alienation, and coldness. The sum of these three is an ideology of intimacy. (p. 259)

Today, most of us subscribe to this ideology. We recognize that having acquaintances, friends, and lovers is a good thing—and the more the merrier. Most authors and professors (including myself) subscribe to this ideology to a greater or lesser degree. Parks (1982) suggests that the appeal of the ideology of intimacy "flows from larger critiques which decry the loss of feeling and the decline of community in modern life. Popular images of people hungry for close, meaningful relationships and of communities fragmented by rapid change and excessive mobility are not new" (p. 85). Parks warns that other values such as privacy, nonintimate relationships, and information control may be lost and that individuals may be propelled into an unending and ultimately unsatisfying quest for intimacy. Paradoxically, effortful striving for intimacy may prevent us from ever finding it—or at least finding it satisfying (more on this later).

Of course, nonintimate relationships, including those between business associates and casual friends, can be very satisfying. However, Spitzberg and Cupach (1994) point out that an ideological assumption is that only closer relationships are valuable.

> Relationships are considered "on track" if they are progressing toward intimacy and togetherness and are disintegrating, decaying, dissipating, declining, dissolving, or dying if they are moving away from intimacy. Yet as the chapters on the dark side have argued, closeness often breeds undue influence, loss of identity, loss of privacy, frustration of individual goals and personal projects, and the possibilities of great psychological and physical harm. (p. 317)

There is, indeed, a dark side to intimate relationships. After all, most violence, including most murders, occurs within the confines of intimate relationships (see Marshall, 1994).

We strive today for more intimacy, yet our busy lives often preclude it. We are suffering from information overload, and our lives are "saturated." In Gergen's (1991) landmark book *The Saturated Self,* he discusses the geographically, interpersonally, and socially fragmented situation of the postmodern age. The multiple selves, fragmented lives, and busy schedules of postmodern humans prevent any "true" intimacy:

> In the context of social situation, one can see why both intimacy and commitment are vanishing from relationships. This began when commitment concepts of the person were ended by modernism. In the romantic period one could build a life around "true love" or "a powerful passion." With the advent of modernism, expressions of mysterious depths began to appear to be dubious. . . . Nowadays, to tell a romantic partner, "It is your soul I thirst" or "My passion is all consuming," might send him or her into a quick retreat. (pp. 175–179)

Although human contact may be increasing dramatically, our intimacy needs are unmet. We may not even know how to achieve intimacy. Moreover, although intimacy is our quest, true intimacy may frighten us.

Intimacy As an Emotion

In our quest for the experience of intimacy, we may think intimate thoughts and feel intimate emotions (Praeger, 1995). Traditionally, intimacy has been conceptualized cognitively as an ideology. Recently, however, scholars have begun conceptualizing intimacy as an emotion.

Reflect for a moment on an intimate interaction: a hug from an old friend or sharing time with family during the holidays. Tune in to your feelings. The emotion of intimacy you may be experiencing is often described as warmth. Andersen and Guerrero (1998a) have suggested that intimacy, or warmth, is a basic emotion. Although it is not listed in most studies as a basic emotion, it may be that English has no word with which to describe the nonverbal, ineffable feeling of intimacy that Andersen and Guerrero call interpersonal *warmth*. The Danish word *hugge* and the German *gemütlichkeit* come the closest in capturing the warm, pleasant, amiable, cozy feelings that are experienced in close relationships.

Most definitions of intimacy include feelings of warmth as a central component. Sternberg's (1986, 1988) theory of love employs three thermal metaphors: *hot* for passion, *cool* for commitment, and *warm* for intimacy. Warmth is the metaphor employed to describe feelings of intimacy, attachment, commitment, validation, closeness, and involvement. Scholars have recognized that intimacy has a distinct emotional component. Acitelli and Duck (1987) recognize that love and intimacy can be located in both thoughts and emotions. In her book on intimacy, Praeger (1995) recognizes the centrality of intimacy as an emotion. It is primarily nonverbal behavior during intimate interaction that generates these warm feelings, although verbal behaviors also play a role. Patterson's (1983) review of research demonstrates that the quality of emotions or affect in close relationships is the result of nonverbal involvement, particularly touch communication, such as kissing, hugging, and holding hands. Intimate, warm feelings can emotionally be experienced only through immediate interpersonal communication in positive situations with relationally significant others.

Intimacy in Relationships

Intimate relationships result from many episodes of warm, immediate interactions. As Praeger (1995) maintains, "At the simplest level, an intimate relationship is one in which intimate interactions occur on a regular and predictable basis" (p. 23). Perhaps the most essential quality of intimate relationships is that each one is unique. Although many of our role relationships (for example, our interactions with supermarket clerks, bank tellers, or fellow citizens) are nonunique and replaceable, intimate relations are difficult, if not impossible, to replace. Hendrick and Hendrick (1992) contend that intimacy "is characterized by genuineness and an absence of formal 'role' relationships" (p. 166). In intimate relationships, a unique pattern of nonverbal behavior develops. Special experiences are shared, and relational intimacy both enhances those experiences and is enhanced by them. More time and higher-quality time is spent together, creating a chronemic bond. Space—work space, home space, and conversational space—is also shared in distinct ways, creating proxemic intimacy. Touch that would be offensive in role relationships is encouraged in intimate relationships, creating a special haptic bond. Intimate interactants display unique, implicit facial expressions whose meanings are clear only to each other. Interaction rhythms begin to merge.

Intimacy is the essence of friendship (Perlman & Fehr, 1987). Friendships are characterized by deep, intimate interconnections (Walster, Walster, & Berscheid, 1978) that are emotional, cognitive, and behavioral. Intimate relationships, including friendships, also involve a powerful, unspoken nonverbal comfortableness and unpretentiousness. Activities, schedules, and movements are highly synchronized and have pleasing, comfortable rhythms to them (see Chapter 8).

Intimate relationships have a history; they often develop slowly over time as trust, warmth and synchrony build. But they also have a future. We expect our intimate relationships to play an important role in our lives for years to come; we want our intimate partners to be lifelong friends who will support us and comfort us, as well as engage us in talk and activity. When intimate relationships end through conflict, geographic separation, or death, we usually feel a deep loss, in part because the termination of a relationship robs our future of happy, intimate interactions with a treasured partner.

A number of studies have shown that nonverbal behaviors are crucial for sustaining intimate relationships. One study by Noller (1980) reveals the importance of gaze behavior in marital relations: well-adjusted, intimate married couples spent less time looking at each other during negative messages than did poorly adjusted couples. This was true for speakers and listeners and suggests that although eye contact is generally positive, it is an intimate, deferent, nonconfrontational behavior to avert eye contact during conflict. Additionally, Noller (1980) reports that poorly adjusted couples tended to look more when speaking and less when listening than did well-adjusted couples, indicating that poorly adjusted couples are more dominant and less intimate (see Chapter 12 for more on the visual dominance ratio). Other research by Noller (1982) shows that well-adjusted couples sent more positive messages, fewer negative messages, and fewer discrepant messages (for example, positive visual behaviors accompanied by negative vocal behaviors) than did poorly adjusted couples. Similarly, several other studies have found that unhappily married couples sent and reciprocated more negative messages than did happily married couples (Fitzpatrick & Badzinski, 1985; Gottman, 1979).

Intimate relationships may be one of our greatest stress reducers, a source of much of our creative energy, and the basis of our important plans and goals. Think of losing the three most intimate relationships you have. Would any of your plans or projects seem very important without them? Probably not. Our very physical and psychological health depends on intimate relationships. Severely depressed people tend to have highly disrupted and negative intimate relationships (Segrin, 1998). It is likely that a lack of intimacy produces depression and that negative, depressed moods destroy feelings of intimacy. Such a negative spiral of depression and lack of intimacy can be difficult to break. Intimacy, however, has the ability to promote optimism and mental health and, consequently, lead to more intimacy.

In this section, we have examined five dimensions of intimacy: as a behavior, as a function of our closest interpersonal interactions, as an ideology, as an emotion, and as a key component of close relationships. Nonverbal immediacy cues are vital to intimacy. Immediacy behaviors that are prolonged and occur repeatedly over the course of a relationship both generate intimacy and result from intimacy. Touch is particularly indicative of intimacy. Intimacy cannot be achieved unilaterally; it must be interactionally reciprocal, held as a part of one's life philosophy, experienced emotionally, and sustained in an intimate interaction.

Verbal and Nonverbal Intimacy

Certainly, verbal behaviors can communicate intimacy. Verbal intimacy behaviors have been summarized by Andersen (in press; Andersen & Guerrero, 1998a). There are several types of verbal intimacy behaviors. *Positive interaction patterns,* in which both partners exert symmetrical or complementary patterns of control, are likely to result from and create close, intimate relationships (see Rogers & Millar, 1988). *Verbal immediacy behaviors,* including first-person plural pronouns (*we* versus *you* and *I*) and other linguistic devices, create relational bonds that help to establish and maintain interpersonal intimacy (Wiener & Mehrabian, 1968). *Self-disclosure* (such as telling your partner about your very personal fears and joys) is a primary means of communicating intimacy and escalating relational closeness (see Derlega, Metts, Petronio, & Margulis, 1993). *Personal forms of address* (for example, Tom as opposed to Mr. Knight or President Knight) have considerable relational significance (see King & Sereno, 1984). Finally, specific verbal *communication about the relationship* often enhances closeness and confirms relational commitment (for example, "I'm glad we're friends," or "I love you"). Despite these important verbal behaviors, it is nonverbal behaviors, with their greater authenticity, multichanneled redundancy, developmental primacy, and general spontaneity, that produce the greatest relational impact.

Cognitive-Valence Theory

How are intimate relationships formed? A number of theories of relationship formation and interpersonal adaptation exist (for summaries see Andersen & Andersen, 1984; Burgoon et al., 1995). Many of these theories have similar components, so we will not review them all here. One theory of intimacy we will focus

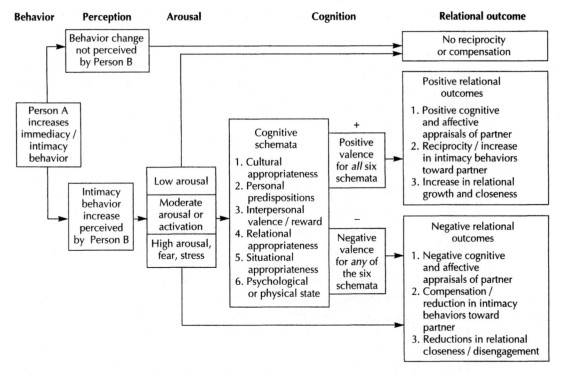

FIGURE 9.1   Cognitive-valence theory

on is *cognitive-valence theory,* a theory that describes and explains the process of intimacy exchange across a variety of relationships, including those between close colleagues, friends, intimate friends, romantic partners, married couples, and family members.

Relationships don't "just happen." They result from numerous positive interaction episodes. Intimate communication behavior is the primary vehicle for developing and increasing relational intimacy. All intimate relations begin with increases in immediacy, particularly nonverbal immediacy, by one of two partners. Of course, a person's immediacy behaviors must be perceived or noticed by her or his interaction partner to have any communicative significance. As the cognitive-valence model (Figure 9.1) indicates, Person B must detect a change in Person A's behavioral immediacy level. In other words, Person B must perceive that Person A's behavior is more intimate than usual. Reis and Shaver (1988) maintain that considerable research on perceptual filters has shown that expectations and schemata profoundly influence a partner's behavior. They also contend, "What matters for B's response is B's construal of A's expression" (p. 378). Perceived increases in intimacy behavior activate receivers physiologically, emotionally, and cognitively and also increase their arousal.

Arousal

Studies have examined the relationship between increases in immediacy communication and arousal. In his summary of twenty-four studies on the relationship between immediacy increases and arousal, Andersen (1985) concludes, "The research generally supports a positive relationship between immediacy increases and increases in arousal" (p. 15). Arousal increases as a function of increased gaze, close proxemic distances, more direct body orientation, greater spatial density and crowding, increased smiling, and more touch. Research by Andersen, Guerrero, Buller, and Jorgensen (1995) reveals that increases in multichanneled immediacy by one person significantly raise a partner's physiological arousal.

According to cognitive-valence theory, when one interactant perceives increased intimacy from another interactant, physiological arousal increases. Very large arousal increases, however, are inherently aversive and stressful and lead to withdrawal and even flight. For example, a stranger invading your space on a dark street would cause you to experience high arousal and, possibly, to flee. Many studies have shown that rapid arousal increases are unpleasant and aversive (see Berlyne, 1960; Cappella & Greene, 1982; Eysenck, 1967, 1976) and that the resulting reactions can occur without any conscious thought (Zajonc, 1980, 1984). By contrast, small arousal changes produce little behavioral change.

Most intimate messages produce moderate increases in arousal that activate cognitive schemata, or social knowledge structures (Brehm, 1985; Mandler, 1975). People store knowledge about a given message's cultural appropriateness, their interpersonal relationship with the interaction partner, their interpersonal valence (positive or negative attitude toward the partner) the situational appropriateness of the message, their present physical or emotional state, and their predisposition toward a particular type of communication. Cognitive-valence theory emphasizes that these cognitive schemata, or social knowledge structures, hold information about expected behavior. If the observed behavior fails to roughly match the expected behavior, the receiver will perceive the behavior as inappropriate, and negative relational outcomes will occur (see Figure 9.1). Six cognitive schemata are described here in detail.

Cognitive Schemata

Research has shown that six cognitive schemata work to determine the valence of an intimacy increase (see Andersen, 1993a, in press). Valence is a term borrowed from chemistry, which means a positive or negative change. Planalp (1985) suggests that relational schemata permit individuals to approach interactions with some sense of what behaviors are appropriate given the specific situation and relationship. The following review will describe six types of cognitive schemata that people employ to valence intimacy increases: cultural schemata, self-schemata, interpersonal schemata, relational schemata, situational schemata, and state schemata.

CULTURAL SCHEMATA

Other than our membership in the human race itself, culture is the most basic force that shapes human development. Culture is such a basic and invisible force that it is often confused with human nature itself (see Chapter 4 for a detailed account on the effects of culture on nonverbal communication). Hall (1976) argues that "there is not one aspect of human life that is not touched and altered by culture" (p. 16). Our cultural knowledge, or schemata, are so deeply ingrained in us that it is virtually impossible to think or behave transculturally.

Cultures differ dramatically in the degree to which they value and display intimacy (see Chapter 4). For example, contact cultures use small interaction distances and considerable interpersonal touch. Noncontact cultures use little or no touch and maintain greater interpersonal distances. As a result of these cultural differences, Americans may view Arabs as pushy and intrusive, and Asians may perceive almost every other culture as too touch-oriented. These cultural communication norms are so automatic and overlearned that when an individual violates these norms, the reaction is negative. Thus, culturally inappropriate immediacy behaviors are negatively valenced by interaction partners.

SELF-SCHEMATA

Self-schemata, or individual schemata, also influence our response to intimacy behaviors. Individuals differ greatly in personality and personal preferences for intimacy. Three groups of stable individual difference variables play a role in the intimacy-exchange process: (1) *personality traits or psychological predispositions* such as dogmatism, dominance, extroversion, and locus of control (whether a person is motivated by self or others); (2) *communication predispositions* such as communication apprehension, predispositions toward verbal behavior, shyness, and touch avoidance; and (3) *trait communication behavior,* or act frequencies (such as amount of eye contact or interpersonal distance) which are consistent, intraindividual patterns of interpersonal actions (Andersen, 1987). Like cultural schemata, self-schemata are used to judge the appropriateness of intimacy behaviors. When an interaction partner's intimacy behaviors are judged to be personally inappropriate, they will be negatively valenced by the receiver. A shy person, for example, might respond negatively to immediacy increases from friends or acquaintances, whereas an extrovert might respond positively to immediacy increases. As indicated in Chapter 7, traits such as communication apprehension and touch avoidance are likely to result in negative valencing of intimacy behaviors.

INTERPERSONAL SCHEMATA

During interpersonal interactions, we are quick to form impressions of other people. Considerable research shows that our perceptions about another person's qualities have dramatic effects on our valencing of intimacy behaviors. Compare these two extremes: being hugged by an unbathed, homeless person and being hugged by your regular dating partner. These personal perceptions, or schemata, represent what we call interpersonal valence (Garrison, Sullivan, & Pate, 1976), an umbrella term that encompasses aspects of credibility (Andersen & Clevenger, 1963; McCroskey, 1966), attraction (McCroskey & McCain, 1974), and homophily, or similarity (Andersen & Todd-Mancillas, 1978; Rogers & Shoemaker, 1971). Burgoon, Buller, and Woodall (1996) call these constructs "reward value." Credible, attractive, homophilous communicators are intrinsically "rewarding." It is important to distinguish reward value, or interpersonal valence, from the construct "relationship." Interpersonal valence is the evaluation of another person's qualities, not one's relationship with that person.

Interpersonal valence is a central construct in communication. Messages are not processed in a vacuum, they are always colored by evaluations of the source. Intimate actions are no exception. Our valencing of the *person* is critical to our evaluation of any attempt he or she makes to increase intimacy. If an immediacy behavior is displayed by a person with very low interpersonal valence, or low reward value, we will valence the immediacy behavior negatively.

RELATIONAL SCHEMATA AND RELATIONAL TRAJECTORIES

In relational communication, the focus is on the dyad, or relationship, rather than the self or the other. Relational schemata are different from interpersonal schemata (Andersen, 1993a; Baldwin, 1992). Chelune, Robinson, & Kommor (1984) maintain that in a relationship, the focus shifts from "you and me" to "us" and thus creates a new system with its own unique properties. Intimate partners develop a sense of "we-ness" and thus create a new metaperspective (Reis & Shaver, 1988). Relational schemata are the store of knowledge we have about our relationships with others as they exist now. For example, a person might say, "We were just acquaintances but now we're getting a lot closer" or "We are engaged."

Evidence suggests that at least two kinds of relational schemata exist: relational type (for example, friend, lover, coworker, spouse, and so on) and relational trajectory (the direction in which the relationship is going; Baxter, 1987). Relational trajectory is a very important kind of relational schemata because it is one's expectation of where the relationship should be heading. Should the relationship be escalating or de-escalating? Should the relationship be on a steady and stable course? Immediacy behaviors that fall along the anticipated trajectory of future intimacy are most likely to be positively valenced. Take, for example, touch. Imagine you are in a new relationship and you *really* like your dating partner, but so far you have only held hands. Because you want the relationship to become more intimate, you will have a positive response when your date holds you close, puts her or his arm around you, and is attentive to you, even at a large party. In other words, you will judge most positively those immediacy behaviors that fall along your preferred relational trajectory, not just those that are appropriate to your current relational state. The key to relational success is to anticipate your partner's desired relational trajectory and to behave accordingly. If your partner desires more space and less intimacy, the relationship will benefit from giving your partner that space. If your partner anticipates and desires more intimacy, your relationship will benefit from being more intimate.

Research shows the importance of relational schemata. Relational history has a powerful effect on the interpretation of specific actions (Altman & Taylor, 1973; Andersen, 1993a; Baldwin, 1992; Knapp, 1978). Relationships are comprised of nonverbal metamessages that have precedence over literal messages (Chelune et al., 1984). Relational attributions that transcend interpersonal or situational attributions color the interpretation of each message. Planalp (1985) contends that this cognitive background helps frame and interpret each message. She states, "Relational schemata, then, are coherent frameworks of relational knowledge that are used to derive relational implications of messages" (p. 9). One way that relational schemata operate is to create expectations about a relationship (Park & Waters, 1988). Researchers believe that deviations from these expectations are essential to our interpretation of particular behaviors. Chelune et al. (1984) suggest, "Discrepancies and/or consistencies between current perceived behavior and expectations derived from past behaviors become meaningful and make a statement (metacommunication) about the relationship between the interactants" (p. 25). King and Sereno (1984) maintain that in more-stable, long-term relationships, we are capable of recognizing deviations from prior patterns, suggesting that relational schemata are more vital to developed relationships.

Research shows the critical importance of relational schemata; they are the *most important* determinants of intimacy acceptance or rejection. Heslin and Alper (1983) have shown that reactions to touch are totally dependent on the nature of the relationship. In very close relationships, intimate touch is expected, comfortable, and pleasurable. In moderately close relationships, intimate touch is unexpected and uncomfortable. Among strangers, most touch is extremely uncomfortable, particularly intimate touch. Studies of touch in the nursing profession have revealed that nurses need to establish a good nurse-patient relationship before using expressive touch. By contrast, instrumental, task-oriented touch requires no such prior relationship (McCann & McKenna, 1993).

In a study of excessive intimacy, Andersen (1992a) asked subjects to describe a situation in which they perceived intimacy to be excessive and to explain why they perceived it to be excessive. Among the many reasons cited, 54 percent attributed their perception of excessive intimacy to the relationship, more than all the other schemata combined. Subjects reported that several nonverbal behaviors were inappropriate except in *very* intimate relationships, including several types of touch, prolonged eye gaze, and invasion of one's personal space. As Andersen (in press) concludes, "People overwhelmingly attribute the appropriateness of another individual's intimate behavior to the relationship, not to other qualities." Relational partners described behavior inappropriate to the relationship in the following ways: "I just didn't think it was right for my boss to touch me that way."

"I saw our relationship as a friendship, nothing more." "The relationship happened too quickly destroying any chance of 'chemistry.'" "Someone I barely knew shouldn't be standing so close." Indeed, in a study of sexual harassment, Wertin and Andersen (1996) found that behavior inappropriate to the relationship was the leading reason recipients perceived unwanted sexual attention as harassment. In the appropriate relational context, almost any immediacy behavior will be perceived positively. The wrong behavior for the relationship's current state or anticipated trajectory will be perceived as negative, excessive, and even harassing.

SITUATIONAL SCHEMATA

The situation, or the context, affects the meaning of every immediacy behavior. The expression "out of context" describes behaviors that are meaningless, difficult to interpret, or misleading. Close interpersonal distances and intimate touch might be appropriate behaviors for the bedroom or even the living room but not for the classroom or the boardroom. Behavior that is appropriate in private may be perceived as excessively intimate in public. Parents are often upset by their teenagers' public displays of affection because these behaviors seem inappropriate in the given context, or situation. Scholars have shown that contextual sensitivity is an essential component of communication competence (Goffman, 1959; Spitzberg & Cupach, 1989).

Some settings are associated with particular actions. Chelune et al. (1984) show that some physical settings are more conducive to intimacy than others. Situational schemata are stored in our memories, along with behaviors judged to be appropriate or inappropriate in a given setting. Acitelli and Duck (1987) believe that intimacy is both personal and situational. Perceptions of the appropriateness of intimacy by participants are critical, "particularly their judgments about the level of intimacy appropriate for a given situation or occasion" (p. 301). "A *situational schema* is structured, intuitive knowledge about one's current context as an instance of a general class of similar contexts" (Andersen, 1993a, p. 20). Familiar contexts are meaningful, and behaviors appropriate to those contexts are easy to determine. Unfamiliar contexts may produce anxiety, require lots of mental effort, and lead to inappropriate nonverbal behaviors. Intimacy inappropriate to a particular situation, like kissing a girlfriend in front of her parents, may be tolerated in close relationships, particularly if the violations are in the direction of the overall relational trajectory. In general, however, intimacy inappropriate to the situation will be negatively valenced.

STATE SCHEMATA

We all experience changing moods, psychological states, and physical conditions. Within a single day, we may feel tired, excited, bored, depressed, sexually stimulated, fearful, angry, and loving. Our thoughts and feelings related to being tired, happy, aroused, fearful, drunk, or sick are state schemata. Physical conditions, moods, and psychological states come and go. Like situations, states are transitory and temporary. States, however, represent intrapersonal, internal dispositions, whereas situations relate to external environments (for a more complete discussion see Andersen, 1988).

States can affect perceptions of intimacy. The most obvious example is the wife who says to her amorous husband, "Not tonight, dear, I have a headache." A fight with one's boss, an illness, a loss by one's favorite basketball team, stress in one's life, noisy children, a hangover, excitement over a new job, an endorphin rush after a run, hunger, and a host of other factors affect how we respond to a partner's nonverbal expressions of intimacy. In general, negative physical or psychological states result in negative reactions to intimacy. Canary and Cody (1993) describe an instance of a state reaction: "If Tracy has the flu, for example, she may not feel up to reciprocating Brad's interactional intimacy" (p. 207). On occasion, negative states may be consistent with positive intimacy behaviors. Massaging a partner's sports injury or holding a sick friend's hand may be perceived quite positively. In general, though, positive, energetic states are most conducive to positive reactions to intimacy.

Valence

As mentioned previously, valence is a chemistry term that refers to positive or negative charges. Relationships, like subatomic particles, can be either negative or positive. Cognitive-valence theory suggests that movement toward intimacy is possible only during positively valenced interaction. This movement toward intimacy is a precarious process: a negative valence in any one schema could arrest the process of intimacy development (see Figure 9.1). This is why Andersen (1989, in press) describes the process of intimacy development as "fragile." Burgoon et al. (1995) summarize how the valencing process works in cognitive-valence theory:

> Positively valenced arousal leads to reciprocity—or increased immediacy. If a *single negative* valence occurs during the valencing process (such as five positive valences and one negative), then the overall valence of the arousal is negative. Thus, negative valencing carries more weight than positive valencing. The negatively valenced arousal leads to compensation and withdrawal. (p. 108)

Thus, showing intimacy too soon in a relationship, violating a person's own preference levels for intimacy, or displaying intimacy in an inappropriate situation will result in negative valence and send the relationship into a negative spiral. Research has shown that negative relational information is weighted more heavily than positive information (Andersen, 1998; Kellerman, 1989). "Precariousness of close relationships is a result of several factors. Negative spirals can result from inappropriate behavior for *any* of the six cognitive schemata" (Andersen, 1998).

Relational Outcomes

Positively valenced intimacy will result in three positive relational outcomes. First, an interactant will experience more positive interpersonal valence toward her or his partner. Positive, appropriate, relational intimacy will create higher attraction levels, more interpersonal closeness, perceived intimacy, and overall reward value for one's partner. Second, positively valenced immediacy behaviors will be reciprocated. Thus, if a person receives an appropriate, positively valenced hug from a relational partner, he or she is likely to return the hug or increase the intimacy in other ways, say, with a kiss or a smile. Numerous studies have shown this reciprocity effect (for summaries see Andersen, 1985; Burgoon et al., 1995; Patterson, 1973a, 1976). Third, appropriate intimacy creates greater relational closeness, not just attraction for one's partner but a feeling of closeness, warmth, and intimacy. This starts a cycle in which positive interpersonal perceptions and a positive relationship lead to a positive valencing of increased behavioral immediacy, which, in turn, leads to increased positive feelings toward one's partner and to the relationship (Andersen, 1998). Relations are built on positive cycles of appropriate, receiver-oriented immediacy behaviors. Close, satisfying relationships are characterized by positive intimacy spirals.

Negatively valenced intimacy will result in three corresponding negative outcomes. First, negative cognitive and affective appraisals of one's partner result from negatively valenced behaviors. An interactant will respond negatively to a partner who is overbearing, shows too much intimacy in inappropriate situations, or shows intimacy prematurely in the relationship. Attraction to this person turns to repulsion. Reward value drops. Second, negatively valenced intimacy causes compensatory reactions, as shown in a whole host of theories (for summaries of research and theory see Andersen & Andersen, 1984; Burgoon et al., 1995). Too much intimacy—especially with the wrong person, at the wrong moment, or at the wrong stage of the relationship—causes the receiver to withdraw or even flee. Such withdrawals or compensatory reactions frequently promote more immediacy behaviors by the sender. Often, these compensatory immediacy behaviors are perceived as desperate attempts to increase intimacy and are met with another round of compensation and flight. When a partner withdraws or compensates, the only possible course of action that will help the relationship is a gradual withdrawal to restore a comfortable level of intimacy to the relationship. Otherwise, the downward spiral of hide and seek, withdraw and approach will continue. Third, inappropriate intimacy also decreases relational closeness. Savvy relational partners look for signs of relational claustrophobia in their partners and give them space. Sensitivity to excessive intimacy is a major predictor of relational success. As Gibran (1923) has said of marriage, "Let there be space in your togetherness . . . for the pillars of the temple stand apart and the oak tree and the cypress grow not in each other's shadow" (pp. 16–17).

Cognitive-valence theory is one way of conceptualizing or modeling relationships and their outcomes. The theory attempts to explain one of the most basic questions regarding human relationships: Why is intimacy appreciated and reciprocated in some instances and rebuffed and compensated in other occasions? The cognitive-valence process attempts to unite the research on immediacy behaviors, perception, physiological arousal, interpersonal cognition, and relational outcomes into a single, unified model of relational intimacy.

Paradoxes of Intimacy

Dialectic Theory

Successful relationships represent a balance between oppositional forces. Too much nonverbal immediacy, such as close interpersonal distances or touch, can cause claustrophobic reactions or interpersonal overload. Too little nonverbal immediacy can cause resentment, loss of closeness, and other relational ills. Dialectic theory has emerged as a way of understanding these oppositional and paradoxical forces.

Dialectics are contradictions, or paradoxes, that reinforce one another. Writing on dialectics, Rawlins (1992) says:

> These antagonistic yet interdependent aspects of communication among friends form the pulse of routine as well as volatile and transitional moments of such dyads . . . configurations of contradictions compose and organize friendships through an ongoing process of change across the life course. (pp. 7–8)

Dialectics are forces for change. They provide the energy by which relationships become more intimate. Likewise, dialectics provide the dynamic balance for relationship maintenance (Baxter, 1994). However, relational breakups also derive their energy from dialectic tension. As Andersen (1993a) has stated: "A primary reason that relationships are dynamic, nonlinear, and even turbulent is the nature of human dialectical cognition" (p. 9).

Human relations themselves are paradoxes. With each new relationship, we become more than we were. The opportunities for companionship, dialog, cooperation, sexuality, reproduction, friendship, support, and intimacy are possible only in interpersonal relationships. At the same time, however, we become less than we were. In relationships, we lose freedom, other relationships, and that precious commodity, time. Relationships can cost money, create risks, and result in emotional distress. Relationships are paradoxical.

Intimacy exists in a set of these dialectical tensions. The fragile nature of intimacy was described earlier in this chapter. Most of our relationships are transitory, impersonal, and nonintimate. Few of our relationships ever attain high intimacy levels. To understand how we attain, maintain, and successfully terminate our intimate relationships, we need to consider relational dialectics.

Although dozens of paradoxes pervade and perplex our relationships, scholars have focused on a set of dialectics with particular significance for intimate relations. We will examine four dialectics here: (1) autonomy-connection, (2) novelty-predictability, (3) openness-closedness, and (4) risk-reward. Although both verbal communication and nonverbal communication are important in managing relational dialectics, this section will focus on the sometimes subtle, but always important, nonverbal aspects of dialectics.

AUTONOMY-CONNECTION

The first and most fundamental relational dialectic has been variously called autonomy/connection (Baxter, 1988), integration/separation (Baxter, 1994), individualism/collectivism (Lustig & Andersen, 1990b), and freedom to be independent/freedom to be dependent (Rawlins, 1992). This dialectic suggests the contradiction between seeking intimacy and avoiding it. As Rawlins (1992) states:

> In forming a relationship, each friend grants the other a pair of contradictory prerogatives. The freedom to be independent is the liberty to pursue one's life interests without the friend's interference or help. In contrast, the freedom to be dependent is the privilege of calling on or relying on one's friend in times of need. Both liberties engender choices for self and other. Yet, exercising individual options of independent or dependent behavior also poses de facto contingencies restricting the other's choices. (p. 16)

Intimate relationships involve sacrifice of one's individuality. As Baxter (1993) states, "No relationship can exist unless the parties forsake individual autonomy. However, too much connection paradoxically destroys the relationship because the individual entities become lost" (p. 89).

The autonomy-connection dialectic manifests itself continuously through nonverbal behaviors. Sharing proxemic space is a sign of togetherness, bonding, and intimacy, but it is also constraining and inhibiting. Relationships can also suffer chronemically: too much time together may make a partner seem intrusive, boring, or inhibiting; however, too little time together may make a partner seem uncaring, and may prevent relational closeness and intimacy. The tension between autonomy and connection is also evident in the eye behavior of newly intimate couples, which is characterized by periods of contact and avoidance. When the connection through eye contact becomes uncomfortable, partners avert their eyes and autonomy is restored. Soon, however, the need to connect returns, and eye contact bonds the couple in nonverbal intimacy.

Research demonstrates the push and pull of autonomy versus connection by showing that nonverbal immediacy behavior varies across relational stages as couples become more and less connected. Studies show that touch increases significantly during the stages of serious dating and engagement (Figure 9.2). By contrast, married couples touch less the longer they are married (Emmers &

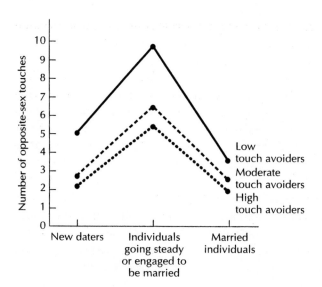

FIGURE 9.2 Effects of relational stage and touch avoidance on interpersonal touch (Guerrero & Andersen, 1991)

Dindia, 1995; Guerrero & Andersen, 1991). Married couples can show less tactile immediacy over the years because their relationship is so intimate.

Touch, however, does not equate with more intimacy. Emmers and Dindia (1995) report that touch increases along with intimacy up to a point, then as relationships become highly intimate touch decreases! Guerrero and Andersen (1994) have found that although the frequency of touch peaks at intermediate stages (during serious dating and engagement), partners match one another's touch more in stable, married relationships. They conclude that the reciprocity of touch behavior, rather than the frequency of touch, may be the key component predicting intimacy in marital relationships. As Guerrero and Andersen (1991) state, "touching may decrease in 'stable' relational stages, not from a loss of psychological intimacy or feelings of closeness but from a reduced need to continually communicate intimacy behaviorally" (p. 160). Sternberg (1986), in his triangular theory of love, discusses a similar process. According to Sternberg, relationships are characterized by both *manifest intimacy,* which is the physical intimacy that we show one another through behavioral displays (such as touching, smiling, and gazing), and *latent intimacy,* which is the psychological intimacy that we feel toward one another but cannot "see." Sternberg theorizes that in satisfying relationships, once the relationship is well established the manifest intimacy will drop off but the latent intimacy level will remain high or increase slightly. Paradoxically, couples may actually need less touch and more autonomy in their established relationships in order to avoid feeling "smothered."

Autonomy-connection is a relational tightrope act we all walk. Baxter (1993) reports that this dialectic is present in 88 percent of all relationships and particularly present in long-term relationships. As we will examine later in this chapter, several methods exist for coping with the fundamental relational dialectic of autonomy and connection.

NOVELTY-PREDICTABILITY

The second relational dialectic that affects intimate relationships is novelty-predictability. Our intimate friends must be predictable in a variety of ways. Loyalty, punctuality, concern for our welfare, reliability, and consistency are prerequisites to the experience of intimacy in a relationship. However, spontaneity, novelty, change, excitement, and adventure create more-attractive, more-interesting intimate relationships.

Theory and research have shown that in all relationships, but particularly in intimate relationships, partners are driven by the need for stability and certainty in their relational partner (Berger, 1988; Berger & Bradac, 1982). According to Baxter (1994), "conditions of intimacy are facilitated when partners have certainty and predictability about one another, their interactions together, and the state of their relationship" (p. 24).

However, research also shows that spontaneity and adventure are also valued. Learning theorists have shown that emotional deadening can result from excess repetition (Baxter, 1993). Sternberg (1988) maintains that "in order for love to survive there has to be some mystery—some degree of doubt about what will happen when" (p. 132).

Nonverbal behaviors are part and parcel of the novelty-predictability dialectic. Chronemic behavior, for example, can establish certainty and predictability, such as being available, being punctual, spending time together, and sharing important events. Conversely, surprises (such as parties, weekend trips, and so on) that break up and energize mundane, repetitive schedules are chronemically novel events. Although established patterns of proxemic and haptic behavior create trust, prevent feelings of sexual harassment, and provide certainty, on some occasions, surprises, sexual spontaneity, and intimate affection provide much-needed novelty in a relationship.

Research has shown that the novelty-predictability dialectic exists for over three-fourths of all relationships and over 80 percent of longer-term relationships (Baxter, 1993). Another study suggests that failure to introduce sufficient novelty can be a major problem in long-term relationships. Hill, Rubin, and Peplau (1976) report that the number one reason for terminating a dating relationship is boredom with the relationship.

OPENNESS-CLOSEDNESS

Another dialectic that is extraordinarily important in intimate relationships is openness-closedness. Openness is the foundation of many theories and models of relational development (Altman & Taylor, 1973; Berger & Bradac, 1982; Knapp, 1978). Presumably, unless one is nonverbally and verbally open, intimacy is impossible to develop. However, critiques of the "ideology of intimacy"(discussed earlier in the chapter) suggest that nonstrategic or insensitive openness is not a recipe for intimacy. Instead, sensitive, strategic, tactical behaviors that maximize the benefits of openness and minimize injury are advised.

Although openness has been equated frequently with verbal behaviors such as self-disclosure, nonverbal behaviors are crucial aspects of openness as well. Open body postures (Andersen, 1985; Morris, 1977) communicate openness, warmth, and intimacy, whereas folded arms, a covered face, and other barrier signals reduce intimacy and immediacy. Similarly, averting touch (see Chapter 7) and eye contact (see Chapter 2) are closed, inaccessible behaviors. Proxemic behaviors such as facing a person directly and maintaining appropriate interaction distances signal openness and lay the foundation for intimacy. Baxter and Montgomery (1996) maintain that behavioral openness includes "a variety of verbal and nonverbal signals that grant permission to explore specified aspects of the personal domain including behaviors such as appropriately timed eye contact, smiling, and other back-channel actions that say to the other person that he or she is being attended to" (p. 135). On the other hand, too much nonverbal openness, from inappropriate nudity to excessive eye contact, does not lay a sound foundation for intimacy.

Baxter (1993) has shown that 72 percent of relational partners report that the openness-closedness dialectic is present in their relationship. This is particularly true for new relationships. Because couples may simultaneously strive for privacy and self-control on the one hand and affiliation and connection on the other, it is not surprising that openness-closedness is an issue that must be dealt with in most intimate relationships.

RISK-REWARD

An old aphorism tells us, "It is better to have loved and lost than never to have loved at all." This optimistic view of relationships suggests that intimacy is unattainable without risk. The poet Gibran (1923) similarly advises, "when love beckons to you, follow him . . . even as he is for your growth so he is for your pruning" (p. 12). Although a partner's trust must be earned, all intimate relationships are ultimately a leap of faith. Holmes and Remple (1989) argue that "issues of trust have their origins in the dialectic between people's hopes and fears as close relationships develop" (p. 187). Wheeless (1978) has shown that trust is essential to relational involvement and interpersonal solidarity. However, trust and intimacy can be unwarranted and risky.

People often fail to trust others. Engaging in immediate nonverbal communication requires trust. In terms of proxemics, going to a new boyfriend's (or girlfriend's) house or apartment requires trust. Touch in new relationships requires a suspension of fear, particularly in the case of sexual touch. Chronemic intimacy requires giving up precious time and excluding other relational opportunities. Most violence, including assault, rape, and even murder, occurs in close, intimate relationships (Marshall, 1994). AIDS, depression, unwanted pregnancies, infidelity, and abuse are only a few of the risks people encounter in intimate relationships. People want the reward to outweigh the risk in intimate relationships. They secretly and strategically test relationships to establish a baseline of trust, fidelity, and loyalty before increasing relational intimacy (Baxter & Wilmot, 1984). Many of these tests include searches for nonverbal cues of deception (see Chapter 11). Relational tests include fidelity checks (such as spying and pushing the redial button on a partner's phone to see who he or she has been talking to) and testing to see if a partner will respond to one's emotional distress (Baxter & Wilmot, 1984; Guerrero, Andersen, Jorgensen, Spitzberg, & Eloy, 1995). Nonetheless, the risks involved with a new relationship may be part of the pleasure, the thrill of the hunt, the arousal of taking risks.

OTHER DIALECTICS

Certainly these aforementioned dialectics aren't the only tensions that exist in intimate relationships. Others include the ideal-real, instrumental-affectional, reciprocal-compensatory, and public-private dialectics (for the best summaries of relational dialectics see Baxter & Montgomery, 1996; Rawlins, 1992). Indeed, scholars have come to recognize that the potential number of relational contradictions is practically infinite (Billig, 1987; Baxter & Montgomery, 1996).

Managing Intimate Paradoxes

How do intimate partners cope with the paradoxes and contradictions present in all relationships? Scholars have found a number of ways—some functional, some dysfunctional—that people cope with intimate paradoxes.

CYCLICAL ALTERNATION

One way we cope with contradiction is to cycle between both dialectical poles to maintain balance. Couples will balance a period of autonomy with a period of connectedness. Openness will be followed by closedness for a time. Baxter (1993) discovered that cyclical alternation was the most common way of coping with the autonomy-connection dialectic and the second most common way to manage the novelty-predictability dialectic. One female respondent in Baxter's (1993) study reported cyclical alternation this way: "we kind of kept floundering around together . . . drifting towards each other and drifting apart again . . . kind of a cycle" (p. 97). These cycles appear to swing in a pendulumlike manner, alternating between autonomy-enhancing efforts and connection-enhancing efforts.

Nonverbal behaviors are critically important in cyclical alternation. Chronemic, proxemic, and haptic behaviors can create patterns of connection and autonomy. Whole clusters of immediacy behaviors signal periods of openness and closedness. Novelty and predictability can be established through touch or facial expressions. Indeed, it is quite normal, perhaps necessary, for relationships to experience cycles across all of the dialectics.

SEGMENTATION

Segmentation involves separating content or activity into distinct domains, appropriate to only one pole of a dialectic. Often, nonverbal behaviors are segmented to manage dialectical tension. For example, the junior-high student struggling with the autonomy-connection dialectic may let her parents kiss her good-bye at home but not at school. Similarly, some parents are very open with their children about politics or religion but completely closed about the "taboo" topics of drugs and sex. Some couples may decide that certain novel behaviors are okay in private but that predictable appropriateness is the only public face to show.

SELECTION

Selection is another method of coping with relational contradiction. In selection, partners perceive the coexistence of contradictions but transcend them by making one pole more dominant (Baxter, 1993). For example, recognizing that autonomy may threaten connection, partners may restrict each other's access to other people. Similarly, a couple may feel that it is more important to have a predictable, secure relationship than an exciting, novel relationship. Selection is a common strategy for coping with autonomy-connection, openness-closedness, and novelty-predictability (Baxter, 1993). Selection is most likely to be successful when both partners value the same side of the dialectic. If one partner values autonomy over connection and the other values connection over autonomy, selection is not a viable option.

UNITY OF OPPOSITES

Perhaps the best way to manage, even appreciate, relational dialectics is through understanding the unity of opposites (see Altman, Vinsel, & Brown, 1981; Hendrick & Hendrick, 1992). This is similar to the Chinese concept of yin (passive, yielding) and yang (dominant, active). Opposites are sustained by one another. Happiness is impossible without sadness; life exists only with death; and freedom couldn't even be a concept without oppression.

Without autonomy, connection would be logically impossible. Without closedness, openness would have no meaning. Relationships need to accept and even embrace paradox and change. It is, after all, separation that makes for a happy reunion or predictability that allows for novelty. Baxter (1988; Baxter & Montgomery, 1996) calls the unity of opposites a process of reframing and reaffirmation; it involves accepting that paradoxic polarities cannot be reconciled, and therefore must be appreciated. From this perspective, the tension is tolerated and the richness afforded by each polarity is celebrated. Moreover, the tensions are reframed so that they are viewed as complementary rather than contradictory. Allen et al. (1996) report that autonomy and connection, novelty and predictability, indeed, all the dialectical poles are correlated in interpersonal relationships. Moreover, each pole of each dialectic is correlated with relational satisfaction. This empirical existence suggests that dialectics are, indeed, unities of opposites.

How can these contradictions create intimacy through communication? One way is to recognize that they are compatible though contradictory. A couple in love, for example, may be separated proxemically and chronemically by distance and time, yet during this separation, the couple may exploit the advantages of autonomy. On the one hand, he might work overtime, watch football (which she hates), and go out with his buddies—unconstrained by the connections and commitments he experiences when she is with him. On the other hand, she may study harder than ever, go to extra dance classes, and read that novel she never has time for. Upon reuniting, they will likely celebrate their connection through all of the multichanneled interconnections of communication. They may hug and kiss, look into each other's eyes longingly, stay with each other for days, manifest their joy through facial expressions of happiness and excitement, and speak with intimate or enthusiastic paralanguage.

Intimacy cannot be found by emphasizing only one dialectical pole. Intimacy involves sharing warmth and togetherness as well as permitting separateness; it means being open and closed, taking risks and receiving rewards, being simultaneously predictable and novel. Intimacy is a process of celebrating change, understanding paradox, and showing closeness through rich multidimensional acts of warm, involving nonverbal communication.

DENIAL

Perhaps the least healthy way to cope with dialectical tension is through denial. Some partners refuse to recognize that their relationships go through any periods of risk, autonomy, or closedness. Baxter and Montgomery (1996) state, "Denial represents an effort to subvert, obscure and deny the presence of a contradiction by legitimizing only one dialectical pole to the virtual exclusion of the other poles" (p. 61). They add, "the denial response is destined to fail, the dominance of one opposing force creates an exigence for the neglected opposition" (p. 61).

Denying autonomy, for example, may propel one partner into a desperate quest for connection, thereby denying the other partner space or time apart. Like small children desperately holding their mothers and not accepting even temporary separation, friends and lovers who cling to their partners or restrict their interactions outside the relationship are viewed as immature, even pathetic. Autonomy should be viewed as a way to enhance connection, and risk as a means to making relational success even more rewarding.

DISORIENTATION

Another dysfunctional response to relational paradox is disorientation. This is a fatalistic response to contradictions, which are regarded as inevitable, negative, and unchangeable (Baxter & Montgomery, 1996). These attitudes often lead to pessimism, helplessness, and a failure to see any rewarding alternatives in one's life. Relational interactants may feel trapped in a pattern of behavior from which they can't escape. Couples who perpetuate dysfunctional cycles are typically experiencing disorientation in some form. Abusive relationships and many conflicted relationships suffer from disorientation. By nature, relationships entail paradox, and creatively dealing with these paradoxes is the only path to increased intimacy.

Summary

Intimacy is located in many places. It exists in immediacy behaviors, especially prolonged nonverbal immediacy that enhances intimate connection. It exists in intimate interactions, especially when intimacy is reciprocated. It exists as an ideology, a widespread belief in our culture that life is incomplete without experiencing intimacy. It exists as a warm, comforting emotion that we experience with intimate friends. Finally, it exists in and characterizes special, close relationships.

Cognitive-valence theory helps explain why intimacy develops—or fails to develop. Intimacy begins with immediacy behaviors that arouse or stimulate interaction partners. On the one hand, very high arousal levels are inherently unpleasant and lead to avoidance and negative valence. Moderate arousal levels, on the other hand, activate cognitive schemata that the receiver uses to assess the appropriateness of the immediacy behaviors. Increases in immediacy behaviors that are culturally, personally, interpersonally, relationally, situationally, and state appropriate lead to attraction, reciprocity, and increased relational intimacy. Increases in immediacy behaviors that violate one or more of the cognitive schemata lead to repulsion, compensatory responses, and reduced relational intimacy.

Intimacy is dialectically balanced along four relational paradoxes: autonomy-connection, novelty-predictability, openness-closedness, and risk-reward. These relational contradictions, or paradoxes, are managed through cyclical alternation, denial, segmentation, selection, the unity of opposites, denial, and disorientation.

10

Persuasive Posturing

Influencing Others through
Nonverbal Communication

IN *THE IMMORTALS*, a novel about John F. Kennedy's romantic affair with Marilyn Monroe, Michael Korda (1992) describes the initial encounter between Senator Kennedy and the starlet Monroe:

> She was wearing a tight black dress of shimmering material, which seemed several sizes too small for her, a white fox stole, costume jewelry earrings, and a cheap black patent-leather handbag. The whole outfit looked as if it might have been purchased from a thrift shop. Not that it mattered—Marilyn was beyond good taste, or bad. At this point in her life she was perhaps the biggest star in Hollywood. I took the opportunity to move closer to Jack, whose expression resembled that of a man getting his first glimpse of the Grand Canyon or Mount Everest—some natural wonder of awesome proportion and reputation. Jack closed the distance, determined to reach Marilyn before I did, took her hand, squeezed it briefly rather than shaking it, and gave her his most dashing smile. She smiled back, "I can't *believe* you're a *Senator*?" she cooed, in her tiny breathless voice. She had a charming habit of ending every sentence as if it were a question. "I thought they were all old men." She hadn't removed her hand from his. (pp. 28–29)

Influence comes in many forms. The erotic power of movie icons or political power brokers—amplified by stunningly good looks and communicated through facial expression, gait, touch, distance, and vocal inflections—makes for virtually irresistible influence. If Korda is to be believed, Jack and Marilyn both got what they wanted that night. She was nonverbally influenced by his power, charm, wealth, and good looks. He was nonverbally influenced by her stunning beauty and Hollywood stardom.

Each day of life is a game of influential moves, from small requests, such as getting one's daughter to be home on time or one's husband to take out the garbage, to major requests, such as getting your lover to accept your proposal for marriage or getting a troubled friend to seek counseling. Much, perhaps most, of our communication is intentionally influential, persuasive, and designed to change the beliefs, attitudes, or behaviors of others. Some persuasive communication is beneficial, enhancing the human spirit and condition. Some is used to cheat, seduce, deceive, or cover up. Regardless of its purpose, nonverbal behavior, in particular, determines the persuasive impact of a message, as we will see in this chapter. Unfortunately, most communication research has been preoccupied with the impact of verbal messages on persuasion. Until recently, this narrow preoccupation has caused many scholars to overlook the important persuasive effects of nonverbal communication. Moreover, the interplay of *both* nonverbal and verbal cues makes it impossible to understand verbal persuasion without considering its nonverbal aspects.

Influencing Attitudes and Changing Behaviors

At one time, the entire field of communication was focused on persuasion. In the late 1960s, when differences in ideology created conflict in our field, much like the rest of the world, communication focused on influence: How can we stop communism and communist propaganda? How can we persuade our leaders to stop the war in Vietnam? How can people of color and women gain influence in patriarchal, white America? The ideological battle was between what Rushing (1993) describes as "power" and "other." All questions seemed to revolve around persuasion and social influence. As a result, the field of communication came to learn a lot about persuasion. As our field matured and branched out into research on such diversified topics as personal relationships, health, organizations, and culture, we became less preoccupied with persuasion. Of course, this does not mean that persuasion is unimportant in society today. Although the issues have changed, public service announcements promote safe sex, regular exercise, cancer prevention, and the benefits of education, not to mention the millions of messages from advertisers urging us to be conspicuous consumers.

In its heyday, persuasion research rarely focused on nonverbal messages. In recent years, however, nonverbal studies, a number of active research programs, and several exciting theories have emerged that have illuminated how nonverbal behavior creates powerful persuasive outcomes. Several of these theories have generated research programs that promise to provide additional insights into the persuasion process. Although these theories have helped explain the nonverbal processes of persuasion, none has provided a great theoretical breakthrough; no theory or model has emerged as dominant. But theory building is cumulative, and nonverbal persuasion is much better understood now than it was a decade ago, as the following theories suggest.

The Direct-Effects Model of Immediacy

Research has shown that increases in nonverbal immediacy substantially enhance a persuader's chance of gaining compliance and having influence on others (for more on immediacy, see Chapter 8). Studies have shown that both single-channeled immediacy increases, such as increased eye contact, and multichanneled immediacy increases are associated with increased persuasion. The so-called direct-effects model (Andersen, 1979; Andersen, 1985) and a similar model of nonverbal immediacy, the social-meaning model (Burgoon, Coker, & Coker, 1986; Burgoon, Manusov, Mineo, & Hale, 1985), predict a linear relationship between immediacy and persuasion. For example, when an interaction partner accompanies a request with a smile, a light touch, and direct eye contact, the sender is using multichanneled immediacy behaviors to increase the likelihood that the receiver will comply.

GAZE AND PERSUASION

Research has provided substantial support for the social-meaning and direct-effects models. This is particularly true for the persuasive effects of gaze (looking at another person) and eye contact (mutual gaze into one another's eyes). In a field study, Kleinke and Singer (1979) observed the effect of gaze or no gaze on subjects' willingness to accept leaflets being distributed on a street. These researchers found that subjects were more likely to accept leaflets in the gaze condition than in the no-gaze condition. This effect was consistent for both males and females and was stronger when experimenters used no verbal communication. In similar field research by Valentine (1980), bystanders were more willing to assist a disabled victim with a broken arm (by picking up change he had dropped) in an experimental gaze condition than in a no-gaze condition. This finding occurred whether the victim was alone or accompanied by a friend.

Burgoon et al. (1986) provide additional empirical support for the social-meaning model for gaze behavior. They tested whether a person was judged as more likely to be hired for a job when gazing versus not gazing. Specifically, they report that gaze aversion carried very negative meaning and was least persuasive, whereas sustained gaze was highly effective in interpersonal persuasion. Gaze is probably effective persuasively because it is simultaneously powerful and immediate (Andersen, 1985; Segrin, 1990). In fact, gaze can command considerable authority. In a study by Bull and Gibson-Robinson (1981), poorly dressed solicitors for charity increased their contributions dramatically when they used direct gaze. Linkey and Firestone (1990) examined a group discussion task, in which group members were asked to influence one another. These researchers found that influence was primarily a function of the visual dominance ratio (the degree to which one person looks at an interaction partner or is looked at by the interaction partner). A study by Liss, Walker, Hazelton, and Cupach (1993) shows that compliance is highly correlated with mutual gaze, indicating that eye contact is a potent predictor of persuasion. Segrin (1993) statistically compiled the results of forty-nine nonverbal studies, including twelve on gaze behavior. Gaze produced greater compliance than averted gaze in every one of the twelve studies. Although the effects of gaze are not overpowering, they are very consistent according to Segrin. Thus, gaze, dominant gaze, and mutual gaze all seem to have significant persuasive effects. In short, when a person is engaged in persuasive communication, looking at one's interaction partner is a major determinant of the persuader's success.

TOUCH AND PERSUASION

Like gaze, touch has positive effects on persuasion. In two compliance experiments by Willis and Hamm (1980), strangers were asked by a petitioner to comply by signing a petition or by filling out a questionnaire. In both experiments, half the strangers received touch and half received no touch; other communication cues remained constant across the two conditions. In the first experiment, strangers signed the petition 81 percent of the time in the touch condition but only 50 percent of the time in the no-touch condition. In the second experiment, strangers complied by completing the questionnaire 70 percent of the time in the touch condition but only 40 percent of the time in the no-touch condition. Results of both experiments demonstrate the significant, positive effects of touch on compliance.

An investigation of touch and foot-in-the-door techniques (where a small request is followed by a larger request) showed that touch increases compliance in most experimental conditions (Goldman, Kiyohara, & Pfannensteil, 1985). In the first step of this study, an experimenter asked subjects for a small favor; the experimenter responded either positively to each subject's compliance by saying "You have been very helpful" or negatively by saying "You have not been very helpful." Next, another experimenter asked the subjects for a bigger favor. If the second experimenter used touch, the subjects were more likely to comply than if no touch accompanied the request for the bigger favor. Touch was even effective in gaining compliance following the negative-response condition. Patterson, Powell, and Lenihan (1986) conducted a touch experiment in which subjects were initially asked to score some test papers. After completing the stacks they had been given, subjects were then asked to stay and score more tests. The results showed that subjects who were touched when asked to score the additional tests were more likely to comply than subjects who were not touched. The researchers attribute the increased compliance to perceptions of greater sensitivity and/or status of the experimenter in the touch condition.

In his statistical summary of thirteen studies examining the influence of touch on compliance, Segrin (1993) reports that touch showed a positive, consistent effect on compliance across the thirteen studies. Virtually all these studies compared the results of an experimenter's either touching a stranger on the arm or not touching a stranger while making a request. Little is known about the effects of persuasive touch in close relationships. Nor have researchers examined the effects of more-intimate types of touch (such as strokes, caresses, or squeezes) or touch on intimate areas of the body (such as the chest and face). Nonetheless, the available research indicates that, in general, interpersonal touch has clear, persuasive effects—a finding that is consistent with the direct-effects model.

TOUCH, GAZE, AND PERSUASION

Interestingly, a number of studies have examined the persuasive impact of both touch and gaze in combination. This type of examination allows researchers to determine (1) whether one of these cues can substitute for the other, (2) their relative persuasive impact, and (3) whether they have additive or cumulative effects. Kleinke (1977) reports two such experiments that examined the effect of gaze and touch on compliance. In the first study, the experimenter left a dime in a phone booth. When a subject found the dime and the experimenter asked to have it back, the experimenter manipulated gaze and touch to produce four experimental conditions: touch and gaze, touch alone, gaze alone, and neither touch nor gaze. The touch-and-gaze condition resulted in more dimes being returned, indicating that touch and gaze have additive effects on compliance. In the second study, experimenters asked strangers in a shopping mall if they would lend them a dime. Consistent with experiment one, four combinations of touch and gaze were employed, and again the touch-and-gaze condition produced the greatest incidence of compliance. Kleinke's explanation is that touch and gaze increase attention and involvement, thereby making noncompliance more difficult. In another article, Kleinke (1980) reports two experiments that replicated the 1977 study, one in which the experimenter made a legitimate request (asking for a dime to make a phone call) and one in which the experimenter made an "illegitimate" request (asking for a dime to buy a candy bar). The results for the legitimate-request experiment reflected the finding of the 1977 study, but those for the illegitimate-request experiment did not. In the illegitimate-request experiment, the no-touch/no-gaze condition secured more compliance, possibly because the experimenter appeared more tactful or humble. A replication of Kleinke's (1977) phone booth experiment by Brockner, Pressman, Cabitt, and Moran (1982) showed that touch and gaze independently increased compliance and that touch and gaze together increased compliance even more.

The data from these five studies suggest additive effects of both touch and eye contact consistent with the direct-effects and social-meaning models. Touch and eye contact are positive immediacy cues for most people that increase others' compliance. These findings have considerable practical importance. When soliciting for charity, requesting signatures for a petition, asking for a favor, or seeking assistance from a stranger, the combination of touch and gaze considerably increases one's chance of achieving compliance.

KINESIC BEHAVIOR AND PERSUASION

What effects do various bodily movements have on persuasion? A few studies provide some answers. In a study of opinion change, McGinley, LeFerve, and McGinley (1975) report that open body positions result in more persuasion than closed body positions (keeping one's knees and feet together and one's arms folded and held close to the body). Other literature, discussed in previous chapters, suggests that communicators are perceived as more friendly, approachable, and warm when they use open body postures. Burgoon, Birk, and Pfau (1990) examined several kinesic behaviors for their impact on persuasion. They found that as kinesic immediacy and expressiveness increased, so did persuasiveness. Among the various kinesic behaviors they examined, facial pleasantness was the most predictive of persuasive success. In addition, more overall bodily movement and animation were correlated with persuasiveness. Liss et al. (1993) examined the effect of smiling on compliance gaining and found that more smiling resulted in greater compliance. Together, these three studies indicate that persuasion can be facilitated by kinesic activity, including open body positions, positive facial affect, and kinesic animation.

VOCAL CUES AND PERSUASION

Several studies also show a positive link between vocal immediacy and persuasion. A series of studies by Buller and his associates shows that vocal immediacy cues such as a pleasant tone of voice and a fast delivery are linked to greater compliance. These effects are particularly true for individuals who are skilled decoders of nonverbal communication (Buller & Aune, 1988a, 1992; Buller & Burgoon, 1986; Buller, LePoire, Aune, & Eloy, 1992). Segrin's (1993) statistical summary of the research shows that both vocal rate and pleasantness are associated with persuasion. Burgoon et al. (1990) report that persuasiveness increases with greater vocal fluency and pitch variety but not greater vocal pleasantness. Employing a fast, pleasant delivery style with vocal variation makes verbal communication more persuasive. This is particularly true while talking on the telephone, when other nonverbal cues are absent.

PHYSICAL APPEARANCE AND PERSUASION

Studies of compliance gaining and physical appearance show that conventional attire has positive persuasive effects. In general, "dressing up" is recommended for most persuasive situations. In a petition-signing experiment by MacNeill and Wilson (1972), experimenters obtained more signatures when dressed conventionally (in a suit and tie with short hair) than unconventionally (in a faded army jacket with long hair). In a similar study, Darley and Cooper (1972) examined the effects of countercultural, or "hippie," appearance on political campaign effectiveness. They found that voters were less likely to take a leaflet from a "hippie" than from a conventionally dressed campaigner; they were also more likely to throw the leaflet away if they accepted it from the hippie rather than the conventionally dressed campaigner. Moreover, voters attributed more radical, less acceptable views to candidates supported by hippies than by conventionally dressed campaigners.

Perhaps the most authoritative sort of dress is the uniform. Certainly, we are much more likely to comply with a police officer's request than a civilian's. Similarly, the uniform of medical personnel communicates authority and ensures a patient's compliance in a variety of ways: going to designated rooms, waiting a long time, taking off one's clothes, and submitting to embarrassing or painful medical procedures. The white coat or white dress is still universally worn by medical professionals to communicate authority and to ensure compliance. In Milgram's (1974) classic experiments in which he successfully persuaded participants to induce shocks (that they believed were real) to other people in laboratory learning studies, compliance was gained by an experimenter in a gray technician's coat worn over a white shirt and tie.

In a related study, Bushman (1988) had a female confederate randomly stop pedestrians and say, "This fellow is overparked at the meter and doesn't have any change. Give him a nickel." The woman wore different clothing in three experimental conditions. When dressed in a uniform, she gained more compliance than when dressed in business attire or casual attire. The nondescript blue uniform produced compliance 72 percent of the time, whereas only 48 percent compliance was gained in the business-attire condition and 52 percent in the casual-attire condition. In his statistical summary of nineteen studies, Segrin (1993) concludes that the more formal or high-status the clothing, the greater the compliance rate obtained. Evidently, we are more likely to permit appropriately and well-dressed individuals to approach us and to gain our trust than inappropriately or less-conventionally dressed individuals.

MULTIDIMENSIONAL IMMEDIACY AND PERSUASION

Persuaders increase immediacy and involvement through multiple channels. Several studies have examined multidimensional immediacy behaviors and persuasion. In a study of classroom compliance employing multiple indices of immediacy, Andersen (1979) found that students in a speech class were more likely to engage in communication practices (such as using an outline, maintaining eye contact, or using gestures) suggested by immediate rather than nonimmediate teachers. Burgoon et al. (1990) reported a similar finding in a study of persuasive speakers. Specifically, they found that greater persuasion was associated with vocalic behaviors (such as longer pauses, vocal pleasantness, and pitch variety), increased gaze, more smiling, greater facial expressiveness, and more overall movement.

Subsequent research has also shown that individuals use nonverbal communication to resist persuasion. In a study of rejection strategies for flirtatious advances, Trost and Engstrom (1994) report that rejectors avoided nonverbal contact, ignored the persuader, maintained larger interpersonal spaces, acted cold and uninterested, displayed alternative relational ties (such as engagement rings), and acted nervous and uneasy.

MULTICHANNELED, MEDIATED PERSUASIVE CUES

What effect do nonverbal cues in the media have on viewers? Studies of television newscasters, for example, have shown that nonverbal behaviors influence viewers in a variety of ways. Newscasters have tremendous influence. We treat them like virtual acquaintances who are nightly guests in our homes. For many years, Walter Cronkite, the anchorman for CBS news, was considered the most credible man in America.

Studies show that the nonverbal behavior of television newscasters affects voting preferences. Friedman, Mertz, and DiMatteo (1980) report that newscasters' facial expressions are consistently biased toward certain candidates at levels unlikely to occur by chance. In the 1976 election, Walter Cronkite, David Brinkley, and Harry Reasoner showed more favorable facial expressions when reporting on Jimmy Carter than on Gerald Ford. John Chancellor and Barbara Walters showed more positive facial affect toward Ford than Carter. Verbal content, however, showed no corresponding bias. Two studies replicate and extend these findings to the 1984 elections and show that newscasters' biased facial expressions were associated with viewers' voting behaviors (Mullen et al., 1986). The first study found that Dan Rather of CBS and Tom Brokaw of NBC showed no facial bias when reporting on Ronald Reagan or Walter Mondale. However, Peter Jennings of ABC exhibited strong facial bias to Reagan over Mondale. The second study, which examined voters in four cities in Ohio, Missouri, Massachusetts, and Pennsylvania, showed that in each city, viewers of ABC had significantly more favorable attitudes toward Reagan than viewers of NBC or CBS. Although pro-Reagan viewers might have tuned in more to ABC, Mullen et al. (1986) believe that this study actually demonstrates a subtle, peripheral route to persuasion that occurs without deliberate, conscious consideration. In either case, this study suggests a strong association among nonverbal behavior, television viewing, and electoral decisions.

Explaining the Direct-Effects Model

Based on the evidence, the direct-effects model (Andersen, 1985) and social-meaning model (Burgoon et al., 1985) best explain nonverbal persuasive effects. Immediacy behaviors have a direct effect on compliance such that increased immediacy results in increased compliance. Moreover, the effects of various nonverbal behaviors are significant and are usually stronger than verbal message variables in their impact. As Segrin (1993) points out:

> The effects of nonverbal behaviors and various verbal message variables on compliance were compared. This comparison revealed that the nonverbal behaviors are as powerful, and, in some cases, more powerful than some of the message strategies that have been studied in producing compliance from others. It appears for example that whether a source gazes at and touches a target while attempting to gain compliance will be as influential in determining the

outcome as whether the source gives supportive information, uses a foot-in-the-door strategy, or a one- versus two-sided message. (pp. 183–184)

But, *why* does nonverbal immediacy have such a substantial impact on compliance? A number of explanations suggest that immediacy behaviors communicate power, attention, warmth, and liking. These explanations are not mutually exclusive. All of them may be valid explanations of the direct-effects model to some degree.

POWER

Immediate, involving nonverbal behaviors may be more persuasive because they convey not warmth and immediacy but rather dominance and power. Burgoon et al. (1985) and Segrin (1990) assert that touch, fast speaking, official uniforms, and direct gaze are effective behaviors of persuasion because they are powerful, not because they are immediate. Nonetheless, although these behaviors certainly are powerful (see Chapter 12), this explanation fails to account for the persuasiveness of open body positions (McGinley et al., 1976), which are more submissive and vulnerable than closed body positions. The literature reviewed in this chapter on facial expressions shows that smiling is highly persuasive even though it is a submissive behavior. Likewise, LaCrosse (1975) reports that head nods, a nondominant signal of affirmation, were shown to increase persuasiveness in a counseling setting. Research by Burgoon et al. (1990) shows that several warm but nondominant nonverbal behaviors enhance persuasiveness, including vocal pleasantness, kinesic/proxemic immediacy, facial expressiveness, and kinesic relaxation. Dominant nonverbal behaviors, such as harsh facial expressions and the dominant "command" tone of voice, definitely give an added persuasive boost to immediacy behaviors.

As Machiavelli (1513/1947) said almost five hundred years ago, "Here the question arises whether it is better to be loved or feared or feared than loved. The answer is it is better to be both" (p. 48). Of course, this still raises questions as to why nondominant immediacy behaviors are persuasive. It may be that immediacy behaviors are persuasive for several reasons; for example, they may increase perceptions of trustworthiness and dynamism, which are both key components underlying credibility. As we will see in the following discussion, immediacy behaviors also command attention and reflect interpersonal warmth and liking.

ATTENTION

Immediacy behaviors get our attention. In virtually every theory of persuasion, attention is a necessary prerequisite to message processing and eventual compliance. For example, Petty and Cacioppo's (1986) elaboration-likelihood model (discussed later in this chapter) requires message processing as a prerequisite to persuasion or attitude change. It is hard to ignore a person's persuasive request when he or she is staring you in the eyes or touching you on the arm. Mehrabian

(1971a) suggests that immediacy behaviors are "approach" behaviors that increase sensory stimulation and thus turn one's focus to another person and her or his behavior. Andersen (1985) maintains that immediacy behaviors are so compelling that they create a condition in which communication must occur: "Eye contact, closer distance, and open positions almost force another person to realize that communication is commencing" (p. 2). Although more research needs to be conducted, current research and theory suggest that some of the direct effects of immediate behavior are attributable to the increased attention that immediacy behaviors produce during interaction.

WARMTH

Research on nonverbal communication shows that immediacy behaviors are perceived as warm, close, and nurturant (see Andersen, 1985; Andersen & Guerrero, 1998a). Humans, from infancy through adulthood, enjoy behaviors such as warm, protective touch, smiles, and openness, which send nonthreatening, supportive messages. Research reveals that the perception of warmth is a particularly important nonverbal behavioral outcome for many professionals, such as therapists, doctors, and trial judges, because it puts people at ease and sends positive messages (Blanck & Rosenthal, 1992; Blanck, Rosenthal, & Vannicelli, 1986). Immediacy behaviors that effectively convey warmth include touch, gaze, smiles, and postural directness. We may react positively to warm behavior because like our parents' warm caregiving, friendly, loving behavior evokes feelings of spontaneous positivity.

Interpersonal warmth may be a basic social emotion. Immediacy behaviors produce warm feelings that are associated with intimacy, attachment, bondedness, and emotional connectedness. Andersen and Guerrero (1998a) maintain that "interpersonal warmth is the pleasant, contented, intimate feeling that occurs during positive interactions" (p. 304). Obviously, anytime a communicator can create such interpersonal warmth, he or she is setting the stage for a positive persuasive outcome.

LIKING

Immediacy behaviors may also have direct, positive effects because they signal that another person likes us. Immediacy behaviors can signal interest, inclusion, or connection even when warmth isn't present in an interaction. In his opening chapter on immediacy, Mehrabian (1971a) contends, "Such behavior patterns and many others can be understood in terms of the *immediacy principle:* People are drawn to persons they like, evaluate highly, and prefer; and they avoid or move away from things they dislike, evaluate negatively, or do not prefer" (p. 1). When people engage in affiliative behavior, we are drawn to them, we experience feelings of interest, inclusion, and attraction, and we seek to treat them positively. The automatic rule of reciprocity is the basis for much human behavior (Cialdini, 1988). A failure to respond positively to someone who is positive to us makes us seem abusive, unfair, and interpersonally isolated.

Several series of studies demonstrate clearly that immediacy behaviors inherently and directly communicate positive affect and harmonious relations (Andersen, 1979; Andersen, 1985; Andersen, Andersen, & Jensen, 1979). Nonverbal immediacy cues have clear social meanings that lead to positive persuasive effects (Burgoon, Buller, Hale, & deTurck, 1984; Burgoon et al., 1985, 1986; Strzyzewski, 1990). These findings suggest that in neutral to positive relationships (including most initial interactions), immediacy behaviors generally have direct positive effects (Andersen, 1985) for many of the reasons previously outlined.

Although the direct-effects model and social-meaning model are supported by the bulk of the evidence for most immediacy behaviors, other theoretical approaches also yield insights into the positive impact of nonverbal behavior on persuasion. We will discuss several of these approaches in the following sections.

Expectancy-Violations Theory

Expectancy-violations theory attempts to explain the persuasive impact of immediacy behavior. Early tests of this theory centered on spatial invasion. Burgoon and Jones (1976) argue that each person has cultural and personal expectations about the normative distances that should be maintained during interpersonal interaction. Research has shown that attractive, or rewarding, individuals are more persuasive if they violate interpersonal distance norms. Burgoon and Jones contend that these violations draw attention to the positive characteristics of high-reward individuals. By contrast, low-reward, or unattractive, individuals are most persuasive at normative distances because they draw less attention to their personal characteristics at such distances.

How has this model fared? In several studies of proxemic invasion, the model received some support. Partial confirmation is provided by Stacks and Burgoon (1979), who found that rewarding communicators were more persuasive at either closer or farther distances than at normative interpersonal distances. As predicted by the model, nonrewarding individuals produced no difference in persuasiveness at close, normal, or far interpersonal distances. Two studies by Burgoon and Aho (1982) provide only partial support for the model. In both studies, distance showed no significant effect on compliance for either low-reward communicators or high-reward communicators, although reward itself produced significant effects and increased the attentiveness of receivers. This study actually supported the direct-effects and social-meaning models. Albert and Dabbs (1970) report that actual persuasion was greater at far interpersonal distances (14 to 15 feet) than at either close or moderate interpersonal distances (1 to 5 feet). Buller (1987) conducted a study in which experimenters assumed close, moderate, or far interpersonal distances while attempting to get subjects to sign petitions. Findings show that close interpersonal distances resulted in the greatest compliance, whereas moderate and far interpersonal distances resulted in less compliance. Neither Albert and Dabbs nor Buller manipulated the reward value, but their results suggest that nonnormative distance increases compliance.

In an extension of expectancy-violations theory to vocalic communication, a study by Buller and Burgoon (1986) found that pleasant voices (a positive norm violation) produced more compliance but only for good decoders. Poor decoders complied more with hostile voices (a negative norm violation) than neutral or pleasant voices. Although reward value was not successfully manipulated, the study provides some support for the expectancy-violations model.

Two studies attempted to extend expectancy-violations theory to eye behavior (Burgoon et al., 1985, 1986). Both studies employed either rewarding confederates or nonrewarding confederates and differing levels of eye gaze. The high-reward interviewees had strong qualifications, including experience, excellent grade point averages, and good references. The low-reward applicants were poorly qualified, had low grade point averages, and had little relevant work experience. Results of these studies provided little support for the expectancy-violations model because the primary results showed direct persuasive effects for increased levels of gaze regardless of reward value. These results support the social-meaning and direct-effects models described earlier.

Overall, although the expectancy-violations model has received some general confirmation, the support for its persuasive effects is mixed. Moreover, few of the related studies have actually tested whether expectations were violated or not; as such, a central tenet of the theory remains untested (Segrin, 1990). The best evidence for the persuasive effects of expectancy-violations theory relates to interpersonal distance. The evidence suggests that rewarding individuals should stand closer or farther than the normative interaction distance for maximal persuasive effects. For nonrewarding communicators, standing at normative interpersonal distances may maximize persuasive effects.

Distraction Models

There is a rival approach to the expectancy-violations theory in explaining the persuasive effects of nonverbal behavior. According to the so-called distraction models, if a sender's nonverbal behavior distracts a receiver, the receiver is more susceptible to persuasion. Stacks and Burgoon (1979) hypothesized that distance violations produced more persuasion because of their distracting properties. Unfortunately, they found that distance violations have no effect on a self-reported distraction measure. However, close and far distance violations were more persuasive than normative distances. Why did these distance violations produce more persuasion? One explanation is that distraction worked even though subjects were unaware of the distraction, so they could not self-report it. Another explanation is that these distance violations produced arousal effects. A subsequent study by Stacks and Burgoon (1981) reports a significant effect of both distance violations and extremes in physical attractiveness on distraction. Small persuasive effects were found for physical attractiveness and none for distance violations, providing better support for the distraction models. Similarly, in a test of the distracting effects of rapidly spoken messages on persuasion,

Woodall and Burgoon (1983) showed that fast messages were more distracting than normal-rate messages, but they found no persuasive effects from the faster messages.

In a metaanalysis of thirty-eight studies conducted by Buller (1986) that examined the distraction-persuasion relationship. Buller reports that communication-irrelevant factors, such as noise or visual distractions, generally reduced persuasion and attitude change because they impeded the receiver's comprehension of the message. Communication-relevant distractions, however, such as highly attractive or credible sources, caused receivers to focus on these positive qualities, producing a positive effect on persuasion. If the source had low attractiveness or credibility, focusing on the speaker reduced attitude change because these negative distractions impeded believability and persuasion. In general, positively regarded sources may benefit from the receiver's focusing her or his attention on the positive characteristics of the source.

Petty and Cacioppo's (1986) work on persuasion and cognition may also help explain the process of distraction. Basically, they have shown that distraction aids the persuasion process if the message is of low quality (that is, containing weak, ambiguous arguments); for example, a distracting appearance, haptic behavior, or oculesic behavior might distract a receiver such that he or she could not concentrate on the many flaws of a low-quality message. High-quality (that is, strong, clear) persuasive arguments, on the other hand, are less effective when a receiver is distracted by conspicuous nonverbal cues; the receiver cannot concentrate on the high-quality message, so its effectiveness is reduced.

Communication-Accommodation Theory

Vocalic aspects of speech are crucial to persuasion. Several studies show that rapid speech enhances persuasion (Apple, Streeter, & Krause, 1979; MacLachlan, 1979; Miller, Maruyama, Beaber, & Valone, 1976), perhaps by increasing the effort it takes to perceive the message or by improving the perceived competence of the source. However, one study (Woodall & Burgoon, 1983) found that fast speech rates did not differ from slow speech rates in their persuasive effect. The regions in which the studies were conducted offer one explanation for these conflicting results. The Apple et al. study and the MacLachlan studies were conducted in New York, and the Miller et al. study was conducted in Los Angeles—both of these cities are locations where fast speech is the norm. The Woodall and Burgoon study, in contrast, was conducted in the southeast, where speech is considerably slower. Thus, slow speakers may be more persuasive in the South, but fast speakers may be more persuasive in the North and on the West Coast.

An even stronger explanation for these results can be found in communication-accommodation theory. According to this theory (Street, 1982; Street & Brady, 1982; Street & Giles, 1982), listeners perceive speech similar to their own as more attractive, pleasant, and intelligible. Moreover, speakers typically adjust or accommodate their speech to the style or rate of the other interactant, even though most speakers are unaware of this accommodation (Street, 1982). Based on this theory, speakers who adjust to the communication rates and styles of their listeners should be more persuasive.

Several studies provide support for the persuasive effects of communication accommodation. In a study by Buller and Aune (1988a), good decoders were most likely to comply with faster messages, whereas poor decoders were not. Why did good decoders prefer faster messages? The authors showed that good decoders spoke faster; thus, as predicted by communication-accommodation theory, faster speakers (that is, good decoders) preferred to listen to and were more influenced by faster speech.

A second study by Buller and Aune (1989) partially replicated the first study. Again, good decoders were found to speak faster than poor decoders. However, no effect was found for actual or perceived similarity of speech rate on compliance. Poor decoders (who generally spoke slowly) complied most with speakers with moderately slow voices, whereas good decoders (who generally spoke fast) complied most with speakers with moderately fast and very fast voices. These findings suggest that people are influenced by those who speak at the same rate as they do.

A study by Burgoon et al. (1987) examined the effects of a number of communication variables on patient compliance with their physician's advice. Among the many communication variables tested, only perceived similarity was significantly related to compliance. A final study by Buller and Burgoon (1986) shows that good nonverbal decoders complied more in pleasant-voice conditions than in neutral- or hostile-voice conditions, whereas poor decoders complied most in the hostile-voice condition, moderately in the neutral-voice condition, and least in the pleasant-voice condition. Because good decoders are more affiliative, composed, and social than are poor decoders, Buller and Burgoon attribute the results to communication accommodation. People comply more with voice tones that are similar to their own.

This review shows that communication-accommodation theory, as applied to nonverbal communication and persuasion, has received some support. Communicators would probably be well advised to use vocalic cues similar to their persuasive target's vocalic cues to maximize compliance. However, speech accommodation is a dynamic process in which both interactants adapt to the other's speaking style. No study of this dyadic type of social interaction has been conducted; the theory remains untested in its most complete form (Segrin, 1990). Finally, research generally shows that, independently, increased gaze, faster speech, and more touch are persuasive. This presents a problem for communication-accommodation theory, which would have to assume that most people are higher-than-average gazers, faster-than-average speakers, and more-frequent-than-average touchers. It seems that more immediacy is probably more important than more accommodation. However, a combination of immediacy and accommodation may be highly effective given that both forms of communication reflect liking.

Emotional Arousal

Considerable evidence demonstrates that nonverbal communication behaviors, particularly immediacy behaviors, are physically and emotionally arousing (see Chapters 7 and 9 for more about arousal). For example, Andersen (1985) provides a review of twenty-four studies that demonstrated that immediacy behaviors such as gaze, closer interpersonal distances, and touch produced increases in measures of physiological arousal, including galvanic skin response and heart rate. Much of the research reviewed previously in both Chapters 8 and 9 suggests that immediacy behaviors result in positive, emotional mood arousal.

Emerging evidence suggests that positive mood arousal is an explanation for the persuasive effects of nonverbal immediacy behaviors. Research has suggested that positive affective (emotional) reactions are automatic and reflect little need for analytic cognitive activity (Zajonc, 1980, 1984). As Zajonc (1984) states:

> Only a few years ago, I published a rather speculative paper entitled "Feeling and Thinking: Preferences Need No Inferences." The argument began with the general hypothesis that affect and cognition are separate and independent systems and that although they ordinarily function conjointly, affect could be generated without a prior cognitive process. (p. 259)

Research and theory have begun to provide support for this position. Petty and Cacioppo's elaboration-likelihood model makes the distinction between thoughtful analysis and "peripheral," or "primitive," affect processing. Petty and Cacioppo's biases toward thoughtful rationality are evident because they characterize "gut" feelings, intuition, and emotional feelings as *peripheral* and *primitive.* Their central argument in the elaboration-likelihood model is an important one: either persuasive cues can be thoughtful, issue-relevant, and logical, or they can be emotional, nonverbal, and contextual. Petty and Cacioppo claim that in the literature "central thought processing" appears to be more enduring. Of course, recent research suggests that these "peripheral" nonverbal cues, like gazing and smiling, are often more persuasive and more enduring than "central," logical, verbal message strategies such as the use of supporting evidence (Segrin, 1993).

Other researchers (Stiff, 1986; Stiff & Boster, 1987) have criticized the elaboration-likelihood model and have proposed alternatives to it such as the elasticity model, which suggests that the parallel processing of information occurs such that we are simultaneously influenced by logical and emotional messages. Evidence seems to support the elasticity model's prediction that both logical and emotional messages are processed simultaneously.

Research on media campaigns also suggests the importance of emotional and affective information. In their research on AIDS information campaigns, Flora and Maibach (1990) report that emotional public-service messages showing families coping with AIDS, a woman pleading with her audience to use condoms, and an intravenous drug user with AIDS explaining what she would have done differently were more effective than rational messages featuring former Surgeon General Koop's testimony in Congress, actors discussing how to use condoms, or narrated descriptions of how AIDS is contracted. This study showed that emotional messages produced more long-term behavioral changes and information-seeking behavior about AIDS than did rational messages.

Chaudhuri and Buck (1995) report that mood arousal strategies in advertisements are highly related to emotional, or affective, cognitions. They suggest:

> Emotional communication in advertising . . . can result in affective cognitions through the use of mood arousal strategies. Repeated pairings of a brand with a mood transfers the affect generated by the mood to the brand itself. The use of "Joe Camel" in cigarette advertising, for example, has recently drawn strong protests from anti-smoking groups. The assumption has been that certain nonverbal mood arousing cues in advertisements, such as the presence of animals, can produce affective responses that, in turn, are transferred to a favorable image for the advertised brand. (p. 425)

Chaudhuri and Buck (1995) used dozens of print and televised advertisements to demonstrate that mood-arousal processes create positive affective reactions to many commercial products.

Studies of political communication reveal the same sorts of patterns. Despite much criticism, Ronald Reagan was the most popular American president in recent decades. Although many voters disagreed with his policies and questioned both his logic and ethics, Reagan racked up huge election victories. McHugo (1985) examined emotional reactions by college students to President Reagan's expressive displays in image-only and sound-and-image conditions. Results, which were the same for both conditions, showed emotional responses consistent with Reagan's expressive displays. Attitudes toward Reagan affected listeners' self-reported emotional reactions; when Reagan was angry, viewers felt anger; when Reagan was happy, viewers reported feeling happy. McHugo (1985) concludes that expressive displays have a direct emotional impact on viewers that suggest "a possible mechanism for nonverbal behavior to influence attitudes" (p. 1526). Reagan was a "feel good" president; he created positive emotional arousal and attained electoral popularity in spite of policies or plans that had little benefit for and low popularity with the electorate in general.

The process of nonverbal emotional arousal has been shown to work in both interpersonal relationships and mass media campaigns. Typically, nonverbal messages have an automatic validity that is virtually irrefutable. A cute baby, a gentle touch, a pretty face, and a warm smile touch our hearts and influence our behavior. Cialdini (1988) calls this our "heart of hearts," a place where our "true" feelings exist before we begin to intellectualize and rationalize a message. Instead of thinking of emotional meaning as peripheral, primitive, or illogical, we should regard it as valid intuitive information that, in addition to logic, should be taken "to heart." Of course, image manipulators both in daily interaction and in the media often employ false smiles and artificial images to exploit our heartfelt responses. My own wife, who weeps at long-distance telephone commercials, is touched by these emotionally exploitative advertisements.

Emotions are contagious. Research has shown that emotions spread quickly from person to person, largely through a nonverbal communication process (Andersen & Guerrero, 1998b; see also Chapter 6). Mob panic, mass euphoria, and contagious laughter are all examples of emotional contagion, a term coined by Hatfield, Cacioppo, and Rapson (1994). People imitate one another's actions and get feedback from their own behavior through a process known as interpersonal facial feedback (Cappella, 1993). Direct viewing of other people's emotional behavior can change our own emotions. For example, seeing a child's face light up with joy when opening a gift usually makes us feel happy, whereas hearing a loved one angrily describe having been treated badly is likely to make us feel mad. Mirroring, or motor mimicry, is another process in which one person mimics another person's anticipated response, such as wincing when someone is about to be hit (Bavelas, Black, Chovil, Lemery, & Mullett, 1988). Although each of these mechanisms probably explains some of the reasons for emotional influence, the bottom line is this: it's easy to become sad around a sad person and to feel happy around a happy person. Contagious emotions are a powerful form of interpersonal influence. Whether it is my wife with tears in her eyes watching a long-distance commercial, my friend sending off a check after seeing a children's fund advertisement and feeling sympathy for hungry kids, or me helping my daughter solve a problem that she is "stressed out" about, we are all influenced by the emotions around us.

Physical-Attraction Theories

Upon meeting another person for the first time—before the first word is spoken and even before we have much of a chance to observe the person's nonverbal actions—we are influenced by that person's appearance (see Chapter 2 for more on physical appearance). We are told, "Don't judge a book by its cover," but we still make judgments about people based on physical beauty, race, age, and biological sex. Moreover, considerable evidence indicates that physically attractive people are far more persuasive than less-attractive people. Burgoon (1983) has written extensively about the so-called reward value of a communicator. Physically attractive people, like it or not, are so "rewarding" that they can violate rules of communication and actually enhance their own reward value. Many social scientists call this a halo effect, in which one positive quality dominates other, unrelated evaluations.

In a classic experiment, a woman gave an identical speech to two similar audiences. For one audience, her hair, skin, and clothing were made to look unattractive; for the other audience, she was attractively presented. The audience viewing the attractive woman was persuaded significantly more than the audience viewing the unattractive woman (Mills & Aronson, 1965). In three experiments,

Physically attractive people, such as Leonardo Di Caprio and Gwyneth Paltrow, are inherently more persuasive than most of us because they are perceived to be more competent, honest, and intelligent than other people.

Burgoon and Aho (1982) manipulated the reward value of a shopper by controlling—among other variables—the person's physical attractiveness. In general, they found that the physically attractive shopper gained more compliance than the physically unattractive shopper.

In a study by Adams and Read (1983), physically attractive women were found to interact more frequently, be less hostile, and exhibit less compliance with another's request. They concluded, "facially attractive women may have the poise or confidence to engage in more frequent influence or persuasion attempts than lesser attractive women" (p. 157). The less attractive women were perceived to use "a highly undesirable influence style which includes demanding, interrupting, opinionated, submissive and antagonistic behavior" (p. 157). This study supports research by Chaiken (1979) that finds that physically attractive communicators are certainly more persuasive due to greater communication skills as well as their attractiveness. These studies suggest that physically attractive persons tend to get more practice at and more rewards from communicating and develop greater social and persuasive competence to complement their already winning looks.

A study by Puckett, Petty, Cacioppo, and Fischer (1983) indicates that physical attractiveness isn't always positively correlated with persuasion. Subjects were provided with a picture of a male author and written arguments, either strong or weak. Subjects found attractive authors to be more persuasive than unattractive authors when the essay was strong but less persuasive than unattractive authors when the essay was weak. This suggests that men's attractiveness and competence interact to produce powerful persuasive effects.

The relationship between physical attractiveness and persuasion can be explained by several theoretical perspectives. One explanation, described earlier, is the halo effect, in which a single positive characteristic dominates other evaluations of the person. The halo effect may explain why physically attractive people are typically perceived as more credible, similar, friendly, powerful, and persuasive than less-attractive people. A second explanation is that we pay more attention to physically attractive people because they are pleasant to observe. The increased personal attention causes us to attend to their requests or arguments, resulting in increased persuasion. A third explanation is that it is reinforcing to interact with physically attractive people; these interactions provide "rewards" that condition us to comply with their requests, according to reinforcement theory. Fourth, cultural stereotypes hold that what is beautiful is good (Dion, Berscheid, & Walster, 1972). This "good" person is expected to produce good, persuasive messages. Finally, some evidence exists that affective responses to persuasion are completely separate from cognitive responses (Swann, Griffith, Piedmore, & Gaines, 1987) and even mediated by different neural modules in the human brain (Stacks & Andersen, 1989). This would explain Efran's (1974) findings (which will be discussed in the following section) that, cognitively, jurors believe physical appearance shouldn't affect their decisions, yet their actual decisions are affectly based and biased by physical appearance.

Several explanations exist for the excessive persuasive power of physical attractiveness. Probably all of the preceding explanations provide part of the picture. Right or wrong, physically attractive people are more persuasive, are used to influencing others, and have the confidence to use persuasive techniques to gain compliance from other people.

Selling Ourselves

It's who you look like, not who you are.—Jackson Browne

The focus of persuasive messages is diverse. Parents seek to influence children. Radio talk-show hosts try to influence our political beliefs. Advertisers attempt to sell us their products. Doctors seek compliance from their patients.

Often, however, persuasion involves a simpler objective: selling ourselves. We want to appear attractive to our dates, competent to our professors, conscientious to our employers, honest to the IRS, and likeable to our friends. Selling ourselves is perhaps the most common objective of persuasion. Most people intuitively understand how to sell themselves. Without much thought, we know to select our best suit for an important job interview or to spend extra time on our hair before a big date. We all sell ourselves—as a date, mate, friend, employee, student, family member, and so on. Image management, once thought to be the sole province of corporate advertisers, is everybody's business. Some critics have decried the superficiality of this interpersonal sales process. In the play *My Dinner with Andre*, Andre decries the shallow roles people assume:

> One of the reasons we don't know what's going on is that when we're at one of these parties we're all too busy performing. We're concentrating on our own roles and giving a good performance, so we *can't* perceive what's going on around us. That was one of the reasons Grotowski gave up the theater, you know. He just felt that people in their lives were performing so well that performance in a theater was sort of superfluous and in a way obscene. (Shawn & Gregory, 1981, p. 69)

According to Herzog (1974), the increased tendency toward fake performances and managed images is a dangerous trend, which he labels the "B.S. factor." He states, "Fakery, in other words, has come to seem a natural, quotidian part of experience. Indeed, that was the object in the first place—to make the unreal appear real, the bizarre seem ordinary, the non-thing or non-person look like a thing or person" (p. 17). If anything, fakery has become an even more refined art in over two decades since Herzog's identification of the B.S. factor. Political candidates are more carefully packaged than ever before. Parents manage their kindergartners' image. Interpersonal relationships turn into sales encounters. Academic resumes have become a clever form of fiction designed to "market" job applicants.

Communication researchers have identified and even condemned the superficial deceptions involved in selling oneself. Nevertheless, communication research may itself be part of the problem. Dozens of different lines of communication research have come to one overriding conclusion: Meanings lie within people; that is, the impressions we form of others are not just part of the communication game, they are the whole game. From a communication perspective, if people believe you are beautiful or credible, then you are beautiful or credible. The manipulation of perceptions in face-to-face communication and in the mass media is continuous. And much of this image manipulation is done through subtle, nonverbal methods. As students of communication, we should be aware of the power of image manipulation. Many people, including scholars, either are unaware of image manipulation or accept it as an inherent aspect of communication.

Traditional persuasion research has focused on how to change other people's attitudes and behaviors. But as Miller and Burgoon (1978) have noted, "most people devote the preponderance of their persuasive energies to selling *themselves*" (p. 33). Certainly, some persuasive messages deal with attitudes or issues. We all attempt to influence friends and relatives about consumer products, political candidates, and social issues. Sometimes we simply want another person to wake up, to go to the store, to go out on a date, or to take her vitamins. However, compared with these sorts of persuasive attempts, we devote much more of our energy to improving our attractiveness and credibility with others. Dressing appropriately, putting on makeup, appearing attentive to one's boss, and smiling at a friend or prospective date are all actions that seek to ingratiate and sell ourselves to other people.

Research shows that many of our nonverbal actions are crucial in determining others' reactions to us. Conversely, scholars have shown that our impressions of other people are largely a function of nonverbal communication. Results of a study by McMahon (1976) showed that in an overwhelming number of cases (84 percent), nonverbal cues were more important in forming initial impressions than verbal cues. Moreover, by creating positive impressions on others, we improve our ability to influence them. So, even when we are seeking compliance, our first task is to get others to like, respect, and believe us. For only then will our messages have much effect.

Selling Our Bodies

Although we do it subtly, most of us use our physical appearance, our bodies and their adornment, to sell ourselves. The right physique, the right "look," and the latest fashions make us more credible and attractive on the basketball court, in the corporate office, in the bedroom, and in the classroom. We spend an inordinate amount of time and money to stay in shape, buy the right clothes, and have the right hairstyle. And it works. A metaanalysis that combined the results of seventy-eight previous experiments reveals that physically attractive people are perceived as more sociable, dominant, sexually warm, mentally healthy, intelligent, socially skilled, and popular than less physically attractive people (Feingold, 1992). These findings show, however, that there is little relationship between these perceptions and people's actual personalities.

Being physically attractive might even be a matter of life and death. Our legal system, like every other institution, is biased by our looks. Juries appear to be persuaded in favor of defendants who are physically attractive as opposed to those who are less attractive. Efran (1974) studied simulated juries who received identical fact sheets and a picture of a defendant; some juries received pictures of attractive defendants, and others were given pictures of unattractive defendants. The physically attractive defendants were evaluated as less likely to be guilty and were given less severe punishments than the unattractive defendants. This occurred despite the fact that 93 percent of the jurors said that physical appearance should not bias their verdicts. These findings suggest that we react unconsciously

Americans spend considerable time exercising for more than good health. They realize that a good appearance is a big part of being influential and successful.

to physical-appearance cues. Cialdini (1988) reviews several studies that show that "unless criminal defendants have used their attractiveness to commit a crime, good looking people are more likely to receive favorable treatment in the legal system" (p. 162). As a recent 20/20 report on "lookism" reported, if you are on trial for a crime, "you better be good looking."

Research on the role of physical appearance in politics generally shows that attractiveness is an advantage, but the research is more equivocal and mixed than research on evaluations of speakers, shoppers, or juries. Some writers have alleged that more physically attractive candidates are more electable. Folklore and research suggest that John Kennedy's physical appearance caused him to win the televised presidential debates and possibly even the presidency against Richard Nixon; allegedly, radio listeners preferred Nixon, whereas television viewers preferred Kennedy. An article by Vancil and Pendell (1987), however, suggests that this conclusion is a myth unsupported by the actual evidence.

Other research on physical attractiveness and electoral outcomes shows a mixed pattern of results. Andersen and Kibler (1978) found some small effects of physical attractiveness on voter preference, but these effects were wiped out by voters' perceptions of the candidates' attitude similarity and competence. Bowman (1980) studied the effect of attractiveness by showing undergraduates photographs of political candidates and asking them who they would vote for. *More*-attractive male candidates overwhelmingly received more votes than less-attractive male candidates. However, *less*-attractive female candidates received more votes than more-attractive female candidates. These findings held up regardless of whether the election was for Congress, the state legislature, the office of mayor, the school board, or a judicial seat.

Research shows a strong relationship between physical attractiveness and competence. In a study by Lewis and Bierly (1990), subjects were asked to rate the competence of forty-four men and women in the U.S. House of Representatives. Whether the politician was a man or a woman, attractive members of Congress were perceived as much more competent than less-attractive members. The effect existed for both male and female respondents, although it was stronger for male respondents.

Research has shown that different styles of dress can alter peoples' image, either favorably or unfavorably. Showing up for a formal dinner in jeans and a T-shirt or going to basketball practice in a tuxedo would not affect one's image positively! Research on women's clothing by Harris et al. (1983) showed that a formal skirt outfit maximized others' perceptions regarding how successful, happy, feminine, interesting, attractive, and intelligent a woman was. Formal pants, however, led to positive perceptions regarding how *active,* happy, and successful a woman was. Dress styles do communicate and clearly enable us to sell ourselves to other people as more competent, appropriate, and attractive.

Several studies, however, have shown that attractiveness is not always an advantage. The general finding that physically attractive communicators are more persuasive does not hold true in certain circumstances. The Bowman (1980) study discussed previously shows one such exception. Regarding political candidates, some voters may perceive that good looks and competence are incompatible. Indeed, women with good looks are perceived to have less need to be competent, but their less-attractive counterparts are perceived to need to develop competence to compensate for their lack of physical benefits. These findings are consistent with an organizational communication study conducted by Heilman and Saruwatari (1979), who found that physical attractiveness was a disadvantage for female job applicants for managerial positions but an advantage at lower-level nonmanagerial positions. Similar results were reported by Hocking, Walker, and Fink (1982), who asked undergraduates to evaluate the morality of two women who allegedly had had premarital sexual intercourse with a man they had never met before or with a man they had been dating for six months. Half the subjects were told the woman was very attractive; the others were told the woman was unattractive. As predicted, the attractive female was perceived as less moral, and this effect was magnified when she had just met her partner.

Unfortunately, according to these studies, attractive women are held to different standards than less-attractive women. As such, both groups are at a distinct disadvantage. An attractive woman is perceived to "have it made," presumably because males will reward her for her physical attractiveness. An attractive woman is perceived not to need to be competent to be a success in business or politics, or to resort to premarital sex to "get her man." An unattractive woman, on the other hand, cannot rely on enticing men with her beauty, so she must become competent, successful, political, and promiscuous to obtain her rewards. These findings confirm the feminist position that women are viewed as objects.

Nonetheless, in politics, employment, dating, business, and every other context, we sell ourselves with our looks. Critics may justifiably deride the superficiality of physical beauty, but it is a unique and salient form of currency in contemporary American society.

Immediacy and Interpersonal Perceptions

When selling ourselves to others, nonverbal immediacy is critical (see Chapter 8). Frowns or tears can make the most beautiful person look ugly. Lack of eye contact or inappropriate interpersonal distances can make a person seem rude, deceptive, or shy. Much of the research on selling oneself reveals the powerful persuasive role of these nonverbal immediacy cues.

Perhaps the most important immediacy cue is eye contact, a behavior that simultaneously creates positive impressions of warmth, confidence, credibility, and attentiveness. Conversely, avoidance of eye contact often leads to attributions of deception, coldness, shyness, disinterest, and rudeness. In a study of interview behavior, Andersen and Coussoule (1980) report that more-continuous lookers were generally perceived as more composed, attractive, extroverted, sociable, and homophilous (similar) than those who averted eye contact.

Employment-interview research shows the importance of eye contact in getting a job. In an employment-interview simulation, Burgoon et al. (1985) found that greater eye contact positively affected the interviewer's perception of the job applicant's competence, composure, sociability, extroversion, task attraction, social attraction, physical attractiveness, intimacy, and immediacy. Most importantly, the study found that moderate to high levels of eye contact increased the likelihood of an individual's being hired, as compared to reduced eye contact.

Other immediacy cues also increase the likelihood of favorable employment interviews. McGovern (1977) experimentally examined the effects of high interviewee immediacy (increased gaze, more energy, and positive tones of voice) on the attitudes of personnel representatives. Results showed that 89 percent of the high-immediacy interviewees were invited back for a second interview, whereas none of the low-immediacy interviewees were invited back. In a similar set of experiments, Young, Beier, and Beier (1979) examined the effect of positive head movements, smiling, and eye contact on job applicants' ratings. Simultaneous use of all three of these immediacy cues by applicants produced the highest ratings. The next-highest ratings were achieved by applicants who employed a combination of eye contact and smiling, followed by eye contact alone. Minimal immediacy produced distinctly lower employment ratings. The same study also found that immediacy cues had a positive effect on employment ratings even for applicants with negative work histories. Another study by Imada and Hakel (1977) also examined the effect of immediacy (including eye contact, smiling, attentive posture, close interpersonal distances, and direct body orientation) in employment interviews. Eighty-six percent of interviewees in the high-immediacy condition were recommended for the job, whereas only 19 percent of the low-immediacy interviewees were recommended. These studies make it clear that increasing one's nonverbal immediacy enhances one's employment opportunities. Similarly, a study of graduate-school selection interviews showed that positive facial nonverbal behavior, particularly eye contact, was critical to graduate-school acceptance (Anderson, 1991). High levels of eye contact fundamentally determined perceptions of competence, strength, and character. Positive facial expressions were linked to both likability and perceptions of motivation.

As was the case with physical appearance, manifesting nonverbal immediacy may even be a matter of life and death! Hemsley and Doob (1978) assessed the effect of direct versus averted gaze during courtroom testimony. For all three defendants in the study, testimony accompanied by averted gaze was significantly associated with guilty verdicts. A similar study by Pryor and Buchanan (1984) created three experimental trial conditions and showed them to real jurors in a Florida courtroom. In one condition, the defendant averted eye contact, exhibited nervous self-touching behaviors, spoke nonfluently, and generally appeared anxious. The defendant in another condition maintained considerable eye contact, exhibited minimal self-touching behaviors, and spoke fluently. The defendant in a third condition exhibited moderate anxiety, between the first two extremes. The immediate, relaxed defendant was less likely to be found guilty than either of the less immediate, more anxious defendants. The more immediate, less anxious defendant was perceived as more competent, trustworthy, pleasant, virtuous, reliable, and intelligent than the more anxious, less immediate defendants. Clearly, jurors judge the nonverbal behavior of trial participants and view immediate, relaxed defendants more favorably.

In the political world, nonverbal immediacy behaviors also significantly increase candidates' credibility and electability. Research on nonverbal behavior in the 1988 Bush-Dukakis debates (Pfau & Kang, 1989) reveals that ratings for both George Bush and Michael Dukakis increased during those segments of the debates when each candidate exhibited immediacy behaviors. Their study revealed that greater nonverbal potency or power played little role in the debates but that greater immediacy played a significant, positive role. This was bad news for Dukakis, who employed fewer immediacy behaviors in general and whose speaking style was perceived by many as "wooden."

A number of additional immediacy behaviors have a positive influence on people's interpersonal perceptions. Interpersonal touch has been shown to have generally positive effects on interpersonal perception (for summaries of this research see Major & Heslin, 1982; see also Chapters 2 and 7). Even nonreciprocal touch can have positive effects. In one study, touchers were rated as significantly higher in status, assertiveness, and warmth than nontouchers (Major & Heslin, 1982). However, several touch-avoidance studies suggest that for highly touch-avoidant individuals, this general pattern may not hold (Andersen, Andersen, & Lustig, 1987; Andersen & Leibowitz, 1978; Sorensen, 1979), because touch avoiders dislike touchers more than nontouchers. Closer proxemic distances also tend to enhance credibility, particularly if the communicator is attractive or has high reward value (Burgoon & Jones, 1976). Several studies have found that even pupil dilation produces increases in physical and social attraction although receivers are unaware of its effects (Andersen, Todd-Mancillas, & DiClemente, 1980; Hess, 1975; Hess & Goodwin, 1974).

Vocalic Influences

A number of studies have examined vocalic, or paralinguistic, influences on interpersonal perceptions. Early research by Miller and Hewgill (1964) discovered that nonfluencies (such as stuttering, false starts, and hesitations) reduce a speaker's credibility. Pearce (1971) reports that more positive, involved, and emotional speaking styles produce perceptions of more dynamism than a scholarly, dispassionate style.

Research by Berry (1990, 1992) demonstrates that people with more attractive voices were judged to be more warm, likeable, honest, dominant, and achievement oriented. Semic, Miller, and Guerrero (1996) extended Berry's research by examining how attractive and unattractive voices are perceived on answering machine messages. Like Berry, these authors found that more attractive voices were perceived as more dominant, competent, likeable, and trustworthy than unattractive voices. Berry (1992) studied the combined effects of vocal attractiveness and vocal maturity. She found that people with less mature, babyish vocal qualities were perceived as less powerful and less competent but warmer and more honest than people with mature-sounding voices.

Several studies have found that faster speaking rates are correlated with more positive impressions and more persuasiveness. One study (Miller et al., 1976) discovered that faster speech increases credibility, which, in turn, increases persuasion. Presumably, people who talk relatively rapidly are confident about what they are saying; they don't hesitate or have to search for the right words because they are knowledgeable. By contrast, Apple et al. (1979) report, slower speakers are judged as less fluent, more passive, and less truthful. MacLachlan (1979) conducted a series of studies that found that fast talkers are regarded much more favorably. Ray and Ray (1988) report that fast-talking doctors are perceived as more competent and socially attractive than slower-talking doctors. The results generally show the benefits of faster speaking rates. However, one study by Woodall and Burgoon (1983) suggests that fast delivery only increases perceived extroversion, has little effect on perceived competence, and may actually decrease both perceived composure and character. Why did Woodall and Burgoon fail to replicate the other studies? One explanation may be found in communication-accommodation theory (Street & Giles, 1982), which has shown that speakers prefer speech styles similar to their own. The initial studies (Apple et al., 1979, MacLachlan, 1979; Miller at al., 1976; Ray & Ray, 1988) were conducted in Cleveland, Los Angeles, and New York, where speech rates tend to be rapid. Woodall and Burgoon (1983) conducted their study in Florida, where the speech rate is relatively slow. Participants in each study may have reacted more favorably to speech similar to their own. In general, though, fast speech rates have more persuasive impact than slow rates. Ketrow's (1990) summary of research on voice and persuasiveness concludes that to maximize one's credibility and social attractiveness, a person should speak fluently and slightly faster than one's listeners and use a moderately loud voice, a standard dialect, and clear diction.

Of course, selling oneself is effective in the corporate, materialistic world, where power and wealth are ultimate values and the "one who dies with the most toys wins." In the final section of this chapter, we will examine the ethics of selling oneself.

Ethics in Persuasion

Years ago, a colleague of mine launched an attack against all persuasion. In his explanation, he railed against persuasion as a form of dominance, enslavement, and autocratic control. He claimed persuasion leads to Nazism and exploitation of the masses. He urged us to repudiate and slay persuasion as a tool of evil dictators. The paradox, of which you may already be aware, is that a persuasive diatribe against persuasion if applied to itself would self-destruct. It is a classic example of the paradoxical struggle between the power structure and the rebel, the establishment and the revolutionary, the modernist and the postmodernist, the religious institution and the atheist, the patriarchy and the feminist, capitalism and communism.

When all is said and done, this is what Rushing (1993) eloquently describes as the battle between "power" and "other." It ultimately results in great power struggles, in which adversaries become increasingly indistinguishable. So the battles between political parties, the war of the century between capitalism and communism, even the war between hegemonic patriarchy and overzealous feminism all emphasize power over "power" or power over "other" in a way that diminishes the human spirit. The third character in Rushing's (1993) mythic trilogy is "spirit." According to Rushing, spirit allows interrelationship among all things.

Bateson (1972) maintains that individual consciousness may pull people out of their ecological niche and disrupt the homeostatic loops of which humans are a part. Persuasion that wins a victory "over" another person, institution, or species weakens our relationships and ultimately threatens all of us.

So my friend who vehemently attempted to persuade us that all persuasion is evil missed the mark. It is egoistic, selfish persuasion, used at the expense of others, that is evil. Persuading a child to stay back from a cliff, a sick friend to see a doctor, a troubled relative to think about counseling, a rich aunt to donate to charity—these are the uses of persuasion that enhance the spirit not diminish it. Persuasion is not the villain. It is persuasion "over" others that is evil—my gain at your expense, my defeat of you for my profit. Persuasion, like fire, can warm, nourish, and illuminate. At the same time, it can also scorch, consume, and incinerate.

The tools of persuasion must be employed wisely with respect for one's receiver and with a recognition of the interrelationship among all people and all things. For what goes around comes around. This is particularly true for the student of persuasion who is acquiring powerful tools from theory and research. My advice to you is this: Use persuasion wisely and ethically.

Persuasion is best used to unite the common interests of all people, of all living things. In your persuasive attempts, ask this question: Will my interaction partner and I *both* be better off as a result of this persuasive effort? If the answer is no, the persuasive message may have ethical problems. To understand and use persuasion is easy. To use it in a way that creates collaboration, promotes symbiosis, and enhances the human spirit is far more challenging.

Summary

Nonverbal communication has often been overlooked by persuasion researchers. As this chapter demonstrates, nonverbal communication is as important as, perhaps more important than, verbal communication in persuading others to change their attitudes and behavior. The evidence best supports the direct-effects model of nonverbal immediacy, which argues that direct gaze, touch, positive facial expression, attractive physical appearance, and combinations of positive, warm cues have clear and consistent persuasive effects. Nonverbal immediacy is effective because it communicates power, captures others' attention, and sends cues of warmth and liking that set the stage for influential behavior.

Other nonverbal-communication/persuasion models have also received some support. Expectancy-violations theory has shown that rewarding communicators are more persuasive when they violate expectancies (for example, by using nonnormative interpersonal distances) but that unrewarding communicators are more persuasive when their behavior is consistent with expectancies (for example, by adopting normative interaction distances). Distraction models suggest that irrelevant distractions (such as traffic noise) reduce persuasion. Distractions in the form of high-status or highly attractive persuaders may enhance attraction and persuasion. This may help explain why rewarding individuals who violate expectations and create a positive distraction are influential. Communication-accommodation theory suggests that we are most persuasive when we adopt our receiver's style of communication. Arousal theories have shown that nonverbal emotional appeals that stimulate receivers are often more persuasive than cool, logical appeals. Physical-attraction theories have shown that attractive communicators experience a "halo effect"; that is, they are perceived by their receivers as more credible, knowledgeable, and competent—qualities that enhance their persuasive efforts. This halo effect appears to exist for both physical and vocal attractiveness.

The most common form of persuasion is selling ourself. In daily life, we strive to appear competent, intelligent, attractive, and credible, primarily through impression management and nonverbal behavior. How and to what ends we use this persuasive power is a matter of ethics. Persuasion has the power to heal or hurt, protect or punish, attract or alienate. The choice is up to us.

11

Concealing and Revealing
Deception and Its Detection
through Nonverbal Cues

DECEPTION RESEARCHER Sissela Bok (1978) poses difficult questions about lying:

> Should physicians lie to dying patients so as to delay the fear and anxiety which the truth might bring them? Should professors exaggerate the excellence of their students on recommendations to give them a better chance in a tight job market? Should parents conceal from children the fact that they were adopted? Should social scientists send investigators masquerading as patients in order to learn about racial and sexual biases in diagnosis and treatment? . . . To lie, equivocate, be silent, or tell the truth in any given situation is often a hard decision. (pp. xv–xvi)

Although we all tell lies, falling victim to a lie can be extremely infuriating, upsetting, and frustrating. Broken marital vows can result in divorce. The uncovered lies of political leaders have led to their impeachment. Lies related to business dealings are the basis of numerous lawsuits. Indeed, labeling someone a "liar" is one of the worst criticisms that can be leveled against a person.

A major paradox surrounds the issue of lying. Despite the fact that lying can destroy friendships, marriages, business deals, and even presidencies, lying actually is quite commonplace! One study reports that 62 percent of all statements made in conversation are deceptive (Turner, Edgley, & Olmstead, 1975). A study by Burgoon, Callister, and Hunsaker (1994) finds that 85 percent of patients conceal or equivocate and about one-third outright lie when talking to their doctor; only 3 percent of patients are completely honest with their doctors. A national survey by Patterson and Kim (1991) reveals that 91 percent of Americans lie regularly! In a recent diary study of lying in everyday life, people reported telling from 0 to 46 lies over one week's time (DePaulo, Kashy, Kirkendol, Wyer, & Epstein, 1996).

Lying is a widespread and central form of influence. Lies are also a method of excusing one's mistakes or being polite to others. The ability to conceal one's true feelings and opinions is an essential part of being a competent communicator; of course, inept or unethical deceptions are considered incompetent. Spitzberg and Cupach (1984) suggest that when deception is both effective and appropriate, it can actually enhance perceptions of a communicator's competence, even when the deception is subsequently discovered. The key is that the deception must be situationally appropriate. It is also likely that many undetected deceptions have numerous interpersonal benefits for the sender. Some individuals, including actors, magicians, nurses, researchers, or politicians, simply could not do their jobs without using deception. A nurse could harm a patient by revealing that his condition was worsening. A head of state cannot divulge state secrets during international negotiations. Even in our close relationships, honesty may not always be the best policy, such as when being asked to comment on your mother-in-law's hideous new dress, when tasting a close friend's disastrous new recipe, or when being asked by your romantic partner if you still feel physical attraction toward an ex-lover. These examples are illustrative of Metts' (1989) research, which demonstrates that individuals often deceive to protect their partners or their relationships.

So, although we loathe being lied to and misled, such deceptions are the stuff of everyday communication. We perpetrate and are exposed to dozens of lies each day! Of course, not all people lie at the same frequency. People with certain personality traits, including manipulativeness and overconcern with self-presentation, tell more lies (Kashy & DePaulo, 1996).

Deception is not limited to human behavior. Indeed, plants and animals employ deceptive coloration to fool enemies, trap prey, and enhance reproduction. Deception provides an evolutionary advantage by increasing the survival rate of a species. Verbal communication, which lends itself to the most easily produced deceptions, probably gave humans an advantage in producing collective deceptions that could dupe less-sophisticated animals. Indeed, humans learned to use this advantage on their own species. Human cooperation and altruism have often been undermined by another aspect of human nature—a desire to gain selective advantages over the group. Archaeologists Leakey and Lewin (1978) maintain:

> During the course of natural selection, individuals are certain to arise who (unconsciously) try to "cheat" in the altruism game. They may produce sham moralistic aggression, sham guilt, sham sympathy, and sham gratitude in an attempt to take more than they give, a situation that could be biologically beneficial in the short term at least. Although an animal without spoken language could indulge in such "cheating" it is much more effective via the spoken word. (p. 192)

Research on chimpanzees has shown that they are capable of intentional deception (Calvin, 1991; Mitchell, 1993). According to Calvin (1991), chimpanzees, under normal circumstances, will call other chimps when they find food in abundance; when only a small amount of food is available, however, they will not call other chimps, or they may even decoy them to the wrong location. Woodruff and Premack (1979) found that chimpanzees deliberately misled "hostile" trainers who were about to steal their food but correctly informed trainers of the food's whereabouts when these trainers had previously shared food with the chimps. Premack and Premack (1983) describe the results of a series of their experiments:

> Did these experiences lead the chimpanzees to lie? In these experiments, the chimpanzees showed two forms of lying: full-fledged lying and a precursor form. Only some of the animals became full-fledged liars. . . . When in the presence of the hostile trainer, all four animals did, in fact, suppress these involuntary movements . . . two of them managed to develop actual lying by misdirecting the hostile trainer to the empty container. (pp. 51–52)

In short, these experiments have shown that chimpanzees engage in two forms of lying: the suppression of nonverbal cues that indicate food location to prevent it from being stolen and a deliberate misdirection to an empty food container. These and numerous other nonverbal actions are effective means of deception. Verbal communication, however, greatly facilitates the act of lying. Indeed, verbal communication is an inherently deceptive system. In Chapter 1, we discussed how difficult it is to fake nonverbal communication. The multichanneled, biologically based, spontaneous, nonverbal system does not easily lend itself to deception. But words are "designed" to inform or to persuade others that the sender's view of reality is correct, an action that always carries with it individual biases, perceptual distortions, and self-serving rationalizations.

Of course, as receivers of verbal messages, we don't blindly accept them. We perform reality checks against what we believe to be true, and we monitor communication behaviors for signs of contradictory messages (see Ekman, 1985). Leakey and Lewin (1978) argue that like deception, detection has great survival advantages: "Just as natural selection inevitably produces would-be cheaters, it will just as inevitably give rise to individuals capable of detecting cheating. And so the game of bluff and double-bluff begins, with the new emotions of trust and suspicion being invented" (p. 192).

Defining Deception

The most widely used definition of *deception* is: a conscious, intentional behavior committed with full knowledge that the information is untrue. Zuckerman, DePaulo, and Rosenthal (1981) define deception as an intentional act that "fosters in another person a belief or understanding which the deceiver considers false"

(p. 3). Knapp and Comadena (1979) note that most studies operationalize deception as "the conscious alteration of information a person believes to be true in order to significantly change another's perceptions from what the deceiver thought they would be without the alteration" (p. 271).

Although these definitions form the basis for most deception research, they may be too narrow to characterize the many kinds of subtle deceptions common in day-to-day interaction. Burgoon, Buller, and Woodall (1996) maintain that although people do intentionally provide false information, they also conceal, omit, or exaggerate information—acts that also can be considered deceptive. Ekman (1985) suggests that there are two primary ways to deceive: to conceal and to falsify. Other scholars also include equivocation in their lists of deceptive acts (see Bavelas, Black, Chovil, & Mullet, 1990; Buller, Burgoon, Buslig, & Roiger, 1996; Burgoon, Buller, Guerrero, Afifi, & Feldman, 1996). Equivocation, for example, might involve giving a vague, ambiguous answer to a question. Certainly, concealment and equivocation can be just as misleading as falsification. Thus, both are considered forms of deception in this chapter.

Another problem with the preceding definitions of deception as an intentional act is the implication that deception occurs primarily through verbal communication. To date, virtually all of the deception research has focused on deliberate, conscious, *verbal* lies. Although considerable research has examined the nonverbal consequences of deception, such as increased anxiety, little research has examined the many subtle, nonverbal acts that constitute deception in and of themselves.

Some forms of nonverbal deception are processed at low levels of awareness. Research by various scholars (Andersen, Andersen, & Landgraf, 1985; Ekman, 1978; Shennum & Bugental, 1982) shows that five types of behavior that could be considered deceptive commonly occur in facial expressions: (1) *simulation,* or showing feelings when you have no feelings; (2) *intensification,* giving the appearance of more feeling than you have; (3) *inhibition,* appearing to have no feelings when you really have feelings; (4) *miniaturization,* giving the appearance of having less feelings than you actually have; and (5) *masking,* covering a feeling with an expression of a feeling you are not having (see Chapter 6 for a detailed discussion of the nonverbal communication of emotions).

A broad conceptualization of deception would include a lengthy list of various acts, including backstabbing, bluffing, conning, concealing, concocting, covering up, crying wolf, distorting, doctoring, entrapping, equivocating, using euphemisms, evading, exaggerating, fabricating, creating false implications, falsifying, fibbing, committing forgery and fraud, playing hoaxes, being hypocritical, impersonating, inventing, lying, masking, playing make-believe, misrepresenting, telling myths, perjuring, teasing, feigning politeness, prevaricating, putting others on, pulling ruses, simulating, spinning tall tales, spying, swindling, being two-faced, and telling untruths and white lies. Hopper and Bell (1984) report that communicators perceive most of these acts to fall into six categories or clusters: (1) *fictions,* including exaggerating and telling tall tales and white lies; (2) *playings,* including teasing, bluffing, and playing hoaxes; (3) *lies,* including fibbing, telling untruths, and making other false verbal statements; (4) *crimes,* including entrapping, covering up, and committing forgery; (5) *masks,* including backstabbing, evading, and concealing; and (6) *unlies,* including being two-faced, backstabbing, and concealing.

Signs of Deception

Finding foolproof cues that accompany deceptive communication has been an age-old goal of judges, juries, professors, and parents. Indeed, examining the behavioral correlates of lying is one of two major streams of communication research on deception. I had an opportunity years ago to do deception consulting with the staff at a law-enforcement academy that trained police officers, detectives, and polygraph operators. Law-enforcement professionals have relied on the polygraph, or lie detector, as an important tool in their work. Over the past couple decades, however, courts and lawmakers have attempted to restrict the use of the polygraph, criticizing the practice as an invasion of privacy, particularly in a new arena, preemployment interviews. In light of these restrictions, law-enforcement professionals have become interested in finding a supplement to the polygraph, a way of detecting deception through nonverbal communication. In consulting with the law-enforcement academy, I focused on teaching the staff the following three important principles of detecting deception: (1) no foolproof means of detecting deception through nonverbal behavior exists now or is likely to in the future; (2) nonetheless, some commonalities in deceptive behavior can aid in its detection; and (3) a complex mixture of unconscious and strategic processes produce subtle changes in behavior during deceptive communication.

The Inconsistency of Deception Cues

Early deception researchers sought to discover a behavioral profile of deceptive communication. They hoped to find certain cues (for example, stuttering or shifty eyes) that always accompany deception. If they had been successful, the theoretical and practical payoffs would have been great. Unfortunately, although a few nonverbal cues have shown consistent associations with deception, these cues are associated with many other behavioral causes.

As you will learn in this chapter, there are good theoretical reasons why no consistent set of deception cues should exist. Kraut (1980) claims that a careful, a-priori theoretical analysis demonstrates why this is so: "People sometimes act differently when they are lying and telling the truth. But these differences are not communicants of deception per se, but instead reflect internal states like heightened cognitive processing, fear, guilt, excitement or arousal" (p. 213). At best, nonverbal cues are indirect indicants of deception. As you will see in the following discussion, research is proceeding on these indirect cues, but the process is much more complex than once believed.

As mentioned, research has found few consistent deception cues. Across twenty-one studies, Kraut (1980) reports that only four of fourteen nonverbal deception cues were consistent across more than one study. Buller and Walther (1989) maintain, "A great deal of the empirical research on deception has searched for behaviors that can reliably discriminate deceivers from truthtellers. By and large, this research has found that deception affects behavior, but few cues uniquely identify deception" (p. 1).

Individual Differences

Individual differences in skill, personality, and behavior are another reason why nonverbal cues are inconsistently related to deception. These individual differences take many forms. Gender, age, communication skill, personality, and behavior patterns determine the extent to which a person manifests deception nonverbally. Thus, it should not be too surprising that a single checklist of deception cues that works for every individual has been hard to construct.

EXPRESSIVENESS

In a study by Riggio and Friedman (1983), dominant, extroverted, and exhibitionistic individuals displayed fewer nervous behaviors during deception than other people. In fact, people displaying these three personality traits were so good at controlling anxiety cues that they overcontrolled them, resulting in more nervous behavior during truth-telling than during deception. Similarly, one study found that expressive and socially tactful people were more successful deceivers (Riggio, Tucker, & Throckmorton, 1987). Burgoon, Buller, and Guerrero (1995) also found that social expressivity was generally associated with partner-perceptions of believability. Another study found that highly expressive people were no more likely to show deception cues when lying than when truthful (DePaulo, Blank, Swaim, & Hairfield, 1992). Conversely, unexpressive people appeared more deceptive when lying.

MACHIAVELLIANISM

Research on Machiavellian individuals (manipulators) has shown an inconsistent relationship with deception. Knapp, Hart, and Dennis (1974) and O'Hair, Cody, and McLaughlin (1981) report little relationship between deceptive behavior and Machiavellianism. However, Buller and Burgoon's (1994) literature review suggests some differences in the deceptive skills of high and low Machiavellians. High Machiavellians were found to compensate manipulatively during deception through the exaggeration of such behaviors as increased eye contact.

ANXIETY

Research suggests that self-conscious and anxious individuals are poorer perpetrators of lies, just as they are poor communicators in general (see Chapter 7). A study by Riggio, Tucker, and Widaman (1987) found that persons high in public self-consciousness fell apart during deception and displayed numerous deception cues, including less verbal fluency, less eye contact, fewer head movements, and more emotional reactions. Riggio, Tucker, and Throckmorton (1987) found socially anxious people to be less successful deceivers. Similarly, O'Hair, Cody, and Behnke's (1985) research showed that high communication-apprehensive individuals displayed more vocal stress during prepared lies than prepared truths, although no difference was found for spontaneous truths and lies.

SELF-MONITORING

Research on self-monitors (individuals who are more situationally sensitive and adaptive) revealed that high self-monitors were more successful deceivers than low self-monitors (Krauss, Geller, & Olson, 1976; Miller, deTurck, & Kalbfleish, 1983). Moreover, their skills improved when they had an opportunity to practice their deceptive strategies (Miller et al., 1983). However, research by Zuckerman et al. (1979) found the opposite relationship: self-monitoring led to less success at deceiving. Burgoon, Buller, Guerrero, and Feldman's (1994) findings may partially explain this inconsistency. They found that high and low self-monitors perceived themselves to be more successful at deception than moderate self-monitors. However, observers saw high self-monitors as the most successful deceivers. These findings indicate that high self-monitoring individuals may be their own toughest critics, in that they try to control the cues that leak deception and notice when they fail to do so. Observers, however, see high self-monitors as the most believable, presumably because they are effective in managing their behavior during deception.

AGE AND NONVERBAL ABILITY

In their review of research, Buller and Burgoon (1994) report that people, especially women, become more skilled at lying as they get older. Evidently, deceptive skills can be learned, and advancing years provide more opportunity for practice. Several studies have found that individuals who score higher in tests of nonverbal skill emit fewer deception cues. Individuals with greater nonverbal sending ability (those who can easily encode emotions nonverbally) are viewed as being more truthful (Riggio & Friedman, 1983). Similarly, studies have found that people scoring high on a measure of "social skill" emit fewer deception cues and are judged as more believable than people who are less socially skilled (Riggio, Tucker, & Widaman, 1987), especially during concealment (Burgoon, Buller, Guerrero, & Feldman, 1994).

OCCUPATION

Even out of character, actors are probably able to pull off deception without much change in their behavior. One study showed that good actors tended to be skilled liars who could deceive observers, especially with their faces (Riggio & Friedman, 1983). Many professions require excellent acting ability to sustain lies and conceal information: not only actors but lawyers, political candidates, diplomats, salespeople, and magicians all rely on deception in their work. These professions probably attract already proficient deceivers who then become even more skilled as they practice their deceptive arts in their livelihoods.

Contextual Factors

In addition to individual differences, variations in context may alter the display of deception cues (see Chapter 3 for more on context and nonverbal communication). Buller and Aune (1988b) report that deceivers behave differently with friends than with strangers. Strangers decrease eye contact during deception, but friends increase it, suggesting that nonimmediacy may be a deceptive strategy limited to strangers. Another explanation is that friends strategically manage their immediacy cues during deception to appear warm and sincere. Recent research shows that deceivers are generally more expressive and less formal when deceiving friends as opposed to strangers. Deception directed toward friends also shows more alterations in behavior than deception directed toward strangers (Buller, Burgoon, White, & Ebesu, 1994), indicating that people may be more active in managing deception when with friends.

As a central part of interpersonal deception theory, Buller and Burgoon (1996) focus on the difference between noninteractive and interactive contexts in which deception occurs. They argue that in noninteractive contexts (such as a videotaped intercommunication, in which the deceiver and potential detector are not present at the same time and place), deceivers are nonimmediate, uninvolved, overaroused, negative, and impaired communicatively but that in interactive contexts, deceivers behave more strategically. Thus, in interactive contexts, deceivers control their nonimmediacy, nervousness, and arousal. The result may be a somewhat stilted performance. However, good deceivers in interactive contexts appear to be telling the truth. Clearly, the search for deception cues must take into account the type of relationship and context in which deception takes place.

Similarly, prepared lies are displayed differently than spontaneous lies. O'Hair et al. (1981) found that during prepared deception, liars used shorter pauses, shorter messages, more head nods, less smiling, and more adaptors than did truth-tellers. During spontaneous lies, only body adaptors increased. A profile of deceptive behavior must take into account these contextual factors.

Emerging Consistencies

Among dozens of possible nonverbal deception cues, a few are emerging as consistent correlates of deception. Even so, none of these cues are *uniquely* associated with deception. Because there are individual and contextual differences in behavior and because emotional displays that are unrelated to deception are often present when one is deceiving, these cues are useful only in general terms, not for identifying deception in specific people in specific circumstances. Given these caveats, what does research reveal as the most likely deception cues?

SPEECH ERRORS

Research has consistently shown that speech errors are one of the most common correlates of deception. Research summaries have consistently shown that speakers manifest more mispronunciations, false starts, stutters, and other disfluencies during deception (Burgoon, Buller, & Woodall, 1989; DePaulo, Stone, & Lassiter, 1985; Kraut, 1980; Vrij & Winkel, 1991; Zuckerman et al., 1981). One study by deTurck and Miller (1985) found that deceivers showed more speech errors than truth-tellers. Moreover, this study found that these errors were not due to arousal, because aroused nondeceivers did not show more speech errors. (Later in this chapter we will examine eleven processes that explain the changes in behavior, such as speech errors, that occur during deception.) Another study found intercultural support for increased speech errors during deception by observing newly arrived immigrants from Taiwan and Hong Kong, who also showed this pattern (Cody, Lee, & Chao, 1988).

SPEAKING TURNS

The duration of a person's speaking turn is a deception variable that constitutes a combination of verbal and chronemic (nonverbal) cues. Most studies show that liars talk less than truth-tellers, particularly in response to questions (Comadena, 1982a; deTurck & Miller, 1985; Knapp et al., 1974; Vrij & Winkel, 1991). Early summaries of research found no significant relationship between deception and speaking turns (Kraut, 1980; Zuckerman et al., 1981), but a more recent statistical summary concludes that shorter responses are associated with deception (DePaulo et al., 1985), suggesting that deceivers are less committed to their lies. Alternatively, deceivers may have more problems constructing messages than do truth-tellers. Chinese-immigrant deceivers were also found to employ shorter responses (Cody et al. 1988), indicating cross-cultural support for this deception cue.

EYE BLINKS

Two of the most extensive statistical summaries of research on deception conclude that increased blinking is associated with deception (Kraut, 1980; DePaulo et al., 1985), although this finding was not replicated for Chinese immigrants (Cody et al., 1988). Increased blinking may be due to increased arousal or cognitive activity during deception.

SMILES

Research on the relationship of smiling to deception has been rather contradictory. Some studies have found increased smiling during deception, whereas others have reported decreased smiling. Research shows no overall statistical relationship between deception and smiling (DePaulo et al., 1985; Kraut, 1980; Zuckerman et al., 1981; Vrij & Winkel, 1991). The prevailing evidence suggests a trend toward less smiling during deception, but the relationship is not statistically significant across twenty studies. Research (Ekman, 1988; Ekman, Friesen, &

O'Sullivan, 1988) suggests that true (felt) smiles are different than deceptive (unfelt) smiles, which mask other emotions (such as anxiety, contempt, or sadness). Deceptive smiles show traces of the masked emotion, and the corners of the eyes remain relatively stationary. Likewise, unfelt smiles are asymmetrical, with the smile usually portrayed more strongly on the right side of the face than the left. Felt, happy smiles, in contrast, are displayed at the corners of the eye, which fold and "smile" when someone is genuinely happy. Had previous research on deception separated these two types of smiles, a decrease in felt, happy smiles and an increase in masking smiles during deception probably would have been found.

ADAPTORS

Adaptors are self-touches or object manipulations, such as twiddling one's fingers, playing with a piece of string, straightening one's clothes, or scratching an itch. Numerous studies reveal that increased adaptors are one of the most powerful correlates of deception. Comprehensive statistical summaries of the deception literature all report that increased adaptors are associated with deception (DePaulo et al., 1985; Kraut, 1980; Vrij & Winkel, 1991; Zuckerman, et al., 1981), although one subsequent study failed to find such increases (Koper & Miller, 1986). In another study, adaptors increased during factual deceptions but decreased during emotional deceptions (Comadena, 1982b). The typical finding of an increase in adaptors during deception is probably due to increased tension. However, Vrij and Winkel (1991) report fewer adaptors during deception. Similarly, Koper and Miller (1986) found that *highly* deceitful people manifested few adaptors, perhaps suggesting that some experienced liars feel little tension and/ or are able to control its outward expression. Motivation may also play a role. Deceivers who are highly motivated to escape detection may carefully control nervous gestures such as adaptors. Unfortunately for the deceiver, however, too much control may lead to a stiff, unnatural-looking manner (see Buller & Burgoon, 1996; Burgoon, Buller, & Guerrero, 1995).

BODY MOVEMENTS

Some research suggests that increased head movements are associated with deception, including up and down nodding behaviors as well as overall head mobility (Donagy & Dooley, 1994). However, other research (Buller, Burgoon, White, & Ebesu, 1994) indicates less nodding during deception.

In a series of studies by Vrij and his colleagues, deceivers displayed fewer finger, hand, and arm movements than truth-tellers (Vrij, 1994; Vrij, Semin, & Bull, 1996; Vrij & Winkel, 1991). This effect was most pronounced while deceivers were listening, suggesting that the cognitive demands of speaking limit the strategic management of limb movement.

VOCAL PITCH

In general, studies report that deception is associated with an increase in vocal pitch (see summaries by Burgoon, Buller, & Woodall, 1996; DePaulo et al., 1985;

Ekman, 1988; and Zuckerman et al., 1981). This increase is probably due to heightened arousal and tension experienced while lying. Streeter, Krauss, Geller, Olson, and Apple (1979) found that highly stressful deceptive acts resulted in the greatest increase in vocal pitch.

GAZE

"You can't hide your lying eyes," is ingrained in our folk wisdom and is even a line from a popular song. Evidently, this adage rests on shaky ground, because three major statistical summaries of deception research show no statistically significant, overall relationship between eye contact and deception (DePaulo et al., 1985; Kraut, 1980; Zuckerman et al., 1981). However, many individual studies have found decreases in gaze during deception. By contrast, other studies (for example, Riggio & Friedman, 1983) have found an increase in eye contact, perhaps because deceivers overcompensate by consciously maintaining more direct gaze when lying. Presumably, people know that deception is stereotypically linked with decreased eye contact, so they make sure to "look into someone's eyes" when deceiving.

PUPIL DILATION

Several studies report increased pupil dilation during deception (see DePaulo et al., 1985; Zuckerman et al., 1981), which is probably due to increased arousal associated with lying. However, pupil dilation usually is correlated with positive arousal (Andersen, Todd-Mancillas, & DiClemente, 1980), so this finding is somewhat surprising. Perhaps pupil dilation is a sign of increased cognitive activity that may occur during lying.

HAND SHRUGS

One of the earliest reported and most interesting deception cues is the hand shrug (Ekman & Friesen, 1972). This gesture involves raising and lowering the hand—palm up—one or more times. Statistical reviews of previous research disagree about whether such gestures are actually associated with deception (DePaulo et al., 1985; Zuckerman et al., 1981). Hand shrugs may unconsciously indicate confusion over what to say or low confidence in what is said.

OTHER CUES

At present, the best available evidence suggests that some other nonverbal cues are indicants of deception, including gestures, speech rate, foot and leg movements, and postural shifts. Unfortunately, no consistent evidence has shown that these cues are trustworthy correlates of deception (DePaulo et al., 1985). In fact, nonverbal behaviors such as smiling and nodding may be almost absent in some deceptive encounters and quite abundant in others. As Burgoon, Buller, & Woodall (1996) stress, there is no single telltale sign that proves a person is deceiving.

Toward a Theory of Deceptive Behavior

As mentioned earlier, a complex mix of unconscious and conscious processes are the cause of behavioral differences during deception. Perhaps the greatest benefit of research on deception is our increased theoretical understanding of many basic processes underlying human communication. Any behavioral theory of deception must account for these numerous processes that occur during deception.

Both physical and mental changes occur during deception to cause cues to "leak." These leaks are usually involuntary, unconscious changes in nonverbal behavior. This leakage hypothesis was the basis for the original research on deception cues (see Ekman & Friesen, 1969a). Recently, scholars have recognized that deceivers also consciously and strategically alter their behavior during deception to conceal their lies, resulting in a second set of processes that produces changes in behavior during deception. As such, the difficulty in producing a profile of deception cues and in detecting deception is a function of the many types of leakage and strategic changes that occur during deception (see Buller & Burgoon, 1994, 1996).

Causes of Leakage during Deception

During deception, unconscious emotional and physical changes occur. Usually, these changes are experienced as guilt, nervousness, and anxiety about getting caught. Researchers have discovered at least five primarily unconscious processes that cause leakage to occur: arousal, anxiety, negative affect, cognitive difficulty, and duping delight. Although the discussion in this chapter is limited to deception, leakage is also likely to occur in situations that evoke anger, sexual arousal, joy, fear, and anxiety (see Chapter 6 for a general discussion of emotion and Chapter 7 for a discussion of anxiety).

AROUSAL

The human mind and body prepare for activity by increasing mental and physiological arousal, including a faster heart rate, increased blood pressure, faster respiration, and changes in the electrical conductivity of the skin (see Chapter 7). If arousal occurs in a negative context or if it reaches very high levels, it is experienced as anxiety. At other times, arousal can be sexual, physiological, or simply exciting. Arousal induces changes in nonverbal behaviors, including increased movement and vocalic modifications.

Polygraphic testing is based on the fact that during deception, key physiological indicators, such as one's heart rate, increase. According to current theory, there are at least six reasons for this increase in physiological arousal. First, because the individual often remembers past deceptions as unpleasant and traumatic, conditioned-response theory predicts that during deception the act of lying is conditioned to and associated with prior unpleasant arousal (Zuckerman et al., 1981). Second, conflict theory predicts that arousal during lying is due to conflicting internal tendencies to lie *and* tell the truth. Third, punishment theory suggests that arousal is the result of anticipated negative consequences should the lie be discovered (Zuckerman et al., 1981). Fourth, the guilt associated with deception can also produce arousal. Fifth, the enhanced motivation to succeed in deceiving another person may be stimulating or arousing (Zuckerman & Driver, 1985). Sixth, some individuals experience arousal because they enjoy deception and especially get pleasure from successful deception.

Many of the deception cues described earlier are due, in part, to increases in arousal. These cues include increased speech errors, blinking, adaptors, vocal pitch, and pupil dilation. Deception research shows that arousal cues are most likely to be associated with deception (Buller & Aune, 1988b; Burgoon & Buller, 1994; Zuckerman & Driver, 1985). Likewise, specific tests of arousal theory have been somewhat supportive. In one experiment, deceivers in swivel chairs showed more "chair twisting"; other arousal cues, however, were actually reduced (Buller & Aune, 1988b).

Deceivers probably attempt to control arousal cues, which explains why all experiments have not found increases in arousal behaviors. Two studies of deception cues among Chinese immigrants failed to support the typical predictions of deception-induced arousal, casting doubt on whether it is a cross-cultural phenomenon (Cody et al., 1988; O'Hair, Cody, Choa, & Wang, 1989). Regardless, a large body of evidence shows that arousal-related changes occur in people's behavior during deception.

ANXIETY

Researchers are not always able to separate arousal from anxiety. We do know, however, that some behavioral changes during deception likely result from specific increases in anxiety rather than general arousal. Guilt about lying or fear of being caught contributes to specific anxiety responses rather than simply to general arousal. One of the behaviors that commonly increases during deception is the use of adaptors, self-touching or object-manipulating behaviors designed to reduce stress and anxiety. The increase in adaptors during deception is probably an attempt to reduce anxiety rather than a result of general arousal.

The most compelling evidence that suggests that nonverbal deception cues result from anxiety rather than general arousal comes from a study comparing aroused deceivers, aroused truth-tellers, and unaroused truth-tellers (deTurck & Miller, 1985). Six cues, including adaptors, hand gestures, speech errors, pauses, response latency, and message duration, distinguished deceivers from *both* unaroused truth-tellers and aroused truth-tellers. "We can conclude that behavioral configurations displayed by deceivers are not attributable to arousal per se but rather are unique to deception-induced arousal" (deTurck & Miller, 1985, p. 197). It is likely that anxiety added to arousal results in many behavioral deception cues.

NEGATIVE AFFECT

For most people, deception is unpleasant. Many deceivers have some negative feelings for the person they are lying to since it's typically an adversarial win-lose situation. Moreover, deceivers may feel guilt, anger, or anxiety during the deceptive act, especially when they are lying rather than concealing or equivocating. Several scholars (Zuckerman & Driver, 1985; Buller & Burgoon, 1994) have suggested that some deception cues involve leaking signs of negative feelings toward others. DePaulo et al. (1985) report that liars make more negative statements than truth-tellers. Ekman and Friesen (1969a) suggest that negative feelings during deception may be leaked via negative micromomentary expressions occurring at a fraction of a second but nonetheless influencing others' perceptions. Two studies found negative vocal cues to be associated with deception. DePaulo, Rosenthal, Green, and Rosenkrantz (1982) report that liars were judged to have more negative tones of voice than truth-tellers. This study used content-filtered speech so that the judges were not aware of what was said, only the tone of voice. Buller and Aune (1988b) report that deceptive strangers were less vocally pleasant than truth-telling strangers. Although evidence is limited, it seems likely that liars communicate more negative affect than do truth-tellers. Research on deception in interactive contexts has also shown that deceivers show more negative affect than truth-tellers (Burgoon & Buller, 1994).

COGNITIVE DIFFICULTY

Lying isn't easy. Deceivers must tell a plausible lie, monitor the receivers' reactions, control their own behavior, and seem confident. Buller and Burgoon (1994) maintain that lying is so difficult that it leads to incompetent performance, characterized by an artificial, halting, or unbelievable style. Several of the deception cues discussed previously, including disfluencies and pupil dilation while speaking, have been found in previous studies to be more common during any difficult or cognitively demanding task (DePaulo et al., 1985; Greene, O'Hair, Cody, & Yen, 1985; Vrij & Winkel, 1991; Zuckerman & Driver, 1985). It follows, then, that these deception cues may result from the cognitive difficulty experienced when lying. Cody et al. (1988) found support for the hypothesis that lying is more difficult than truth-telling. Among their Chinese-immigrant sample, deceivers used briefer messages with fewer details and higher rates of speech errors than truth-tellers—a finding that is consistent with the fact that lying produces signs of cognitive difficulty. Although research is still needed, these results seem to suggest that some deception cues are caused by cognitive difficulty or overload. In their recent theoretical overview of the deception phenomenon, Buller and Burgoon (1996) conclude that deception is a complex task that adds

further cognitive demands beyond those associated with conducting conversation. Deceivers must strategically manipulate information to craft plausible messages "on-line" all while attending to partner reactions for information about success or failure. These tasks alone are demanding and are made more so by the special demands of creating false impressions. (p. 210)

So, conversational demands on cognitive resources are substantially increased in deceptive situations, often diverting these resources from other features of competent communication.

DUPING DELIGHT

Some liars are overconfident. Smug, excited, and pleased with their success at the deception game, these deceivers begin to emit signs of pleasure, excitement, and overconfidence, which Ekman (1985, 1988) labels duping delight. These feelings may produce increased arousal, contributing further to the overstimulation many liars experience. Duping delight may be responsible for the occasional finding that deception produces positive affect, such as gleeful vocal tones or smiles.

Strategic Deception Cues

The five processes just described result in the involuntary leakage of deception cues. But humans are strategic creatures who influence, plan, scheme, and strategize during their deceptive attempts. Strategic deception cues are aimed at concealing deception. Buller and his colleagues (Buller & Burgoon, 1994, 1996; Buller, Burgoon, & Guerrero, 1994) argue that deception cues are a mixture of leaked (unplanned) and strategic (planned) cues. "Deceivers are concerned with appearing credible, allaying receiver suspicions, minimizing their responsibility for deceit and avoiding unpleasant consequences if deception is detected" (Buller, Burgoon, & Guerrero, 1994, p. 10). These strategic attempts to deceive produce additional changes in behavior, including reductions and (sometimes) increases in immediacy, image manipulation, arousal reduction, ambiguity increases, and leakage control.

NONIMMEDIACY

Immediacy behaviors communicate involvement, approach, and physical or psychological closeness (see Chapter 8). Deception researchers have frequently witnessed reductions in immediacy by liars or attempts to disaffiliate from the target of their lies (Buller & Burgoon, 1994; DePaulo et al., 1985). Buller and Burgoon (1994) believe that nonimmediacy, or withdrawal, behaviors are strategic, intentional behaviors used to distance oneself from the target of a lie, to disaffiliate, and to reduce the scrutiny of probing communication. Deception research has shown that deceivers sometimes smile less, stand or sit farther away, reduce gaze, stand at less-direct body angles, and use shorter statements and answers (Buller, 1988; Buller & Burgoon, 1994; Burgoon & Buller, 1994; DePaulo et al., 1985). Similarly, research on equivocation reveals that equivocators show less pleasant, more negative cues than nonequivocators (Buller, Burgoon, Buslig, & Roiger, 1994). Although equivocation is a mild form of deception, it is interesting that equivocators, like outright liars, manifest less immediacy.

Several deception studies have tested for immediacy effects. In their statistical summary of prior research, Zuckerman and Driver (1985) found that "deceptive statements were more nonimmediate than truthful ones, perhaps signaling withdrawal from the content of the message" (p. 138). In a study by Buller and Aune (1988b), deceivers were significantly less immediate and involved than truth-tellers, and this effect occurred throughout an entire deceptive episode. In a study of paralinguistic cues, Cody, Marsten, and Foster (1984) reported that liars used fewer words, shorter messages, and longer pauses than truth-tellers. Ironically, by attempting to conceal their lies through the strategy of dissociation and nonimmediacy, deceivers actually produce an additional deception cue for the attentive observer to detect.

IMMEDIACY

Paradoxically, some studies have actually found immediacy to increase during deception (DePaulo et al., 1985; Riggio & Friedman, 1983). Evidently, deceivers use pleasant, immediate behaviors to ingratiate receivers and make them buy their deceptive communication. Surprisingly, some studies have even found simultaneous increases and decreases in immediacy during deception and equivocation (see Buller, Burgoon, Buslig, & Roiger, 1994). Although nonimmediacy is a more typical response in deceptive communication, some deceivers overcompensate to create a positive image. The fact that immediacy behaviors both increase and decrease during deception is paradoxical and confusing. Nonetheless, it typifies the complexity of nonverbal deception cues and illustrates why a simple profile of deceptive behaviors has remained so elusive (see Chapter 8 for more about immediacy).

IMAGE MANIPULATIONS

Deceivers want to make a good impression on others; they want to be viewed as nice, honest people. To accomplish this goal, deceivers may strategically change their behavior. These image-protecting or image-management behaviors may comprise yet another set of deception cues (Buller & Burgoon, 1994, 1996; Burgoon, Buller, & Guerrero, 1995; DePaulo et al., 1985). These behaviors include pleasant, affiliative, expressive actions such as smiles, nods, vocal and kinesic expressiveness, and an avoidance of interrupting the other person (Burgoon et al., 1995; DePaulo et al., 1985). But evidence for image protection during deception is mixed, with some studies finding more image-protecting behaviors but more studies finding reductions or no differences in these behaviors (Buller, 1988). Buller and Aune (1988b) specifically tested the hypothesis that image-protecting behaviors such as head nodding, head shaking, and general pleasantness would increase during deception; however, they found no support for that hypothesis. Burgoon, Buller, & Guerrero (1995) found that more-skilled deceivers are better able to manage their image and are more effective at deception. Thus, although not all studies indicate that image-manipulation is a strategic alteration during deception, some evidence indicates that deceivers do try to maintain a more positive image in deceptive than in nondeceptive situations.

AROUSAL REDUCTION

One of the major causes of leakage, discussed previously, is arousal. People feel increased tension, stimulation, and arousal while deceiving. Buller and Aune (1988b) suggest that arousal-related leakage may be moderated by the extent to which deceivers can control this arousal. Deceivers may also actually suppress bodily activity so as not to appear nervous, aroused, or active. Contrary to the leakage hypothesis, Buller and Aune (1988b) found that deceivers displayed significantly fewer head and face adaptors, fewer total adaptors, less gestural animation, and softer voices than truth-tellers. Moreover, they reduced those signs of arousal across the entire deceptive interaction. Buller, Strzyzewski, and Comstock (1991) report that deceivers attempted to conceal their deceit by masking nonverbal nervousness and arousal cues. Masking was particularly evident when a receiver showed signs of suspicion. This limited evidence supports the notion that deceivers strategically reduce arousal cues. Ironically, reductions in nervous behaviors may actually constitute an additional set of deception cues.

AMBIGUITY INCREASES

One of the primary strategies employed by liars to avoid detection is to create vague, unverifiable, and uncertain messages (Buller & Burgoon, 1994). Although research suggests that this strategy involves mainly linguistic tactics, such as ambiguous or equivocal messages, some signs of uncertainty may be communicated nonverbally. One statistical summary of deception research (Zuckerman et al., 1981) reported significantly more hand shrugs (a sign of uncertainty) during deception than during truth-telling. Subsequent statistical summaries report that hand shrugs fall just short of statistical significance as a deception cue. Buller and Aune (1988b) reported that hand shrugs were more prevalent among deceptive friends than truthful friends, although this comparison did not hold up for interactions with strangers or intimates. This limited evidence suggests that future research on deception should explore other signs of vagueness or equivocation as a strategic deception cue.

LEAKAGE CONTROL

Perhaps the most common strategy employed by deceivers is to control leakage and deception cues. Zuckerman and Driver (1985) contend, "Since deceivers try not to disclose what they really think, they must exercise greater control over their behavior than do truth-tellers" (p. 131). Hocking and Leathers's (1980) theory of deception cues based on leakage control argues that deceivers control those behaviors that (1) receivers stereotype as deception cues, (2) the deceiver can most easily monitor, and (3) are most susceptible to conscious control. Hocking and Leathers suggest that Class I behaviors—including head, arm, leg, and body movements and signs of nervousness—meet all of these criteria and are most susceptible to control. Class II behaviors (such as facial expressions) are more difficult to monitor and to control. Class III behaviors (such as disfluencies, speech rate, and vocal nervousness) cannot be consciously controlled. Considerable research supports this model (Cody et al., 1984; Hocking & Leathers, 1980; Buller & Burgoon, 1996). Thus, as mentioned earlier, eye contact is often managed during deceptive interaction. Deceivers know that people expect liars to avert their gaze. Furthermore, eye contact is a fairly easy behavior to control. Hocking and Leathers's model also explains why some studies have found deceivers to become very still, perhaps as a way to control their nervous movements.

In the absence of conscious leakage control by deceivers, one would expect lies to be accompanied by signs of arousal and nervousness, such as increases in gestures, leg and foot movements, body movements, head movements, and postural shifts. Surprisingly, statistical summaries of research do not show increases in these behaviors during deception (DePaulo et al., 1985; Zuckerman & Driver, 1985). In fact, they reveal slight, though nonsignificant, decreases! Moreover, these statistical summaries of psychological studies unfortunately fail to include some communication studies that show *significant decreases* in these behaviors. Hocking and Leathers (1980) report significantly fewer foot movements, one of the most controllable deception-related behaviors. Greene et al. (1985) showed that people who were asked to lie not only exhibited less foot and leg movement than truth-tellers, they also continued to manifest fewer of these behaviors when they stopped lying, as compared to those who told the truth all along.

The best way to control strong emotions during deception, according to Ekman (1985), is to mask the emotions. Masks may include facial covering or turning away to conceal the emotional display. The best masks, of course, are false emotions, which provide camouflage to mislead the receiver. So, leakage control may also include feigned warmth or happiness or mock outrage. Evidence suggests that leakage is controlled in many ways (Ekman, 1985).

Any emerging theory of deceptive behavior needs to account for the many varieties of nonverbal leakage cues and strategic nonverbal behaviors outlined here. The complexity of these eleven interwoven processes demonstrates the theoretical basis for the inability to provide a simple taxonomy of nonverbal deception cues. Similarly, as we will learn in the next section, it is part of the reason why deception detection is so difficult.

Deception Detection

How well can ordinary folks detect lies? The previous discussion indicates that even the experts, compiling extensive lists of nonverbal correlates of deception, are far from perfect accuracy in their detection of deception. Intuition would suggest, and research shows, that ordinary, untrained observers are usually even poorer deception detectors. In some cases, however, individuals who attempt to detect deception as a part of their occupations are the poorest deception detectors. For example, police officers, professional interrogators, and customs inspectors sometimes have *lie biases*. In other words, because these individuals deal with deceivers on a frequent basis, they tend to think people are lying to them more often than not, which makes them inaccurate deception detectors. For most people, the opposite is true: we think that people are telling us the truth more often than not. This tendency leads to a *truth bias*, which can also lead to deception-detection inaccuracies.

In a number of laboratory studies, naive, untrained observers were asked to determine whether another person was lying or telling the truth, a situation with a fifty-fifty chance of a correct guess. Research shows that people do little better than chance, even when they are highly attentive to the fact a lie may be occurring. Because we don't look for lies in most everyday interactions, we probably detect far fewer than half of all the lies we're told.

Actually, as Miller and Stiff (1993) point out, deception detection is something of a misnomer. Virtually all of the experiments in this area of research employ both truthful and deceptive communication and ask subjects to determine if the communicator is telling the truth or not. So, most of these studies are actually investigations of truth detection as well as deception detection. Indeed, studies reveal that accuracy is higher for truth detection than for deception detection, probably because of the truth bias mentioned earlier (Burgoon, Buller, Ebesu, & Rockwell, 1994; Feeley & Young, 1995).

Statistical summaries of research confirm that people are poor lie detectors. Kraut (1980) reports that although people can detect lies at slightly above chance level, the mean accuracy rate across previous studies was about 57 percent, with accuracy rates rarely reaching 65 percent. Other studies corroborate this figure. Littlepage, Maddox, and Pineault (1985) report 58 percent accuracy in their deception study, with respondents judging true statements correctly 67 percent of the time and false statements correctly 51 percent of the time. Similarly, Mc-Cornack and Parks's (1987) participants correctly judged deception 59 percent of the time, even though the participants were dating partners, who should have been able to detect deception more easily than strangers. With dating partners, however, the truth bias is probably firmly entrenched. O'Sullivan, Ekman, and Friesen (1988) conducted a study in which participants viewed an honest interview and a deceptive interview. When the honest interview was shown first, the mean detection accuracy rate was 59.67, but when the deceptive interview was shown first, accuracy dropped to 48 percent and only 3 of 109 observers were 70 percent accurate in their judgments. Although the detection rate in both conditions was unimpressive, honest baseline data increased detection accuracy slightly. Additional research shows that even people trained to detect deception, including polygraphers, judges, and customs inspectors, demonstrate little increased ability to detect deception (Kraut & Poe, 1980; Ekman & O'Sullivan, 1991).

Of course, people's poor ability at detection does not mean that most people believe themselves to be poor deception detectors. People consistently report high levels of confidence in their ability to detect deception (Miller & Stiff, 1993). Thus, most people think they are better at detecting deception than they actually are. In the following section, we will explore some of the key reasons for people's overconfidence and poor detection ability.

Truth and Lie Biases

The biases that people hold shape the way they perceive various communication events. When deception is a possibility, truth and lie biases often dictate whether a receiver will actively try to detect deception in the first place. When a truth bias is operating, receivers are unlikely to look for deception unless the sender does something to "tip them off" that deception could be occurring. When a lie bias is operating, receivers are likely to be suspicious and guarded even when the sender is telling the truth. In fact, a receiver's suspicious behavior might lead a truth-teller to become nervous and, thus, to appear deceptive. Alternatively, a receiver's suspicious behavior might cause a deceiver to manage her or his deceptive behavior more carefully in an attempt to avoid being detected. Either way, these biases can lead to a string of processes that ultimately result in inaccurate judgments regarding whether or not deception is occurring.

Most of us believe that others generally tell us the truth. To think that every statement is a lie would make us overly skeptical, cynical, even paranoid. Researchers have shown that a truth bias exists during everyday interactions (Levine & McCornack, 1992; McCornack & Parks, 1986; Stiff, Kim, & Ramesh, 1989). It takes an unusual event—such as receiving information that doesn't make sense or observing odd behavior on the part of an interactant—to make us suspicious. Several studies suggest that our truth biases result in low levels of suspicion in interpersonal encounters (Buller & Burgoon, 1996; Levine & McCornack, 1992). This truth bias is particularly strong for familiar and likeable individuals, such as friends and lovers (Burgoon, Buller, Ebesu, & Rockwell, 1994).

Similarly, certain individuals, such as used-car salespeople, politicians, and telemarketers, may violate our normal truth bias. In other words, they alert our lie biases: we *expect* a used-car salesperson to conceal certain facts about cars, and we *expect* politicians to have "no comment" when confronted by incriminating evidence. We are suspicious of their words and actions. Thus, ordinary

Famous cheater Charles Van Doren, who was given the answers prior to his appearances on the popular TV gameshow *Twenty-One*, successfully deceived the American public. Does his manner appear to be deceptive in these photos?

individuals who normally have truth biases can exhibit lie biases under certain circumstances.

Those who are in the business of detecting deception, however, may more routinely exhibit lie biases. For example, police detectives and prison guards may expect people to lie to them on a day-to-day basis, making them highly suspicious and vigilant. Interestingly, a study of prisoners, police detectives, patrol police, customs officers, and college students revealed that only prisoners could correctly identify deception cues, probably because they receive the best feedback about the success or failure of their deception strategies (Vrij & Semin, 1996).

Erroneous Stereotypes

Each of us has beliefs or stereotypes about how liars behave during deception. Being "shifty-eyed" is an example of a behavior commonly associated with deception. Nonetheless, eye behavior usually is *not* associated with deception (DePaulo et al., 1985; Kraut, 1980; Riggio, Tucker, & Throckmorton, 1987; Zuckerman &

Driver, 1985). One statistical summary of deception research reports that eight behaviors are *believed* to be associated with deception: increased speech hesitations, higher vocal pitch, more speech errors, longer response times, slower speech rates, decreased eye contact, more postural shifts, and less smiling. Unfortunately, only three of these (speech hesitations, vocal pitch, and speech errors) are actually associated with deception (DePaulo et al., 1985). Similar surveys, not included in the former summary, have found that liars are believed to exhibit defensive gestures, shakiness, excessive movements, unnatural gestures, excessive swallowing, slow responses, and reduced eye contact; none of these behaviors, however, have been consistently associated with actual deception (Hocking, Bauchner, Kaminski, & Miller, 1979; Hocking & Leathers, 1980). One study even reports that more-attractive communicators are perceived as less deceptive (Aune, Ching, Levine, & Yanai, in press).

In one study, researchers discovered that any weird behavior during interaction led observers to conclude that deception was occurring (Bond et al., 1992). These weird behaviors included staring excessively, closing the eyes, raising the arms, and raising the shoulders. Probably any weird or unusual behavior that violates expectancies of how people normally communicate can lead to attributions of deception.

Research has shown that receivers often falsely perceive that deception is occurring. The most common reason for disbelieving the truth is the *Othello error*, which occurs when a truth-teller is falsely accused of deception based on emotional responses (such as nervousness or concern) that appear to be deceptive. The term Othello error derives from Shakespeare's famous play in which Othello misinterprets Desdemona's fear and distress over Cassio's death as evidence of her infidelity (Ekman, 1985). The Othello error illustrates that nervous movements and increases in pitch can be erroneously perceived as deception cues, even though such behavior changes are frequently the result of anger, fear, or anything that feels uncomfortable. Burgoon, Buller, Ebesu, White, and Rockwell (1996) report that suspicion fails to improve detection accuracy. They maintain that an Othello-type error may be responsible, because when truth-tellers are falsely accused, they display behaviors that seem like deception. Suspicion creates a self-fulfilling prophecy: suspicion probing leads the accused to display "deceptive-seeming" behaviors, which the accuser mistakes for deceptive behavior.

People, in general, are terrible lie detectors, yet they may be better in some contexts than most of the laboratory studies have indicated. A British researcher designed an intriguing experiment called the megalab truth test (Wiseman, 1995). Frustrated that most prior experiments had typically been conducted in research laboratories with university students, Wiseman designed a study to see if lies could be detected in the media. Wiseman filmed an interview with Sir Robin Day, a well-known British political commentator, about his favorite films. In one interview, Day told the truth; in the other, he lied. The transcript of the interview was printed in the *Daily Telegraph,* a large London newspaper, and the taped interview was broadcast on both national radio and television. The public was asked to indicate by telephone which interview was truthful. Over 40,000 people responded. Radio listeners detected the lying interview 73.4 percent of the time; newspaper readers, 64.2 percent; and television viewers, only 51.8 percent. One explanation for the large discrepancy among the different forms of media is that nonverbal, visual cues actually act as distractors that enable deceivers to cover their lies with convincing nonverbal displays. These findings also suggest that in some contexts, such as radio, detection accuracy is well above the commonly reported 50 percent range. Of course, in this case, respondents knew that Sir Day was telling the truth in one situation and not the other. Without this knowledge, the truth bias may have operated so that most people would have assumed Day was telling the truth, causing the accuracy rate to go down.

Sometimes, we have a feeling that someone is lying to us but we can't know for sure. When this happens, we become suspicious. Recent studies that measure the degree of suspicion also suggest that we may be better at deception detection than prior studies have suggested. Several studies have found that we are more suspicious of deceptive communicators than truthful ones (Buller, Strzyzewski, & Comstock, 1991; Buller, Strzyzewski, & Hunsaker, 1991; Burgoon, Buller, Dillman, & Walther, 1995).

Although our strategies frequently throw us off track in detecting deception, liars may send signals that we do perceive accurately, at least enough to make us suspicious. Stereotypes, however, probably do not increase our accuracy. Remember: widely held stereotypes about lie detection are also shared by liars. During deception, liars are most likely to control the very cues that we most commonly look for to catch them. The communication game of hide and seek continues, with the liar frequently winning.

Collaborative Deceptions

The fact that many lies are actually cooperative and collusive is another factor that prevents or reduces overt deception detection. "Deception, like other communications, is mutually negotiated. Deceiver and deceived collaborate" (Knapp & Comadena, 1979, p. 272). Collaborative deception takes a number of forms. First, situations exist in which lies are expected. Bluffing in poker is a prime example of collaborative deception. Lies are expected in many sales encounters; the customer may claim limited financial resources or the existence of a better deal elsewhere, and the salesperson may quote a "rock-bottom" price. Both parties recognize the virtual certainty of deception but—as with poker—regard it as part of the sales game. Second, lies may be mutually advantageous. Consider two buddies bragging to a group about the girls they picked up or the touchdowns they once scored; they may both profit from each other's deceptions. Third, many lies, especially trivial ones, are accepted to avoid embarrassment. Morris (1977) provides the following example of such socially comfortable deception:

> If, at a dinner party, our hostess offers us a second helping of a horribly unpalatable dish, we refuse it with a polite lie. Instead of telling her the truth, we may say we are full up or on a diet. If she detects the lies and appreciates the reason for it, she is likely to let us get away with it, rather than risk introducing a note of discord into the evening. . . . Now both sides are lying and both sides know it, but the charade is allowed to run its course. (p. 107)

A fourth reason for deceptive collusion is to avoid the consequences of uncovering a lie. Parents may adopt the attitude that "ignorance is bliss" rather than probing to find out whether their daughter smokes marijuana or lives with her boyfriend. Spouses who suspect extramarital affairs may choose not to ask rather than have their lives shattered by such a revelation. Collusive lies often result in psychological denial. They are particularly common when the consequence of discovery is relational conflict or destruction.

A final type of collusive lie is the requested lie. "The most explicit form of fabrication collaboration is a formal request to be told a lie if a particularly undesirable event should occur" (Knapp & Comadena, 1979, p. 273). Thus, patients sometimes tell doctors, "Don't tell me if it's malignant." Spouses may say, "I don't want to know about your affair." This overt request to be lied to is more common than many people realize.

Collaborative lies may create a shared distorted perception of reality. Collaborative liars may actually begin to believe their fabrications (O'Hair & Cody, 1994). There is some evidence that whole groups sometimes come to believe collaborative lies. In the early twentieth century, both blacks and whites commonly believed in the "inherent inferiority of blacks." Citizens of most nations believe the lie that their country is always right. Collaborative lies are more common than most of us realize and deserve more investigation.

Lack of Vigilance

Most of us are unprepared to detect lies. We start with a truth bias, which for most of us is fairly persistent. Moreover, being constantly skeptical takes too much effort; in our daily lives, we are forced to sift through so many messages— from our numerous face-to-face encounters, from computers and message machines, from news media and advertising. So we go through life not particularly vigilant about lies, tending to accept what we're told.

One study reports that when receivers were warned about the possibility of deception, their accuracy improved (Buller, 1989). Another study shows that when receivers were told to suspect lies, they tended to look away from the more deceptive face and tuned in to the "leakier" body to look for deception cues (Zuckerman, Spiegel, DePaulo, & Rosenthal, 1982). These findings demonstrate that vigilance increases when lies are anticipated. But as Levine (1994) argues, "recent deception research suggests that *receivers* may be decidedly unmotivated to detect deception" (p. 14).

(Un)familiarity

Because each person behaves somewhat differently during deception, unfamiliarity should make deception detection difficult. Research has generally shown that behavioral familiarity is associated with improved deception detection. Miller et al. (1981) summarized several studies that show that familiarity with a particular individual provides a baseline of observable truthful behavior that a receiver can use to contrast with deceptive behavior. Research by Zuckerman, Koestner, and Alton (1984) shows that people can learn to detect deception from a particular person. Subjects who were shown a person's behavior during lying and truth-telling were the most accurate in detecting subsequent lies.

A study by Feeley and Young (1995) found that increased exposure to a person's truthful behavior resulted in greater judgment accuracy for the detection of both truthful and deceptive communicators. Comadena (1982a) reported that familiarity tended to produce more detection accuracy, particularly for female observers. Female spouses were especially good deception detectors.

Interestingly, another body of research shows that we're not always better at picking up friends' lies because we have a truth bias, as indicated in our earlier discussion. Research has shown that relational familiarity is a two-edged sword. In close relationships, we are less vigilant of deception and more likely to hold truth biases. Recent summaries of research (Levine, 1994; Millar & Millar, 1995) suggest that we may be less accurate in deception detection in our close, familiar relationships. Truth biases also tend to reduce suspiciousness in close relationships. One study found that truth biases increase with familiar partners but also that these relational truth biases were even stronger when the receiver was suspicious (Burgoon, Buller, Ebesu, & Rockwell, 1994). Levine and McCornack (1992) conclude:

> As individuals become increasingly involved in relationships, there is an increase in confidence in ability to judge a partner's behavior. It is likely that when individuals are highly confident in their ability to detect deception they are less likely to scrutinize a partner's behavior actively, and more likely to rely on judgmental heuristics such as a truth bias. (p. 152)

Recent research also suggests that different cues are useful for detecting the deception of friends and family as opposed to strangers. Voice and physical behavior aid in the detection of strangers' deception. Voice alone, however, is superior for detecting the deception of friends and relatives, evidently because focusing on a single channel can undermine the truth bias (Millar & Millar, 1995).

In sum, our deception-detection ability seems to improve when we develop familiarity through repeated exposure to an unfamiliar individual's behavior; in short, observable baseline data improve detection. For people we know very well, however, we have relational familiarity, and observable data are overridden by truth biases. Therefore, we might be better at detecting deception in acquaintances and casual friends, as compared to strangers (for whom we have no behavioral familiarity) and close friends, family, and lovers (for whom we have truth biases).

Individual Differences

Earlier in this chapter we examined individual differences, such as social skill, Machiavellianism, and self-consciousness, that affect people's ability to conceal their lies. But do individual differences have an effect on the ability to detect lies? Based on early evidence, personality differences seem not to play an important role in deception detection. Kraut (1980) summarizes the research on individual differences and concludes, "A number of findings suggest the lack of both stability and generality of individual differences in the detection of deception" (p. 213). In a summary of research on deception detection, Buller and Burgoon (1996) suggest that receivers' sensitivity skills increase their ability to detect deception. Future research, however, needs to investigate which receiving skills are most critical in the detection of deception.

Gender does appear to be related to the ability to detect deception; females are generally more accurate than males. A statistical summary of prior research showed that women were better overall detectors of deception but that detection rates were also higher in same-sex rather than opposite-sex dyads (Zuckerman et al., 1981). Other studies, not included in the former statistical summary, reveal the same pattern. Comadena (1982a) found that wives were better deception detectors than husbands. Two studies, however, found no clear gender effect in deception (Hurd & Noller, 1988; Manstead, Wagner, & MacDonald, 1984), but they did find that women were better at detecting honesty. McCornack and Parks (1987) found women to be consistently more accurate then men in detecting deception at all stages of a relationship. However, because women are generally more sensitive and polite communicators, they may decode the intended (rather than actual) message and thus be less accurate deception detectors (Burgoon, Buller, & Woodall, 1996). Although current research suggests that women are better deception detectors, more research needs to be conducted (see Chapter 5 for a detailed discussion of sex and gender).

Overattribution

Overattribution occurs when prior information biases what we see. Overattribution is the basis of self-fulfilling prophecies, expectancy effects, a failure to process contradictory information, and rationalization. Often what we see is the result of what we *expect* to see rather than what we actually see! This is true in the detection of deception.

Overattribution, or anchoring as it is sometimes called, is the tendency to make a final judgment too close to an initial one. Research shows that initial anchors, or attributions, distort respondents' own personal judgments of deception. In two studies, respondents were asked to judge whether a person was lying or telling the truth about that person's attitude toward a third person (Koestner, Colella, & Alton, 1984; Zuckerman, Fischer, Osmun, Winkler, & Wolfson, 1987). When respondents are asked to judge another's attitudes toward the third person before judging whether the other was lying, they are not as likely to conclude that the other is lying than if the judgment about lying comes first. When the possibility of deception is salient, we are prone to perceive deception. Several studies have shown that in long-term or trusting relationships, detectors are less likely to make attributions of lying (Buller, 1989; Buller & Walther, 1989; McCornack & Parks, 1987). These positive relational anchors produce overattributions of honesty.

Indirect Attributions

Earlier in this chapter we discussed how people's stereotypes about lying aren't very accurate. Research suggests that attributions about deception come indirectly from other sets of cues. Buller (1988) shows that receivers make deception attributions when a sender is highly aroused or lacking in intimacy or immediacy. Hale and Stiff (1989) report that incongruence between verbal and nonverbal cues leads to attributions of deception. Although these indirect attributions that judge incongruent, aroused, or nonimmediate cues as deception may occasionally be correct, arousal, incongruence, and nonimmediacy are frequently the result of factors other than deception, contributing further to inaccurate deception detection. Despite the fact that detecting deception may have very profound relational consequences for most individuals (Aune, Metts, & Ebesu, 1990), people are very poor at discovering acts of deception.

Imagining a World without Deception

This chapter may seem to have concluded on a pessimistic note. Ordinary people have considerable difficulty detecting the lies of others. Undoubtedly, this means that a considerable amount of deception occurs. Certainly, over the last thirty years, the public has learned that many politicians lie. Vietnam, Watergate, the Iran-Contra controversy, and the Lewinsky affair—to name only a few examples—have demonstrated that U.S. presidents tell a number of lies to the American public. This should remind us not to trust every word emanating from high places, although it doesn't mean that all politicians are congenital liars.

Deception is often covered by strategic immediacy cues such as smiling. The American public only gradually came to see through the deception of former President Richard Nixon.

Certainly, advertisers, salespeople, brokers, agents, and bankers engage in a considerable amount of deceptive behavior in an attempt to influence us. When financial gain is involved, the motivation to lie is substantial, particularly in a society where money and material objects are highly valued. Deception even occurs in personal relationships, when lying may save face, improve one's image, permit exploitation of another sexually or economically, or create artificial closeness through flattery or ingratiation.

The fact that we are all dupes of such deceptions from time to time is disturbing indeed. Our inability to separate truth from falsehood may make us wish for a world in which deception is easily detected—an appealing idea until we consider what such a world would be like. George Orwell (1949), in his novel *1984*, written half a century ago, describes a society in which thoughts can be monitored and deception detected:

> There was of course no way of knowing whether you were being watched at any given moment. How often, or on what system, the Thought Police plugged in on any individual wire was guesswork. It was even conceivable that they watched everybody all the time. But at any rate they could plug in your wire

whenever they wanted to. You have to live—did live, from habit that became instinct—in the assumption that every sound you made was overheard, and except in darkness, every movement scrutinized. . . . Thoughtcrime was not a thing that could be concealed forever. You might dodge successfully for a while, even for years, but sooner or later they were bound to get you. (pp. 4, 20)

Certainly, living in paranoid fear of being caught in a lie would be far worse than living in a society in which our freedom sometimes permits exploitation. In the following passage, Orwell (1949) describes facecrime, the revelation of our deceptions through nonverbal communication!

It was terribly dangerous to let your thoughts wander when you were in any public place or within a range of a telescreen. The smallest thing could give you away. A nervous tic, an unconscious look of anxiety, a habit of muttering to yourself—anything that carried with it the suggestion of abnormality, or having something to hide. In any case, to wear an improper expression on your face (to look incredulous when a victory was announced, for example) was itself a punishable offense. There was even a word for it in Newspeak: *facecrime*, it was called. (p. 20)

Although it seems at first that the detection and regulation of deception would be a wonderful idea, Orwell's vision of such a society should convince us otherwise.

Summary

Deception, a widespread communication phenomenon, involves intentionally misleading another person. Although deception is a communication skill that has advantages for both individuals and species, it also can have extremely negative consequences. Researchers have made some strides in identifying a set of nonverbal deception cues, although considerable behavioral inconsistencies exist; these inconsistencies are due to individual differences, contextual factors, and the diverse origins of deception cues. Deception has been associated with increased speech errors, shorter speaking turns, increased blink rate, both more and less smiling, increased adaptors, both more and fewer body movements, increased vocal pitch, increased gaze, more pupil dilation, and increased hand shrugs.

Deception cues comprise both leakage behaviors and strategic behavioral changes. During deception, increases may occur in arousal, anxiety, and negative affect, resulting in leakage cues. Deceivers may also leak their emotional states due to the cognitive difficulty of lying and to duping delight, the joy and excitement of successful lying. Liars also behave strategically by increasing and/or reducing immediacy, manipulating their image, attempting to reduce arousal, increasing the ambiguity of their message, and attempting to control leakage. The combination of these leakage and strategic behaviors results in a complex and often inconsistent set of deception cues.

People are poor deception detectors. Most of us (1) operate with truth biases in the majority of our interactions (only occasionally do lie biases take over), (2) possess erroneous stereotypes about deception cues, and (3) are often willing collaborators in deception. Behavioral unfamiliarity with strangers prevents good deception detection; at the same time, however, relational familiarity in close relationships creates truth biases that also prevent accurate deception detection. Overattribution is an additional cause for our inaccuracy in detecting deception.

Although we all wish we could detect deception more easily, social politeness and interpersonal effectiveness depend, to some degree, on deception. It would certainly be beneficial to be able to detect deception in salespeople and politicians, but the universal detection of deception would probably have as many disadvantages as advantages.

12

Positions of Power
The Nonverbal Communication of
Control, Power, and Status

Iₙ ʜɪs ᴄʟᴀssɪᴄ book, *The Power Elite*, C. Wright Mills (1956) observes:

> As the means of information and power are centralized, some men come to
> occupy positions in American society from which they can look down, upon,
> so to speak, and their decisions mightily affect, the everyday worlds of men
> and women. (p. 3)

Over forty years later, things have changed little. An elite exists in America with
access to its powerful institutions: business, banking, communications, education, and politics.

Status hierarchies have existed in every human culture throughout history.
At one time, raw muscle power probably determined an individual's status and
power. In modern times, however, as Morris (1977) notes, "muscle power has
given way to inherited power, manipulative power, and creative power. The top
muscle-men have been superseded by the top inheritors, top fixers, and top tal-
ents" (p. 121).

Although the nature of power has certainly changed, its importance has
not. Holders of power still exert dominance over those with less power. Indeed,
one of the two most important dimensions of human relationships is the power
dimension. Bertrand Russell (1938) understood the importance of this dimension when he stated, "The fundamental concept in social science is *Power*, in
the same sense in which *Energy* is the fundamental concept in physics" (italics
added, p. 10).

How does a person acquire power? Certainly, money, social class, education,
neighborhood, and family provide disproportionate access to power and status.
However, an individual's own subtle behaviors can have a major effect on others'
perceptions of her or his power. The charisma of some prominent people, such

305

as John F. Kennedy, Ronald Reagan, Mother Teresa, Walter Cronkite, Bob Dylan, Michael Jordan, Robin Williams, or Madonna, involves more than money, social class, or education.

It is appropriate that this chapter on power concludes this book, for power is one of the most basic functions of communication and social behavior. Power is manifested in every nonverbal code, and in this chapter we will have a chance to review the many codes of nonverbal communication as they relate to the communication of power. Power and dominance hierarchies exist in every human culture and in other primate groups as well. Rajecki (1983) points out that the "dominance hierarchies seem to be a pervasive phenomenon in the primate world" (p. 86). Establishing power structures and dominance hierarchies, as you will see, is often accomplished through nonverbal codes: eye behavior, kinesic displays, material possessions, proxemic behavior, and other "positions of power."

Research on power, status, and dominance reveals that nonverbal communication plays an important role in establishing one's position and determining one's degree of interpersonal influence (Andersen & Bowman, 1990; Burgoon & Hale, 1984; Duran, Jensen, Prisbell, & Rosoff, 1979; Mehrabian, 1972). *Power* typically refers to the ability to influence others to do what one wants and to control interactions (Andersen & Bowman, 1990; Berger, 1985; Ellyson & Dovidio, 1985; Patterson, 1983). *Status* refers to one's position in society, which generally contributes to power and dominance (Henley, 1977; Patterson, 1983; Ridgeway, 1987). *Domineering* behaviors are actions on the part of one person to assert control, or dominance, over another (Millar, Rogers-Millar, & Courtright, 1979). If accepted by another person, then domineering behaviors become dominant ones. Often, domineering behaviors are exhibited by a domineering individual who seeks to control others. (At the end of this chapter is a checklist entitled "Behaviors That Reveal." Before reading the following sections, you might want to complete the checklist and compare your responses with the research findings discussed in this chapter.) *Dominance* refers to one's position of power in relation to others (Duran et al., 1979; Patterson, 1983) and can represent either the actual state of affairs or a perceived judgment (Ellyson & Dovidio, 1985). All these terms relate to a single dimension of interpersonal behavior often labeled *control* (Burgoon & Hale, 1984; Duran et al., 1979); alternative terms for this dimension include *influence, authority, assertiveness, superiority,* and *leadership* (Duran et al., 1979; Henley, 1977).

All humans, indeed all animals, establish power and status hierarchies. Even in the most liberal democracies, more political and economic power resides in the hands of some people than others. Both humans and animals manifest power through nonverbal behaviors. Subtle power cues tell us who is in charge and provide guidelines as to how to behave in the presence of powerful or powerless others.

In the following sections, the various codes of nonverbal communication are examined with respect to the hierarchical structure of human interaction. We begin where most interactions begin—upon meeting a person for the first time, when we make judgments regarding the person's physical appearance.

Physical Appearance

Prior to the initiation of verbal interaction, people communicate their status and power through their physical appearance, and this information often is used as the basis for powerful first impressions (P. A. Andersen, 1984). As noted in Chapter 2, the inferences we make about another person's character and status are made from how we perceive her or his appearance. Among the various impressions communicated through appearance, the nonverbal messages of dominance and status, conveyed through dress and physical size, have a major impact on interpersonal power perceptions.

Dress

One's style of dress sends a variety of messages and is often the major determinant of first impressions. Fowles (1974) contends, "Our clothes broadcast our sex, our rank and our up-to-dateness" (p. 348). Of the many statements a person makes through clothing, often the clearest messages are those regarding power and status.

Formal dress increases perceptions of dominance and control (Bickman, 1974; Brown, 1965; Mehrabian, 1976; Molloy, 1976; Morris, 1977). Mehrabian (1976) asserts that people who select formal dress are tapping the dominance dimension. The suit, in particular, is a symbol of dominance (Mehrabian, 1976; Molloy, 1976). Molloy, in his best-selling book, *Dress for Success,* claims that most authority is conveyed by a dark suit but warns that black should be avoided due to its funereal overtones. He states that the dark solid-blue suit provides particularly high credibility with the lower middle class, although he provides no specific reason for this assertion. Molloy also claims that the pinstripe is the most authoritative pattern and that an expensive, conservative tie is a vital suit accessory, for it symbolizes respectability and responsibility (Molloy, 1976). Over two decades later, the pinstripe suit is still a symbol of authority and status. Despite a lack of supporting data, Molloy's claims are so widely read and quoted by the American business establishment that they have become the guidelines that dictate U.S. business fashion.

Expensive, immaculately polished shoes are also a symbol of high status (Morris, 1977). Curiously, shoes can connote dominance or submission. Mehrabian (1976) claims that "shoes in particular can be selected to be noisy and rough (high load in dominant ways), hushed and smooth sounding, or almost totally silent (low load and submissive)" (p. 64). Similarly, expensive, high-fashion, or high-technology shoes (such as aerobic, basketball, or running shoes) can also signal power and status. Indeed, there have been reports of children resorting to crime to get basketball shoes that cost $100 or more, prompting civil rights groups to object to the marketing of shoes to poor customers through "power ads."

A uniform is a special kind of attire that both reveals and conceals power. It identifies the wearer as part of a group structure, making the wearer's status

The uniform is a nonverbal certificate of legitimate authority and power.

within the group highly visible while suppressing other status cues (Joseph & Alex, 1972). The suppression of status and individuality is the reason behind the great school uniform debate in the United States. Proponents argue that school uniforms reduce socioeconomic status differences and reduce gang influence because "gang" attire would be prohibited by a uniform code. Opponents agree that uniforms reduce differences in status and individuality but argue that they suppress expression, creative individuality, and free speech.

The uniform is also a certificate of legitimacy and can elicit conformity if it symbolizes authoritative power, as do military or police uniforms. Uniforms conceal and reveal power by suppressing individual status symbols while signaling powerful messages of authority and group status. Through the use of its uniform, a group certifies an individual as its representative and assumes responsibility for her or his behavior (Joseph & Alex, 1972). In a study by Bickman (1974), people more often complied with requests made by an experimenter dressed as a guard than one dressed as a civilian or milkman. Although a uniform affords the wearer certain authority at times, paradoxically, people who work in uniform generally have lower status than individuals who work in professional clothes (Koehler, Anatol, & Applbaum, 1981). For example, airline employees, including flight attendants, baggage handlers, and even pilots, usually wear uniforms, but the CEO of the airline is likely to wear a business suit. Low-status workers in establishments such as fast-food restaurants or grocery stores are also likely to wear uniforms.

High-status attire simultaneously creates perceptions of both leadership and conformity. In a study of pedestrian traffic, Lefkowitz, Blake, and Mouton (1955) report that when a high-status person (communicated by that person's dress) violated a law by walking against a red light, there was a significant increase in the rate of violations by other pedestrians; by contrast, when the same person dressed in low-status clothing walked against a red light, significantly fewer pedestrians followed suit. Another study of pedestrian behavior found that passersby resisted penetrating the boundaries of an interacting social group when the group members wore clothing of high status (Knowles, 1973). In an uncrowded college library, students fled more rapidly when their space was invaded by a well-dressed man than when invaded by a casually dressed man (Barash, 1973). In a moderately crowded library, however, the speed of flight responses was not statistically significant. Various nonverbal cues operate at a very low level of awareness. It appears that under conditions of moderate crowding, people expect to have less space, so they are less likely to react negatively. It is also unlikely that the college students (or the pedestrians in the two previous studies) were very consciously aware of the attire worn by the confederates in this experiment, but it analogically and nonlinguistically affected their attitudes and behavior nonetheless.

Not surprisingly, people of great wealth and high status have the prerogative to break the rules of dress. We all know that the super rich can afford to dress expensively, but they also have the freedom to dress shabbily and still maintain their well-established position (Henley, 1977). In addition, they can wear eccentric clothing with impunity (Morris, 1977). In short, high-status individuals have the nonverbal prerogative to dress however they please.

Gender differences in dress demonstrate an element of dominance and submission. Both men's and women's clothing is rigidly prescribed in many cultures and is governed more by fashion and social convention than by comfort or freedom of movement. Some men's dress clothing, including ties and hard-soled shoes, is not designed for comfort, but women's clothing, in particular, is often quite restrictive and designed to create a submissive demeanor. In our culture, women's clothing often is tailored to emphasize bodily contours and is made of delicate materials associated with femininity (for example, silk chiffon). The frailty of fabric and close-fitting design combine to restrict a woman's movement. A skirt, for instance, prevents certain physical activities and sitting positions, and fine fabrics compel a woman to avoid getting dirty. Restrictive corsets of the past made it almost impossible to breathe; today, some fashionable shoes make it almost impossible to walk. Additionally, the close-fitting design of women's clothing often precludes the incorporation of pockets, a functional aspect of most men's clothing. By being forced to carry a purse, a woman is further restricted in physical movement (Henley, 1977).

Over time, women have begun to adopt greater variety in their clothing. The fact that women can wear either traditionally feminine clothing or more-masculine, unisex clothing is indicative of the "liberation" of contemporary women. Men, however, are relegated to traditionally male clothing. For example, most men in the United States would not wear a dress (although some men do sport earrings). This suggests that insofar as clothing is concerned, men are not as "liberated" as women because their clothing choices are more narrowly prescribed (see Chapter 5 for more on gender and nonverbal communication).

Height and Size

Height and physical size are important components of power. Tallness and largeness indicate dominance and status (Mehrabian, 1972). These attributions may derive from the physical advantage these characteristics gave our ancestors during hand-to-hand combat (Henley, 1977). The "height is power" phenomenon places short men and most women at a disadvantage; having to look up to taller people suggests lower status and a perception of submissiveness.

Measures that give the appearance of being tall or large, however, can increase a person's dominance (Scheflen, 1972). "Standing tall is in itself a good way of achieving dominance" (Henley, 1977, p. 89). In a confrontation, the act of "standing over another or the more abbreviated displays of height (i.e., raising one's head or brow while looking down) have the effect of 'cutting an opponent down to size' symbolically" (Remland, 1982a, p. 84). Beards and long hair make one's head appear larger, thereby increasing dominance (Mehrabian, 1976). Not surprisingly, a slumped posture or a curled-up position is submissive because it creates a smaller appearance (Morris, 1977).

Physical size has particular significance in the business world, where height goes hand in hand with success. Tall men are more likely to be hired and to gain larger salaries and prominent positions than are shorter men (Henley, 1977). Morris (1977) agrees that being tall improves one's chances of success; here, he elaborates on the stereotypical obstacles that face a short person:

> Short men who are intensely ambitious are notorious for the savagery of their "assertiveness" when they have struggled to the top, indicating the need to compensate for their small stature. Where a tall man at the top can afford to relax, the short tyrant must remain tense, forever reestablishing his position. (p. 142)

Although the messages of power and status conveyed by physical size date back to a time when size was more directly related to survival, being tall and large today still produces perceptions of power.

Kinesics

Kinesic behavior communicates messages of power and status via bodily positions, movements, gestures, and facial expressions (P. A. Andersen, 1984; see Chapter 2). The way we move and position our bodies has a powerful, reciprocal relationship with power: dominance is reflected in kinesic behavior, and kinesic behavior produces perceptions of dominance.

Positions

The positions in which people stand and sit reveal their relative power. Generally, powerful people occupy more space (see Chapter 2). Remland (1982b) reports that powerful people are more expansive while both sitting and standing. Observe people who hold their arms away from their body and their legs apart; these people exhibit power.

One particular example of an expansive body position is the arms-akimbo (hands-on-hips) position. Mehrabian (1968b) finds that people have a greater tendency to use the arms-akimbo position when addressing a low-status person than a high-status person. Likewise, Scheflen (1972) notes that individuals who hook their thumbs in their belt or use the arms-akimbo position are asserting dominance. Henley (1977) cites research studies in which receivers characterize the arms-akimbo position as a bossy and imperious behavior.

Relaxation is another power cue. Generally, higher-status individuals are more relaxed. This is probably due to the fact that those of higher power can afford to relax, whereas the weak must remain watchful (Andersen & Bowman, 1990; Burgoon, Buller, & Woodall, 1996; Prisbell, 1982). Research confirms that when two strangers meet, the more relaxed individual is of higher status (Mehrabian, 1971a; Mehrabian & Friar, 1969). Likewise, high-status listeners are more relaxed than low-status listeners. Mehrabian (1969, 1972) reports that the degree of reclining and the asymmetry of limbs are important correlates of high status among seated individuals and that rocking movements and leg and foot movements are cues emitted by high-status individuals when standing. These cues are in marked contrast to the extremely submissive cues of bodily rigidity and symmetry, such as soldiers are required to exhibit while standing at attention (Mehrabian, 1976). Similarly, people are most relaxed when interacting with a person of low status, moderately relaxed when interacting with a person of equal status, and least relaxed with a person of high status (Mehrabian, 1968a, 1968b, 1972).

As mentioned, a kinesic cue associated with higher status is limb asymmetry, that is, extending the arms or legs askew (LaFrance & Mayo, 1978; Mehrabian, 1972, 1976). Superiors have the prerogative to sprawl, put their feet up, stretch, and drape their arms over the back of a chair. Leaning is another kinesic status marker. High-status individuals can lean back and appear relaxed, whereas low-status individuals must sit erect. Mehrabian (1972) maintains that status is conveyed by the expansive position, a set of high-status behaviors characterized by a backward leaning trunk as well as other cues. Henley (1977) asserts that dominant persons have the freedom to lean forward to express negative opinions, whereas subordinates should lean forward only to ingratiate themselves or to express positiveness. Remland (1981) reports that higher-status individuals can behave in a more relaxed and inattentive fashion than those of lower status. It is not unusual during an interaction for superiors to lean back in their chairs and to look around the room while they appear to be listening.

Several other kinesic behaviors signal power and dominance. Scheflen (1972) suggests that a sideways head tilt is a submissive posture, whereas holding the head erect signals dominance. Mehrabian and Friar (1969) find that closed, as opposed to open, arm positions are associated with higher status, at least for females. Mehrabian (1971a) maintains that because standing is less relaxed than sitting, seated positions are high-status positions. Perhaps this explains why conventional etiquette requires people to stand in the presence of a superior.

Movements

Several movement patterns are associated with status and power. Mehrabian (1971a) summarizes research that demonstrates that higher-status persons have access to more people and locations than lower-status persons. Indeed, it is difficult to gain access to politicians, executive officers, and celebrities, even though these individuals typically have access to their followers. Another action that conveys status is going first through a door. Traditionally, the higher-status person is permitted to enter first (Goffman, 1967). But allowing someone to enter first can also be an act of politeness and respect, as when a man opens a door for a woman and follows her through it. This commonplace act is a source of confusion in a world where power relationships are changing. Today, some women object to having a door opened for them because it implies their weakness or lack of equality. Other women, however, view it as polite behavior.

Actions that help others but require effort are called inconvenience displays. These behaviors communicate both respect and low status. Serving another person, walking someone to the door, and helping someone find a lost item are all behaviors typically performed by persons of low status but are also perceived as polite and respectful acts. Morris (1977) maintains that low-ranking individuals must lower their bodies in the presence of a high-ranked person. However, it is also customary to rise in the presence of a high-status person. This kinesic contradiction may cause confusion among low-status people and is often resolved by placing the high-status person in a seated but elevated position with her or his inconvenienced and uncomfortable subordinates standing around—take, for example, a judge in a courtroom or a queen on a throne.

Pacing is another submissive behavior, which connotes waiting for a high-status person or being imprisoned, like a Bengal tiger at the zoo. Mehrabian (1976) suggests that pacing, even the relaxed sort of pacing done by college lecturers, indicates distress, avoidance, and low status. Pacing may imply an attempt to remove oneself from the environment, thus signaling submissiveness.

Gestures

A few studies have examined the relationship between gesture and power. Henley (1977) reviews research in which drawings of gesticulating males were judged as most superordinate and important among a group of drawings. The one judged most subordinate, insignificant, and humble was off to the side of the group, with his hands behind his back. Steepling, the gesture of touching the fingertips together in a raised position, is perceived as a confident, smug, and proud gesture associated with professionals and other high-status individuals (Henley, 1977).

Pointing is a high-status, directive gesture that is often perceived as rude or excessively dominant. Pointing at someone is a gesture that Scheflen (1972) suggests is an act of spatial intrusion, which often occurs in escalating verbal conflicts that have the potential to end in acts of physical violence. Remland (1981) argues that pointing is an intrusion that communicates disrespect for another's body and can be used only by a high-status person. Pointing directions is also highly dominant—but not necessarily disrespectful. According to Henley (1977), directing another person from a distance is a prerogative reserved for authority figures. Pointing is a primary nonverbal control behavior used to "order" another person (Siegel, Friedlander, & Heatherington, 1992). Dominant persons can direct others gesturally by pointing, beckoning, or halting their subordinates.

Facial Expressions

The face communicates emotional and affective states better than any other part of the body (P. A. Andersen, 1984; Andersen & Guerrero, 1998b). In fact, the face actually evolved as an affective communication channel. Facial expressions are evident in all primate species, including humans (Mitchell & Maple, 1985). Not surprisingly, dominance and submission messages are sent frequently via facial expressions.

Smiling is usually an appeasement gesture among humans and nonhuman primates. But no simple relationship exists between status and smiling. Among primates, smiling is a submissive gesture often displayed by a prostrate animal to appease a dominant aggressor. Considerable research suggests that smiling indicates appeasement, subordination, and submission (Henley, 1977; Keating, 1985). Smiles also communicate responsiveness, warmth, cooperativeness, and docility. Not surprisingly, women smile considerably more than men. This sex difference probably reflects women's traditionally submissive status, as well as their ability to nurture and provide comfort and interpersonal warmth to others. Smiling functions as both a submissive cue and an intimacy cue (see Chapter 9) and in some situations can show power.

Several studies describe contexts in which smiling connotes submissiveness or, alternatively, power. In a study by Kennedy and Camden (1983), smiling women were more likely to be interrupted than smiling men, indicating that female smiles are seen as a uniquely submissive cue. Women smiled significantly more than men when taking their speaking turn, evidently using the smile as an apology for taking their turn or as an act of submission (Kennedy & Camden, 1983). However, there are times when laughing or smiling can symbolize power. In adversarial situations (such as arguments, debates, or courtroom proceedings), smiling ridicules the claims of another and suggests that the argument should not be taken seriously (Remland, 1982a). Likewise, sarcastic smiles and disrespectful giggles may be used by a high-status but not a low-status person. In the 1996 presidential debates, both Bill Clinton and Bob Dole could be seen sarcastically or smugly smiling at each other's claims. The effect was to politely and nonverbally dispute the opponent's claim. As Burgoon, Buller, and Woodall (1996) point out, sometimes nonverbal cues express sentiments that would be inappropriate or impolite to express verbally.

Other facial expressions more clearly communicate power and status. Scheflen (1972) argues that a protruded jaw is a masculine dominance expression. Henley (1977) maintains that the jutting chin, accompanied by overhanging eyebrows, a frown, drawn muscles, and the unwavering stare, constitute the stern face of authority. After observing that lowered eyebrows were a dominance and status display among nonhuman primates, Keating, Mazur, and Segall (1977) showed subjects two photographs of nearly identical faces—the only difference being that in one photograph the eyebrows were raised and in the other they were lowered. Subjects overwhelmingly selected the photographs with lowered brows as manifesting more dominance. Considerable research suggests that lowered brows are dominant, threatening signals in both human and nonhuman primates (Keating, 1985). The "win face" or "plus face," consisting of raised eyebrows, raised chin, open eyes, and a smug expression, is a common preadolescent dominance expression (Henley, 1977; Zivin, 1982). Koehler et al. (1981) describe a facial expression that is commonly used by supervisors who are trying to refrain themselves from berating a delinquent employee: a reddened face and furrowed brow, in addition to tightened shoulders, nonverbally convey control and dominance.

A comparative study of politicians in both France and the United States reveals that facial expressions are crucial to voters' perceptions of dominance in both countries (Masters & Sullivan, 1989). It appears that a leader's dominance is a function of strong, joyful, and interested facial expressions and an absence of confused or fearful ones. Candidates who convey a sense of strength, happiness, and connectedness to voters are perceived as powerful and dominant, whereas candidates who exhibit confusion and fear are perceived as weak.

The manner in which each one of us employs facial expressions signals our power and status. Exaggerated signs of displeasure such as boredom or disgust emphasize disagreement and disrespect for another individual (Remland, 1982a). Henley (1977) maintains that the prohibition or regulation of another person's facial expressions is a dominant move used to subordinate others. Females and particularly children are frequently told, "don't stare, don't pout, and don't be angry," although they are permitted to cry (Henley, 1977). Controlling another's kinesic behavior can be a real power trip because it increases the subordinate's tension and anxiety (Buck, 1982).

Although subordinates are prohibited from showing certain facial expressions to higher-status persons, in general, some studies suggest low-status persons must be more facially responsive to high-status people. Hottenstein (1978) found that high-status persons emitted the same facial expressions to both high- and low-status recipients but that low-status persons showed more facial expressions to people of higher status than persons of their own rank. Evidently, facial responsiveness is required of low-status individuals, perhaps as a way to signal attentiveness and interest.

Oculesics

The study of oculesics has shown that eye contact, or gaze, can communicate attentiveness, warmth, intimacy, control, power, and a number of other messages. Generally, recipients of prolonged gazes perceive the looker to be more dominant than recipients of brief gazes (Thayer, 1969). This perception may have early origins, because direct gaze is a fairly universal dominance display for nonhuman primates in primitive societies—as it is in contemporary human societies (Burgoon & Saine, 1978; Ellsworth, Carlsmith, & Henson, 1972; LaFrance & Mayo, 1978). Research has shown that when senders increase eye contact, receivers perceive them to be more confident, effective, and of higher status (Cook, 1979; Ridgeway, Berger, & Smith, 1985; Tessler & Sushelsky, 1978).

Studies find that people with dominant personalities employ more gaze (Kendon & Cook, 1969; Rosa & Mazur, 1979; Strongman & Chapness, 1968), although Crouch and Koll (1979) failed to replicate this finding. Fromme and Beam (1974) report that highly dominant subjects move closer when gazed at, whereas less-dominant subjects move farther away, although this behavior seems to be more pronounced in males than females. People who are self-abasing and lack self-esteem tend to look downward and sideways during conversations more than their higher-esteem counterparts (Libby & Yanklevich, 1973).

Averting eye contact at key moments in a conversation may signal submissiveness, especially in women. Similarly, blinking frequently during conversations implies weakness and submissiveness (Mehrabian, 1971a). Kennedy and Camden (1983) report that during a group discussion, women were interrupted significantly more often than men when they did not look at their conversation partner. Lamb (1981) found that women were also more likely to avert gaze during simultaneous attempts to speak first in a group. Men often gain access to the floor through the use of increased gaze, which is perceived as a powerful, dominant behavior. Averted gaze also accompanies disfluencies, such as fragmented sentences and vocalized pauses (Cegala, Alexander, & Sokovitz, 1979), thereby reducing the fluency and credibility of a speaker's message.

Social status can be determined by who looks at whom. Argyle (1975) contends that individuals who receive gaze are perceived as the most powerful group members. Research shows that lower-status persons are more likely to look at persons of higher status (Burroughs, Schultz, & Autrey, 1973; Exline, Ellyson, & Long, 1975; Exline & Fehr, 1979; Mehrabian, 1971a; Mehrabian & Friar, 1969). This pattern is more pronounced if the high-status person shows approval (Efran, 1968; Fugita, 1974). Similarly, subjects low in assertiveness exhibit longer-duration gaze than highly assertive subjects (Alexander, 1980). In a study of a military organization, cadets who paid visual attention to low-status persons were rated lower in status (Exline et al., 1975). This finding suggests that people do not feel obligated to look at a lower-status person and may actually lose status by doing so. So, lower-status, less-dominant persons must remain visually attentive, particularly as listeners, whereas high-status individuals have the prerogative to ignore others.

Higher-status persons look more when speaking and less when listening than lower-status persons (Exline et al., 1975; Exline & Fehr, 1979; LaFrance & Mayo, 1978; Patterson, 1983). Exline et al. (1975) developed an index of visual dominance called the dominance ratio. Dominance ratio is computed by dividing the length of time spent looking when listening (a polite, submissive behavior) by the length of time spent looking when speaking (a bold, dominant behavior). Lower dominance-ratio scores indicate more dominance. Research shows that people with a control orientation have lower dominance ratios, indicating that their behavior reflects their orientation (see Fehr & Exline, 1987). High-status individuals have both the ability and prerogative to maintain visual attentiveness while speaking but are not obligated to reciprocate eye contact when listening.

Proxemics

The interpersonal distances and spatial arrangements that occur during interactions are important indicators of power and status. "Getting in someone's face," "invading someone's space," and "keeping one's distance" are expressions that reveal the relationship between proxemics and power.

Interpersonal Distance

Most of the research on interpersonal distance and status is quite consistent; we provide higher-status individuals with more personal space. Mehrabian's (1969) summary of early research in this area concludes, "The distance between two communicators is positively correlated with their status discrepancy" (p. 371).

Likewise, Argyle (1975) reports that "the only direct connection between dominance or status and spatial behavior is the deference shown to high-status people by keeping at a distance from them" (p. 308). Dean, Willis, and Hewitt (1975) demonstrate that interaction distance is greater when people initiate an interaction with a superior than with a peer. The initiated distance with a subordinate does not differ from peer interactions. Moreover, as the status differential becomes greater, the interaction distance increases even more (Dean, Willis, & Hewitt, 1975). One study reports that commuters at a train station accorded taller, higher-status people more space than their shorter, lower-status counterparts (Caplan & Goldman, 1981). Compared to high-status people, lower-status people fail to defend their personal space (Bethel & Bethel, 1974). In a study by Strube and Werner (1984), type-A (control-oriented, time-pressed) individuals maintained larger personal spaces and exerted more control, regardless of their assigned role in the experiment, than type-B (more laid back) individuals. Clearly, more space is afforded to persons of high status and high control.

The prerogative to invade others' space clearly lies with people of high power and status. Eisenberg and Smith (1971) state that the power to defend one's own territory and the right to invade another person's space are certain signs of dominance and prestige. "For a subordinate to enter the boss's office without his consent would be a clear breach of etiquette, but it is expected that the boss will saunter into the realm of any subordinate without there being the slightest complaint" (Eisenberg and Smith, 1971, p. 103). Similarly, Goldhaber's (1974) second and third rule of organizational status are: "The higher up you are in the organization, the better protected your territory is. The higher up you are in the organization, the easier it is to invade the territory of lower-status personnel." These principles are echoed by Henley (1977) and Remland (1981). In an experiment by Leffler, Gillespie, and Conaty (1982), participants temporarily assigned to high-status roles used more space with both their bodies and possessions than low-status participants. These findings suggest that subordinates must be careful not to violate these proxemic rules. Limited violations may create perceptions of increased status, but obvious violations may result in overt sanctions against the offending employee.

In a study of interviewee behavior, Patterson and Sechrest (1970) show that interviewees were perceived as most dominant at a distance of four feet, least dominant at a distance of eight feet, and moderately dominant at a distance of two and six feet. Evidently, increasingly closer distances convey more dominance until excessive closeness is perceived as a violation. The result is a curvilinear relationship between dominance and distance, with close but appropriate distances conveying the most dominance.

Finally, evidence suggests that the control of interpersonal distance resides with the high-status person, who can choose to be intimate or aloof. In a study of dominance and distance, Dean et al. (1975) conclude that a superior can choose a formal or an intimate distance. A subordinate must choose a formal distance.

Henley (1977) summarizes this research: "the proper distance to be kept in an interaction is under the control of the more powerful person" (p. 33).

Body Orientation

Another critical proxemic power variable is the degree of body orientation between two communicators. More-direct orientations reduce the angle between two communicators; a face-to-face orientation is the most direct. Likewise, the angle of leaning (forward or backward) plays a role as well. In a study by Mehrabian (1968b), standing subjects maintained a more direct shoulder orientation to a high-status addressee than to a low-status addressee. Mehrabian (1968a) reports that body orientation is least direct toward women with low status and most direct toward disliked men of high status. In a study by Jorgenson (1975), equal-status dyads assumed a significantly more direct angle of orientation than did discrepant-status pairs; low-status pairs assumed a less direct angle of orientation than high-status pairs. Burgoon and Saine (1978) assert that in group communication, the individual who is faced by most people probably has the most influence.

Haptics

Haptics, the study of tactile communication, is both the most intimate and the most powerful form of nonverbal communication. Touch has the power to repel, disgust, insult, threaten, console, reassure, love, and arouse (P. A. Andersen, 1984; Prisbell, 1982).

Dominance and control are sometimes communicated through the initiation of touch, although touch is more likely to be perceived as an immediacy cue (see Chapter 8). Touchers are perceived as more dominant and assertive than recipients of touch (Burgoon & Saine, 1978; Major, 1981; Major & Heslin, 1982). The person who initiates touch controls the interaction. The more powerful person determines whether both parties touch and what forms of touch are acceptable (Burgoon & Saine, 1978). Some specific touch behaviors indicate dominance or submission. Scheflen (1972) states that direct poking with the index finger is a dominant, controlling act. In contrast, a person who "cuddles" to the touch of another is perceived as submissive (Henley, 1977).

A series of studies show that, in general, people of objectively high status touch more than those of low status. A field study of people on the streets of a large city showed that higher-status people more frequently touched lower-status people than the reverse (Henley, 1973). People randomly assigned to the role of instructor in one study touched significantly more than people assigned to the role of student (Leffler, Gillespie, & Conaty, 1982). Remland (1981) reports that in organizations, superiors touch subordinates considerably more than subordinates touch superiors. Similarly, Street and Buller (1988) find that physicians socially touch patients significantly more than the reverse, signaling their superior status. One study (Goldstein & Jeffords, 1981), conducted in a state legislature, however, reports the reverse pattern: lower-status lawmakers touched older, higher-status lawmakers more than the reverse, perhaps because they were of a less-formal generation than their seniors. The general pattern of the results is summarized nicely by Henley (1977), who states, "When there's a disparity of status, we observe the higher-status person to have more touch privilege than the lower-status person, who is covertly forbidden to touch at all" (p. 107).

Several specific tactile behaviors are associated with dominance and power. Jones (1994) reports several studies of romantic couples that show that one partner will touch or put her or his arm around the other partner to signal possessiveness or togetherness. Interestingly, this is often done with the dominant hand (right for right-handers, left for left-handers). Siegel, Friedlander, and Heatherington (1992) report that one touch behavior, restraining another person, is perceived as a highly controlling behavior. Obviously, any touch that constrains another person's movement is a highly dominant and controlling act. Do not be surprised if relational partners react negatively to such control.

In his book *The Right Touch*, Jones (1994) identifies four progressive touch strategies that constitute power moves in interpersonal relationships (see also Jones & Yarbrough, 1985). The first is the *affection-to-compliance sequence*, in which one person softens up another with affectionate touch and then touches the person again while making a request. Jones provides this example:

> A couple was watching television together on a couch. The female first cuddled against the male. A minute later the male kissed the female. Several minutes later, the commercials came on, and the male put his arm around the female and said, "Will you get me some water, sweetie?" (p. 125)

She complied.

A second progressive touch-power sequence is the *seduction-and-rejection game* (Jones, 1994). This occurs when one person initiates flirtatious touch and then rejects the other's reciprocal approach. For example, a woman blows in her date's ear. When he attempts to engage in intimate touch, she says, "I'm not ready for that kind of relationship."

A third progressive touch-power sequence is the *power-matching move* (Jones, 1994). In this sequence, one person initiates a power touch. For instance, one male may punch another in the arm while saying, "How ya doin',?" creating a power discrepancy. The receiver of the punch then tries to equalize the relationship by punching the initiator back while saying, "Fine, how are you?"

The final touch-power sequence is the *irritate-and-mollify sequence* (Jones, 1994), in which one person initially employs a demanding or aggressive touch that is rejected because it interrupts or irritates the other; the initiator then follows up with an affectionate touch in an attempt to compensate for the first touch. A slap on a friend's butt followed by a hug or mock wrestling followed by a kiss are examples of these power sequences.

Touch is a powerful form of nonverbal behavior. Alhough it can convey power, the very power of touch makes it dangerous to use outside of close relationships. Certainly, intimidating touch is not particularly effective and may provoke retaliatory touch or even legal action.

Vocalics

Status and dominance are reflected in the way we use our voices. Studies show that social status can be detected accurately from paralinguistic cues. Harms (1961) reports that vocal cues enable listeners to distinguish among individuals who had been objectively rated for status on the Hollingshead social status index, a standard measure of status. Moe (1972) successfully replicated Harms's findings and extended them by showing that certain vocal characteristics are perceived to reflect high status and credibility. Vocal characteristics associated with higher social status include clearer articulation, sharper enunciation of consonants, and more vocal intonation (Argyle, 1975).

Two studies have examined receivers' ability to judge dominance from vocal cues with limited success. Research by Scherer (1972) shows that listeners are able to judge dominant personalities from vocal cues in German speakers. However, Markel (1969) reports nonsignificant correlations between listeners' perceptions of vocal dominance and dominant personality types from the Minnesota Multiphasic Personality Index (MMPI). Thus, the voice is not necessarily a reliable indicant of actual dominance.

Can people alter their vocal behavior to create perceptions of more (or less) power? One experiment suggests that perceptions of leadership in women continually increase as vocal rate increases (Stang, 1973). Burgoon and Saine (1978) also note that a fast vocal rate, high volume, and full resonance carry the sound of authority. Low pitch is also a vocal power cue, whereas high pitch is often associated with childish immaturity and submissiveness.

Several researchers report that power and status are associated with louder speaking. Scheflen (1972) asserts that "over-loud paralanguage" is often a part of dominance or high-status displays. Similarly, Mehrabian (1972) suggests that low speech volume is a metaphorical sign of weakness. Remland (1982a) argues that talking loudly is one of a cluster of behaviors that signals disrespect for another and communicates physical dominance.

One vocalic behavior that has received little attention is laughing. Henley (1977) maintains that laughter is a behavior that subordinates exhibit to persons higher in status. It is advisable for subordinates to laugh at their bosses' jokes, but laughing at someone in an awkward situation or laughing at a superior's faux pas is hardly a submissive behavior. Indeed, depending on the situation and relationship, laughing can reflect nervousness or submission, yet at times laughter can be an extremely dominant behavior.

Tone of voice is extraordinarily important in interpersonal interaction. One study reports that women use more-competent, dominant tones of voice when communicating with their bosses as compared to their peers or subordinates, probably in an attempt to impress. Men use their most competent, dominant voice with peers, perhaps reflecting a certain competitiveness with those of the same rank (Steckler & Rosenthal, 1985). Koehler et al. (1981) recommend that supervisors exercise caution when communicating to a subordinate who is a friend; a friendly tone of voice could undermine the perceived importance of a request.

Chronemics

Our culture is extremely time-conscious. As discussed in Chapter 3, we view time as a precious commodity (P. A. Andersen, 1984). The American slogan "Time is money" is indicative of how we treasure time. We try to save time, to spend it on worthwhile activities, and to avoid wasting it. As with anything valuable, the possession of time is correlated with power and status, and this association has significant communicative implications.

Waiting Time

Like money and property, the rich, the powerful, and the dominant control time. By contrast, the lives of the less privileged are filled with waiting—in crowded health care clinics and in long lines for unemployment checks, welfare food stamps, and temporary employment. Waiting time decreases as status increases, and the super rich are provided with luxurious facilities on the rare occasions when they must wait (Henley, 1977). Obtaining or appropriating others' time is also more easily achieved by people of high status. In many parts of the country, the person who can get a doctor's appointment on short notice is either very important or near death (Huseman, Lahiff, & Hatfield, 1976). Letting people "cool their heels" by forcing them to wait in an office is a power play that is quite effective in asserting one's authority.

Talk Time

Power and status also affect the chronemic patterns of talk time, a resource that is scarce and valuable across many interaction situations. Powerful, dominant individuals will talk more (Kendon & Cook, 1969) and hold the floor for a greater proportion of the time than will a low-dominance person (Rogers & Jones, 1975). High-status persons communicate more frequently and speak longer in group discussions (Hurwitz, Zander, & Hymovitch, 1968; Remland, 1981; Stephan, 1952;

Weins, Thompson, Matarazzo, Matarazzo, & Saslow, 1965). When lower-status individuals finally do participate, their communications are more frequently directed toward those of higher status (Hurwitz et al., 1968) and often contain questions. These behaviors provide additional opportunity for high-status persons to regain the floor and spend even more time talking.

Not only do high-status individuals engage in more talk time, they interrupt more often as well (Burgoon & Saine, 1978; Henley, 1977; Weins et al., 1965). Even experimental subjects temporarily assigned to higher-status positions interrupt more than those assigned to low-status positions (Leffler et al., 1982). Individuals with dominant personalities interrupt more frequently (Rogers & Jones, 1975). This interruption pattern is prevalent in business organizations, where subordinates may not interrupt a boss but must immediately cede the floor when the superior interrupts them (Henley, 1977).

Higher-status people influence the actual speech patterns of lower-status individuals. Koehler et al. (1981) claim that response latency is shorter for a subordinate, whereas a superior may take her or his time in answering. Furthermore, the length of one's speaking turn is affected by the relative status of one's interaction partner. According to Mehrabian (1968a):

> Utterance duration, for example, is a very stable quality in a person's speech, about 30 seconds long on the average. But when someone talks to a partner whose status is higher than his own, the more the high-status person nods his head the longer the speaker's utterances become. If the high-status person changes his own customary speech pattern toward longer or shorter utterances, the lower-status person will change his own speech in the same direction. (p. 54)

Mehrabian (1968a) asserts that a subordinate who does not follow the customary low-status pattern will tend to be negatively perceived by a superior.

Greetings and Meetings

Initiating or terminating a conversation is also a prerogative of the powerful, high-status person (Mehrabian, 1971a), who dictates the chronemic patterns of the interaction as well (Burgoon & Saine, 1978). The more powerful individual will decide when the meeting will take place, the length of the interaction, and how much time is devoted to each discussion topic (Henley, 1977). Interactions are usually terminated nonverbally, although the high-status individual can explicitly indicate that an interaction is over through verbal communication.

Work Time

Flexibility of one's work schedule is associated with status, as it symbolizes control over time. Lower-status, hourly workers are regulated by a time clock, whereas those in higher-status, managerial positions can control time by setting their own hours. The ability to control the time of others further increases one's status and power. Henley (1977) states, "Some people have the power to annex other people's time, and the more they can annex, the more powerful they become; the more powerful they are, the more of others' time they can annex" (p. 49).

The high-status person's time in an organization is considered more valuable than that of the low-status person (Koehler et al., 1981; Remland, 1981). Higher-status individuals have the freedom to waste the time of others, yet they expect others to strictly adhere to their schedules (Goldhaber, 1974). Punctuality is demanded of subordinates, whereas superiors have the prerogative to arrive late to meetings (Koehler et al., 1981; Henley, 1977; Remland, 1981). Hurt, Scott, and McCroskey (1978) state that waiting time in academic settings is associated with status. Increased tardiness is a perk of higher rank. A myth exists at many universities that requires one to wait longer for a full professor than an associate professor, and to wait longer for an associate professor than an assistant professor. Although no such rule really exists, most undergraduates can recite it verbatim.

Spending Time

How an individual spends time conveys power and status within an organization. As Koehler et al. (1981) describe:

> When members of an organization are willing to devote considerable time (including spare time) in meetings, on committees, developing contacts, and the like with the aim of influencing decisions, they are likely to have an effect. They provide scarce energy reserves; they may become major information sources; they are more likely to be present when something important is under consideration. (p. 197)

Additionally, the more an individual spends time with the boss, the more her or his organizational status increases (Huseman et al., 1976).

The irreversibility of time gives it inherent value, but the particular monetary worth that business organizations place on it has made time itself a status symbol. High-status organization members are awarded more control over time, and this power enables them to attain further power and prestige within the organization.

Environment

We are constantly under the influence of our physical surroundings. Environmental conditions can affect an individual's thoughts, emotions, and behavior in a variety of ways. Therefore, it is not surprising that organizational communication is greatly influenced by the setting in which it occurs. Surroundings can communicate directly by projecting a particular image; they can also regulate the quality and quantity of interpersonal or group communication (P. A. Andersen, 1984). Furthermore, various characteristics of the environment can be manipulated intentionally to express dominance and status.

Territory

As indicated previously, superior height is associated with power and status; thus, it is not surprising that the height of an individual's territory symbolizes her or his relative importance (Henley, 1977). Persons of greater social or organizational value are often referred to as "high-ups," whereas persons of lesser value are referred to as "underlings" (Brown, 1965). The design of most office buildings clearly demonstrates this hierarchy: "High-rise office buildings designed to be occupied by one corporation invariably set aside the top floors for the executive echelons, frequently with the president or chairman of the board and a few key assistants occupying the topmost or penthouse floor" (Mehrabian, 1976, p. 141). Sitting in a higher position also communicates superiority—suggesting perhaps a throne—and can be achieved by offering visitors very low, soft chairs, into which they sink (Morris, 1977). Similarly, being "up front" is a position of privilege and control. First-class airplane seats are up front; lower-class seating is to the rear (Brown, 1965). In the 1950s, African Americans throughout the South were required to sit in the back of the bus, which symbolized their subservient status and lack of equality. African Americans' refusal to sit in the back of the bus was an opening shot in the battle for civil rights, but it also increased power for people of color in American society.

The possession of a larger space or territory is a sign of power and status. The poor must live in cramped quarters in crowded cities, whereas the rich and powerful are able to escape high density by purchasing spacious accommodations (Zlutnick & Altman, 1972). Larger territory is also a function of status within the business organization; the most important executive usually has the largest office (Eisenberg & Smith, 1971; Mehrabian, 1976; Goldhaber, 1974; Huseman et al., 1976).

Quantity of space is not the only index of high status; the elite have quality environments as well (Goldhaber, 1974). The most desirable locations, such as an office with many windows or one next to the company president, signal importance within an organization (Eisenberg & Smith, 1971; Mehrabian, 1976), as does a convenient, reserved parking space (Huseman et al., 1976). A study by Haber (1982) reveals that in the classroom, dominant individuals are most likely to occupy the center seats, whereas marginal, less-dominant individuals sit on the periphery.

Not only do high-status, high-power people possess more and better quality space, they have the prerogative to invade the territory of the lower-status, as mentioned earlier (Burgoon, Buller, & Woodall, 1996; Henley, 1977; Mehrabian, 1971a). In addition to the exclusive right to invade the territory of others, high-power people have the ability to defend their own territory (Eisenberg & Smith, 1971; Goldhaber, 1974). Low power and low status in the office are indicated by the unprotected quality of open work pits or cubicles made from temporary partitions; by contrast, the "real" walls of a closed office blocked by a reception-ist's desk provide effective protection from territory invasion (Goldhaber, 1974; Huseman et al., 1976).

Executive seclusion has many advantages, but it also has drawbacks. The inaccessibility of the elite results in isolation; indeed, it is lonely at the top (Mehrabian, 1976). Some executives attempt to overcome this isolation by taking occasional walks through their subordinates' dominion, but often they find that they have become so isolated that the subordinates become anxious, clam up, feel they're being evaluated, or otherwise exhibit avoidance behavior (Mehrabian, 1976). Another detrimental consequence of upper-echelon isolation is the cre-ation of barriers to vital upward information flow. Mehrabian (1976) states that "management consultants are often amazed at how little many senior executives know about fairly significant interoffice matters" (p. 143).

Seating Patterns

In Chapter 3 we learned that certain seating arrangements lead to increased inter-action. Group seating patterns can also be employed to express dominance and status nonverbally. Research shows that high-power individuals select the most focal position in a group, particularly the end seat at a table (Heckel, 1973; Som-mer, 1967). Not only is a highly visual position positively correlated with in-creased interaction (Hearn, 1957; Ward, 1968), it also provides more control of interaction patterns. LaFrance and Mayo (1978) assert that "leaders must be in a position where they can see and be seen by all. This allows for more direct at-tempts to influence others and more efficient monitoring of the responses" (p. 100).

Not surprisingly, persons who occupy focal positions, such as the end seat of a table, are perceived as leaders (Ward, 1968) and are more likely to be selected as forepersons of juries (Strodtbeck & Hook, 1961). According to Strodtbeck and Hook, "the jurors felt that there was some intrinsic 'propriety' about the foreman being at the head of the table" (1961, p. 400).

The seating pattern of followers is quite different from that of leaders. In-dividuals who wish to avoid interaction choose the least focal positions. In an early study, Hare and Bales (1963) reported that persons who sit at the corners of rectangular tables tend to contribute least to the conversation. Additionally, Sommer (1961) noted that followers will sit as close as possible to the leader. Later research on seating patterns and relative status, however, has found that many people will not attain a close position to a higher-status person but instead sit far away, closer to peers, and face the high-status person directly (Lott & Sommer, 1967). Similar behavior was noted in a study of cafeteria seating patterns, in which individuals involved in a cooperative task chose seats that were corner to corner, whereas individuals involved in a competitive task sat opposite one another (Sommer, 1965). Possibly, the more distant position with visual contact represents a challenge, a play for dominance through direct gaze.

Artifacts

It should not be surprising that objects and possessions are viewed as status symbols. Even before much research on the nonverbal communication of status and power was conducted, the suburban family of the 1950s knew that large houses, boats, and cars were symbols of success that connoted status and power.

Today, business and organizational leaders can be identified by the artifacts that accompany their status. Korda (1983) tells a story about an owner of a company being wooed by a larger conglomerate. The conglomerate offered him everything: stock, a lifetime seat on the board of directors, a plane, and a limousine. But he turned it all down. It was only after offering him a couple of floors in a new building with a private elevator, a private bath and shower, and a heated towel rack that he finally accepted! Koehler et al. (1981) list organizational status symbols, including special parking places, luxury company cars, and office furnishings.

The latest and most expensive pieces of office equipment, such as personal computers and fax machines, are power symbols, although expertise in using them is often limited to lower-power individuals (Korda, 1983). Really high-status individuals have subordinates who operate and maintain office equipment. Considerable status revolves around the possession and use of communication devices such as telephones, fax machines, cell phones, beepers, and computers. Having more telephones and computers displayed on one's desk than is necessary is a status symbol (Morris, 1977). However, really high-status persons do not actually dial the telephones; someone else does that for them. Operating any mechanical device has a tinge of manual labor and a low-status flavor (Morris, 1977). Furthermore, in an age when the telephone is often an environmental invader, a secretary, an answering service, or voice mail increases an individual's control and dominance. When one executive secretary reaches another executive secretary, a status battle of who speaks first ensues. High status requires the other person to come on the line first (Morris, 1977). Morris maintains that a top executive can manifest special status with a car phone, which implies how busy and important he or she is. This is such a status symbol that one phone company has marketed dummy aerials for phoneless vehicles, a form of dominance mimicry (Morris, 1977). Today, cellular phones are the status symbol for the mobile and upwardly mobile executive. Likewise, not having a fax machine and e-mail may cause others to think of you as old-fashioned, poor, or laggardly.

Briefcases are another organizational status symbol (Korda, 1983; Morris, 1977). Bulky briefcases are a sign of low status because only peons have to lug

The limousine, like a large office and house, is a status symbol that conveys power and prestige.

around paperwork. Slimmer briefcases are much higher in status because high-status individuals need carry only vital papers. The ultimate status symbol, of course, is no briefcase at all; when you possess real power, all they want is you (Korda, 1983). As humorous as some of these examples are, status symbols have real meaning to high-power individuals. A sudden loss of these hard-won status symbols would cause feelings of hurt and reprimand.

Immediacy

Up to this point, we have examined nonverbal status and power cues individually. Obviously, in real interaction, nonverbal cues are sent and received simultaneously through multiple channels and perform multiple functions. Most perceptions of status and power are the result of the receiver's gestalt perception of clusters of nonverbal cues rather than single, isolated behaviors.

One such multichanneled construct is nonverbal immediacy. In Chapter 8, immediacy behaviors were defined as clusters of cues that simultaneously communicate approach as opposed to avoidance, signal availability for communication, increase sensory stimulation and arousal, and communicate interpersonal warmth in most relationships (Andersen, Andersen, & Jensen, 1979; Andersen, 1985). Research suggests that persons of high status and power have all the options for increasing or decreasing immediacy (Andersen, 1985; Duran et al., 1979).

Remember, high-status persons have the prerogative to increase or decrease distance, touch, and eye contact. Additionally, Mehrabian (1971) contends, "Generally, the option to increase or decrease immediacy by initiating or terminating a conversation is left to the person of high status" (p. 32). In his summary of research on power and dominance, Patterson (1983) states:

> The pattern of findings related to encoded power and dominance suggests that high status individuals have greater flexibility in the instrumental use of nonverbal involvement than low status individuals. Thus, a high status person can typically relate to others with variable involvement and not risk the censure or disapproval a low status person would. (p. 103)

This is particularly true for initiating increased immediacy. Likewise, a movement toward intimacy is typically initiated by the person of higher status (Brown, 1965; Mehrabian, 1971a).

In addition to the general rule that high-status individuals have all of the immediacy options, several other findings are of interest. A study reported by Hurwitz et al. (1968) concludes that individuals with little power generally perceive they are liked more by those with more power than the situation actually justifies. Those with little power evidently reduce the threat associated with the powerful by distorting their perceptions of powerful people. Furthermore, it is possible that powerful people soften their power manipulations through increased immediacy behaviors, which lead low-status individuals to perceive they are liked.

High-status individuals use immediacy to dominate others in several ways. In a study by Geller, Goodstein, Silver, and Steinberg (1974), reducing immediacy by ignoring a person caused subjects to feel alone, withdrawn, and shy and to rate themselves less favorably than control subjects. Druckman, Rozelle, and Baxter (1982) argue that immediacy cues are interpreted quite differently in competitive as opposed to cooperative situations. In competitive settings, immediacy may be perceived as an attempt to intimidate or dominate. Burgoon and Saine (1978) report that low-status people are likely to mirror the posture and gestures of high-status individuals, possibly in an effort to establish harmony and immediacy and to get "in sync" with the valued higher-status person. Finally, Kennedy and Camden (1983) show that positive-affect displays help men avoid being interrupted and enable them to hold the floor. For women, however, positive affect serves as an invitation for men to interrupt them!

Power Principles

It is important to understand that power is always a relational construct. There can be no powerful people without powerless people. High status exists only in contrast to low status. Likewise, power is a fuzzy construct because power balances can change. Formal power can yield to informal power. Following are some power principles to keep in mind.

First, *assigned power does not equal actual power.* Organizations often produce covert power structures that have more real power than positions at the top of the organizational chart. In fact, subordinates often have far more power than they realize. Powerlessness is a state of mind that can be overcome with a change in actions and attitudes. Subordinates can organize and act collectively in their mutual interest. The power to quit, strike, or revolt resides in all subordinates. Short of acts of defiance, subordinates still have power options. Each individual has a range of power, jointly or separately. Nevertheless, although occasionally exceeding power latitudes may be advantageous, subordinates who continually challenge power and status nonverbally will irritate their superiors and usually be put in their place (Dean et al., 1975). By contrast, though, subordinates who display little or no nonverbal power relegate themselves to continuous powerlessness. Every subordinate must maintain a delicate balance between too little and too much power. A study by Remland (1982b) reports that subordinates who increase their nonverbal status displays also increase their perceived satisfaction with the superior and the organization. Low status is as much a self-inflicted phenomenon as one that is controlled by superiors.

Second, *models of power and status must be relationally based.* The rules of status and power are quite different for superiors, peers, and subordinates. As just described, the least number of options are available to the subordinate; exhibiting too much visible power is offensive and inappropriate to one's superiors. In peer relationships, however, one's latitude of options expands. Nonetheless, even among peers, too much visible power can make one seem arrogant, manipulative, greedy, or inappropriate. The latitude for peers may be greater, but sanctions still exist for consistently manifesting power inappropriate to one's position. Superiors have the widest latitudes, yet even CEOs, presidents, and dignitaries have limits on their power.

Third, *power is paradoxical.* One paradox many women face in an organization is that many of their dominance or power behaviors are interpreted as something other than power (see Chapter 5 for more on this issue). Loud, assertive women are still sometimes perceived as "bitchy" or "nagging," whereas men who engage in the same behavior are perceived as powerful. A study by Henley and Harmon (1985) reveals that when dominance behaviors are performed by women, they're perceived as sexual rather than dominant. These attributions deny dominance to women.

Fourth, *the less power individuals exhibit, the more power they actually have.* One study reports that when status differentials are reduced, either by decreasing the superior's nonverbal power displays or by increasing the subordinate's, the superior is rated more considerate and less aversive but no less effective (Remland, 1982b). Thus, superiors who show some nonverbal deference to subordinates may have more power in the long run by instilling satisfaction and loyalty in the subordinate. In any organization, where you stand in the power structure, who you communicate with, how much power they have, and what you can do within the appropriate behavioral parameters are essential factors in gaining and maintaining control.

Power is an interesting and elusive construct that is only beginning to be fully understood. Part of the elusiveness of power is that so much of it is conveyed nonverbally. In his major review of power research, Berger (1985) states:

> It can be argued that these nonverbal behaviors are more significant in determining the experience of power than are variables related to verbal content. One conclusion drawn here is that failure to take into account nonverbal behavior in the study of communication and power relationships is to doom oneself to study the tip of a very large iceberg. (p. 483)

Hopefully, this chapter has enabled you to examine a bit more of the iceberg. Future research will probe the depths of covert power that is expressed through nonverbal communication.

Summary

Power and control are two of the most fundamental aspects of human behavior. Both animals and humans convey power and dominance primarily through nonverbal behavior. Prior to any verbal interaction, physical appearance communicates power and status. Our clothing broadcasts our status, wealth, fashion consciousness, and power. Formal dress, polished shoes, uniforms, and expensive basketball shoes all communicate power and leadership, as well as conformity. Very rich and high-status individuals can break the rules of dress. Some clothing, particularly women's clothing, severely restricts movement and creates subordination. Tallness and largeness also signal power and status.

Kinesic behavior sends messages of power and status through posture, position, gestures, and facial expressions. Powerful people use more space; for example, the hands-akimbo position is a particularly effective behavior for conveying power. Relaxation is another sign of dominance, whereas tension is a subordination display. Serving another person is a sign of subordination, as is lowering one's body or bowing in the presence of another. Larger, more frequent gestures generally communicate power, although pointing is often perceived as a powerful but rude behavior. Smiling is a submissive behavior in most circumstances, whereas a protruding jaw and lowered eyebrows, like the anger expression, communicate power. Happy, confident expressions are powerful, whereas fearful or confused expressions are subordinate.

People whose oculesic behavior includes more overall eye contact and staring are judged to be more powerful. Blinking and averting eye contact are signs of submissiveness. In groups, people are more likely to look at leaders and powerful people. High-status people look more while speaking and less when listening.

Proxemic behavior provides many cues of power and dominance. High-status people are accorded more personal space and have the prerogative to invade the space of others. Likewise, the higher people are in an organization, the more space they are afforded in terms of their office or car and at meetings. Subordinates directly face more-dominant individuals.

High-status and powerful people possess haptic freedom. They can choose to touch or not to touch other people. Low-status people have few touch prerogatives. The initiation of touch and restraining touch are signs of power, as are four touch behavioral sequences: the affection-to-compliance sequence, the seduction-and-rejection game, the power-matching move, and the irritate-and-mollify sequence. Touch is dangerous to use outside of close relationships.

Vocalic characteristics associated with power and status include clear articulation, vocal intonation, loudness, and deeper pitch. Research shows that faster-speaking individuals, particularly women, are more credible and powerful. Very high-pitched voices are associated with childish immaturity and submissiveness. Laughing is generally a subordination behavior. For example, lower-status individuals are expected to laugh at their superiors' jokes.

Power and status are related to chronemic behaviors, particularly in a time-conscious culture such as the United States, where time is money. Thus, low-status, but not high-status, individuals can be kept waiting. High-status people have greater access to talk time and interrupt more than low-status people. Powerful and high-status people can arrange meeting times and decide when a meeting will end. Flexibility of schedules is associated with high-status individuals, whereas lower-status individuals must punch clocks and be on time. For low-status people, spending time with higher-status people increases their power and status.

Environments can also convey power and status. Higher positions and larger territories are associated with greater power. Higher-status people have the right to invade the territories of others, but the reverse is not true. Power positions include the head of a table, the front of a room, and other, more visually focal locations.

Artifacts are some of the most important status symbols in today's materialistic culture. Modern communication technology, private parking spaces, and isolated offices are signs of status. Car phones, expensive cars, jewelry, and slimmer briefcases are among the many objects that convey power and status.

Paradoxically, immediacy behaviors constitute their own form of power. Immediacy behaviors, which increase interpersonal closeness, are the prerogative of the powerful. Likewise, because other people value warmth and immediacy, immediacy behaviors enhance the power of an individual.

There are several principles associated with power: assigned power does not equal actual power; power and status are relationally based; power is paradoxical; and the less power individuals exhibit, the more power they actually have.

Behaviors That Reveal*

This activity focuses on gestures of dominance and submission. In a psychological sense, the term *dominance* is used here to describe a personality tendency to seek influence and have authority over others. It is important to keep in mind that there is a difference between "symbols of dominance" and "gestures of dominance." The former would include cues from the nonverbal environment, such as symbols of office, authoritative clothing, or significant height. By contrast, dominance gestures are used to assert oneself and to influence others. *Submission,* on the other end of the continuum, is defined as the act of yielding or surrendering. Submissive behaviors are associated with resignation, obedience, and meekness. Based on these definitions, rate the following behaviors as behaviors of dominance, behaviors of submission, or behaviors that are neither dominant nor submissive.

BEHAVIORS OF DOMINANCE	BEHAVIORS OF SUBMISSION	NEITHER DOMINANT NOR SUBMISSIVE	BEHAVIOR
_____	_____	_____	1. Staring
_____	_____	_____	2. Lowering one's eyes
_____	_____	_____	3. Interrupting
_____	_____	_____	4. Frowning
_____	_____	_____	5. Smiling
_____	_____	_____	6. Cocking (tilting) one's head
_____	_____	_____	7. Pointing
_____	_____	_____	8. Yielding (moving out of another person's way)
_____	_____	_____	9. Cuddling to another person's touch
_____	_____	_____	10. Averting another person's gaze
_____	_____	_____	11. Taking up a large amount of space
_____	_____	_____	12. Initiating touch

BEHAVIORS OF DOMINANCE	BEHAVIORS OF SUBMISSION	NEITHER DOMINANT NOR SUBMISSIVE	BEHAVIOR
_____	_____	_____	13. Pausing during a conversation (allowing another person to interrupt)
_____	_____	_____	14. Crowding another person's space
_____	_____	_____	15. Blinking
_____	_____	_____	16. Holding one's head erect or forward (chin-up position)

*Does this checklist look familiar? After completing it, go back to Chapter 5, page 130, and match up these responses with those from the earlier checklist. Which gender uses more dominant behaviors? Which gender exhibits more submission? affection? Is the relationship between gender and dominance changing? Are you and others of your generation different from your parents' generation?

References

Abbey, A., & Melby, C. (1986). The effects of nonverbal cues on perceptions of sexual intent. *Sex Roles, 15,* 283–298.

Acitelli, L. K., & Duck, S. W. (1987). Intimacy as the proverbial elephant. In D. Perlman & S. W. Duck (Eds.), *Intimate relationships: Development, dynamics, and deterioration* (pp. 297–308). Beverly Hills, CA: Sage.

Adams, G. R. (1977). Physical attractiveness research: Toward a developmental social psychology of beauty. *Human Development, 20,* 217–239.

Adams, G. R., & Read, D. (1983). Personality and social influence styles of attractive and unattractive college women. *Journal of Psychology, 114,* 151–157.

Addington, D. W. (1968). The relationship of selected vocal characteristics to personality. *Speech Monographs, 35,* 492–505.

Afifi, W. A., & Johnson, M. L. (1993, November). *The nonverbal display of affection: Cross-sex interactions in bars.* Paper presented at the annual convention of the Speech Communication Association, Miami, FL.

Aida, Y. (1993). Communication apprehension and power strategies in marital relationships. *Communication Reports, 6,* 116–121.

Aiello, J. R. (1976, April). *Effects of episodic crowding: A developmental perspective.* Paper presented at the Eastern Psychological Association Convention, New York, NY.

Aiello, J. R. (1987). Human spatial behavior. In D. Stools & I. Altmann (Eds.), *Handbook of environmental psychology* (Vol. 1, pp. 389–504). New York: Wiley.

Aiello, J. R., Epstein, Y. M., & Karlin, R. A. (1975, May). *Field experimental research on human crowding.* Paper presented at the Eastern Psychological Association Convention, New York, NY.

Aiken, L. R. (1963). The relationship of dress to selected measures of personality in undergraduate women. *Journal of Social Psychology, 59,* 119–128.

Albert, S., & Dabbs, J. M. (1970). Physical distance and persuasion. *Journal of Personality and Social Psychology, 15,* 265–270.

Alexander, A. (1980, April). *An investigation of eye gaze and its relation to assertiveness.* Paper presented to the Nonverbal Division at the Eastern Communication Association Conference, Ocean City, MD.

Allen, M. (1995, November). *Dialectical theory: Testing the relationships between tensions and relational satisfaction.* Paper presented at the Speech Communication Association Convention, Chicago, IL.

Altman, I., & Taylor, D. A. (1973). *Social penetration: The development of interpersonal relationships.* New York: Holt, Rinehart & Winston.

Altman, I., Vinsel, A., & Brown, B. B. (1981). Dialectic conceptions in social psychology: An application to social penetration and privacy regulation. In L. Berkowitz (Ed.) *Advances in experimental social psychology* (Vol. 14, pp. 107–160). New York: Academic Press.

Amabile, T. M., & Kabat, L. G. (1982). When self-descriptions contradict behavior: Actions to speak louder than words. *Social Cognition, 1*(4), 311–335.

Andersen, J. F. (1979). Teacher immediacy as a predictor of teaching effectiveness. In D. Nimmo (Ed.), *Communication yearbook 3* (pp. 543–559). New Brunswick, NJ: Transaction Books.

Andersen, J. F. (1984, April). *Nonverbal cues of immediacy and relational affect.* Paper presented at the annual convention of the Central States Speech Association, Chicago, IL.

Andersen, J. F., & Andersen, P. A. (1987). Never smile

until Christmas? Casting doubt on an old myth. *Journal of Thought, 22,* 57–61.

Andersen, J. F., Anderson, P. A., & Jensen, A. D. (1979). The measurement of nonverbal immediacy. *Journal of Applied Communication Research, 7,* 153–180.

Andersen, J. F., Andersen, P. A., & Landgraf, J. (1985, May). *The development of nonverbal communication competence in childhood.* Paper presented at the annual convention of the International Communication Association, Honolulu, HI.

Andersen, J. F., Andersen, P. A., & Lustig, M. W. (1987). Opposite-sex touch avoidance: A national replication and extension. *Journal of Nonverbal Behavior, 11,* 89–109.

Andersen, J. F., Andersen, P. A., Murphy, M. A., & Wendt-Wasco, N. (1985). Teachers' reports of students' nonverbal communication in the classroom: A developmental study in grades K–12. *Communication Education, 34,* 292–307.

Andersen, J. F., Norton, R. W., & Nussbaum, J. F. (1981). Three investigations exploring relationships between perceived teacher communication behaviors and student learning. *Communication Education, 30,* 377–392.

Andersen, J. F., & Withrow, J. G. (1981). The impact of lecturer nonverbal expressiveness on improving mediated instruction. *Communication Education, 30,* 342–353.

Andersen, K., & Clevenger, T., Jr. (1963). A summary of experimental research in ethos. *Speech Monographs, 30,* 59–78.

Andersen, P. A. (1984). Nonverbal communication in the small group. In R. S. Cathcart & L. A. Samovar (Eds.), *Small group communication* (4th ed., pp. 258–275). Dubuque, IA: Brown.

Andersen, P. A. (1985). Nonverbal immediacy in interpersonal communication. In A. W. Siegman & S. Feldstein (Eds.), *Multichannel integrations of nonverbal behavior* (pp. 1–36). Hillsdale, NJ: Erlbaum.

Andersen, P. A. (1986). Consciousness, cognition, and communication. *Western Journal of Speech Communication, 50,* 87–101.

Andersen, P. A. (1987). The trait debate: A critical examination of the individual differences paradigm in intercultural communication. In B. Dervin &

M. J. Voigt (Eds.), *Progress in communication sciences* (Vol. 8, pp. 47–82). Norwood, NJ: Ablex.

Andersen, P. A. (1988). Explaining intercultural differences in nonverbal communication. In L. A. Samovar & R. E. Porter (Eds.), *Intercultural communication: A reader* (5th ed., pp. 272–281). Belmont, CA: Wadsworth.

Andersen, P. A. (1989, May). *A cognitive valence theory of intimate communication.* Paper presented at the International Network on Personal Relationships Conference, Iowa City, IA.

Andersen, P. A. (1991). When one cannot not communicate: A challenge to Motley's traditional communication postulates. *Communication Studies, 42,* 309–325.

Andersen, P. A. (1992a, July). *Excessive intimacy: An account analysis of behaviors, cognitive schemata, affect, and relational outcomes.* Paper presented at the 6th International Conference on Personal Relationships, Orono, ME.

Andersen, P. A. (1992b). Nonverbal communication in the small group. In R. S. Cathcart & L. A. Samovar (Eds.), *Small group communication* (6th ed., pp. 272–286). Dubuque, IA: Brown.

Andersen, P. A. (1993a). Cognitive schemata in personal relationships. In S. Duck (Ed.), *Individuals in relationships* (pp. 1–29). Newbury Park, CA: Sage.

Andersen, P. A. (1993b, July). *Steps to a communication of ecology: The interrelationships of systems in the global environmental crisis.* Paper presented at the Conference on Communication and the Environment, Big Sky, MT.

Andersen, P. A. (1997). Cues of culture: The basis of intercultural differences in nonverbal communication. In L. A. Samovar and R. E. Porter (Eds.), *Intercultural communication: A reader* (8th ed., pp. 244–256). Belmont, CA: Wadsworth.

Andersen, P. A. (1998a). Researching sex differences within sex similarities: The evolutionary consequences of reproductive differences. In D. J. Canary & K. Dindia (Eds.), *Sex differences and similarities in communication* (pp. 83–100). Mahwah, NJ: Erlbaum.

Andersen, P. A. (1998b). The cognitive valence theory of intimate communication. In T. M. Palmer & G. A. Barnett (Eds.), *Progress in Communication*

Sciences, Volume XIV: Mutual Influence in Interpersonal Communication: Theory and Research in Cognition, Affect, and Behavior (pp. 39–72). Stanford, CT: Ablex.

Andersen, P. A., & Andersen, J. F. (1982). Nonverbal immediacy in instruction. In L. L. Barker (Ed.), *Communication in the classroom: Original essays* (pp. 98–120). Englewood Cliffs, NJ: Prentice-Hall.

Andersen, P. A., & Andersen, J. F. (1984). The exchange of nonverbal immediacy: A critical review of dyadic models. *Journal of Nonverbal Behavior, 8,* 327–349.

Andersen, P. A., Andersen, J. F., & Mayton, S. M. (1985). The development of nonverbal communication in the classroom: Teachers' perceptions of students in grades K–12. *Western Journal of Speech Communication, 49,* 188–203.

Andersen, P. A., Andersen, J. F., Wendt, N. J., & Murphy, M. A. (1981, May). *The development of nonverbal communication behavior in school children grades K–12.* Paper presented at the annual convention of the International Communication Association, Minneapolis, MN.

Andersen, P. A., & Bowman, L. (1990). Positions of power: Nonverbal influence in organizational communication. In J. A. DeVito & M. L. Hecht (Eds.), *The nonverbal communication reader* (pp. 391–411). Prospect Heights, IL: Waveland Press.

Andersen, P. A., & Coussoule, A. R. (1980). The perceptual world of the communication apprehensive: The effect of communication apprehension and interpersonal gaze on interpersonal perception. *Communication Quarterly, 28,* 44–54.

Andersen, P. A., Eloy, S. V., Guererro, L. K., & Spitzberg, B. H. (1995). Romantic jealousy and relational satisfaction: A look at the impact of jealousy experience and expression. *Communication Reports, 8,* 77–85.

Andersen, P. A., Garrison, J. P., & Andersen, J. F. (1975, November). *Defining nonverbal communication: A neurophysiological explanation of nonverbal information processing.* Paper presented at the annual meeting of the Western Speech Communication Association, Seattle, WA.

Andersen, P. A., Garrison, J. P., & Andersen, J. F. (1979). Implications of a neurophysiological approach for the study of nonverbal communication. *Human Communication Research, 6,* 74–89.

Andersen, P. A., & Guerrero, L. K. (1989, February). *Avoiding communication: Verbal and nonverbal dimensions of defensiveness.* Paper presented at the annual convention of the Western Speech Communication Association, Spokane, WA.

Andersen, P. A., & Guerrero, L. K. (1998a). The bright side of relational communication: Interpersonal warmth as a social emotion. In P. A. Andersen & L. K. Guerrero (Eds.), *Handbook of communication and emotion: Research, theory, applications, and contexts* (pp. 303–324). San Diego, CA: Academic Press.

Andersen, P. A., & Guerrero, L. K. (1998b). Principles of communication and emotion in social interaction. In P. A. Andersen & L. K. Guerrero (Eds.), *Handbook of communication and emotion: Research, theory, applications, and contexts* (pp. 49–96). San Diego, CA: Academic Press.

Andersen, P. A., Guerrero, L. K., Buller, D. B., & Jorgensen, P. F. (1998). An empirical comparison of three theories of nonverbal immediacy exchange. *Human Communication Research, 24,* 501–535.

Andersen, P. A., & Kibler, R. J. (1978). Candidate valence as a predictor of voter preference. *Human Communication Research, 5,* 4–14.

Andersen, P. A., & Leibowitz, K. (1978). The development and nature of the construct touch avoidance. *Environmental Psychology and Nonverbal Behavior, 3,* 89–106.

Andersen, P. A., Lustig, M. W., & Andersen, J. A. (1986). *Communication patterns across the United States: A theoretical perspective.* Paper presented at the annual convention of the International Communication Association, Chicago, IL.

Andersen, P. A., Lustig, R., & Andersen, J. A. (1990). Changes in latitude, changes in attitude: The relationship between climate and interpersonal communication predispositions. *Communication Quarterly, 38,* 291–311.

Andersen, P. A., & Singleton, G. W. (1978, March). *The relationship between body-type and communication avoidance.* Paper presented at the annual convention of the Eastern Communication Association, Boston, MA.

Andersen, P. A., & Sull, K. K. (1985). Out of touch,

out of reach: Tactile predispositions as predictors of interpersonal distance. *The Western Journal of Speech Communication, 49,* 57–72.

Andersen, P. A., & Todd-Mancillas, W. R. (1978). Scales for the measurement of homophily with public figures. *Southern Speech Communication Journal, 43,* 169–179.

Andersen, P. A., Todd-Mancillas, W. R., & Di-Clemente, L. (1980). The effects of pupil dilation in physical, social, and task attraction. *Australian Scan: Journal of Human Communication, 7 & 8,* 89–95.

Anderson, N. R. (1991). Decision making in the graduate selection interview: An experimental investigation. *Human Relations, 44,* 403–417.

Angier, N. (1995, February 22). Studying sense that picks up scents. *The San Diego Union Tribune,* p. E3.

Apple, W., Streeter, L. A., & Krauss, R. M. (1979). Effects of pitch and speech rate on personal attributions. *Journal of Personality and Social Psychology, 37,* 715–727.

Archer, D., & Akert, R. M. (1977). Words and everything else: Verbal and nonverbal cues in social interpretation. *Journal of Personality and Social Psychology, 35,* 443–449.

Argyle, M. (1972). Non-verbal communication in human social interaction. In R. A. Hinde (Ed.), *Nonverbal communication* (pp. 248–268). Cambridge: Cambridge University Press.

Argyle, M. (1975). *Bodily communication.* New York: International Universities Press.

Aronoff, J., Woike, B. A., & Hyman, L. M. (1992). Which are the stimuli in facial displays of anger and happiness? Configurational bases of emotion recognition. *Journal of Personality and Social Psychology, 62,* 1050–1066.

Asendorpf, J. B., & Scherer, K. R. (1983). The discrepant repressor: Differentiation between low anxiety, high anxiety, and repression of anxiety by autonomic-facial-verbal patterns of behavior. *Journal of Personality and Social Psychology, 45,* 1334–1346.

Aune, K. S., & Aune, R. K. (1997, May). *Effects of relationship level and biological sex on motives for emotion management.* Paper presented at the annual meeting of the International Communication Association, Montreal, Quebec.

Aune, R. K., Ching, P. U., Levine, T. R., & Yanai, O. T. (in press). Attributions of deception as a function of reward value: A response to a nonverbal expectancy violation or the use of a cognitive heuristic? *Communication Quarterly.*

Aune, R. K., Metts, S., & Ebesu, A. S. (1990, November). *Managing the discovery of deception.* Paper presented at the annual meeting of the Speech Communication Association, Chicago, IL.

Badzinski, D. M. (1986, November). *Towards understanding the effects of mood on interaction processes.* Paper presented at the annual convention of the Speech Communication Association, Chicago, IL.

Bakan, P. (1971). The eyes have it. *Psychology Today, 4,* 64–67.

Bakan, P., & Strayer, F. F. (1973). On reliability of conjugate lateral eye movements. *Perceptual and Motor Skills, 36,* 429–430.

Baldwin, M. W. (1992). Relational schemas and the processing of social information. *Psychological Bulletin, 112,* 461–484.

Bandler, R., & Grinder, J. (1979). *Frogs into Princes.* Moab, UT: Real People Press.

Barash, D. P. (1973). Human ethology: Personal space reiterated. *Environmental Behavior, 5,* 67–73.

Barbee, A. P., Rowatt, T. L., & Cunningham, M. R. (1998). When a friend is in need: Feelings about seeking, giving, and receiving social support. In P. A. Andersen & L. K. Guerrero (Eds.), *Handbook of communication and emotion: Research, theory, applications, and contexts* (pp. 281–301). San Diego, CA: Academic Press.

Barker, L. L., Cegala, D. J., Kibler, R. J., & Wahlers, K. J. (1979). *Groups in process: An introduction to small group communication.* Englewood Cliffs, NJ: Prentice-Hall.

Barker, L. L., & Collins, N. B. (1970). Nonverbal and kinesic research. In P. Emmert & W. D. Brooks (Eds.), *Methods of research in communication.* Boston: Houghton Mifflin.

Barnland, D. C. (1978). Communication styles in two cultures: Japan and the United States. In A. Kendon, R. M. Harris, & M. R. Key (Eds.), *Organizational behavior in face to face interaction* (pp. 427–456). The Hague: Mouton.

Barrett, K. C. (1995). A functionalist approach to shame and guilt. In J. P. Tangney & K. W. Fischer (Eds.), *Self-conscious emotions: The psychology of shame, guilt, embarrassment and pride* (pp. 25–63). New York: Guilford.

Bate, B. (1988). *Communication and the sexes.* New York: Harper & Row.

Bateson, G. (1972). *Steps to an ecology of mind.* New York: Balantine Books.

Baum, A., Davis, G. E., & Valins, S. (1979). Generating behavioral data for the design process. In J. R. Aiello & A. Baum (Eds.), *Residential crowding and design* (pp. 175–196). New York: Plenum Press.

Baumeister, R. F., Reis, H. T., & Delaspaul, P. (1995). *Personality and Social Psychology Bulletin, 21,* 1256–1258.

Baumeister, R. F., Stillwell, A. M., & Heatherton, T. F. (1994). Guilt: An interpersonal approach. *Psychological Bulletin, 115,* 243–267.

Baumeister, R. F., & Wotman, S. R. (1992). *Breaking hearts: The two sides of unrequited love.* New York: Guilford Press.

Bavelas, J. B. (1990). Behaving and communicating: A reply to Motley. *Western Journal of Speech Communication, 54,* 593–602.

Bavelas, J. B., Black, A., Chovil, N., Lemery, C. R., & Mullett, J. (1988). Form and function in motor mimicry: Topographic evidence that the primary function is communicative. *Human Communication Research, 14,* 275–299.

Bavelas, J. B., Black, A., Chovil, N., & Mullet, J. (1990). *Equivocal communication.* Newbury Park, CA: Sage.

Bavelas, J. B., Black, A., Lemery, C. R., & Mullett, J. (1986). "I'll show how you feel": Motor mimicry as a communicative act. *Journal of Personality and Social Psychology, 50,* 322–329.

Bavelas, J. B., Chovil, N., Coates, L., & Roe, L. (1995). Gestures specialized for dialogue. *Personality and Social Psychology Bulletin, 21,* 394–405.

Baxter, L. A. (1987). Cognition and communication in the relationship process. In P. McGhee, D. Clarke, & R. Burnett (Eds.), *Accounting for relationships: Social relationships of interpersonal links* (pp. 192–212). London: Methuen.

Baxter, L. A. (1988). A dialectical perspective on communication strategies in relationship development. In S. Duck (Ed.), *Handbook of personal relationships* (pp. 257–259). New York: Wiley & Sons.

Baxter, L. A. (1993). Dialectical contradictions in relationship development. In S. Petronio, J. K. Alberts,

M. L. Hecht, & J. Buley (Eds.), *Contemporary perspectives on interpersonal communication.* Madison, WI: Brown & Benchmark.

Baxter, L. A. (1994). A dialogic approach to relationship maintenance. In D. Canary & L. Stafford (Eds.), *Communication and relational maintenance* (pp. 233–234). San Diego, CA: Academic Press.

Baxter, L. A., & Montgomery, B. M. (1996). *Relating: Dialogues and dialectics.* New York: Guilford.

Baxter, L. A., & Ward, J. (1975). Newsline. *Psychology Today, 8*(8), 28.

Baxter, L. A., & Wilmot, W. W. (1984). "Secret tests": Social strategies for acquiring information about the state of the relationship. *Human Communication Research, 11,* 171–201.

Bayes, M. A. (1970). An investigation of the behavioral cues of interpersonal warmth (Doctoral dissertation, University of Miami, 1970). *Dissertation Abstracts International, 31,* 2272B.

Beck, W. W., & Lambert, G. E. (1977). First impressions and classroom climate. *Kappa Delta Pi Record, 13*(4), 121–122.

Becker, F. D. (1973). Study of spatial markers. *Journal of Personality and Social Psychology, 26,* 439–445.

Beebe, S. A. (1980). Effects of eye contact, posture and vocal inflection upon credibility and comprehension. *Australian Scan: Journal of Human Communication, 7–8,* 57–70.

Begley, S. (1995, March 27). Gray matters. *Newsweek,* pp. 48–54.

Beier, E. G., & Sternberg, D. P. (1977). Marital communication: Subtle cues between newlyweds. *Journal of Communication, 27,* 92–97.

Bell, R. A., & Daly, J. A. (1984). The affinity-seek function in communication. *Communication Monographs, 51,* 91–115.

Bellah, R. N., Madsen, R., Sullivan, W. M., Swidler, A., & Tipton, S. (1985). *Habits of the heart: Individualism and commitment in American life.* New York: Harper & Row.

Bem, S. L. (1974). The measurement of psychological androgyny. *Journal of Counseling and Clinical Psychology, 42,* 155–162.

Benson, T. W., & Frandsen, K. D. (1976). *An orientation to nonverbal communication.* Chicago: Science Research Associates.

Berger, C. R. (1985). Social power and interpersonal communication. In M. L. Knapp & G. R. Miller

(Eds.), *Handbook of interpersonal communication* (pp. 439–499). Beverly Hills, CA: Sage.

Berger, C. R. (1988). Uncertainty and information exchange in developing relationships. In S. Duck (Ed.), *Handbook of personal relationships* (pp. 239–255). New York: Wiley & Sons.

Berger, C. R., & Bradac, J. J. (1982). *Language and social knowledge: Uncertainty in interpersonal relations.* London: Edward Arnold.

Berger, C. R., & Calabrese, R. J. (1975). Some explorations in initial interaction and beyond: Toward a theory of interpersonal communication. *Human Communication Research, 1,* 99–112.

Berlyne, D. E. (1960). *Conflict, arousal, and curiosity.* New York: McGraw-Hill.

Berry, D. S. (1990). Vocal attractiveness and vocal babyishness: Effects on stranger, self and friend impressions. *Journal of Nonverbal Behavior, 14,* 141–153.

Berry, D. S. (1992). Vocal types and stereotypes: Joint effects of vocal attractiveness and vocal maturity on person perception. *Journal of Nonverbal Behavior, 16,* 41–54.

Berscheid, E., & Walster, E. M. (1978). *Interpersonal attraction* (2nd ed.). Reading, MA: Addison-Wesley.

Bethel, E. R., & Bethel, J. A. (1974, December). *Superordinate-subordinate status relationships and defense of personal space.* Paper presented at the annual meeting of the Speech Communication Association, Chicago, IL.

Bickman, L. (1974). The social power of a uniform. *Journal of Applied Social Psychology, 4,* 47–61.

Billig, M. (1987). *Arguing and thinking: A rhetorical approach to social psychology.* New York: Cambridge University Press.

Birdwhistell, R. L. (1970). *Kinesics and context.* Philadelphia: University of Pennsylvania Press.

Biswas, A. K. (1984). *Climate and development.* Dublin, Ireland: Tycooly.

Blanck, P. D., & Rosenthal, R. (1982). Developing strategies for decoding "leaky" messages: On learning how and when to decode discrepant and consistent social communications. In R. S. Feldman (Ed.), *Development of nonverbal behavior in children* (pp. 203–229). New York: Springer Verlag.

Blanck, P. D., & Rosenthal, R. (1992). Nonverbal behavior in the courtroom. In R. S. Feldman (Ed.),

Applications of nonverbal behavioral theories and research (pp. 89–115). Hillsdale, NJ: Erlbaum.

Blanck, P. D., Rosenthal, R., & Vannicelli, M. (1986). Talking to and about patients: The therapist's tone of voice. In P. D. Blanck, R. Buck, & R. Rosenthal (Eds.), *Nonverbal communication in the clinical context* (pp. 99–143). University Park, PA: Pennsylvania State University Press.

Blumstein, P., & Schwartz, P. (1983). *American couples: Money, work, sex.* New York: Morrow.

Boderman, A., Freed, D. W., & Kinnucan, M. T. (1972). Touch me, like me: Testing an encounter group assumption. *Journal of Applied Behavioral Science, 8,* 527–533.

Bogen, J. E. (1977). Some educational implications of hemispheric specialization. In W. C. Wittrock, *The human brain* (pp. 133–152). Englewood Cliffs, NJ: Prentice-Hall.

Bok, S. (1978). *Lying: Moral choice in public and private life.* New York: Random House.

Bond, C. F., Omar, A., Pitre, U., Lashley, G. R., Skaggs, L. M., & Kirk, C. T. (1992). Fishy-looking liars: Judgment from expectancy violation. *Journal of Personality and Social Psychology, 63,* 969–977.

Bond, M. H. (1993). Emotions and their expression in Chinese culture. *Journal of Nonverbal Behavior, 17,* 245–262.

Bowlby, J. (1979). *The making and breaking of affectional bonds.* London: Tavistock.

Bowman, A. (1980, April). *Physical attractiveness and electability: Looks and votes.* Paper presented at the annual meeting of the Midwest Political Science Association.

Breed, G., Christiansen, E., & Larson, D. (1972). Effect of a lecturer's gaze direction upon teaching effectiveness. *Catalog of Selected Documents in Psychology, 2,* 115.

Breed, G., & Ricci, J. S. (1973). "Touch me, like me" artifact. *Proceedings of the 81st Annual Convention of the American Psychological Association, 8,* 153–154.

Brehm, S. S. (1985). *Intimate relationships.* New York: Random House.

Briton, N. J., & Hall, J. A. (1995). Beliefs about female and male nonverbal communication. *Sex Roles, 32,* 70–90.

Brockner, J., Pressman, B., Cabitt, J., & Moran, P. (1982). Nonverbal intimacy, sex and compliance:

A field study. *Journal of Nonverbal Behavior, 6,* 253–258.

Brody, L., & Hall, J. A. (1993). Gender and emotion. In M. Lewis & J. Haviland (Eds.), *Handbook of emotions* (pp. 447–460). New York: Guilford.

Broverman, I. K., Vogel, S. R., Broverman, D. M., Clarkson, F. E., & Rosenkrantz, P. S. (1972). Sex role stereotypes: A current appraisal. *Journal of Social Issues, 28,* 59–78.

Brown, D. E. (1991). *Human universals.* Philadelphia: Temple University Press.

Brown, L. R., Kane, H., & Roodman, D. M. (1994). *Vital signs 1994: The trends that are shaping our future.* New York: Norton.

Brown, R. (1965). *Social psychology.* New York: Free Press.

Bruneau, T. (1979). The time dimension in intercultural communication. In D. Nimmo (Ed.), *Communication yearbook 3* (pp. 423–433). New Brunswick, NJ: Transaction Books.

Buck, R. (1979). Individual differences in nonverbal sending accuracy and electrodermal responding: The externalizing-internalizing dimension. In R. Rosenthal (Ed.), *Skill in nonverbal communication: Individual differences.* Cambridge, MA: Oelgeschlager, Gunn, & Hain.

Buck, R. (1982). Spontaneous and symbolic nonverbal behavior and the ontogeny of communication. In P. S. Feldman (Ed.), *Development of nonverbal behavior in children* (pp. 29–62). New York: Springer Verlag.

Buck, R. (1984). *The communication of emotion.* New York: Guilford Press.

Buck, R. (1988). Nonverbal communication: Spontaneous and symbolic aspects. *American Behavioral Scientist, 31,* 341–354.

Buck, R. (1995). Review of human facial expression: An evolutionary view. *Communication Theory, 5,* 393–396.

Buck, R., Miller, R. E., & Caul, W. F. (1974). Sex, personality, and physiological variables in the communication of emotion via facial expression. *Journal of Personality and Social Psychology, 30,* 587–596.

Bull, P. E. (1987). *Posture and gesture.* Oxford: Pergamon Press.

Bull, R., & Gibson-Robinson, E. (1981). The influence of eye-gaze, style of dress, and locality on the amounts of money donated to charity. *Human Relations, 34,* 895–905.

Buller, D. B. (1986). Distraction during persuasive communication: A meta-analytic review. *Communication Monographs, 53,* 91–114.

Buller, D. B. (1987). Communication apprehension and reactions to proxemic violations. *Journal of Nonverbal Behavior, 11,* 13–25.

Buller, D. B. (1988, November). *Nonverbal predictors of attributions during deception.* Paper presented at the annual meeting of the International Communication Association, New Orleans, LA.

Buller, D. B. (1989). *Deception by strangers, friends, and intimates: Attributional biases due to relationship development.* Unpublished manuscript, University of Arizona.

Buller, D. B., & Aune, R. K. (1988a). The effects of vocalics and nonverbal sensitivity on compliance: A speech accommodation theory explanation. *Human Communication Research, 14,* 301–332.

Buller, D. B., & Aune, R. K. (1988b, February). *Nonverbal cues to deception among friends and strangers.* Paper presented at the annual meeting of the Western Speech Communication Association, San Diego, CA.

Buller, D. B., & Aune, R. K. (1989, May). *The effects of vocalics and nonverbal sensitivity on compliance: Further tests of the speech accommodation explanation.* Paper presented at the annual meeting of the International Communication Association Convention, San Francisco, CA.

Buller, D. B., & Aune, R. K. (1992). The effects of speech rate similarity on compliance: Application of communication accommodation theory. *Western Journal of Communication, 56,* 37–53.

Buller, D. B., & Burgoon, J. K. (1986). The effects of vocalics and nonverbal sensitivity on compliance. *Human Communication Research, 13,* 126–144.

Buller, D. B., & Burgoon, J. K. (1994). Deception: Strategic and nonstrategic communication. In J. Daly & J. M. Wiemann (Eds.), *Interpersonal communication* (pp. 191–213). Hillsdale, NJ: Erlbaum.

Buller, D. B., & Burgoon, J. K. (1996). Interpersonal deception theory. *Communication Theory, 6,* 203–242.

Buller, D. B., & Burgoon, J. K. (1998). Emotional expression in the deception process. In P. A. Andersen & L. K. Guerrero (Eds.), *Handbook of communication and emotion: Research, theory, applications, and contexts* (pp. 379–402). San Diego, CA: Academic Press.

Buller, D. B., Burgoon, J. K., Buslig, A. L., & Roiger, J. F. (1994). Interpersonal deception: VIII. Further analysis of nonverbal and verbal correlates of equivocation from the Bavelas et al. (1990) research. *Journal of Language and Social Psychology, 13,* 396–417.

Buller, D. B., Burgoon, J. K., Buslig, A. L., & Roiger, J. F. (1996). Testing interpersonal deception theory: The language of interpersonal deception. *Communication Theory, 6,* 268–288.

Buller, D. B., Burgoon, J. K., & Guerrero, L. K. (1994, November). *Behavioral sequences in interpersonal deception.* Paper presented at the annual meeting of the Speech Communication Association Convention, New Orleans, LA.

Buller, D. B., Burgoon, J. K., White, C. H., & Ebesu, A. S. (1994). Interpersonal deception: VII. Behavioral profiles of falsification, equivocation, and concealment. *Journal of Language and Social Psychology, 13,* 366–395.

Buller, D. B., Jorgensen, P. F., Andersen, P. A., & Guerrero, L. K. (1995, June). *Correspondence among physiological, nonverbal, and perceptual measures of arousal.* Paper presented at the meeting of the International Network on Personal Relationships, Williamsburg, VA.

Buller, D. B., LePoire, B. A., Aune, R. K., & Eloy, S. V. (1992). Social perceptions as mediators of the effect of speech rate on compliance. *Human Communication Research, 19,* 286–311.

Buller, D. B., Strzyzewski, K. D., & Comstock, J. (1991). Interpersonal deception: I. Deceivers' reactions to receivers' suspicions and probing. *Communication Monographs, 58,* 1–24.

Buller, D. B., Strzyzewski, K. D., & Hunsaker, F. G. (1991). Interpersonal deception: II. The inferiority of conversational participants as deception detectors. *Communication Monographs, 58,* 25–40.

Buller, D. B., & Walther, J. B. (1989). *Deception in established relationships: Application of schema theory.* Paper presented at the annual meeting of the Western Speech Communication Association, Spokane, WA.

Bullis, C., & Horn, C. (1995). Getting a little closer:

Further examination of nonverbal comforting strategies. *Communication Reports, 8,* 10–17.

Burgoon, J. K. (1978). Attributes of a newscaster's voice as predictors of his credibility. *Journalism Quarterly, 55,* 276–281.

Burgoon, J. K. (1980). Nonverbal communication research in the 1970s: An overview. In D. Nimmo (Ed.), *Communication yearbook 4* (pp. 179–197). New Brunswick, NJ: Transaction books.

Burgoon, J. K. (1983). Nonverbal violations of expectations. In J. M. Wiemann & R. P. Harrison (Eds.), *Nonverbal interaction* (pp. 77–111). Beverly Hills, CA: Sage.

Burgoon, J. K. (1985a). Nonverbal signals. In M. L. Knapp & G. R. Miller (Eds.), *Handbook of interpersonal communication* (pp. 344–390). Beverly Hills, CA: Sage.

Burgoon, J. K. (1985b). The relationship of verbal and nonverbal codes. In B. Dervin & M. J. Voight (Eds.), *Progress in communication sciences* (Vol. 6, pp. 263–298). Norwood, NJ: Ablex.

Burgoon, J. K. (1994). Nonverbal signals. In M. L. Knapp & G. R. Miller (Eds.), *Handbook of interpersonal communication* (2nd ed., pp. 229–285). Thousand Oaks, CA: Sage.

Burgoon, J. K., & Aho, L. (1982). Three field experiments on the effects of violations of conversational distance. *Communication Monographs, 49,* 71–88.

Burgoon, J. K., Birk, T., & Pfau, M. (1990). Nonverbal behaviors, persuasion, and credibility. *Human Communication Research, 17,* 140–169.

Burgoon, J. K., & Buller, D. B. (1994). Interpersonal deception: III. Effects of deceit on perceived communication and nonverbal behavior dynamics. *Journal of Nonverbal Behavior, 18,* 155–184.

Burgoon, J. K., Buller, D. B., Dillman, L., & Walther, J. B. (1995). Interpersonal deception: IV. Effects of suspicion on perceived communication and nonverbal behavior dynamics. *Human Communication Research, 22,* 163–196.

Burgoon, J. K., Buller, D. B., Ebesu, A. S., & Rockwell, P. A. (1994). Interpersonal deception: V. Accuracy in deception detection. *Communication Monographs, 61,* 303–325.

Burgoon, J. K., Buller, D. B., Ebesu, A. S., White, C. H., & Rockwell, P. A. (1996). Testing interpersonal deception theory: Effects of suspicion on communication behaviors and perceptions. *Communication Theory, 6*, 243–267.

Burgoon, J. K., Buller, D. B., & Guerrero, L. K. (1995). Interpersonal deception: IX. Effects of social skill and nonverbal communication on deception success and detection accuracy. *Journal of Language and Social Psychology, 14*, 289–311.

Burgoon, J. K., Buller, D. B., Guerrero, L. K., Afifi, W. A., & Feldman, C. M. (1996). Interpersonal deception: XII. Information management dimensions underlying deceptive and truthful messages. *Communication Monographs, 63*, 50–69.

Burgoon, J. K., Buller, D. B., Guerrero, L. K., & Feldman, C. M. (1994). Interpersonal deception: VI. Effects on preinteractional and interactional factors on deceiver and observer perceptions of deception success. *Communication Studies, 45*, 263–280.

Burgoon, J. K., Buller, D. B., Hale, J. L., & deTurck, M. A. (1984). Relational messages associated with nonverbal behaviors. *Human Communication Research, 10*, 351–378.

Burgoon, J. K., Buller, D. B., & Woodall, W. G. (1989). *Nonverbal communication: The unspoken dialogue.* New York: Harper & Row.

Burgoon, J. K., Buller, D. B., & Woodall, W. G. (1996). *Nonverbal communication: The unspoken dialogue.* New York: McGraw-Hill.

Burgoon, J. K., & Coker, D. A. (1988, May). *Nonverbal expectancy violations and conversational involvement.* Paper presented at the annual convention of the International Communication Association, New Orleans, LA.

Burgoon, J. K., Coker, D. A., & Coker, R. A. (1986). Communicative effects of gaze behavior: A test of two contrasting explanations. *Human Communication Research, 12*, 495–524.

Burgoon, J. K., Dillman, L., & Stern, L. A. (1993). Adaptation in dyadic interaction: Defining and operationalizing patterns of reciprocity and compensation. *Communication Theory, 3*, 295–316.

Burgoon, J. K., & Hale, J. L. (1984). The fundamental topoi of relational communication. *Communication Monographs, 51*, 193–214.

Burgoon, J. K., & Jones, S. B. (1976). Toward a theory of personal space expectations and their violations. *Human Communication Research, 2*, 131–146.

Burgoon, J. K., Kelley, D. L., Newton, D. A., & Keeley-Dyerson, M. P. (1989). The nature of arousal and nonverbal indices. *Human Communication Research, 16*, 217–255.

Burgoon, J. K., & Koper, R. J. (1984). Nonverbal and relational communication associated with reticence. *Human Communication Research, 10*, 601–626.

Burgoon, J. K., & LePoire, B. A. (1992). A reply from the heart: Who are Sparks and Greene and why are they saying all these horrible things? *Human Communication Research, 18*, 472–482.

Burgoon, J. K., LePoire, B. A., Beutler, L. E., Bergan, J., & Engle, D. (1992). Nonverbal behaviors as indices of arousal: Extensions to the psychotherapy context. *Journal of Nonverbal Behavior, 16*, 159–178.

Burgoon, J. K., Manusov, V., Mineo, P., & Hale, J. L. (1985). Effects of gaze on hiring, credibility, attraction and relational message interpretation. *Journal of Nonverbal Behavior, 9*, 133–146.

Burgoon, J. K., & Newton, D. A. (1991). Applying a social meaning model to relational message interpretations of conversational involvement: Comparing observer and participant perspectives. *Southern Communication Journal, 66*, 96–113.

Burgoon, J. K., Pfau, M., Birk, T., & Manusov, V. (1987). Non-verbal communication performance and perceptions associated with reticence: Replications and classroom implication. *Communication Education, 36*, 119–130.

Burgoon, J. K., Pfau, M., Parrott, R., Birk, T., Coker, R., & Burgoon, M. (1987). Relational communication, satisfaction, compliance-gaining strategies, and compliance in communication between physicians and patients. *Communication Monographs, 54*, 307–324.

Burgoon, J. K., & Saine, T. (1978). *The unspoken dialogue: An introduction to nonverbal communication.* Boston: Houghton Mifflin.

Burgoon, J. K., Stern, L. A., & Dillman, L. (1995). *Interpersonal adaptation: Dyadic interaction patterns.* New York: Cambridge University Press.

Burgoon, J. K., Walther, J. B., & Baesler, E. J. (1992). Interpretations, evaluations, and consequences of interpersonal touch. *Human Communication Research, 19*, 237–263.

Burgoon, M., Callister, M., & Hunsaker, F. G. (1994). Patients who deceive: An empirical investigation of patient-physician communication. *Journal of Language and Social Psychology, 13*, 443–468.

Burleson, B. R., & Goldsmith, D. J. (1998). How the comforting process works: Alleviating emotional distress through conversationally induced re-appraisals. In P. A. Andersen & L. K. Guerrero (Eds.), *Handbook of communication and emotion: Research, theory, applications, and contexts* (pp. 245–280). San Diego, CA: Academic Press.

Burleson, B. R., Kunkel, A. W., Samter, W., & Werking, K. J. (1996). Men's and women's evaluations of communication skills in personal relationships: When sex differences make a difference—and when they don't. *Journal of Social and Personal Relationships, 13*, 201–224.

Burroughs, W. A., Schultz, W., & Autrey, S. (1973). Quality of argument, leaders, votes, and eye contact in three-person leaderless groups. *Journal of Social Psychology, 90*, 89–93.

Burton, R. (1976). *The language of smell.* Boston: Routledge & Kegan Paul.

Bush, D. F., & Connolly, R. (1984, May). *Physician gender and nonverbal cues influence memory for health information and attitudes toward the practitioner.* Paper presented at the annual meeting of the International Communication Association, San Francisco, CA.

Bushman, B. J. (1988). The effects of apparel on compliance: A field experiment with a female authority figure. *Personality and Social Psychology Bulletin, 14*, 459–467.

Buss, D. M. (1988). From vigilance to violence: Tactics of mate retention in American undergraduates. *Ethology and Sociobiology, 9*, 291–317.

Byers, E. S., & Heinlein, L. (1989). Predicting initiations and refusals of sexual activities in married and cohabiting heterosexual couples. *Journal of Sex Research, 26*, 210–231.

Cain, W. S. (1990). Educating your nose. In J. A. Devito & M. L. Hecht (Eds.), *The nonverbal communication reader* (pp. 279–290). Prospect Heights, IL: Waveland Press.

Calhoun, J. B. (1962). Population density and social pathology. *Scientific American, 26*(2), 139–148.

Calvin, W. H. (1991). *The ascent of mind.* New York: Bantam Books.

Camras, L. A. (1982). Ethological approaches to non-verbal communication. In R. S. Feldman (Ed.), *Development of nonverbal behavior in children* (pp. 3–28). New York: Springer Verlag.

Canary, D. J., & Cody, M. J. (1993). *Interpersonal communication: A goals-based approach.* New York: St. Martin's Press.

Canary, D. J., Emmers-Sommer, T. M., & Faulkner, S. (1997). *Sex and gender differences in personal relationships.* New York: Guilford.

Canary, D. J., & Hause, K. S. (1993). Is there any reason to study sex differences in communication? *Communication Quarterly, 41*, 129–144.

Canary, D. J., Spitzberg, B. H., & Semic, B. A. (1998). The experience and expression of anger in interpersonal settings. In P. A. Andersen & L. K. Guerrero (Eds.), *Handbook of communication and emotion: Research, theory, applications, and contexts* (pp. 189–213). San Diego, CA: Academic Press.

Caplan, M. E., & Goldman, M. (1981). Personal space violations as a function of height. *Journal of Social Psychology, 114*, 167–171.

Caporael, L. R. (1981). The paralanguage of caregiving: Baby talk to institutionalized aged. *Journal of Personality and Social Psychology, 40*, 876–884.

Cappella, J. N. (1981). Mutual influence in expressive behavior: Adult-adult and infant-adult dyadic interaction. *Psychological Bulletin, 89*, 101–132.

Cappella, J. N. (1983). Conversational involvement: Approaching and avoiding others. In J. M. Wiemann & R. P. Harrison (Eds.), *Nonverbal interaction* (pp. 113–148). Beverly Hills, CA: Sage.

Cappella, J. N. (1985). Production principles for turn-taking rules in social interaction: Socially anxious vs. socially secure persons. *Journal of Language and Social Psychology, 4*, 193–212.

Cappella, J. N. (1991a). The biological origins of automated patterns of human interaction. *Communication Theory, 1*, 4–35.

Cappella, J. N. (1991b). Mutual adaptation and relativity of measurement. In B. M. Montgomery & S. Duck (Eds.), *Studying interpersonal interaction* (pp. 103–117). New York: Guilford.

Cappella, J. N. (1993). The facial feedback hypothesis in human interaction: Review and speculation. *Journal of Language and Social Psychology, 12,* 13–29.

Cappella, J. N., & Greene, J. O. (1982). A discrepancy-arousal explanation of mutual influence in expressive behavior for adult and infant-adult interaction. *Communication Monographs, 49,* 89–114.

Cappella, J. N., & Palmer, M. T. (1990). Attitude similarity, relational history, and attraction: The mediating effect of kinesic and vocal behaviors. *Communication Monographs, 57,* 161–181.

Cardot, J., & Dodd, C. (1979, November). *Communication apprehension as a predictor of proxemic establishment.* Paper presented at the annual meeting of the Speech Communication Association, San Antonio, TX.

Carducci, B. J., & Webber, A. W. (1979). Shyness as a determinant of interpersonal distance. *Psychological Reports, 44,* 1075–1078.

Cassidy, P. (1993, November). *The influence of notation on the development of Western music.* Paper presented at the annual convention of the Speech Communication Association, Miami, FL.

Cegala, D. J., Alexander, A. F., & Sokovitz, S. (1979). An investigation of eye gaze and its reaction to selected verbal behavior. *Human Communication Research, 5,* 99–108.

Cegala, D. J., & Sillars, A. L. (1989). Further examination of nonverbal manifestations of interaction involvement. *Communication Reports, 2,* 39–47.

Chaiken, S. (1979). Communicator physical attractiveness and persuasion. *Journal of Personality and Social Psychology, 37,* 1387–1397.

Chaudhuri, A., & Buck, R. (1995). Affect, reasoning, and persuasion. *Human Communication Research, 21,* 422–441.

Chelune, G. J., Robinson, J. T., & Kommor, M. J. (1984). A cognitive interactional model of intimate relationships. In V. Derlega (Ed.), *Communication, intimacy, and close relationships* (pp. 11–40). Orlando, FL: Academic Press.

Cherry, C. (1966). *On human communication.* Cambridge, MA: MIT Press.

Chinoy, E. (1967). *Society.* New York: Random House.

Christiansen, C. M. (1960). Relationships between pupil achievement, pupil affect-need, teacher warmth, and teacher permissiveness. *Journal of Educational Psychology, 51,* 169–174.

Cialdini, R. B. (1984). *Influence: How and why people agree to things.* New York: Quill.

Cialdini, R. B. (1988). *Influence, science and practice.* New York: Harper Collier.

Clark, M. S., Milberg, S., & Erber, R. (1984). Effects of arousal on the judgments of others' emotions. *Journal of Personality and Social Psychology, 46,* 551–560.

Coates, E. J., & Feldman, R. S. (1996). Gender differences in nonverbal correlates of social status. *Personality and Social Psychology Bulletin, 22,* 1014–1022.

Coats, W. D., & Smidchens, U. (1966). Audience recall as a function of speaker dynamism. *Journal of Educational Psychology, 57,* 189–191.

Cody, M. J., Lee, W. S., & Chao, E. Y. (1988, September). *Telling lies: Correlates of deception among Chinese.* Paper presented at the International Congress of Psychology, Sydney, Australia.

Cody, M. J., Marsten, P. J., & Foster, M. (1984, May). *Paralinguistic and verbal leakage of deception as a function of attempted control of timing of questions.* Paper presented at the annual meeting of the International Communication Association, San Francisco, CA.

Coker, D. A., & Burgoon, J. K. (1987). The nature of conversational involvement and nonverbal encoding patterns. *Human Communication Research, 13,* 463–494.

Comadena, M. E. (1982a). Accuracy in detecting deception: Intimate and friendship persons. In M. Burgoon (Ed.), *Communication yearbook 6* (pp. 446–472). Beverly Hills, CA: Sage.

Comadena, M. E. (1982b, May). *Nonverbal cues in the perception of deception.* Paper presented at the annual meeting of the Eastern Communication Association, Hartford, CT.

Comadena, M. E., & Andersen, P. A. (1978, April). Kinesic correlates of communication apprehension: An analysis of hand movements. Paper presented at the annual convention of the International Communication Association, Chicago, IL.

Comstock, J., Rowell, E., & Bowers, J. W. (1995).

Food for thought: Teacher immediacy, student learning and curvilinearity. *Communication Education, 44,* 251–266.

Condon, J. C., & Yousef, F. (1983). *An introduction to intercultural communication.* Indianapolis, IN: Bobbs-Merrill.

Condon, W. S., & Ogston, W. D. (1966). Sound film analysis of normal and pathological behavior patterns. *Journal of Nervous and Mental Disease, 143,* 338–347.

Condra, M. B. (1988, November). *Flirtation in developing relationships.* Paper presented at the annual convention of the Speech Communication Association, New Orleans, LA.

Conlee, C. J., Olvera, J., & Vagim, N. M. (1993). The relationship among physician nonverbal immediacy and measures of patient satisfaction with physician care. *Communication Reports, 6,* 25–33.

Cook, M. (1979). Gaze and mutual gaze in social encounters. In S. Weitz (Ed.), *Nonverbal communication: Readings with commentary* (2nd ed., pp. 77–86). New York: Oxford University Press.

Cortés, J. B., & Gatti, F. M. (1965). Physique and self-description of temperament. *Journal of Consulting Psychology, 29,* 432–439.

Coutts, L. M., & Schneider, F. W. (1976). Affiliative conflict theory: An investigation of the intimacy equilibrium and compensation hypothesis. *Journal of Personality and Social Psychology, 34,* 1135–1142.

Coutts, L. M., Schneider, F. W., & Montgomery, S. (1980). An investigation of the arousal model of interpersonal intimacy. *Journal of Experimental Social Psychology, 16,* 545–561.

Crawford, C. B. (1994). Effects of sex and sex-roles on avoidance of same- and opposite-sex touch. *Perceptual and Motor Skills, 70,* 107–112.

Crawford, M. (1995). *Talking difference: On gender and language.* London: Sage.

Crouch, W. W. (1980, April). *Consistency of selected eye behaviors across conversations with nine different partners.* Paper presented at the annual convention of the Eastern Communication Association, Ocean City, MD.

Crouch, W. W., & Koll, M. (1979, May). *The function of behavior in signaling dominance and submission in dyadic interactions.* Paper presented at the Eastern Communication Association, Philadelphia, PA.

Crusco, A. H., & Wetzel, C. G. (1984). The Midas touch: The effects of interpersonal touch on restaurant tipping. *Personality and Social Psychology, 10,* 512–517.

Cupach, W. R., & Metts, S. (1990). Remedial processes in embarrassing predicaments. In J. A. Anderson (Ed.), *Communication yearbook 13* (pp. 323–352). Beverly Hills, CA: Sage.

Cupach, W. R., & Metts, S. (1991). Sexuality and communication in close relationships. In K. McKinney & S. Sprecher (Eds.), *Sexuality in close relationships* (pp. 93–110). Hillsdale, NJ: Erlbaum.

Cupach, W. R., & Metts, S. (1994). *Facework.* Thousand Oaks, CA: Sage.

Daly, J. A., & Stafford, L. (1984). Correlates and consequences of social-communicative anxiety. In J. A. Daly & J. C. McCroskey (Eds.), *Avoiding communication: Shyness, reticence, and communication apprehension* (pp. 125–143). Beverly Hills, CA: Sage.

Daly, M., & Wilson, M. (1987). Evolutionary psychology and family violence. In C. Crawford, M. Smith, & D. Krebs (Eds.), *Sociobiology and psychology: Ideas, issues and applications* (pp. 293–309). Hillsdale, NJ: Erlbaum.

Daly, S. (1978). Behavioral correlates of social anxiety. *British Journal of Social and Clinical Psychology, 17,* 117–120.

Darley, J. M., & Cooper, J. (1972). The "clean for gene" phenomenon: The effect of students' appearance on political campaigning. *Journal of Applied Social Psychology, 2,* 24–33.

Darwin, C. (1872/1904). *The expression of emotion in man and animals.* London: John Murray.

Davis, C. (1992). Illinois: Crossroads and cross section. In J. H. Madison (Ed.), *Heartland: Comparative histories of midwestern states* (pp. 127–157). Bloomington: Indiana University Press.

Davis, F. (1973). *Inside intuition.* NY: McGraw-Hill.

Dean, L. M., Pugh, W. M., & Gundersen, E. K. E. (1975). Spatial and perceptual components of crowding: Effects on health and satisfaction. *Environment and Behavior, 7,* 225–236.

Dean, L. M., Willis, F. N., & Hewitt, J. (1975). Initial distance among individuals equal and unequal in military rank. *Journal of Personality and Social Psychology, 32,* 294–299.

Deethardt, J. F., & Hines, D. G. (1983). Tactile communication and personality differences. *Journal of Nonverbal Behavior, 8,* 143–156.

DePaulo, B. M. (1992). Nonverbal behavior and self-presentation. *Psychological Bulletin, 111,* 203–243.

DePaulo, B. M., Blank, A., Swaim, G. W., & Hairfield, J. G. (1992). Expressiveness and expressive control. *Personality and Social Psychology Bulletin, 18,* 276–285.

DePaulo, B. M., Kashy, D. A., Kirkendol, S. E., Wyer, S. M., & Epstein, J. A. (1996). Lying in everyday life. *Journal of Personality and Social Psychology, 70,* 979–995.

DePaulo, B. M., Rosenthal, R., Green, C. R., & Rosenkrantz, J. (1982). Diagnosing deceptive and mixed messages from verbal and nonverbal cues. *Journal of Experimental Social Psychology, 18,* 433–446.

DePaulo, B. M., Stone, J. I., & Lassiter, G. D. (1985). Deceiving and detecting deceit. In B. Schlenker (Ed.), *The self and social life* (pp. 323–370). New York: McGraw-Hill.

DePaulo, B. M., Zuckerman, M., & Rosenthal, R. (1980). Humans as lie detectors. *Journal of Communication, 30*(2), 129–139.

Derlega, V. J., Lewis, R. J., Harrison, S., Winstead, B. A., & Costanza, R. (1989, May). *Gender differences in the initiation and attribution of tactile intimacy.* Paper presented at the meeting of the International Network on Personal Relationships, Iowa City, IA.

Derlega, V. J., Metts, S., Petronio, S., & Margulis, S. T. (1993). *Self-disclosure.* Newbury Park, CA: Sage.

deTurck, M. A., & Miller, G. R. (1985). Deception and arousal: Isolating the behavioral correlates of deception. *Human Communication Research, 12,* 181–201.

DeVito, J. A., & Hecht, M. L. (1990). *The nonverbal communication reader.* Prospect Heights, IL: Waveland.

Dillard, J. P. (1994). Rethinking the study of fear appeals: An emotional perspective. *Communication Theory, 4,* 295–323.

Dillard, J. P. (1998). The role of affect in communication, biology, and social relationships. In P. A. Andersen & L. K. Guerrero (Eds.), *The handbook of communication and emotion: Research, theory, applications, and contexts* (pp. xvii–xxxii). San Diego, CA: Academic Press.

Dindia, K. (1987). The effects of sex of subject and sex of partner on interruptions. *Human Communication Research, 13,* 345–371.

Dindia, K. (1997, November). *Men are from North Dakota, women are from South Dakota.* Paper presented at the annual meeting of the National Communication Association, Chicago, IL.

Dindia, K., Fitzpatrick, M. A., & Attridge, M. (1989, November). *Gaze and mutual gaze: A social relations analysis.* Paper presented at the annual convention of the Speech Communication Association, San Francisco, CA.

Dinnerstein, L., & Reimers, D. M. (1975). *Ethnic Americans: A history of immigration and assimilation.* New York: Harper & Row.

Dion, K. L. E., Berscheid, E., & Walster, E. (1972). What is beautiful is good. *Journal of Personality and Social Psychology, 24,* 285–290.

Dittman, A. T. (1972). Developmental factors in conversational behavior. *Journal of Communication, 22,* 404–423.

Dolin, D., & Booth-Butterfield, M. (1993). Reach out and touch someone: An analysis of nonverbal comforting responses. *Communication Quarterly, 41,* 383–393.

Donagy, W. C., & Dooley, B. (1994). Head movement, gender, and deceptive communication. *Communication Reports, 7,* 76–87.

Doty, R. L. (Producer) (1974, November 10). Olfaction. *NOVA.* New York and Washington, DC: Public Broadcasting Service.

Doty, R. L., Snyder, P. J., Huggins, G. R., & Lowry, L. D. (1981). Endocrine, cardiovascular, and psychological correlates of olfactory sensitivity changes during the human menstrual cycle. *Journal of Comparative and Physiological Psychology, 95,* 46–60.

Druckman, D., Rozelle, R. M., & Baxter, J. C. (1982). *Nonverbal communication: Survey, theory, and research.* Beverly Hills, CA: Sage.

Duck, S. (1988). *Relating to others.* Chicago: Dorsey Press.

Duck, S., & Miell, E. E. (1986). Charting the development of relationships. In R. Gilmour & S. Duck

(Eds.), *The emerging field of personal relationships*. Hillsdale, NJ: Erlbaum.

Duran, R. L., Jensen, A. D., Prisbell, M., & Rosoff, J. M. (1979, February). *The control dimension of interpersonal relationships: Conceptualization, behavioral correlates and measurement.* Paper presented at the annual meeting of the Western Speech Communication Association convention, Los Angeles, CA.

Eagly, A. H., Makhijani, M. G., & Klonsky, B. G. (1992). Gender and the evaluation of leaders: A meta-analysis. *Psychological Bulletin, 111*, 3–22.

Earthworks Group (1990). *50 simple things kids can do to save the earth.* Kansas City, MO: Andrews and McMeel.

Eckman, B. K. (1978, March). *Nonverbal correlates of anxiety.* Paper presented at the annual meeting of the Eastern Communication Association, Boston, MA.

Edmonds, E. M., & Cahoon, D. D. (1986). Attitudes concerning crimes related to clothing by female victims. *Bulletin of the Psychonomic Society, 24*, 444–446.

Efran, J. S. (1968). Looking for approval: Effects on visual behavior of approbation from persons differing in importance. *Journal of Personality and Social Psychology, 10*, 21–25.

Efran, M. G. (1974). The effect of physical appearance on the judgment of guilt, interpersonal attraction and severity of recommended punishment in a simulated jury task. *Journal of Research in Personality, 8*, 45–54.

Egland, K. L., Stelzner, M. A., Andersen, P. A., & Spitzberg, B. H. (1995). Perceived understanding, nonverbal communication, and relational satisfaction. In J. Aitken (Ed.), *Interpersonal communication processes* (pp. 1–28). Westeland, MI: Hayden-McNeill.

Egland, K. L., Stelzner, M. A., Andersen, P. A., & Spitzberg, B. H. (1997). Perceived understanding, nonverbal communication and relational satisfaction. In J. Aitken & L. Shedletsky (Eds.), *Intrapersonal communication processes* (pp. 386–395). Annandale, VA: The Speech Communication Association.

Ehrlichman, H., & Weinberger, A. (1978). Lateral eye movements and hemispheric asymmetry: A critical review. *Psychological Bulletin, 85*, 1080–1101.

Ehrlichman, H., Weiner, S. L., & Baker, A. H. (1974). Effects of verbal and spatial questions on initial gaze shifts. *Neuropsychologica 12*, 266–277.

Eibl-Eibesfeldt, I. (1972). Similarities and differences between cultures in expressive movements. In R. A. Hinde (Ed.), *Nonverbal communication* (pp. 297–312). London: Cambridge University Press.

Eibl-Eibesfeldt, I. (1974). *Love and hate: The natural history of behavior patterns.* New York: Holt, Rinehart & Winston.

Eibl-Eibesfeldt, I. (1979). Universals in human expressive behavior. In A. Wolfgang (Ed.), *Nonverbal behavior, applications and cultural implications* (pp. 17–30). New York: Academic Press.

Eisenberg, A. M., & Smith, R. R., Jr. (1971). *Nonverbal communication.* Indianapolis: Bobbs-Merrill.

Ekman, P. (1965). Communication through nonverbal behavior: A source of information about an interpersonal relationship. In S. S. Tomkins & C. E. Izard (Eds.), *Affect, cognition and personality* (pp. 390–442). New York: Spring.

Ekman, P. (1972). Universal and cultural difference in the facial expression of emotion. In J. R. Cole (Ed.), *Nebraska symposium on motivation* (pp. 207–283). Lincoln: University of Nebraska Press.

Ekman, P. (1976). Movements with precise meanings. *Journal of Communication, 26*(3), 14–26.

Ekman, P. (1978). Facial expression. In A. W. Siegman & S. Feldstein (Eds.), *Nonverbal behavior and communication* (pp. 97–116). Hillsdale, NJ: Erlbaum.

Ekman, P. (1982). *Emotion in the human face.* Cambridge, England: Cambridge University Press.

Ekman, P. (1985). *Telling lies: Clues in the marketplace, politics, and marriage.* New York: Norton.

Ekman, P. (1988). Lying and nonverbal behavior: Theoretical issues and new findings. *Journal of Nonverbal Behavior, 12*, 163–175.

Ekman, P. (1993). Facial expression and emotion. *American Psychologist, 48*, 384–392.

Ekman, P., & Friesen, W. V. (1969a). Nonverbal leakage and clues to deception. *Psychiatry, 32*, 88–106.

Ekman, P., & Friesen, W. V. (1969b). The repertoire of nonverbal behavior: Categories, origins, usage and coding. *Semiotica, 1*, 49–98.

Ekman, P., & Friesen, W. V. (1972). Hand movements. *Journal of Communication, 22*, 353–374.

Ekman, P., & Friesen, W. V. (1975). *Unmasking the face: A field guide to recognizing emotions from facial clues.* Englewood Cliffs, NJ: Prentice-Hall.

Ekman, P., & Friesen, W. V. (1986). A new pancultural facial expression of emotion. *Motivation and Emotion, 10,* 159–168.

Ekman, P., Friesen, W. V., & Ellsworth, P. (1972). *Emotion in the human face: Guidelines for research and integration of findings.* New York: Pergamon Press.

Ekman, P., Friesen, W. V., & O'Sullivan, M. (1988). Smiles when lying. *Journal of Personality and Social Psychology, 54,* 414–420.

Ekman, P., & O'Sullivan, M. (1991). Who can catch a liar? *American Psychologist, 46,* 913–920.

Elazar, D. J. (1972). *American federalism: A view from the states.* New York: Thomas P. Crowell.

Elliot, S., & Jensen, A. D. (1979, May). *A summary of literature in olfactory communication: Special attention to pheromones.* Paper presented at the annual meeting of the Eastern Communication Association, Philadelphia, PA.

Elliot, S., Scott, M. D., Jensen, A. D., & McDonough, M. (1982). Perceptions of reticence: A cross-cultural investigation. In M. Burgoon (Ed.), *Communication yearbook 5* (pp. 591–602). New Brunswick, NJ: Transaction Books.

Ellsworth, P. C., Carlsmith, J. M., & Henson, A. (1972). The stare as a stimulus of flight in human subjects. *Journal of Personality and Social Psychology, 21,* 302–311.

Ellyson, S. L., & Dovidio, J. F. (1985). Power, dominance, and nonverbal behavior: Basic concepts and issues. In S. L. Ellyson & J. F. Dovidio (Eds.), *Power, dominance, and nonverbal behavior* (pp. 1–27). New York: Springer Verlag.

Eman, V. A., & Dierks-Stewart, K. J., & Tucker, R. K. (1978, November). *Implications of sexual identity and sexually identified situations on nonverbal touch.* Paper presented at the annual meeting of the Speech Communication Association, Minneapolis, MN.

Emmers, T. M., & Dindia, K. (1995). The effect of relational stage and intimacy on touch: An extension of Guerrero and Andersen. *Personal Relationships, 2,* 225–236.

Engen, T. A. (1973). The sense of smell. *Annual Review of Psychology, 24,* 187–206.

Engen, T. A. (1987). Remembering odors and their names. *American Scientist, 75,* 497–503.

Ervin, F. R., & Martin, J. (1986). Neuropsychological bases of the primary emotions. In R. Plutchik and H. Kellerman (Eds.), *Emotion: Theory, research and experience* (Vol. 3, pp. 145–170). Orlando, FL: Academic Press.

Esp, B. A. (1978). The effects of teacher kinesic communication upon student learning and attitudes. *Dissertations Abstracts International, 39*(5-A), 2828.

Exline, R. V., Ellyson, S. L., & Long, B. (1975). Visual behavior as an aspect of power role relationships. In P. Pliner, L. Drames, & T. Alloway (Eds.), *Nonverbal communication of aggression* (Vol. 2, pp. 21–52). New York: Plenum.

Exline, R. V., & Fehr, B. J. (1979). *Person and context in interpretation of gaze behavior.* Paper presented at the annual convention of the American Psychological Association, New York.

Exline, R. V., & Winters, L. C. (1965). Affective relations and mutual glances in dyads. In S. Tomkins & C. E. Izard (Eds.), *Affect, cognition, and personality.* New York: Springer.

Eysenck, H. J. (1963). *Experiments with drugs.* Oxford: Pergamon Press.

Eysenck, H. J. (1967). *The biological basis of personality.* Springfield, IL: Charles C. Thomas.

Eysenck, H. J. (1971). *Readings in extroversion-introversion: Bearings on basic psychological processes.* London: Staples Press.

Eysenck, H. J. (1976). Arousal, learning and memory. *Psychological Bulletin, 83,* 389–404.

Feeley, T. H., & Young, M. J. (1995, May). *Baseline familiarity in lie detection.* Paper presented at the annual meeting of the International Communication Association Convention, Albuquerque, NM.

Fehr, B., & Russell, J. A. (1984). Concept of emotion viewed from a prototype perspective. *Journal of Experimental Psychology, 113,* 464–486.

Fehr, B. J., & Exline, R. V. (1987). Social visual interaction: A conceptual and literature review. In A. W. Siegman & S. Feldstein (Eds.), *Nonverbal behavior and communication* (2nd ed., pp. 225–236). Hillsdale, NJ: Erlbaum.

Feingold, A. (1990). Gender differences in effects of physical attraction on romantic attraction: A comparison across five research paradigms. *Journal of Personality and Social Psychology, 59,* 981–993.

Feingold, A. (1992). Good looking people are not what we think. *Psychological Bulletin, 3,* 304–341.

Feldstein, S. (1972). Temporal patterns of dialogue. In A. W. Siegman & B. Pope (Eds.), *Studies in dyadic communication* (pp. 91–114). Oxford: Pergamon Press.

Ferguson, C. A. (1964). Baby talk in six languages. *American Anthropologist, 66,* 103–114.

Ferguson, T. J., & Stegge, H. (1995). Emotional states and traits in children: The case of shame and guilt. In J. P. Tangney & K. W. Fischer (Eds.), *Self-conscious emotions: The psychology of shame, guilt, embarrassment and pride* (pp. 174–197). New York: Guilford.

Feyereisen, P. (1987). Brain pathology, lateralization, and nonverbal behavior. In R. S. Feldman & B. Rime (Eds.), *Fundamentals of nonverbal communication* (pp. 31–70). Cambridge: Cambridge University Press.

Fielding, G. J. (1974). *Geography as a social science.* New York: Harper & Row.

Fischer, K. W., & Tangney, J. P. (1995). Self-conscious emotions and the affect revolution: Framework and overview. In J. P. Tangney & K. W. Fischer (Eds.), *Self-conscious emotions: The psychology of shame, guilt, embarrassment and pride* (pp. 3–22). New York: Guilford.

Fisher, J. D., Rytting, M., & Heslin, R. (1976). Hands touching hands: Affective and evaluative effects of an interpersonal touch. *Sociometry, 39,* 416–421.

Fitzpatrick, M. A., & Badzinski, D. (1985). All in the family: Communication in kin relationships. In M. L. Knapp & G. R. Miller (Eds.), *Handbook of interpersonal communication* (pp. 687–736). Beverly Hills, CA: Sage.

Flora, J. A., & Maibach, E. W. (1990). Cognitive responses to AIDS information: The effect of issue involvement and message appeal. *Communication Research, 17,* 759–774.

Forden, C. (1981). The influence of sex-role expectations on the perception of touch. *Sex Roles, 7,* 889–894.

Fowles, J. (1974). Why we wear clothes, ETC. *A Review of General Semantics, 31,* 343–352.

Frank, L. K. (1957). Tactile communication. *Genetic Psychology Monographs, 56,* 209–255.

Frank, O. H. (1952). *Anne Frank: The diary of a young girl.* New York: Random House.

Freud, S. (1930/1961). *Civilization and its discontents* (J. Strachey, Trans.). New York: Norton.

Frick, R. W. (1985). Communicating emotion: The role of prosodic features. *Psychological Bulletin, 97,* 412–429.

Fridlund, A. J. (1991). Evolution and facial action in reflex, social motive, and paralanguage. *Biological Psychology, 32,* 3–100.

Friedman, H. S., Mertz, T. J., & DiMatteo, M. R. (1980). Perceived bias in the facial expressions of television news broadcasters. *Journal of Communication, 30,* 103–111.

Friedman, M. (1985). Toward a reconceptualization of guilt. *Contemporary Psychoanalysis, 21,* 501–547.

Frijda, N. H., Kuipers, P., & ter Schure, E. (1989). Relations between emotion, appraisal, and emotional action readiness. *Journal of Personality and Social Psychology, 57,* 212–228.

Fromme, D. K., & Beam, D. C. (1974). Dominance and sex differences in nonverbal responses to differential eye contact. *Journal of Research in Personality, 8,* 76–87.

Fromme, D. K., Fromme, M. L., Brown, S., Daniell, J., Taylor, D. K., & Rountree, J. R. (1986). Attitudes toward touch: Cross-validation and the effects of gender and acquaintanceship. *Rassegna di Psicologia, 3,* 49–63.

Fromme, D. K., Jaynes, W. E., Taylor, D. K., Harold, E. G., Daniell, J., Rountree, J. R., & Fromme, M. L. (1989). Nonverbal behavior and attitudes toward touch. *Journal of Nonverbal Behavior, 13,* 3–14.

Frymier, A. B. (1994). A model of immediacy in the classroom. *Communication Quarterly, 42,* 133–144.

Fugita, S. S. (1974). Effects of anxiety and approval on visual interaction. *Journal of Personality and Social Psychology, 29,* 586–592.

Funder, D. C., & Ozer, D. J. (1983). Behavior as a function of the situation. *Journal of Personality and Social Psychology, 44,* 107–112.

Gaines, S. O., et al., (1998). Communication of emotions in friendships. In P. A. Andersen & L. K. Guerrero (Eds.), *Handbook of communication and emotion: Research, theory, applications, and contexts* (pp. 507–532). San Diego, CA: Academic Press.

Gaines, S. O., Rusbult, C. E., Wexler, M. O., & Cox, C. L. (1995, June). *Self-monitoring as a moderator of the link between interpersonal traits and re-sponses to dissatisfaction.* Paper presented at the meeting of the International Network on Personal Relationships, Williamsburg, VA.

Galbraith, J. K. (1951). Conditions for economic change in underdeveloped countries. *American Journal of Farm Economics, 33,* 693.

Gallaher, P. E. (1992). Individual differences in non-verbal behavior: Dimensions of style. *Journal of Personality and Social Psychology, 63,* 133–145.

Galle, O. R., & Gove, W. R. (1979). Crowding and social behavior in Chicago, 1940–1970. In J. R. Aiello & A. Baum (Eds.), *Residential crowding and design* (pp. 23–39). New York: Plenum Press.

Garreau, J. (1981). *The nine nations of North America.* New York: Avon Books.

Garrison, J. P., Sullivan, D. L., & Pate, L. E. (1976, December). *Interpersonal valence dimensions as discriminators of communication contexts: An empirical assessment of dyadic linkages.* Paper presented at the annual meeting of the Speech Communication Association, San Francisco, CA.

Gauger, P. W. (1952). The effect of gesture and the presence or absence of the speaker on the listening comprehension of eleventh and twelfth grade high school pupils. Cited in C. W. Dow (Ed.), Abstracts of theses in the field of speech and drama, *Speech Monographs, 19,* 116–117.

Gaulin, S. J. C. (1992). Evolution of sex differences in spatial ability. *Yearbook of Physical Anthropology, 35,* 125–151.

Geertz, C. (1973). *The interpretations of cultures.* New York: Basic Books.

Geller, D. M., Goodstein, L., Silver, M., & Steinberg, W. C. (1974). On being ignored: The effects of the violation of implicit rules of social interaction. *Sociometry, 37,* 541–556.

Gendrin, D. M., & Honeycutt, J. M. (1988, November). *The relationship between self-reported affinity-seeking competence and nonverbal immediacy behaviors among strangers and acquaintances.* Paper presented at the annual convention of the Speech Communication Association, New Orleans, LA.

Gerbner, G., Gross, L., Morgan, M., & Signiorelli, N. (1986). Living with television: The dynamics of the cultivation process. In J. Bryant & D. Zillman (Eds.), *Perspectives on media effects* (pp. 17–41). Hillsdale, NJ: Erlbaum.

Gergen, K. J. (1991). *The saturated self: Dilemmas of identity in contemporary life.* New York: Basic Books.

Gergen, K. J., Gergen, M., & Barton, W. H. (1973). Deviance in the dark. *Psychology Today, 7,* 129–130.

Gibran, K. (1923). *The prophet.* New York: Alfred A. Knopf.

Gifford, R. (1994). A lens-mapping framework for understanding the encoding and decoding of interpersonal dispositions in nonverbal behavior. *Journal of Personality and Social Psychology, 66,* 398–412.

Giglio, K., & Lustig, M. W. (1987, February). *Teacher immediacy and student expectations as predictors of learning.* Paper presented at the annual convention of the Western Speech Communication Association, Salt Lake City, UT.

Gilbert, A. N., & Wysocki, C. J. (1987). The smell survey: Its results. *National Geographic, 174*(4), 514–525.

Giles, H., & Street, R. L. (1994). Communicator characteristics and behavior. In M. L. Knapp & G. R. Miller (Eds.), *Handbook of interpersonal communication* (2nd ed., pp. 103–161). Thousand Oaks, CA: Sage.

Goffman, E. (1959). *The presentation of self in everyday life.* Garden City, NY: Doubleday-Anchor.

Goffman, E. (1967). *Interaction Ritual.* Garden City, NY: Anchor Books.

Goldberg, G. N., Kiesler, C. A., & Collins, B. E. (1969). Visual behavior and face-to-face distance during interaction. *Sociometry, 32,* 43–53.

Goldhaber, G. M. (1974). *Organizational communication.* Dubuque, IA: William C. Brown.

Goldman, M., Kiyohara, O., & Pfannensteil, D. A. (1985). Interpersonal touch, social labeling, and the foot-in-the-door effect. *The Journal of Social Psychology, 125,* 143–147.

Goldstein, A. G., & Jeffords, J. (1981). Status and touching behavior. *Bulletin of the Psychonomic Society, 17*(2), 79–81.

Goodall, H. L. (1995, April). *Spiritual teachings as organizing: Learning to read directions from the signs of postmodern deadends.* Paper presented at the annual meeting of the Southern States Communication Association Convention, New Orleans, LA.

Gore, A. (1992). *Earth in the balance: Ecology and the human spirit.* New York: Plume Book.

Gorham, J. (1988). The relationship between verbal teacher immediacy behaviors and student learning. *Communication Education, 37,* 40–53.

Gorham, J., & Azkahi, W. R. (1990). A comparison of teacher and student perceptions of immediacy and learning: Monitoring process and product. *Communication Education, 39,* 354–368.

Gorham, J., & Christofel, D. M. (1988, November). *The relationship of teachers' use of humor in the classroom to immediacy and student learning.* Paper presented at the annual convention of the Speech Communication Association, New Orleans, LA.

Gottman, J. M. (1979). *Marital interaction: Empirical investigations.* New York: Academic Press.

Grayson, B., & Stein, M. I. (1981). Attracting assault: Victim's nonverbal cues. *Journal of Communication, 31,* 68–75.

Greene, J. O., O'Hair, H. D., Cody, M. J., & Yen, C. (1985). Planning and control of behavior during deception. *Human Communication Research, 11,* 335–364.

Greene, J. O., & Sparks, G. G. (1983). Explication and test of a cognitive model of communication apprehension: A new look at an old construct. *Human Communication Research, 9,* 349–366.

Greene, J. O., & Sparks, G. G. (1992). Intellectual scrutiny as an alternative to replies from the heart: Toward clarifying the nature of arousal and its relation to nonverbal behavior. *Human Communication Research, 18,* 483–488.

Greenwood, J. D. (1994). *Realism, identity, and emotion: Reclaiming social psychology.* Thousand Oaks, CA: Sage.

Griffitt, W. (1970). Environmental effects on interpersonal affective behavior: Ambient effective temperature and attraction. *Journal of Personality and Social Psychology, 15,* 240–244.

Gudykunst, W. B., & Kim, Y. Y. (1992). *Communicating with strangers: An approach to intercultural communication* (2nd ed.). New York: Random House.

Gudykunst, W. B., Ting-Toomey, S., & Chua, E. (1988). *Culture and Interpersonal Communication.* Newbury Park, CA: Sage.

Guerrero, L. K. (1994). "I'm so mad I could scream": The effects of anger expression on relational satisfaction and communication competence. *Southern Communication Journal, 59,* 125–141.

Guerrero, L. K. (1996). Attachment-style differences in intimacy and involvement: A test of the four-category model. *Communication Monographs, 63,* 269–292.

Guerrero, L. K. (1997). Nonverbal involvement across interactions with same-sex friends, opposite-sex friends, and romantic partners: Consistency or change? *Journal of Social and Personal Relationships, 14,* 31–59.

Guerrero, L. K., & Andersen, P. A. (1991). The waxing and waning of relational intimacy: Touch as a function of relational stage, gender and touch avoidance. *Journal of Social and Personal Relationships, 8,* 147–165.

Guerrero, L. K., & Andersen, P. A. (1994). Patterns of matching and initiation: Touch behavior and avoidance across romantic relationship stages. *Journal of Nonverbal Behavior, 18,* 137–153.

Guerrero, L. K., & Andersen, P. A. (1998). Jealousy experience and expression in romantic relationships. In P. A. Andersen & L. K. Guerrero (Eds.), *Handbook of communication and emotion: Research, theory, applications, and contexts* (pp. 155–188). San Diego, CA: Academic Press.

Guerrero, L. K., Andersen, P. A., Jorgensen, P. F., Spitzberg, B. H., & Eloy, S. V. (1995). Coping with the green-eyed monster: Conceptualizing and measuring communicative responses to romantic jealousy. *Western Journal of Communication, 59,* 270–304.

Guerrero, L. K., Andersen, P. A., & Trost, M. (1998). Communication and emotion: Basic concepts and approaches. In P. A. Andersen & L. K. Guerrero (Eds.), *Handbook of communication and emotion: Research, theory, applications, and contexts* (pp. 3–28). San Diego, CA: Academic Press.

Guerrero, L. K., & Ebesu, A. S. (1993, May). *While at play: An observational analysis of children's touch behavior.* Paper presented at the annual convention of the International Communication Association, Miami, FL.

Guerrero, L. K., & Miller, T. A. (1996, May). *The role of nonverbal involvement cues in videotaped distance education courses: Associations with behavioral intent and positive affective learning.* Paper presented at the annual convention of the International Communication Association, Albuquerque, NM.

Guerrero, L. K., & Reiter, R. L. (1998). Expressing emotion: Sex differences in social skills and communicative responses to anger, sadness, and jealousy. In D. J. Canary & K. Dindia (Eds.), *Sex differences and similarities in communication* (pp. 321–350). Mahwah, NJ: Erlbaum.

Gur, R., & Gur, R. (1977). Correlates of conjugate lateral eye movements in man. In S. Harnad, R. W. Doty, L. Goldstein, J. Jaynes, & G. Krauthamer (Eds.), *Lateralization in the nervous system* (pp. 261–281). New York: Academic Press.

Gutsell, L. M., & Andersen, J. F. (1980, May). *Perceptual and behavioral responses to smiling.* Paper presented at the annual convention of the International Communication Association, Acapulco, Mexico.

Haber, G. M. (1982). Spatial relations between dominants and marginals. *Social Psychological Quarterly, 45,* 219–228.

Halberstadt, A. G., & Saitta, M. B. (1987). Gender, nonverbal behavior, and perceived dominance: A test of the theory. *Journal of Personality and Social Psychology, 53,* 257–272.

Hale, D., & Eisen, J. (1968). *The California dream.* New York: Collier.

Hale, J. L., Lundy, J. C., & Mongeau, P. A. (1989). Perceived relational intimacy and relational message content. *Communication Research Reports, 6,* 94–99.

Hale, J. L., & Stiff, J. B. (1989). *Judgments of honesty and deceit: The impact of cue incongruence and normative influence.* Paper presented to the annual meeting of the International Communication Association, San Francisco, CA.

Hall, E. T. (1959). *The silent language.* New York: Doubleday.

Hall, E. T. (1966a). *The hidden dimension.* New York: Doubleday.

Hall, E. T. (1966b). A system of the notation of proxemic behavior. *American Anthropologist, 65,* 1003–1026.

Hall, E. T. (1968). Proxemics. *Current Anthropology, 9,* 83–109.

Hall, E. T. (1976). *Beyond culture.* Garden City, NY: Anchor Books.

Hall, E. T. (1984). *The dance of life: The other dimension of time.* Garden City, NY: Anchor Press.

Hall, J. A. (1978). Gender effects in decoding nonverbal cues. *Psychological Bulletin, 85,* 845–857.

Hall, J. A. (1979). Gender, gender roles and nonverbal communication skills. In Rosenthal (Ed.), *Skill in nonverbal communication* (pp. 31–97). Cambridge, MA: Oelgeschlager, Gunn, & Hain.

Hall, J. A. (1984). *Nonverbal sex differences: Communication, accuracy and expressive styles.* Baltimore, MD: Johns Hopkins University Press.

Hall, J. A. (1985). Male and female nonverbal behavior. In A. W. Siegman & S. Feldstein (Eds.), *Multichannel integrations of nonverbal behavior* (pp. 195–225). Hillsdale, NJ: Erlbaum.

Hall, J. A. (1996). Touch, status, and gender at professional meetings. *Journal of Nonverbal Behavior, 20,* 23–44.

Hall, J. A. (1998). How big are nonverbal sex differences? The case of smiling and sensitivity to nonverbal cues. In D. J. Canary & K. Dindia (Eds.), *Sex differences and similarities in communication* (pp. 155–177). Mahwah, NJ: Erlbaum.

Hall, J. A., & Halberstadt, A. G. (1994). "Subordination" and sensitivity to nonverbal cues: A study of married working women. *Sex Roles, 31,* 149–165.

Hall, J. A., & Halberstadt, A. G. (1997). Subordination and nonverbal sensitivity: A hypothesis in search of support. In M. R. Walsh (Ed.), *Women, men, & gender: Ongoing debates* (pp. 120–133). New Haven, CT: Yale University Press.

Hall, J. A., & Veccia, A. M. (1990). More "touching" observations: New insights on men, women, and interpersonal touch. *Journal of Personality and Social Psychology, 59,* 1155–1162.

Hall, J. A., & Veccia, A. M. (1992). Touch asymmetry between the sexes. In C. L. Ridgeway (Ed.), *Gender, interaction, and inequality* (pp. 81–96). New York: Springer Verlag.

Halpern, D. F. (1986). *Sex differences in cognitive abilities.* Hillsdale, NJ: Erlbaum.

Hare, A., & Bales, R. (1963). Seating position and small group interaction. *Sociometry, 26,* 480–486.

Harms, L. S. (1961). Listener judgments of status cues in speech. *Quarterly of Speech, 47,* 164–168.

Harner, D. P. (1973). *A review of research concerning the thermal environment and its effects on learning.*

Unpublished doctoral dissertation, University of Mississippi.

Harper, R. G., Wiens, A. N., & Matarazzo, J. D. (1978). *Nonverbal communication: The state of the art.* New York: John Wiley.

Harrigan, J. D., Oxman, T. E., & Rosenthal, R. (1985). Rapport expressed through nonverbal behavior. *Journal of Nonverbal Behavior, 9,* 95–110.

Harrington, G. M. (1955). Smiling as a measure of teacher effectiveness. *Journal of Education Research, 48,* 715–717.

Harris, M. B., James, J., Chavez, J., Fuller, M. L., Kent, S., Massanari, C., Moore, C., & Walsh, F. (1983). Clothing: Communication, compliance, and choice. *Journal of Applied Social Psychology, 13,* 88–97.

Harrison, R. P. (1974). *Beyond words: An introduction to nonverbal communication.* Englewood Cliffs, NJ: Prentice-Hall.

Hatfield, E. (1984). The dangers of intimacy. In V. J. Derlega (Ed.), *Communication, intimacy, and close relationships* (pp. 207–220). New York: Academic Press.

Hatfield, E., Cacioppo, J. T., & Rapson, R. L. (1994). *Emotional contagion.* Cambridge, England: Cambridge University Press.

Hatfield, E., & Sprecher, S. (1986). *Mirror, mirror.* Albany, NY: SUNY Press.

Hayes, D., & Metzger, L. (1972). Interpersonal judgments based upon talkativeness: Fact or artifact. *Sociometry, 35,* 538–561.

Hays, R. B. (1985). A longitudinal study of friendship development. *Journal of Personality and Social Psychology, 48,* 909–924.

Hearn, G. (1957). Leadership and the spatial factor in small groups. *Journal of Abnormal and Social Psychology, 54,* 269–272.

Hecht, M. L., Andersen, P. A., & Ribeau, S. A. (1989). The cultural dimensions of nonverbal communication. In M. K. Asante & W. B. Gudykunst (Eds.), *Handbook of international and intercultural communication* (pp. 163–185). Newbury Park, CA: Sage.

Hecht, M. L., Foster, S. H., Dunn, D. J., Willimans, J. K., Anderson, D. R., & Pulbratek, D. (1986). Nonverbal behavior of young abused and neglected children. *Communication Education, 35,* 134–142.

Heckel, R. V. (1973). Leadership and voluntary seating choice. *Psychological Reports, 32,* 141–142.

Heft, H. (1979). Background and focal environmental conditions of the home and attention in young children. *Journal of Applied Social Psychology, 9,* 47–69.

Hegstrom, T. G. (1979). Message impact: What percentage is nonverbal? *Western Journal of Speech Communication, 43,* 134–142.

Heilman, M. E., & Saruwatari, L. R. (1979). When beauty is beastly: The effects of appearance and sex on evaluations of job applicants for managerial and nonmanagerial jobs. *Organizational Behavior and Human Performance, 23,* 360–372.

Helgeson, V. S., Shaver, P., & Dyer, M. (1987). Prototypes of intimacy and distance in same-sex and opposite-sex relationships. *Journal of Social and Personal Relationships, 4,* 195–233.

Hemsley, G., & Doob, A. (1978). The effect of looking behavior on perceptions of a communicator's credibility. *Journal of Applied Social Psychology, 8,* 136–144.

Henchy, V. L., & Falk, E. S. (1995, February). *Public touch in lesbian and "straight" settings: An exploratory study.* Paper presented at the annual convention of the Western States Communication Association, Portland, OR.

Hendrick, S. S., & Hendrick, C. (1992). *Liking, loving, and relating* (2nd ed.). Pacific Grove, CA: Brooks/Cole.

Henley, N. M. (1973). Status and sex: Some touching observations. *Bulletin of the Psychonomic Society, 2,* 91–83.

Henley, N. M. (1977). *Body politics: Power, sex, and nonverbal communication.* Englewood Cliffs, NJ: Prentice-Hall.

Henley, N. M., & Harmon, S. (1985). The nonverbal semantics of power and gender. In S. L. Ellyson & J. F. Dovidio (Eds.), *Power, dominance, and nonverbal behavior* (pp. 151–164). New York: Springer Verlag.

Hensley, W. E. (1991). Pupillary dilation revisited: The constriction of a nonverbal cue. In J. W. Neuliep (Ed.), *Replication research in the social sciences* (pp. 97–104). Newbury Park, CA: Sage.

Herzog, A. (1974). The B.S. factor: The theory and

technique of faking it in America. Baltimore, MD: Penguin Books.

Heslin, R. (1974, May). *Steps toward a taxonomy of touching*. Paper presented at the annual convention of the Midwestern Psychological Association, Chicago, IL.

Heslin, R., & Alper, T. (1983). Touch: A bonding gesture. In J. M. Wiemann & R. Harrison (Eds.), *Nonverbal interaction* (pp. 47–75). Beverly Hills, CA: Sage.

Heslin, R., & Boss, D. (1980). Nonverbal intimacy in arrival and departure at an airport. *Personality and Social Psychology Bulletin, 6*, 248–252.

Hess, E. H. (1965). Attitude and pupil size. *Scientific American, 212*, 46–54.

Hess, E. H. (1975). The role of pupil size in communication. *Scientific American, 233*, 110–119.

Hess, E. H., & Goodwin, E. (1974). The present state of pupilometrics. In M. P. Janisse (Ed.), *Pupillary dynamics and behavior* (pp. 209–246). New York: Plenum Press.

Hess, E. H., & Petrovich, S. B. (1987). Pupillary behavior in communication. In A. W. Siegman & S. Feldstein (Eds.), *Nonverbal behavior and communication* (pp. 327–348). Hillsdale, NJ: Erlbaum.

Hess, E. H., Seltzer, A. L., & Schlien, J. M. (1965). Pupil response of hetero and homosexual males to pictures of men and women: A pilot study. *Journal of Abnormal Psychology, 70*, 165–168.

Heston, J. K., & Garner, P. (1972, April). *A study of personal spacing and desk arrangement in a learning environment*. Paper presented at the International Communication Association Convention, Atlanta, GA.

Hickson, M. L., & Stacks, D. W. (1993). *NVC nonverbal communication: Studies and applications* (3rd ed.). Dubuque, IA: William C. Brown.

Hill, C. T., Rubin, C., & Peplau, L. A. (1976). Breakups before marriage: The end of 103 affairs. *Journal of Social Issues, 32*, 147–168.

Hill, R. D., Blackman, R. E., & Crane, D. R. (1982). The effect of the marital relationship on personal space orientation in married couples. *Journal of Social Psychology, 11*, 23–28.

Hocking, J. E., Bauchner, J., Kaminski, E. P., & Miller, G. R. (1979). Detecting deceptive communication from verbal and paralinguistic cues. *Human Communication Research, 6*, 33–46.

Hocking, J. E., & Leathers, D. G. (1980). Nonverbal indicators of deception: A new theoretical perspective. *Communication Monographs, 47*, 119–131.

Hocking, J. E., Walker, B., & Fink, E. L. (1982). The effects of physical attractiveness on the communication of attributional information. *Psychological Reports, 51*, 111–116.

Hoffner, C., Cantor, J., & Thornson, E. (1988). Children's understanding of a televised narrative: Developmental differences in processing video and audio content. *Communication Research, 15*, 227–245.

Hofstede, G. (1982). *Culture's consequences* (abridged ed.). Beverly Hills, CA: Sage.

Holmes, J. G., & Rempel, J. K. (1989). Trust in close relationships. In C. Hendrick (Ed.), *Close relationships* (pp. 187–220). Newbury Park, CA: Sage.

Honeycutt, J. M., Cantrill, J. G., & Greene, R. W. (1989). Memory structures for relational escalation: A cognitive test of the sequencing of relational actions and stages. *Human Communication Research, 16*, 62–70.

Hopper, R., & Bell, R. A. (1984). Broadening the deception construct. *Quarterly Journal of Speech, 70*, 288–300.

Hottenstein, M. P. (1978). An exploration of the relationship between age, social status and facial gesturing. (Doctoral dissertation, University of Pennsylvania, 1977). *Dissertation Abstracts International, 38*, 5648B–5649B. (University Microfilms No. 78-06, 598)

Huntington, E. (1945). *Mainsprings of civilization*. New York: Wiley & Sons.

Hupka, R. B. (1981). Cultural determinants of jealousy. *Alternative Lifestyles, 4*, 310–356.

Hurd, K., & Noller, P. (1988). Decoding deception: A look at the process. *Journal of Nonverbal Behavior, 12*, 217–233.

Hurt, H. T., Scott, M. D., & McCroskey, J. C. (1978). *Communication in the classroom*. Reading, MA: Addison-Wesley.

Hurwitz, J. J., Zander, A. F., & Hymovitch, B. (1968). Some effects of power on the relations among group members. In D. Cartwright & A. Zander

(Eds.), *Group dynamics* (pp. 291–297). New York: Harper & Row.

Huseman, R. C., Lahiff, J. M., & Hatfield, J. D. (1976). *Interpersonal communication in organizations.* Boston: Holbrook Press.

Hyman, R. T. (1968). The concept of an ideal teacher-student relationship: A comparison and critique. In R. T. Hyman (Ed.), *Teaching: Vantage points for study.* Philadelphia: Lippincott.

Imada, A. S., & Hakel, M. D. (1977). Influence of nonverbal communication and rater proximity on impressions and decisions in simulated employment interviews. *Journal of Applied Psychology, 62,* 295–300.

Insel, P. M., & Lindgen, A. C. (1978). *Too close for comfort: The psychology of crowding.* Englewood Cliffs, NJ: Prentice-Hall.

Izard, C. E. (1977). *Human emotions.* New York: Plenum.

Izard, C. E. (1992). Basic emotions, relationship among emotions, and emotion-cognition relations. *Psychological Review, 99,* 561–565.

Jaffe, J. (1987). Parliamentary procedure and the brain. In A. W. Siegman and S. Feldstein (Eds.), *Nonverbal behavior and communication* (2nd ed., pp. 21–33). Hillsdale, NJ: Erlbaum.

Jaffe, J., & Anderson, S. W. (1979). Prescript to chapter 1: Communication rhythms and the evolution of language. In A. W. Seigman & S. Feldstein (Eds.), *Of speech and time: Temporal speech patterns in interpersonal contexts* (pp. 17–32). Hillsdale, NJ: Erlbaum.

Jandt, F. E. (1995). *Intercultural communication: An introduction.* Thousand Oaks, CA: Sage.

Jensen, A. D., & Andersen, P. A. (1979, May). *The relationship among communication traits, communication behaviors, and interpersonal perception variables.* Paper presented at the annual convention of the International Communication Association, Philadelphia, PA.

Jensen, J. V. (1985). Perspective on nonverbal intercultural communication. In L. A. Samovar & R. E. Porter (Eds.), *Intercultural communication: A reader* (pp. 256–272). Belmont, CA: Wadsworth.

Johnson, K. L., & Edwards, R. (1991). The effects of gender and type of romantic touch on perceptions of relational commitment. *Journal of Nonverbal Behavior, 15,* 43–54.

Jones, S. E. (1994). *The right touch: Understanding and using the language of physical contact.* Cresshill, NJ: Hampton Press.

Jones, S. E., & Brown, B. C. (1996). Touch attitudes and touch behaviors: Recollections of early childhood touch and social self-confidence. *Journal of Nonverbal Behavior, 20,* 147–163.

Jones, S. E., & Yarbrough, E. (1985). A naturalistic study of the meanings of touch. *Communication Monographs, 52,* 19–56.

Jones, T. S., & Remland, M. S. (1982, May). *Cross cultural differences in self-reported touch avoidance.* Paper presented at the annual convention of the Eastern Communication Association, Hartford, CT.

Jorgenson, D. O. (1975). Field study of the relationship between status discrepancy and proxemic behavior. *Journal of Social Psychology, 97,* 173–179.

Joseph, N., & Alex, N. (1972). The uniform: A sociological perspective. *American Journal of Sociology, 77,* 719–730.

Jourard, S. M. (1966). An exploratory study of body-accessibility. *British Journal of Social and Clinical Psychology, 5,* 221–231.

Jourard, S. M., & Rubin, J. E. (1968). Self-disclosure and touching: A study of two modes of interpersonal encounter and their inter-relation. *Journal of Humanistic Psychology, 8,* 39–48.

Kahn, A., & McGaughey, T. A. (1977). Distance and liking: When moving close produces increased liking. *Sociometry, 40,* 138–144.

Kanter, R. M. (1979). How the top is different. In R. M. Kanter & B. A. Stein (Eds.), *Life in organizations* (pp. 20–35). New York: Basic Books.

Kappas, A., Hess, U., & Scherer, K. R. (1991). Voice and emotion. In R. S. Feldman & B. Rime (Eds.), *Fundamentals of nonverbal communication* (pp. 200–237). Cambridge, England: Cambridge University Press.

Kashy, D. A., & DePaulo, B. M. (1996). Who lies? *Journal of Personality and Social Psychology, 70,* 1037–1051.

Keating, C. F. (1985). Human dominance signals: The primate in us. In S. J. Ellyson & J. F. Dovidio (Eds.), *Power, dominance and nonverbal behavior* (pp. 89–108). New York: Springer Verlag.

Keating, C. F., Mazur, A., & Segall, M. H. (1977). Facial gestures which influence the perception of status. *Sociometry, 40,* 374–378.

Keeley-Dyerson, M. P., Bailey, W., & Burgoon, J. K. (1988, May). *The effects of stress and gender on nonverbal decoding accuracy in kinesic and vocalic channels.* Paper presented at the International Communication Association Convention, New Orleans, LA.

Keeley-Dyerson, M. P., Burgoon, J. K., & Bailey, W. (1991). The effects of stress and gender on nonverbal decoding accuracy in kinesic and vocalic channels. *Human Communication Research, 17,* 584–605.

Kellerman, K. (1989). The negativity effect in initial interaction: It's all in your point of view. *Human Communication Research, 16,* 147–183.

Kelley, D. K., & Gorham, J. (1988). Effects of immediacy on recall of information. *Communication Education, 37,* 198–207.

Keltner, D. (1995). Signs of appeasement: Evidence for the distinct displays of embarrassment, amusement, and shame. *Journal of Personality and Social Psychology, 68,* 441–454.

Kendon, A. (1967). Some functions of gaze direction in social interaction. *Acta Psychologica, 26,* 22–63.

Kendon, A. (1983). Gesture and speech. In J. M. Wiemann & R. P. Harrison (Eds.), *Nonverbal interaction* (pp. 13–45). Beverly Hills, CA: Sage.

Kendon, A., & Cook, M. (1969). The consistency of gaze patterns in social interaction. *British Journal of Psychology, 60,* 481–494.

Kennedy, C. W., & Camden, C. (1983). Interruptions and nonverbal gender differences. *Journal of Nonverbal Behavior, 8,* 91–108.

Kenrick, D. T., & Keefe, R. C. (1992). Age preferences in mates reflect sex differences in human reproductive strategies. *Behavioral and Brain Sciences, 15,* 75–137.

Ketrow, S. M. (1990). Attributes of a telemarketer's voice and persuasiveness: A review and synthesis of the literature. *Journal of Direct Marketing, 4,* 7–21.

Kimura, D. (1973). The asymmetry of the human brain. *Scientific American, 231,* 70–76.

King, S. W., & Sereno, K. K. (1984). Conversational appropriateness as a conversational imperative. *The Quarterly Journal of Speech, 70,* 264–273.

Kleck, R. (1970). Interaction distance and nonverbal agreeing responses. *British Journal of Social and Clinical Psychology, 9,* 180–182.

Kleinfeld, J. S. (1974). Effects of nonverbal warmth on the learning of Eskimo and White students. *Journal of Social Psychology, 92,* 3–9.

Kleinke, C. L. (1977). Compliance to requests made by gazing and touching experimenters in field settings. *Journal of Experimental Social Psychology, 13,* 218–223.

Kleinke, C. L. (1980). Interaction between gaze and legitimacy of request on compliance in a field setting. *Journal of Nonverbal Behavior, 5,* 3–12.

Kleinke, C. L., Meeker, F. B., & Fong, C. L. (1974). Effects of gaze, touch, and use of name on evaluation of "engaged" couples. *Journal of Research in Personality, 7,* 368–373.

Kleinke, C. L., & Singer, D. A. (1979). Influence of gaze on compliance with demanding and conciliatory requests in a field setting. *Personality and Social Psychology Bulletin, 5,* 386–390.

Klinnert, M. D., Campos, J. J., Sorce, J. F., Emde, R. N., & Svejda, M. (1983). Emotions as behavioral regulators: Social referencing in infancy. In R. Plutchik & H. Kellerman (Eds.), *Emotion: Theory, research, and experience: Vol. 2. Emotions in early development* (pp. 57–86). New York: Academic Press.

Kloek, J. (1961). The smell of some steroid sex hormones and their metabolities: Reflections and experiments concerning the significance of smell for the mutual relation of the sexes. *Psychiatria, Neurologia, Neurochirugia, 64,* 309–344.

Klopf, D. W., & Thompson, C. A. (1991). Nonverbal immediacy differences among Japanese, Finnish, and American university students. *Perceptual and Motor Skills, 73,* 209–210.

Knapp, M. L. (1972/1978). *Nonverbal communication in human interaction.* New York: Holt, Rinehart & Winston.

Knapp, M. L. (1978). *Social intercourse: From greeting to goodbye.* Boston, MA: Allyn & Bacon.

Knapp, M. L. (1984). *Interpersonal communication and human relationships.* Boston, MA: Allyn & Bacon.

Knapp, M. L., & Comadena, M. E. (1979). Telling it like it isn't: Deceptive communications. *Human Communication Research, 5,* 270–285.

Knapp, M. L., & Hall, J. A. (1997). *Nonverbal communication in human interaction* (3rd ed.). Fort Worth, TX: Harcourt Brace.

Knapp, M. L., Hart, R. P., & Dennis, H. S. (1974). Deception as a communication construct. *Human Communication Research, 1,* 15–29.

Knowles, E. S. (1973). Boundaries around group interaction: The effect of group size and member status on boundary permeability. *Journal of Personality and Social Psychology, 26,* 327–332.

Koehler, J. W., Anatol, K. W. E., & Applbaum, R. L. (1981). *Organizational communication & behavioral perspectives.* New York: Holt, Rinehart & Winston.

Koermer, C., Goldstein, M., & Forston, D. (1993). How supervisors communicatively convey immediacy to subordinates: An exploratory, qualitative investigation. *Communication Quarterly, 41,* 296–281.

Koneya, M. (1977). Query on Ekman: Nonverbal movements or verbal surrogates? *Journal of Communication, 27,* 235–237.

Konner, M. (1987, March). The enigmatic smile. *Psychology Today, 21*(3), 42–46.

Koper, R. J., & Miller, G. R. (1986, May). *Motivation and Machiavellianism as predictors of nonverbal behavior and deception success.* Paper presented at the annual meeting of the International Communication Association, Chicago, IL.

Korda, M. (1983). Status marks—A gold-plated thermos is a man's best friend. In A. M. Katz & V. T. Katz (Eds.), *Foundations of nonverbal communication* (pp. 164–169). Carbondale, IL.: Southern Illinois University Press.

Korda, M. (1992). *The immortals.* New York: Poseidon Press.

Krauss, R. M., Geller, V., & Olson, C. (1976, September). *Modalities and cues in the detection of deception.* Paper presented at the annual convention of the American Psychological Association, Washington, DC.

Kraut, R. E. (1980). Humans as lie detectors: Some second thoughts. *Journal of Communication, 30*(4), 209–218.

Kraut, R. E., & Johnson, R. E. (1979). Social and emotional messages of smiling: An ethological approach. *Journal of Personality and Social Psychology, 37,* 1539–1553.

Kraut, R. E., & Poe, D. (1980). On the line: The deception judgments of customs inspectors and laymen. *Journal of Personality and Social Psychology, 39,* 784–798.

LaBarre, W. (1985). Paralinguistics, kinesics, and cultural anthropology. In L. A. Samovar & R. E. Porter (Eds.), *Intercultural communication: A reader* (pp. 272–279). Belmont, CA: Wadsworth.

LaCrosse, M. B. (1975). Nonverbal behavior and perceived counsellor attractiveness and persuasiveness. *Journal of Counseling Psychology, 22,* 536–566.

LaFrance, M., & Henley, N. M. (1997). On oppressing hypotheses: Or, differences in nonverbal sensitivity revisited. In M. R. Walsh (Ed.), *Women, men, & gender: Ongoing debates* (pp. 104–119). New Haven, CT: Yale University Press.

LaFrance, M., & Mayo, C. (1978). *Moving bodies: Nonverbal communication in social relationships.* Monterey, CA: Brooks/Cole.

Lakoff, R. (1975). *Language and women's place.* New York: Harper & Row.

Lamb, T. A. (1981). Nonverbal and paraverbal control in dyads and triads: Sex or power differences. *Social Psychology Quarterly, 44*(1), 49–53.

Larsen, K. S., & LeRoux, J. (1984). A study of same-sex touching attitudes: Scale development and personality predictors. *The Journal of Sex Research, 20,* 264–278.

Leakey, R. E., & Lewin, R. (1978). *People of the lake: Mankind and its beginnings.* Garden City, NY: Anchor Press.

Leary, M. R., & Meadows, S. (1991). Predictors, elicitors, and concomitants of social blushing. *Journal of Personality and Social Psychology, 60,* 254–262.

Leary, M. R., & Kowalski, R. M. (1995). *Social anxiety.* New York: Guilford.

Leathers, D. G. (1976). *Nonverbal communication systems.* Boston: Allyn & Bacon.

Leeds, C. H. (1950). A scale for measuring teacher-pupil attitudes and teacher-pupil rapport. *Psychological Monographs, 64,* 6.

Leffler, A., Gillespie, D. L., & Conaty, J. C. (1982). The effects of status differentiation on nonverbal behavior. *Social Psychology Quarterly, 45*(3), 161.

Lefkowitz, M., Blake, R., & Mouton, J. (1955). Status factors in pedestrian violation of traffic signals. *Journal of Abnormal and Social Psychology, 51,* 704–706.

Leibowitz, K., & Andersen, P. A. (1976, December).

The development and nature of the construct touch avoidance. Paper presented at the annual meeting of the Speech Communication Association, San Francisco, CA.

Lemerise, E. A., & Dodge, K. A. (1993). The development of anger and hostile interactions. In M. Lewis and J. M. Haviland (Eds.), *Handbook of emotions* (pp. 537–546). New York: Guilford.

Leone, C., & Ensley, E. (1983). Self-generated attitude change: Another look at the effects of thought and cognitive schemata. *Representative Research in Social Psychology, 15,* 2–10.

Levine, T. R. (1994, May). *Conceptualizing interpersonal and relational deception.* Paper presented at the annual meeting of the Speech Communication Association, New Orleans, LA.

Levine, T. R., & McCornack, S. A. (1992). Linking love and lies: A formal test of the McCornack & Parks model of deception detection. *Journal of Social and Personal Relationships, 9,* 143–154.

Levinger, G. (1980). Toward the analysis of close relationships. *Journal of Experimental Social Psychology, 16,* 510–544.

Lewis, K. E., & Bierly, M. (1990). Toward a profile of the female voter: Sex differences in perceived physical attractiveness and competence of political candidates. *Sex Roles, 22,* 1–11.

Lewis, M. (1995). Embarrassment: The emotion of self-exposure and evaluation. In J. P. Tangney & K. W. Fischer (Eds.), *Self-conscious emotions: The psychology of shame, guilt, embarrassment and pride* (pp. 198–218). New York: Guilford.

Lewis, M., & Rosenblum, L. A. (Eds.). (1974). *The effect of the infant on its caregiver.* New York: Wiley.

Lewis, P. F. (1972). Small town in Pennsylvania. *Annals of the Association of American Geographers, 62,* 323–351.

Libby, W. L., Jr., & Yanklevich, D. (1973). Personality determinants of eye contact and direction of gaze aversion. *Journal of Personality and Social Psychology, 27*(2), 197–206.

Linkey, H. E., & Firestone, I. J. (1990). Dyad dominance composition effects, nonverbal behaviors, and influence. *Journal of Research in Personality, 24,* 206–215.

Liss, B., Walker, M., Hazelton, V., & Cupach, W. D. (1993, February). *Mutual gaze and smiling as correlates of compliance-gaining success.* Paper presented

at the annual meeting of the Western States Communication Association, Albuquerque, NM.

Littlepage, G. E., Maddox, J., & Pineault, M. A. (1985). Recognition of discrepant nonverbal messages and detection of deception. *Perceptual and Motor Skills, 60,* 119–124.

Lomax, A. (1968). *Folk song style and culture.* New Brunswick, NJ: Transaction Books.

Lott, D. F., & Sommer, R. (1967). Seating arrangements and status. *Journal of Personality and Social Psychology, 7,* 90–95.

Lower, H. M. (1980). Fear of touching as a form of communication apprehension in professional nursing students. *Australian Scan: Journal of Human Communication, 7–8,* 71–78.

Lustig, M. W., & Andersen, P. A. (1990a). Generalizing about communication apprehension and avoidance: Multiple replications and meta-analyses. *Journal of Social Behavior and Personality, 5,* 309–340.

Lustig, M. W., & Andersen, P. A. (1990b, February). *The influence of individualism on interpersonal communication behavior and research: A synoptic view from the United States.* Paper presented at the annual meeting of the Western Speech Communication Association, Sacramento, CA.

Lustig, M. W., & Koester, J. (1993). *Intercultural competence: Interpersonal communication across culture.* New York: Harper Collins.

Machiavelli, N. (1513/1947). *The prince* (T. G. Bergin, Trans.). New York: Appleton-Century-Crofts.

MacLachlan, J. (1979). What people really think of fast talkers. *Psychology Today, 13*(6), 112–117.

MacNeill, L., & Wilson, B. (1972). *A field study of the effects of conventional and unconventional dress on petition signing behavior.* Unpublished manuscript, Illinois State University, Normal, IL.

Magai, C., & McFadden, S. H. (1995). *The role of emotions in social and personality development: History, theory and research.* New York: Wiley.

Major, B. (1981). Gender patterns in touching behavior. In C. Mayo & N. M. Henley (Eds.), *Gender and nonverbal behavior* (pp. 15–38). New York: Springer Verlag.

Major, B., & Heslin, R. (1982). Perceptions of cross-sex and same-sex nonreciprocal touch: It is better to give than to receive. *Journal of Nonverbal Behavior, 6,* 148–162.

Major, B., Schmidlin, A. M., & Williams, L. (1990). Gender patterns in social touch: The impact of setting and age. *Journal of Personality and Social Psychology, 58,* 634–643.

Malandro, L. A., & Barker, L. (1983). *Nonverbal communication.* Reading, MA: Addison-Wesley.

Malandro, L. A., Barker, L., & Barker, D. A. (1989). *Nonverbal communication.* New York: Random House.

Mandler, G. (1975). *Mind and emotion.* New York: Wiley.

Manning, P., & Ray, G. (1993). Shyness, self-confidence, and social interaction. *Social Psychology Quarterly, 56,* 178–192.

Manstead, A. S. R., Wagner, H. L., & MacDonald, C. J. (1984). Face, body, and speech as channels of communication in the detection of deception. *Basic and Applied Social Psychology, 5,* 317–332.

Manusov, V. (1991). Perceiving nonverbal messages: Effects of immediacy and encoded intent on receiver judgments. *Western Journal of Speech Communication, 55,* 235–253.

Markel, N. N. (1969). Relationship between voice-quality profiles and MMPI profiles in psychiatric patients. *Journal of Abnormal Psychology, 74,* 61–66.

Marsden, P. J., Hecht, M. L., & Robers, T. (1987). "True love ways": The subjective experience and communication of romantic love. *Journal of Social and Personal Relationships, 4,* 387–407.

Marshall, J. E. (1984). Multiple perspectives on modularity. *Cognition, 17,* 209–242.

Marshall, L. L. (1994). Physical and psychological abuse. In W. R. Cupach & B. S. Spitzberg (Eds.), *The dark side of interpersonal communication* (pp. 281–311). Hillsdale, NJ: Erlbaum.

Martin, J. G., & Westie, F. R. (1959). The intolerant personality. *American Sociological Review, 24,* 521–528.

Mascolo, M. E., & Fischer, K. W. (1995). Developmental transformations in appraisals for pride, shame, and guilt. In J. P. Tangney & K. W. Fischer (Eds.), *Self-conscious emotions: The psychology of shame, guilt, embarrassment and pride* (pp. 64–113). New York: Guilford.

Maslow, A. H. (1968). *Toward a psychology of being* (2nd ed.). New York: Van Nostrand.

Masters, R. D., & Sullivan, D. G. Facial displays and political leadership in France. *Behavioural Processes, 19,* 1–30.

Masters, W. H., & Johnson, V. E. (1966). *Human sexual response.* Boston: Little, Brown.

Matarazzo, J. D., Weins, A. N., & Saslow, G. (1965). Studies in interviewer speech behavior. In L. Krasner & U. P. Ullman (Eds.), *Research in behavior modification.* New York: Holt, Rinehart & Winston.

Matsumoto, D. (1991). Cultural influences on facial expressions of emotion. *Southern Communication Journal, 56,* 128–137.

McAdams, D. P. (1988). Personal needs and personal relationships. In S. Duck (Ed.), *Handbook of personal relationships* (pp. 7–22). New York: Wiley & Sons.

McCann, C. D., & Lalonde, R. N. (1993). Dysfunctional communication and depression: Social cognitive processes. *American Behavioral Scientist, 36,* 271–287.

McCann, K., & McKenna, H. P. (1993). An examination of touch between nurses and elderly patients in a continuing care setting in Northern Ireland. *Journal of Advanced Nursing, 18,* 838–846.

McClintock, M. K. (1971). Menstrual synchrony and suppression. *Nature, 229,* 244–245.

McCormick, N. B., & Jones, A. J. (1989). Gender differences in nonverbal flirtation. *Journal of Sex Education and Therapy, 15,* 271–282.

McCornack, S. A., & Parks, M. R. (1986). Deception detection and relationship development: The other side of trust. In M. L. McLaughlin (Ed.), *Communication Yearbook 9* (pp. 377–389). Beverly Hills, CA: Sage.

McCornack, S. A., & Parks, M. R. (1987, May). *What women know that men don't: Sex differences in determining the truth behind deceptive messages.* Paper presented at the annual meeting of the International Communication Association, Montreal, Quebec.

McCroskey, J. C. (1966). Scales for the measurement of ethos. *Speech Monographs, 33,* 65–72.

McCroskey, J. C. (1976). The effects of communication apprehension on nonverbal behavior. *Communication Quarterly, 24,* 39–44.

McCroskey, J. C. (1982). Oral communication apprehension: A reconceptualization. *Communication yearbook, 6,* 136–170.

McCroskey, J. C., & McCain, T. A. (1974). The measurement of interpersonal attraction. *Speech Monographs, 41,* 261–266.

McCroskey, J. C., & McVetta, R. W. (1978). The relationship between communication apprehension and classroom seating preferences. *Communication Education, 27,* 99–111.

McCroskey, J. C., Richmond, V. P., & Young, T. J. (1977, March). *Interpersonal space preferences as a function of sex and communication apprehension.* Paper presented at the annual convention of the Eastern Communication Association, New York.

McCroskey, J. C., & Sheahan, M. E. (1976, April). *Seating position and participation: An alternative theoretical explanation.* Paper presented at the International Communication Association Convention, Portland, OR.

McDaniel, E. R., & Andersen, P. A. (1995, May). *Intercultural variations in tactile communication: An empirical field study.* Paper presented at the annual convention of the International Communication Association, Albuquerque, NM.

McDaniel, E. R., & Andersen, P. A. (1998). Intercultural variations in tactile communication: A field study. *Journal of Nonverbal Behavior,* 59–75.

McDowell, E. E., McDowell, C. E., & Hyendahl, J. (1980, November). *A multivariate study of teacher immediacy, teaching effectiveness, and student attentiveness at the junior and senior high levels.* Paper presented at the Speech Communication Association Convention, New York.

McDowell, E. E., McDowell, C. E., Hyendahl, J., & Steil, L. K. (1980). A multivariate study of demographics, psychological sex roles, and communication apprehension. *Resources in Education,* 1–18.

McGinley, H., LaFerve, R., & McGinley, A. (1975). The influence of the communicator's body position on opinion change in others. *Journal of Personality and Social Psychology, 31,* 686–690.

McGovern, T. V. (1977). The making of a job interviewee: The effect of nonverbal behavior on an interviewer's evaluations during a selection interview (Doctoral dissertation, Southern Illinois University, 1976). *Dissertation Abstracts International* Vol.

374740B-4741B (University Microfilms No. 77-6239).

McHugo, G. J. (1985). Emotional reactions to a political leader's expressive displays. *Journal of Personality and Social Psychology, 49,* 1513–1529.

McLuhan, M. (1969). *Understanding media: The extensions of man.* New York: Penguin.

McMahon, E. M. (1976). Nonverbal communication as a function of attribution in impression formation. *Communication Monographs, 43,* 287–294.

McNeill, D. (1985). So you think gestures are nonverbal? *Psychological Review, 92,* 350–371.

Medley, D. M., & Mitzel, H. E. (1958). A technique for measuring classroom behavior. *Journal of Educational Psychology, 49,* 86–92.

Meerloo, J. A. M. (1971). A world of smells. In J. A. DeVito (Ed.), *Communication: Concepts and processes* (pp. 134–138). Englewood Cliffs, NJ: Prentice-Hall.

Mehrabian, A. (1968a). Communication without words. *Psychology Today, 2,* 52–55.

Mehrabian, A. (1968b). Inference of attitudes from the posture, orientation, and distance of a communicator. *Journal of Consulting and Clinical Psychology, 32,* 296–308.

Mehrabian, A. (1968c). Relationship of attitude to seated posture, orientation, and distance. *Journal of Personality and Social Psychology, 10,* 26–30.

Mehrabian, A. (1969). Significance of posture and position in the communication of attitude and status relationships. *Psychological Bulletin, 71,* 359–372.

Mehrabian, A. (1970). A semantic space for nonverbal behavior. *Journal of Consulting and Clinical Psychology, 35,* 248–257.

Mehrabian, A. (1971a). *Silent messages.* Belmont, CA: Wadsworth.

Mehrabian, A. (1971b). Verbal and nonverbal interactions of strangers in a waiting situation. *Journal of Experimental Research in Personality, 5,* 127–138.

Mehrabian, A. (1972). *Nonverbal communication.* Chicago: Aldine-Atherton.

Mehrabian, A. (1976). *Public places, private spaces.* New York: Basic Books.

Mehrabian, A. (1981). *Silent messages: Implicit communication of emotions and attitudes.* Belmont, CA: Wadsworth.

Mehrabian, A., & Diamond, S. G. (1971). Seating arrangement and conversation. *Sociometry, 34,* 281–289.

Mehrabian, A., & Ferris, S. R. (1967). Inference of attitudes from nonverbal communication in two channels. *Journal of Consulting Psychology, 31,* 248–252.

Mehrabian, A., & Friar, J. T. (1969). Encoding of attitude by a seated communicator via posture and position cues. *Journal of Consulting and Clinical Psychology, 33,* 330–336.

Mehrabian, A., & Ksionsky, S. (1970). Models for affiliative and conformity behavior. *Psychological Bulletin, 74,* 110–126.

Mehrabian, A., & Weiner, M. (1967). Decoding of inconsistent communications. *Journal of Personality and Social Psychology, 6,* 109–114.

Metha, P., & Clark, M. S. (1994). Toward understanding emotions in intimate relationships. In A. I. Weber & J. H. Harvey (Eds.), *Perspectives on close relationships* (pp. 88–109). Boston, MA: Allyn & Bacon.

Metts, S. (1989). An exploratory study of deception in close relationships. *Journal of Personal and Social Relationships, 6,* 159–179.

Metts, S. (1994). Relational transgressions. In W. R. Cupach & B. H. Spitzberg (Eds.), *The dark side of interpersonal communication* (pp. 217–239). Hillsdale, NJ: Erlbaum.

Metts, S., Cupach, W. R., & Imahori, T. T. (1992). Perceptions of sexual compliance-resisting messages in three types of cross-sex relationships. *Western Journal of Communication, 56,* 1–17.

Metts, S., & Spitzberg, B. H. (1996). Sexual communication in interpersonal contexts: A scripts-based approach. In B. Burleson (Ed.), *Communication yearbook* (pp. 49–91). Thousand Oaks, CA: Sage.

Metts, S., Sprecher, S., & Regan, P. C. (1998). Communication and sexual desire. In P. A. Andersen & L. K. Guerrero (Eds.), *Handbook of communication and emotion: Research, theory, applications, and contexts* (pp. 353–378). San Diego, CA: Academic Press.

Mezzakappa, D., & Andersen, P. A. (1996, February). *Nonverbal cues of crime victims: Perceptions of convicted criminals.* Paper presented at the annual meeting of the Western States Communication Association, Pasadena, CA.

Milgram, S. (1974). *Obedience to authority.* New York: Harper & Row.

Millar, F. E., Rogers-Millar, L. E., & Courtright, J. A. (1979). Relational control and dyadic understanding: An exploratory predictive regression model. In D. Nimmo (Ed.), *Communication yearbook 3* (pp. 213–224). Beverly Hills, CA: Sage.

Millar, M., & Millar, K. (1995). Detection of deception in familiar and unfamiliar persons: The effects of information restriction. *Journal of Nonverbal Behavior, 19,* 69–84.

Miller, G. R., Bauchner, J. E., Hocking, J. E., Frontes, N. E., Kaminski, E. P., & Brandt, D. R. (1981). ". . . and nothing but the truth": How well can observers detect deceptive testimony? In B. D. Sales (Ed.), *Perspectives in law psychology: Vol. 3. The jury, judicial and trial process.* New York: Plenum.

Miller, G. R., & Burgoon, M. (1978). Persuasion research: Review and commentary. In B. D. Ruben (Ed.), *Communication yearbook 2* (pp. 29–47). New Brunswick, NJ: Transaction Books.

Miller, G. R., deTurck, M. A., & Kalbfleish, P. J. (1983). Self-monitoring, rehearsal, and self-deceptive communication. *Human Communication Research, 10,* 97–117.

Miller, G. R., & Hewgill, M. A. (1964). The effect of variations in nonfluency on audience ratings of source credibility. *Quarterly Journal of Speech, 50,* 36–44.

Miller, G. R., & Stiff, J. B. (1993). *Deceptive communication.* Newbury Park, CA: Sage.

Miller, L. C., Cody, M. J., & McLaughlin, M. L. (1994). Situations and goals as fundamental constructs in interpersonal communication research. In M. L. Knapp & G. R. Miller (Eds.), *Handbook of interpersonal communication* (pp. 162–198). Thousand Oaks, CA: Sage.

Miller, N., Maruyama, G., Beaber, R., & Valone, K. (1976). Speed of speech and persuasion. *Journal of Personality and Social Psychology, 34,* 615–624.

Miller, R. S., & Leary, M. R. (1992). Social sources and interactive functions of emotion: The case of embarrassment. In M. S. Clark (Ed.), *Review of personality and social psychology* (Vol. 14, pp. 202–221). Newbury Park, CA: Sage.

Millham, J., & Kellogg, R. W. (1980). Need for social

approval: Impression management or self-deception? *Journal of Research in Personality, 14,* 445–457.

Mills, C. W. (1956). *The power elite.* London: Oxford University Press.

Mills, J., & Aronson, E. (1965). Opinion change as a function of the communicator's attractiveness and desire to influence. *Journal of Personality and Social Psychology, 1,* 173–177.

Milmoe, S., Novey, M. S., Kagan, J., & Rosenthal, R. (1974). The mother's voice: Postdicotor of aspects of her baby's behavior. In S. Weitz (Ed.), *Nonverbal communication: Readings with commentary* (pp. 250–265). New York: Oxford University Press.

Milmoe, S., Rosenthal, R., Blane, H. T., Chafetz, M. E., & Wolf, I. (1979). The doctor's voice: Postdicotor of successful referral of alcoholic patients. In S. Weitz (Ed.), *Nonverbal communication: Readings with commentary* (pp. 266–275). New York: Oxford University Press.

Milne, A. A. (1957). *The world of Pooh.* New York: Dutton.

Mitchell, G., & Maple, T. L. (1985). Dominance in nonhuman primates. In S. L. Ellyson & J. F. Dovidio (Eds.), *Power, dominance, and nonverbal behavior* (pp. 49–66). New York: Springer Verlag.

Mitchell, R. W. (1993). Animals as liars: The human face of nonhuman duplicity. In M. Lewis & C. Saarni (Eds.), *Lying and deception in everyday life* (pp. 59–89). New York: Guilford.

Moe, J. D. (1972). Listener judgments of status cues in speech: A replication and extension. *Speech Monographs, 39,* 144–147.

Molloy, J. T. (1976). *Dress for success.* New York: Warner Books.

Monsour, M. (1992). Meanings of intimacy in cross- and same-sex friendships. *Journal of Social and Personal Relationships, 9,* 277–295.

Montagu, A. (1971/1978). *Touching: The human significance of the skin.* New York: Harper & Row.

Montepare, J. M., Goldstein, S. B., & Clausen, A. (1987). The identification of emotions from gait information. *Journal of Nonverbal Behavior, 11,* 33–42.

Montgomery, B. M. (1988). Quality communication in personal relationships. In S. Duck (Ed.), *Handbook of personal relationships* (pp. 343–362). New York: Wiley & Sons.

Moore, M. M., & Butler, D. L. (1989). Predictive as-

pects of nonverbal courtship behavior in women. *Semiotica 76,* 205–215.

Morris, D. (1971). *Intimate behavior.* New York: Random House.

Morris, D. (1977). *Manwatching: A field guide to human behavior.* New York: Harry N. Abrams.

Morris, D. (1985). *Bodywatching.* New York: Crown.

Morton, T. L. (1977). The effects of acquaintances and distance on intimacy and reciprocity. (Doctoral dissertation, University of Utah, 1976). *Dissertation Abstracts International, 37,* 3680B.

Motley, M. T. (1990). Whether one can(not) communicate: An examination through traditional communication postulates. *Western Journal of Speech Communication, 54,* 1–20.

Motley, M. T. (1991). How one may not communicate: A reply to Andersen. *Communication Studies, 42,* 326–339.

Muehlenhard, C. L., Koralewski, M. A., Andrews, S. L., & Burdick, C. A. (1986). Verbal and nonverbal cues that convey interest in dating: Two studies. *Behavior Therapy, 17,* 404–419.

Mulac, A., Studley, L. B., Wiemann, J. M., & Bradac, J. J. (1987). Male/female gaze in same-sex and mixed-sex dyads: Gender-linked differences in mutual influence. *Human Communication Research, 13,* 323–343.

Mulac, A., & Wiemann, J. M. (1984). Observer-perceived communicator anxiety. In J. A. Daly & M. C. McCroskey (Eds.), *Avoiding communication: Shyness, reticence, and communication apprehension* (pp. 107–121). Beverly Hills, CA: Sage.

Mullen, B. Futrell, D., Stairs, D., Tice, D., Baumeister, R., Dawson, K., Riordan, C., Radioff, C., Goethals, G., Kennedy, J., & Rosenfeld, P. (1986). Newscasters' facial expressions and voting behavior of viewers: Can a smile elect a president? *Journal of Personality and Social Psychology, 51,* 291–295.

Murphy, E. H., & Venables, P. H. (1970). Ear asymmetry in the threshold of fusion of two clocks: A signal detection analysis. *Quarterly Journal of Experimental Psychology, 22,* 288.

Murzynski, J., & Degelman, D. (1996). Body language of women and judgments of vulnerability of sexual assault. *Journal of Applied Social Psychology, 26,* 1617–1626.

Noller, P. (1978). Sex differences in the socialization

of affectionate expression. *Developmental Psychology, 14,* 317–319.

Noller, P. (1980). Gaze in married couples. *Journal of Nonverbal Behavior, 5,* 115–129.

Noller, P. (1982). Channel consistency and inconsistency in the communications of married couples. *Journal of Personality and Social Psychology, 53,* 432–441.

Noller, P. (1984). *Nonverbal communication and marital interaction.* Oxford: Pergamon Press.

Noller, P. (1986). Sex differences in nonverbal communication: Advantage lost or supremacy regained? *Australian Journal of Psychology, 38,* 23–32.

Noller, P. (1987). Nonverbal communication in marriage. In D. Perlman & S. Duck (Eds.), *Intimate relationships: Development, dynamics, and deterioration* (pp. 149–175). Beverly Hills, CA: Sage.

Oatley, K., & Johnson-Laird, P. N. (1987). Toward a cognitive theory of emotions. *Cognition and Emotion, 1,* 29–50.

O'Brien, M. (1979). *The idea of the American South, 1920–1941.* Baltimore: Johns Hopkins University Press.

Ogden, J. A. (1989). Visuospatial and other "right hemispheric" functions after long recovery periods in left-hemispherectomized subjects. *Neuropsychologia, 6,* 765–776.

O'Hair, D., & Cody, M. J. (1994). Deception. In W. R. Cupach & B. H. Spitzberg (Eds.), *The dark side of interpersonal communication* (pp. 181–213). Hillsdale, NJ: Erlbaum.

O'Hair, D., Cody, M. J., & Behnke, R. R. (1985). Communication apprehension and vocal stress as indices of deception. *Western Journal of Speech Communication, 49,* 286–300.

O'Hair, D., Cody, M. J., Choa, E. Y., & Wang, X. (1989, February). *Vocal stress and deception detection among Chinese.* Paper presented at the annual meeting of the Western Speech Communication Association, Spokane, WA.

O'Hair, D., Cody, M. J., & McLaughlin, M. L. (1981). Prepared lies, spontaneous lies, Machiavellianism, and nonverbal communication. *Human Communication Research, 7,* 325–339.

Ohman, A. (1993). Fear and anxiety as emotional phenomena: Clinical phenomenology, evolutionary perspectives, and information-processing mechanisms. In M. L. Lewis & J. M. Haviland (Eds.), *Handbook of emotions* (pp. 511–536). New York: Guilford Press.

Orwell, G. (1949). *1984.* San Diego, CA: Harcourt Brace Jovanovich.

O'Sullivan, M., Ekman, P., & Friesen, W. V. (1988). The effect of comparisons on detecting deceit. *Journal of Nonverbal Behavior, 12,* 203–215.

Palmer, M. T., & Simmons, K. B. (1995). Communicating intentions through nonverbal behaviors: Conscious and nonconscious encoding of liking. *Human Communication Research, 22,* 128–160.

Park, K. A., & Waters, E. (1988). Trait and relationships in developmental perspective. In S. Duck (Ed.), *Handbook of personal relationships* (pp. 161–176). New York: Wiley & Sons.

Parks, M. (1982). Ideology in interpersonal communication: Off the couch and into the world. In M. Burgoon (Ed.), *Communication yearbook 5* (pp. 79–107). New Brunswick, NJ: Transaction Books.

Parks, M. R., & Floyd, K. (1996). Meanings for closeness and intimacy in friendship. *Journal of Social and Personal Relationships, 13,* 85–107.

Patterson, J., & Kim, P. (1991). *The day America told the truth.* New York: Prentice-Hall.

Patterson, M. L. (1973a). Compensation in nonverbal immediacy behaviors: A review. *Sociometry, 36,* 237–252.

Patterson, M. L. (1973b). Stability of nonverbal immediacy behaviors. *Journal of Experimental Social Psychology, 7,* 97–101.

Patterson, M. L. (1976). An arousal model of interpersonal intimacy. *Psychological Review, 83,* 235–245.

Patterson, M. L. (1977). Interpersonal distance, affect, and equilibrium theory. *Journal of Social Psychology, 101,* 205–214.

Patterson, M. L. (1978). The role of space in social interaction. In A. W. Siegman & S. Feldstein (Eds.), *Nonverbal behavior and communication* (pp. 265–290). Hillsdale, NJ: Erlbaum.

Patterson, M. L. (1983). *Nonverbal behavior: A functional perspective.* New York: Springer Verlag.

Patterson, M. L. (1988). Functions of nonverbal behavior in close relationships. In S. Duck (Ed.), *Handbook of personal relationships* (pp. 41–56). New York: Wiley & Sons.

Patterson, M. L. (1995). A parallel process model of nonverbal communication. *Journal of Nonverbal Communication, 19,* 330.

Patterson, M. L., & Edinger, I. A. (1987). A functional analysis of space in social interaction. In A. W. Seigman & S. Feldstein (Eds.), *Nonverbal behavior and communication* (pp. 523–562). Hillsdale, NJ: Erlbaum.

Patterson, M. L., Powell, J. L., & Lenihan, M. G. (1986). Touch, compliance, and interpersonal affect. *Journal of Nonverbal Behavior, 10,* 41–50.

Patterson, M. L., & Ritts, V. (1997). Social and communicative anxiety: A review and meta-analysis. In B. Burleson (Ed.), *Communication yearbook 20* (pp. 263–303). Thousand Oaks, CA: Sage.

Patterson, M. L., & Sechrest, L. B. (1970). Interpersonal distance and impression formation. *Journal of Personality, 38,* 161–166.

Pearce, W. B. (1971). The effect of vocal cues on credibility and attitude change. *Western Speech, 35,* 176–184.

Pearce, W. B., and Conklin, F. (1971). Nonverbal vocalic communication and perception of a speaker. *Speech Monographs, 38,* 235–241.

Pearson, J. C., West, R. L., & Turner, L. H. (1995). *Gender and communication* (3rd ed.). Madison, WI: Brown & Benchmark.

Pennebaker, J. W., Rime, B., & Sproul, G. (1994). *Stereotype of emotional expressiveness of northerners and southerners: A cross-cultural test of Montesquieu's hypotheses.* Unpublished manuscript: Southern Methodist University.

Perlman, D., & Fehr, B. (1987). The development of intimate relationships. In D. Perlman & S. Duck (Eds.), *Intimate relationships* (pp. 13–42). Newbury Park, CA: Sage.

Petronio, S. (1993). Communication boundary management: A theoretical model of managing disclosure of private information between married couples. In S. Petronio, J. K. Alberts, M. L. Hecht, & J. Buley (Eds.), *Contemporary perspectives on interpersonal communication* (pp. 221–240). Madison, WI: Brown, Benchmark.

Petty, R. E., & Cacioppo, J. (1986). The elaboration likelihood model of persuasion. In L. Berkowitz (Ed.), *Advances in experimental social psychology* (Vol. 19, pp. 123–205). New York: Academic Press.

Pfau, M., & Kang, J. G. (1989, November). *The impact of relational and nonverbal communication in political debate influence.* Paper presented at the annual meeting of the Speech Communication Association, San Francisco, CA.

Philpot, J. S. (1983). *The relative contribution to meaning of verbal and nonverbal channels of communication: A meta-analysis.* Unpublished master's thesis, University of Nebraska.

Pisano, M. D., Wall, S. M., & Foster, A. (1986). Perceptions of nonreciprocal touch in romantic relationships. *Journal of Nonverbal Behavior, 10,* 29–40.

Pittam, J., & Scherer, K. R. (1993). Vocal expression and the communication of emotion. In M. Lewis & J. M. Haviland (Eds.), *Handbook of emotions* (pp. 185–198). New York: Guilford.

Planalp, S. (1985). Relational schemata: A test of alternative forms of relational knowledge as a guide to communication. *Human Communication Research, 12,* 3–29.

Planalp, S. (1998). Communicating emotion in everyday life: Cues, channels, and processes. In P. A. Andersen & L. K. Guerrero (Eds.), *Handbook of communication and emotion: Research, theory, applications, and contexts* (pp. 29–48). San Diego, CA: Academic Press.

Planalp, S., DeFrancisco, V. L., & Rutherford, D. (1996). Varieties of cues to emotion occurring in naturally occurring situations. *Cognition and Emotion, 10,* 137–153.

Plax, T. G., Kearney, P., McCroskey, J. C., & Richmond, V. P. (1986). Power in the classroom IV: Verbal control strategies, nonverbal immediacy, and affective learning. *Communication Education, 35,* 43–55.

Plutchik, R. (1980). *Emotion: A psychoevolutionary synthesis.* New York: Harper & Row.

Poizner, H., Klima, E. S., & Bellugi, U. (1987). *What the hands reveal about the brain.* Cambridge, MA: MIT Press.

Porter, R. E., & Samovar, L. A. (1998). Cultural differences in emotional expression: Implications for intercultural communication. In P. A. Andersen & L. K. Guerrero (Eds.), *Handbook of communication and emotion: Research, theory, applications, and contexts* (pp. 452–472). San Diego, CA: Academic Press.

Portnoy, E. J. (1993). The impact of body type on perceptions of attractiveness by older individuals. *Communication Reports, 6,* 101–108.

Portnoy, E. P., & Gardner, J. M. (April, 1980). *A perceptual measure of children's development of somotypic preferences.* Paper presented at the annual meeting of the Eastern Communication Association, Ocean City, MD.

Powell, R. G., & Harville, B. (1990). The effects of teacher immediacy and clarity on instructional outcomes: An intercultural assessment. *Communication Education, 39,* 369–379.

Praeger, K. J. (1995). *The psychology of intimacy.* New York: Guilford.

Premack, A. J., & Premack, D. (1983). *The mind of an ape.* New York: Norton.

Priest, R. F., & Sawyer, J. (1967). Proximity and peership: Bases of balance in interpersonal attraction. *American Journal of Sociology, 72,* 633–649.

Prisbell, M. (1982, May). *Nonverbal communication attributes of power and status in the organizational setting.* Paper presented at the annual convention of the Eastern Communication Association, Hartford, CT.

Prosser, M. H. (1978). *The cultural dialogue: An introduction to intercultural communication.* Boston, MA: Houghton Mifflin.

Pryor, B., & Buchanan, R. W. (1984). The effects of a defendant's demeanor on juror perceptions of credibility and guilt. *Journal of Communication, 34*(3), 92–99.

Puckett, J. M., Petty, R. E., Cacioppo, J. T., & Fischer, D. L. (1983). The relative impact of age and attractiveness stereotypes on persuasion. *Journal of Gerontology, 38,* 340–343.

Ragan, P. C., & Berscheid, E. (1996). Beliefs about state, goals and objects of sexual desire. *Journal of Sex and Marital Therapy, 22,* 110–120.

Rajecki, D. W. (1983). Successful comparative psychology: Four case histories. In D. W. Rajecki (Ed.), *Comparing behavior: Studying man studying animals* (pp. 67–108). Hillsdale, NJ: Erlbaum.

Rathus, S. A., Nevid, J. S., & Fichner-Rathus, L. (1993). Human sexuality in a world of diversity. Boston: Allyn & Bacon.

Rawlins, W. K. (1992). *Friendship matters: Communication, dialectics, and the life course.* New York: Aldine de Gruyler.

Ray, G. B., & Ray, E. B. (1988, November). *The relationship of paralinguistic cues to impression formation and the recall of medical messages.* Paper presented at the annual meeting of the Speech Communication Association, New Orleans, LA.

Reece, M. M., & Whitman, R. N. (1961). Warmth and expressive movements. *Psychological Reports, 8,* 76.

Reece, M. M., & Whitman, R. N. (1962). Expressive movements, warmth, and verbal reinforcement. *Journal of Abnormal and Social Psychology, 64,* 234–236.

Register, L. M., & Henley, T. B. (1992). The phenomenology of intimacy. *Journal of Social and Personal Relationships, 9,* 467–481.

Reis, H. T., & Shaver, P. (1988). Intimacy as an interpersonal process. In S. Duck (Ed.), *Handbook of personal relationships* (pp. 367–389). New York: Wiley & Sons.

Remland, M. S. (1981). Developing leadership skills in nonverbal communication: A situational perspective. *Journal of Business Communication, 18,* 17–29.

Remland, M. S. (1982a). The implicit ad hominem fallacy: Nonverbal displays of status in the argumentative discourse. *Journal of the American Forensic Association, 19,* 79–86.

Remland, M. S. (1982b, November). *Leadership impressions and nonverbal communication in a superior-subordinate interaction.* Paper presented at the annual meeting of the Speech Communication Association, Louisville, KY.

Remland, M. S., & Jones, T. S. (1989). The effects of nonverbal involvement and communication apprehension on state anxiety, interpersonal attraction, and speech duration. *Communication Quarterly, 37,* 170–183.

Remland, M. S., Jones, T. S., & Brickman, H. (1991). Proxemic and haptic behavior in three European countries. *Journal of Nonverbal Behavior, 15,* 215–232.

Rich, A. L. (1974). *Interracial communication.* New York: Harper & Row.

Richards, L., Rollerson, B., & Phillips, J. (1992). Perceptions of submissiveness: Implications for victimization. *Journal of Psychology, 125,* 407–411.

Richardson, J. T. E., & Zucco, G. M. (1989). Cognition and olfaction: A review. *Psychological Bulletin, 105,* 352–360.

Richmond, V. P. (1985). *Communication apprehension, avoidance, and effectiveness.* Scottsdale, AZ: Gorsuch Scarisbrick.

Richmond, V. P., Gorham, J. S., & McCroskey, J. C. (1987). The relationship between selected immediacy behaviors and cognitive learning. In M. L. McLaughlin (Ed.), *Communication yearbook 10* (pp. 574–590). Beverly Hills, CA: Sage.

Richmond, V. P., & McCroskey, J. C. (1985). *Communication: Apprehension, avoidance, and effectiveness.* Scottsdale, AZ: Gorsuch Scarisbrick.

Richmond, V. P., & McCroskey, J. C. (1995). *Nonverbal behavior in interpersonal relations.* Boston, MA: Allyn & Bacon.

Richmond, V. P., McCroskey, J. C., & Payne, S. K. (1987). *Nonverbal communication in interpersonal relations.* Englewood Cliffs, NJ: Prentice-Hall.

Richmond, V. P., McCroskey, J. C., Plax, T. G., & Kearney, P. (1986, November). *Teacher immediacy training and student affect.* Paper presented at the annual convention of the Speech Communication Association, Denver, CO.

Ridgeway, C. L. (1987). Nonverbal behavior, dominance, and the basis of status in task groups. *American Sociological Review, 52,* 683–694.

Ridgeway, C. L., Berger, J., & Smith, L. (1985). Nonverbal cues and status: An expectation states approach. *American Journal of Sociology, 90,* 955–977.

Riggio, R. E., & Friedman, H. S. (1983). Individual differences and cues to deception. *Journal of Personality and Social Psychology, 45,* 899–915.

Riggio, R. E., Tucker, J., & Throckmorton, B. (1987). Social skills and deception ability. *Personality and Social Psychology Bulletin, 13,* 568–577.

Riggio, R. E., Tucker, J., & Widaman, K. F. (1987). Verbal and nonverbal cues as mediators of deception ability. *Journal of Nonverbal Behavior, 11,* 126–145.

Rime, B., Mesquita, B., Philipott, P., & Boca, S. (1991). Beyond the emotional event: Six studies of the social sharing of emotion. *Cognition and Emotion, 5,* 435–465.

Ritts, V., & Patterson, M. L. (1996). Effect of social anxiety and action identification on impressions and thoughts in interaction. *Journal of Social and Clinical Psychology, 15,* 191–205.

Rogers, L. E., & Millar, F. E. (1988). Relational communication. In S. Duck (Ed.), *Handbook of personal relationships* (pp. 289–306). New York: Wiley & Sons.

Rogers, L. E., & Shoemaker, F. F. (1971). *Communication of innovations: A cross-cultural approach.* New York: The Free Press.

Rogers, W. T., & Jones, S. E. (1975). Effects of dominance tendencies on floor holding and interruption behavior in dyadic interaction. *Human Communication Research, 3,* 291–302.

Rosa, E., & Mazur, A. (1979). Incipient status in small groups. *Social Forces, 58,* 18–37.

Rosenfeld, H. M. (1965). Effect of an approval-seeking induction on interpersonal proximity. *Psychological Reports, 17,* 120–122.

Rosenfeld, H. M. (1966a). Approval-seeking and approval-inducing functions of verbal and nonverbal responses in the dyad. *Journal of Personality and Social Psychology, 4,* 597–605.

Rosenfeld, H. M. (1966b). Instrumental affiliative functions of face and gestural expressions. *Journal of Personality and Social Psychology, 4,* 65–72.

Rosenfeld, H. M. (1967). Nonverbal reciprocation of approval: An experimental analysis. *Journal of Experimental and Social Psychology, 3,* 102–111.

Rosenfeld, L., & Civikly, J. (1976). *With words unspoken.* New York: Holt, Rinehart & Winston.

Rosenthal, R., & DePaulo, B. M. (1979). Sex differences in accommodation in nonverbal communication. In R. Rosenthal (Ed.), *Skill in nonverbal communication: Individual differences* (pp. 68–103). Cambridge, MA: Oelgeschlager, Gunn, & Hain.

Rosenthal, R., Hall, J. A., Dimatteo, M. R., Rogers, P. L., & Archer, D. (1979). *Sensitivity to nonverbal communication: The PONS test.* Baltimore, MD: Johns Hopkins University Press.

Rosenthal, R., & Jacobson, L. (1968). *Pygmalion in the classroom: Teacher expectations and pupils' intellectual development.* New York: Holt, Rinehart & Winston.

Rostkowski, M. I. (1986). *After the dancing days.* New York: Harper Trophy.

Rushing, J. H. (1993). Power, other, and spirit in cultural texts. *Western Journal of Communication, 57,* 159–168.

Russell, B. (1938). *Power: A new social analysis.* London: Allen & Unwin.

Russell, J. A. (1989). Measures of emotion. In R. Plutchik & H. Kellerman (Eds.), *Emotion: Theory, research, and experience* (pp. 83–111). New York: Academic Press.

Russell, J. A. (1991). Confusions about context in the judgment of facial expressions: A reply to the contempt expression and the relativity thesis. *Motivation and Emotion, 15*, 17–184.

Russo, N. (1967). Connotation of seating arrangement. *Cornell Journal of Social Relations, 2*, 37–44.

Ryan, E. B., Bourhis, R. Y., & Knops, U. (1991). Evaluating perceptions of patronizing speech to elders. *Psychology and Aging, 6*, 442–450.

Ryans, D. G. (1960). *Characteristics of teachers.* Washington, DC: American Council on Education.

Ryans, D. G. (1964). Research on teacher behavior in the context of the teacher characteristic study. In B. J. Biddle & W. J. Ellena (Eds.), *Contemporary research on teacher effectiveness.* New York: Holt, Rinehart & Winston.

Saarni, C. (1985). Indirect processes in affect socialization. In M. Lewis & C. Saarni (Eds.), *The socialization of emotions* (pp. 187–209). New York: Plenum.

Saarni, C. (1993). Socialization of emotion. In M. Lewis & J. M. Haviland (Eds.), *Handbook of emotions* (pp. 435–446). New York: Guilford.

Sabatelli, R. M., & Rubin, M. (1986). Nonverbal expressiveness and physical attractiveness as mediators of interpersonal perceptions. *Journal of Nonverbal Behavior, 10*, 120–133.

Sadalla, E. K. (1978). Population size, structural differentiation and human behavior. *Environment and Behavior, 10*, 271–289.

Samovar, L. A., & Porter, R. E. (1985). Nonverbal interaction. In L. A. Samovar & R. E. Porter (Eds.), *Intercultural communication: A reader.* Belmont, CA: Wadsworth.

Samovar, L. A., Porter, R. E., & Jain, N. C. (1981). *Understanding intercultural communication.* Belmont, CA: Wadsworth.

Sanders, J. A., & Wiseman, R. L. (1990). The effect of verbal and nonverbal teacher immediacy on perceived cognitive, affective, and behavioral learning in the multicultural classroom. *Communication Education, 39*, 341–353.

Sapir, E. (1928). The unconscious patterning of behavior in society. In E. S. Drummer (Ed.), *The unconscious* (pp. 114–142). New York: Knopf.

Saral, T. (1977). Intercultural communication theory and research: An overview. In B. D. Ruben (Ed.), *Communication yearbook 1* (pp. 389–396). New Brunswick, NJ: Transaction Books.

Scafidi, F. A., Field, T. M., Schanberg, S. M., & Bauer, C. R. (1990). Massage stimulates growth in preterm infants: A replication. *Infant Behavior & Development, 13*, 167–188.

Scheff, T. J. (1995). Conflict in family systems: The role of shame. In J. P. Tangney & K. W. Fischer (Eds.), *Self-conscious emotions: The psychology of shame, guilt, embarrassment and pride* (pp. 393–442). New York: Guilford.

Scheflen, A. E. (1965). Quasi-courtship behavior in psychotherapy. *Psychiatry, 27*, 245–257.

Scheflen, A. E. (1972). *Body language and the social order: Communication as behavior control.* Englewood Cliffs, NJ: Prentice-Hall.

Scheflen, A. E. (1974). *How behavior means.* Garden City, NY: Anchor Books.

Scherer, K. R. (1972). Judging personality from voice: A cross-cultural approach to an old issue in interpersonal perception. *Journal of Personality, 40*, 191–210.

Scherer, K. R. (1979). Acoustic noncomitants of emotional dimensions: Judging affect from synthesized tone sequences. In S. Weitz (Ed.), *Nonverbal communication: Readings with commentary* (pp. 249–253). New York: Oxford University Press.

Scherer, K. R., & Wallbott, H. G. (1994). Evidence for universality and cultural variation of differential emotional response patterning. *Journal of Personality and Social Psychology, 66*, 310–328.

Scherwitz, L., & Helmreich, R. (1973). Interactive effects of eye contact and verbal content on interpersonal attraction in dyads. *Journal of Personality and Social Psychology, 25*, 6–14.

Schiffenbauer, A., & Schiavo, R. S. (1976). Physical distance and attraction: An intensification effect. *Journal of Experimental Social Psychology, 12*, 274–282.

Schlenker, B. R., & Leary, M. R. (1982). Social anxiety and self-presentation: A conceptualization and model. *Psychological Bulletin, 92*, 641–669.

Schlenker, B. R., & Leary, M. R. (1985). Social anxiety and communication about the self. *Journal of Language and Social Psychology, 4,* 171–192.

Schwarzwald, J., Kavish, N., Shoham, M., & Waysman, M. (1977). Fear and sex-similarity as determinants of personal space. *Journal of Psychology, 96,* 55–61.

Seager, J., & Olson, A. (1986). *Women in the world atlas.* New York: Simon & Schuster.

Segrin, C. (1990, November). *Nonverbal behavior and compliance: Affiliation, arousal or dominance.* Paper presented at the annual meeting of the Speech Communication Association, Chicago, IL.

Segrin, C. (1993). The effects of nonverbal behavior on outcomes of compliance-gaining attempts. *Communication Studies, 44,* 169–187.

Segrin, C. (1998). Interpersonal communication problems associated with depression and loneliness. In P. A. Andersen & L. K. Guerrero (Eds.), *Handbook of communication and emotion: Research, theory, applications, and contexts* (pp. 216–242). San Diego, CA: Academic Press.

Selye, H. (1956). *The stress of life.* New York: McGraw-Hill.

Semic, B. A., Miller, T. A., & Guerrero, L. K. (1996, May). *The attractive voice as heard on the answering machine: Vocal determinants of first impressions.* Paper presented at the annual meeting of the International Communication Association, Chicago, IL.

Sennett, R. (1977). *The fall of public man.* New York: Vintage Books.

Shaver, P., Schwartz, J., Kirson, D., & O'Connor, C. (1987). Emotional knowledge: Further explorations of a prototype approach. *Journal of Personality and Social Psychology, 52,* 1061–1086.

Shaver, P., Wu, S., & Schwartz, J. C. (1992). Cross-cultural similarities and differences in emotion and its representation: A prototype approach. In M. S. Clark (Ed.), *Review of personality and social psychology: Emotion* (Vol. 13, pp. 175–212). Newbury Park, CA: Sage.

Shaver, P. R., & Hazan, C. (1988, November). A biased overview of the study of love. *Journal of Social and Personal Relationships, 5,* 473–501.

Shawn, W., & Gregory, A. (1981). *My dinner with Andre.* New York: Grove Press.

Sheldon, W. N. (1940). *The varieties of human physique.* New York: Harper.

Shennum, W. A., & Bugental, D. B. (1982). The development of control over affective expression in nonverbal behavior. In R. S. Feldman (Ed.), *Development of nonverbal behavior in children* (pp. 101–122). New York: Springer Verlag.

Shevrin, H., & Toussieng, P. W. (1965). Vicissitudes of the need for tactile stimulation in instinctual development. *The Psychoanalytic Study of the Child, 20,* 310–339.

Siegel, S. M., Friedlander, M. L., & Heatherington, L. (1992). Nonverbal relational control in family communication. *Journal of Nonverbal Behavior, 16,* 117–139.

Siegman, A. W., & Feldstein, S. (1978). Nonverbal behavior and communication (2nd ed.). New York: Halsted Press.

Silberman, E. K., & Weingartner, H. (1986). Hemispheric lateralization of functions related to emotion. *Brain and Cognition, 5,* 322–353.

Silver, C. A., & Spitzberg, B. H. (1992, July). *Flirtation as social intercourse: Developing a measure of flirtatious behavior.* Paper presented at the Sixth International Conference on Personal Relationships, Orono, ME.

Silverman, A. F., Pressman, H. E., & Bartell, H. W. (1973). Self-esteem and tactile communication. *Journal of Humanistic Psychology, 13,* 73–77.

Sitaram, K. S., & Codgell, R. T. (1976). *Foundations of intercultural communication.* Columbus, OH: Merrill.

Skuse, D. H., James, R. S., Bishop, D. V. M., & Coppin, B. (1997). Evidence from Turner's syndrome of an imprinted X-linked locus affecting cognitive function. *Nature, 387,* 705–708.

Slane, S., Dragan, W., Crandall, J., & Payne, P. (1980). Stress effects on the nonverbal behavior of sensitizers and repressors. *Journal of Psychology, 106,* 101–109.

Smith, D. E., Gier, J. A., & Willis, F. N. (1982). Interpersonal touch and compliance with a marketing request. *Basic and Applied Social Psychology, 3,* 35–38.

Smith, T. W., Ingram, R. E., & Brehm, S. S. (1983). Social anxiety, anxious self-preoccupation, and recall of self-relevant information. *Journal of*

Personality and Social Psychology, 44, 1276–1283.

Sommer, R. (1961). Leadership and group geography. *Sociometry, 24,* 99–110.

Sommer, R. (1965). Leadership and small group ecology. *Sociometry, 28,* 337–348.

Sommer, R. (1967a). Small group ecology. *Psychological Bulletin, 67,* 145–151.

Sommer, R. (1967b). Sociofugal space. *American Journal of Sociology, 72,* 654–660.

Sommer, R. (1969). *Personal space.* Englewood Cliffs, NJ: Prentice-Hall.

Sorensen, G. A. (1979, May). *The effects of touch on interpersonal perceptions.* Paper presented at the annual meeting of the Eastern Communication Association, Philadelphia, PA.

Sparks, G. G., & Greene, J. O. (1992). On the validity of nonverbal indicators as measures of physiological arousal: A reply to Burgoon, Kelley, Newton, and Keeley-Dyerson. *Human Communication Research, 18,* 445–471.

Spiegel, J. P., & Machotka, P. (1974). *Messages of the body.* New York: Free Press.

Spitzberg, B. H. (in press). Sexual coersion in courtship relations. In B. Spitzberg & W. Cupach (Eds.), *The dark side of close relationships.* Mahwah, NJ: Erlbaum.

Spitzberg, B. H., & Cupach, W. R. (1984). *Interpersonal communication competence.* Beverly Hills, CA: Sage.

Spitzberg, B. H., & Cupach, W. R. (1989). *Handbook of interpersonal competence research.* New York: Springer Verlag.

Spitzberg, B. H., & Cupach, W. R. (1994). Dark side denouement. In W. R. Cupach & B. H. Spitzberg (Eds.), *The dark side of interpersonal communication* (pp. 315–320). Hillsdale, NJ: Erlbaum.

Spradlin, J., & Fromme, D. K. (1989). *Parental influences on attitudes toward touch.* Unpublished manuscript, Oklahoma State University.

Stacks, D. W., & Andersen, P. A. (1989). The modular mind: Implications for intrapersonal communication. *Southern Communication Journal, 54,* 273–293.

Stacks, D. W., & Burgoon, J. K. (1979, April). *The persuasive effects of violating spacial distance expectations in small groups.* Paper presented at the

annual meeting of the Southern Speech Communication Association Convention, Biloxi, MS.

Stacks, D. W., & Burgoon, J. K. (1981). The role of nonverbal behaviors as distractors in resistance to persuasion in interpersonal contexts. *Central States Speech Journal, 32,* 61–73.

Stang, D. J. (1973). Effect of interaction rate on ratings of leadership and liking. *Journal of Personality and Social Psychology, 27,* 405–408.

Steckler, N. A., & Rosenthal, R. (1985). Sex differences in nonverbal and verbal communication with bosses, peers, and subordinates. *Journal of Applied Psychology, 70,* 157–163.

Steinem, G. (1994). *Moving beyond words.* New York: Simon & Schuster.

Stelzner, M. A., & Egland, K. L. (1995, February). *Perceived understanding, nonverbal communication, relational satisfaction, and relational stage.* Paper presented at the annual convention of the Western States Communication Association, Portland, OR.

Stephan, F. F. (1952). The relative rate of communication between members of small groups. *American Sociological Review, 17,* 482–486.

Stern, D. (1980). The first relationship: Mother and infant. Cambridge, MA: Harvard University Press.

Sternberg, R. J. (1986). A triangular theory of love. *Psychological Review, 93,* 119–135.

Sternberg, R. J. (1987). *The triangle of love: Intimacy, passion, commitment.* New York: Basic Books.

Steward, A. L., & Lupfer, M. (1987). Touching as teaching: The effect of touch on students' perceptions and performance. *Journal of Applied Psychology, 17,* 800–809.

Stier, D. S., & Hall, J. A. (1984). Gender differences in touch: An empirical and theoretical review. *Journal of Personality and Social Psychology, 47,* 440–459.

Stiff, J. B. (1986). Cognitive processing of persuasive messages: A meta-analysis review of the effects of supporting information on attitudes. *Communication Monographs, 53,* 75–89.

Stiff, J. B., & Boster, F. J. (1987). Cognitive processing: Additional thoughts and a reply to Petty, Kasner, Haugtvedt, and Cacioppo. *Communication Monographs, 54,* 233–249.

Stiff, J. B., Kim, H. J., & Ramesh, C. N. (1989, May). *Truth biases and aroused suspicion in relational de-*

ception. Paper presented at the annual meeting of the International Communication Association, San Francisco, CA.

Street, R. L. (1982). Evaluation of noncontent speech accommodation. *Language and Communication, 2,* 13–31.

Street, R. L., & Brady, R. M. (1982). Speech rate acceptance ranges as a function of evaluative domain, listener speech rate and communication context. *Communication Monographs, 49,* 290–308.

Street, R. L., & Buller, D. B. (1988, November). *Nonverbal response patterns in physician-patient interactions: A functional analysis.* Paper presented at the annual convention of the Speech Communication Association, New Orleans, LA.

Street, R. L., & Giles, H. (1982). Speech accommodation theory: A social cognitive approach to language and speech behavior. In M. Roloff & C. Berger (Eds.), *Social cognition and communication* (pp. 193–226). Beverly Hills, CA: Sage.

Streeter, L. A., Krauss, R. M., Geller, V., Olson, C., & Apple, W. (1979). Pitch changes during attempted deception. In S. Weitz, (Ed.), *Nonverbal communication: Readings with commentary* (pp. 254–267). New York: Oxford University Press.

Strodtbeck, F. L., & Hook, L. H. (1961). The social dimensions of a twelve-man jury table. *Sociometry, 24,* 397–415.

Strongman, K. T., & Chapness, B. F. (1968). Dominance hierarchies and conflict in eye contact. *Acta Psychologica, 28,* 376–386.

Strube, M. J., & Werner, C. (1984). Personal space claims as a function of interpersonal threat: The mediating role of need for control. *Journal of Nonverbal Behavior, 8,* 195–209.

Strzyzewski, K. (1990, November). *A model of effective expression as interpersonal influence.* Paper presented at the annual meeting of the Speech Communication Association, Chicago, IL.

Swann, W. B., Griffith, J. J., Predmore, S. C., & Gaines, B. (1987). The cognitive-affective crossfire: When consistency confronts self-enhancement. *Journal of Personality and Social Psychology, 52,* 881–889.

Takala, M. (1977). Consistencies and perception of consistencies in individual psychomotion behav-

ior. In D. Magnusson & N. S. Endler (Eds.), *Personality at the crossroads: Current issues in interactional psychology.* Hillsdale, NJ: Erlbaum.

Tangney, J. P. (1995). Shame and guilt in interpersonal relationships. In J. P. Tangney & K. W. Fischer (Eds.), *Self-conscious emotions: The psychology of shame, guilt, embarrassment and pride* (pp. 114–139). New York: Guilford.

Taraban, C. B., Hendrick, S. S., & Hendrick, C. (1998). Loving and liking. In P. A. Andersen & L. K. Guerrero (Eds.), *Handbook of communication and emotion: Research, theory, applications, and contexts* (pp. 331–351). San Diego, CA: Academic Press.

Tessler, R., & Sushelsky, L. (1978). Effects of eye contact and social status on the perception of a job applicant in an employment interviewing situation. *Journal of Vocational Behavior, 13,* 138–147.

Thayer, S. (1969). The effect of interpersonal looking duration on dominance judgments. *Journal of Social Psychology, 79,* 285–286.

Thayer, S. (1986a). History and strategies of research on social touch. *Journal of Nonverbal Behavior, 10,* 12–28.

Thayer, S. (1986b). Touch: Frontier of intimacy. *Journal of Nonverbal Behavior, 10,* 7–11.

Thayer, S., & Schiff, W. (1974). Observer judgment of social interaction: Eye contact and relationship inferences. *Journal of Personality and Social Psychology, 30,* 110–114.

Thompson, H. S. (1971). *Fear and loathing in Las Vegas: A savage journey to the heart of the American dream.* New York: Random House.

Thompson, J. J. (1973). *Beyond words: Nonverbal communication in the classroom.* New York: Citation.

Thorson, J. A., & Kasworm, C. (1984). Sunshine and suicide: Possible influences of climate on behavior. *Death Education, 8,* 125–136.

Ting-Toomey, S. T. (1991). Intimacy expressions in three cultures: France, Japan, and the United States. *International Journal of Intercultural Relations, 15,* 29–46.

Tocqueville, A. D. (1835/1945). Democracy in America (Vol. 1). New York: Vintage Books.

Todd-Mancillas, W. R. (1982). Classroom environments and nonverbal behavior. In L. L. Barker (Ed.), *Communication in the classroom: Original essays* (pp. 77–97). Englewood Cliffs, NJ: Prentice-Hall.

Tomkins, S. S. (1962). *Affect, imagery, consciousness: Vol. 1. The positive affects.* New York: Springer Verlag.

Tomkins, S. S. (1963). *Affect, imagery, consciousness: Vol. 2. The negative affects.* New York: Springer Verlag.

Tomkins, S. S. (1984). Affect theory. In K. R. Scherer & P. Ekman (Eds.), *Approaches to emotion* (pp. 163–195). Hillsdale, NJ: Erlbaum.

Trager, G. L. (1958). Paralanguage: A first approximation. *Studies in Linguistics, 13,* 1–12.

Trenholm, S., & Petrie, C. R. (1980). Reexamining body accessibility. *Australian Scan: Journal of Human Communication, 7–8,* 33–42.

Trost, M. R., & Engstrom, C. (1994, February). *"Hit the road Jack": Strategies for rejecting flirtatious advances.* Paper presented at the annual meeting of the Western States Communication Association, San Jose, CA.

Trout, D. L., & Rosenfeld, H. M. (1980). The effect of postural lean and body congruence on the judgment of psychotherapeutic rapport. *Journal of Nonverbal Behavior, 4,* 176–190.

Tucker, D. M. (1981). Lateral brain function, emotion, and conceptualization. *Psychological Bulletin, 89,* 19–46.

Turner, R. E., Edgley, C., & Olmstead, G. (1975). Information control in conversations: Honesty is not always the best policy. *Kansas Journal of Sociology, 11,* 69–89.

Ullman, S. E., & Knight, R. A. (1992). A multivariate model for predicting rape and physical injury outcomes during sexual assaults. *Journal of Consulting and Clinical Psychology, 60,* 28.

Vaid, J., Bellugi, U., & Poizner, H. (1989). Hand dominance for signing: Clues to brain lateralization of language. *Neuropsychologia, 27,* 949–960.

Valentine, M. E. (1980). The attenuating influence of gaze upon the bystander intervention effect. *Journal of Social Psychology, 3,* 197–203.

Vancil, D. L., & Pendell, S. D. (1987). The myth of viewer-listener disagreement in the first Kennedy-Nixon debate. *Central States Speech Journal, 38,* 16–27.

Vangelisti, A. L., & Daly, J. A. (1997). Gender differences in standards for romantic relationships. *Personal Relationships, 4,* 203–219.

Vangelisti, A. L., & Sprague, R. J. (1998). Guilt and hurt: Similarities, distinctions, and conversational strategies. In P. A. Andersen & L. K. Guerrero (Eds.), *Handbook of communication and emotion: Research, theory, applications, and contexts* (pp. 123–153). San Diego, CA: Academic Press.

Van Hoofe, J. A. R. A. M. (1972). A comparative approach to the phylogeny of laughter and smiling. In R. A. Hinde (Ed.), *Non-verbal communication* (pp. 209–238). Cambridge, England: Cambridge University Press.

Vollmer, J. J., & Gordon, S. A. (1975). Chemical communication. *Chemistry, 48,* 6–11.

Vrij, A. (1994). The impact of information and setting on detection of deception by police detectives. *Journal of Nonverbal Behavior, 18,* 117–136.

Vrij, A., & Semin, G. R. (1996). Lie experts' beliefs about nonverbal indicators of deception. *Journal of Nonverbal Behavior, 20,* 65–80.

Vrij, A., Semin, G. R., & Bull, R. (1996). Insight into behavior displayed during deception. *Human Communication Research, 22,* 544–562.

Vrij, A., & Winkel, F. W. (1991). Cultural patterns in Dutch and Surinam nonverbal behavior: An analysis of simulated police citizen encounters. *Journal of Nonverbal Behavior, 15,* 169–184.

Waller, R. J. (1992). *The bridges of Madison County.* New York: Warner Books.

Walster, E., Walster, G. W., & Berscheid, E. (1978). *Equity: Theory and research.* Boston, MA: Allyn & Bacon.

Ward, C. D. (1968). Seating arrangement and leadership emergence in small discussion groups. *Journal of Social Psychology, 74,* 83–90.

Ward, R. D. (1918). *Climate: Considered especially in relation to man.* New York: Putnam.

Warner, R. M., Malloy, D., Schnieder, K., Knoth, R., & Wilder, B. (1987). Rhythmic organization of social interaction and observer ratings of positive affect and involvement. *Journal of Nonverbal Behavior, 11,* 57–74.

Watson, D., & Clark, L. A. (1984). Negative affectivity: The disposition to experience aversive emotional states. *Psychological Bulletin, 96,* 465–490.

Watzlawick, P., Beavin, J. H., & Jackson, D. D. (1967).

Pragmatics of human communication. New York: Norton.

Weiner, A. N. (1973). *Machiavellianism as a predictor of group interaction and cohesion.* Unpublished master's thesis, West Virginia University, Morgantown, WV.

Weiner, H. (1966). External chemical messengers: Emission and reception in man. *New York State Journal of Medicine, 66,* 3153–3170.

Weins, A. N., Thompson, S. M., Matarazzo, J. A., Matarazzo, R. G., & Saslow, G. (1965). Interview interaction behavior of supervisors, head nurses, and staff nurses. *Nursing Research, 14,* 322–329.

Weiss, K. R. (1997, January 13). Survey finds record stress in the class of 2000. *Los Angeles Times,* p. 1.

Wells, W., & Siegel, B. (1961). Stereotyped somatypes. *Psychological Reports, 8,* 77–78.

Wertin, L., & Andersen, P. A. (1995). *Sexual harassment and cognitive schemata: A test of cognitive-valence theory.* Unpublished study, School of Communication, San Diego State University.

Wertin, L., & Andersen, P. A. (1996, February). *Cognitive schemata and perceptions of sexual harassment: A test of cognitive valence theory.* Paper presented at the annual convention of the Western States Communication Association, Pasadena, CA.

Wheeler, D. L. (1994, November). Lessons in the signs: Researchers explore the world of the deaf to study the evolution of language. *Chronicle of Higher Education,* A6–A14.

Wheeless, L. R. (1978). A follow-up study of the relationships among trust, disclosure, and interpersonal solidarity. *Human Communication Research, 4,* 143–157.

Whicker, M. L., & Kronenfeld, J. J. (1986). *Sex role changes: Technology, politics, and policy.* New York: Praeger.

White, G. L., & Mullen, P. E. (1989). *Jealousy: Theory, research, and clinical strategies.* New York: Guilford.

Whybrow, P. (1984). Contributions from neuroendocrinology. In K. R. Scherer & P. Ekman, *Approaches to emotion* (pp. 59–75). Hillsdale, NJ: Erlbaum.

Weiner, M., Devoe, S., Rubinow, S., & Geller, J. (1972). Nonverbal behavior and nonverbal communication. *Psychological Review, 79,* 185–214.

Weiner, M., & Mehrabian, A. (1968). *Language within language: Immediacy, a channel in verbal communication.* New York: Appleton-Century-Crofts.

Wilden, A. (1972). Analog and digital communication. *Semiotica, 10,* 50–82.

Wilden, A. (1980). *System and structure.* New York: Tavistock.

Wilkins, B. M., & Andersen, P. A. (1991). Gender differences and similarities in management communication: A meta-analysis. *Management Communication Quarterly, 5,* 6–35.

Willis, F. N., & Hamm, H. (1980). The use of interpersonal touch in security compliance. *Journal of Nonverbal Behavior, 5,* 49–55.

Willis, F. N., & Rawdon, V. A. (1994). Gender and national difference in attitude toward same-gender touch. *Perceptual and Motor Skills, 78,* 1027–1034.

Wilson, B. J., & Smith, S. L. (1998). Children's responses to emotional portrayals on television. In P. A. Andersen & L. K. Guerrero (Eds.), *Handbook of communication and emotion: Research, theory, applications, and contexts* (pp. 533–569). San Diego, CA: Academic Press.

Wiseman, R. (1995). The megalab truth test. *Science, 373,* 391.

Witte, K. (1998). Fear as motivator, fear as inhibitor: Using the extended parallel process model to explain fear appeal successes and failures. In P. A. Andersen & L. K. Guerrero (Eds.), *Handbook of communication and emotion: Research, theory, applications, and contexts* (pp. 423–450). San Diego, CA: Academic Press.

Wood, J. T. (1996). Gender, relationships, and communication. In J. T. Wood (Ed.), *Gendered relationships* (pp. 3–19). Mountain View, CA: Mayfield.

Wood, J. T. (1997a). Clarifying the issues. *Personal Relationships, 4,* 221–228.

Wood, J. T. (1997b). *Gendered lives: Communication, gender, and culture.* Belmont, CA: Wadsworth.

Wood, J. T., & Inman, C. T. (1993). In another mode: Masculine styles of communicating closeness. *Journal of Applied Communication Research, 21,* 279–295.

Woodall, W. G., & Burgoon, J. K. (1981). The effects of nonverbal synchrony on message comprehension and persuasiveness. *Journal of Nonverbal Behavior, 5,* 207–223.

Woodall, W. G., & Burgoon, J. K. (1983). Talking fast and changing attitudes: A critique and clarification. *Journal of Nonverbal Behavior, 8,* 126–142.

Woodruff, C., & Premack, D. (1979). Intentional communication in the chimpanzee: The development of deception. *Cognition, 7,* 333–362.

Wooley, S. C., & Wooley, O. W. (1984, February). Feeling fat in a thin society. *Glamour,* 198–252.

Young, D. M., Beier, E. G., & Beier, S. (1979). Beyond words: Influence of nonverbal behavior of female job applicants in the employment interview. *Personnel and Guidance Journal, 57,* 346–350.

Zajonc, R. B. (1980). Feeling and thinking: Preferences need no inferences. *American Psychologist, 35,* 151–175.

Zajonc, R. B. (1984). On primacy of affect. In K. S. Scherer & P. Ekman (Eds.), *Approaches to emotion* (pp. 259–270). Hillsdale, NJ: Erlbaum.

Zelinsky, W. (1973). *The cultural geography of the United States.* Englewood Cliffs, NJ: Prentice-Hall.

Ziegler-Kratz, N., & Marshall, L. L. (1990). Impressions of therapists: The effects of gaze, smiling, and gender. *Journal of Psychology and the Behavioral Sciences, 5,* 115–129.

Zivin, G. (1982). Watching the sands shift: Conceptualizing development of nonverbal mastery. In R. S. Feldman (Ed.), *Development of nonverbal behavior in children* (pp. 63–98). New York: Springer Verlag.

Zlutnick, S., & Altman, F. (1972). Crowding and human behavior. In J. F. Wohlwill & D. H. Carson (Eds.), *Environment and the social sciences: Perspectives and applications.* Washington, DC: American Psychological Association.

Zuckerman, M., DePaulo, B. M., & Rosenthal, R.

(1981). Verbal and nonverbal communication of deception. In L. Berkowitz (Ed.), *Advances in experimental social psychology* (Vol. 14, pp. 2–59). New York: Academic Press.

Zuckerman, M., & Driver, R. E. (1985). Telling lies: Verbal and nonverbal correlates of deception. In A. W. Siegman & S. Feldstein (Eds.), *Multichannel integrations of nonverbal behavior* (pp. 129–148). Hillsdale, NJ: Erlbaum.

Zuckerman, M., & Driver, R. E. (1989). What sounds beautiful is good: The vocal attractiveness stereotype. *Journal of Nonverbal Behavior, 13,* 67–82.

Zuckerman, M., Fischer, S. A., Osmun, R. W., Winkler, B. A., & Wolfson, L. R. (1987). Anchoring in lie detection revisited. *Journal of Nonverbal Behavior, 11,* 4–12.

Zuckerman, M., Hodgins, H., & Miyake, K. (1990). The vocal attractiveness stereotype: Replication and elaboration. *Journal of Nonverbal Behavior, 14,* 97–112.

Zuckerman, M., Koestner, R., & Alton, A. O. (1984). Learning to detect deception. *Journal of Personality and Social Psychology, 46,* 519–528.

Zuckerman, M., Koestner, R., Colella, M. J., & Alton, A. O. (1984). Anchoring in the detection of deception and leakage. *Journal of Personality and Social Psychology, 47,* 301–311.

Zuckerman, M., Spiegel, N. H., DePaulo, B. M., & Rosenthal, R. (1982). Nonverbal strategies for decoding deception. *Journal of Nonverbal Behavior, 6,* 171–187.

Zweigenhaft, R. L. (1976). Personal space in the faculty office: Desk placement and the student-faculty interaction. *Journal of Applied Psychology, 61,* 529–532.

Credits

Text Credits

Chapter 2 pp. 33, 51, from J. B. Cortes and F. M. Gatti, "Physique and self-description of temperament," *Journal of Consulting Psychology, 29,* 434, 1965. Used with permission; p. 60, T 3.1, from J. K. Burgoon and T. J. Saine, *The Unspoken Dialogue: An Introduction to Nonverbal Communication.* Copyright © 1978 Houghton Mifflin Company. Reprinted by permission. **Chapter 5** p. 130 and **Chapter 12** p. 332, from Dr. Loretta Malandro, *Your Every Move Talks,* Gorsuch Scarisbrick Publishers, Dubuque, IA. Copyright © 1977 Loretta Malandro. Used with permission from the author.

Photo Credits

Chapter 1 p. 8, © Myrleen Ferguson/PhotoEdit; p. 20, © Cleo/PhotoEdit. **Chapter 2** p. 37, © Joel Gordon; p. 39, Courtesy of the author. **Chapter 3** p. 57, © Bonnie Kamin/PhotoEdit; p. 59, © Mark Richards/PhotoEdit. **Chapter 4** p. 79, © Anna E. Zuckerman/PhotoEdit; p. 80, © Cindy Charles/PhotoEdit; p. 87, © A. Ramey/PhotoEdit; p. 88, © Markham Johnson/Robert Holmes Photography; p. 90, © Figaro Magahn/Photo Researchers, Inc. **Chapter 5** p. 112, © Nancy Sheehan/PhotoEdit; p. 117, © Amy C. Etra/PhotoEdit; p. 119, © Joel Gordon. **Chapter 6** p. 138, © Chester Higgins, Jr./Photo Researchers, Inc.; p. 140, © Joel Gordon; p. 141, © Robert Brenner/PhotoEdit; p. 142, © Joel Gordon; p. 144, © Michael Newman/PhotoEdit; p. 145, © Michael Newman/PhotoEdit. **Chapter 7** p. 172, © Tony Freeman/PhotoEdit; p. 182, © Barbara Rowell/Mountain Light. **Chapter 8** p. 188, © Paul Conklin/PhotoEdit; p. 196, © Ursula Markus/Photo Researchers, Inc. **Chapter 9** p. 220, © Barbara Rios/Photo Researchers, Inc.; p. 222, Courtesy of the author. **Chapter 10** p. 263, Everett Collection; p. 267, © Melanie Carr/Zephyr Pictures. **Chapter 11** p. 295, © UPI/Corbis-Bettmann; p. 302, © UPI/Corbis-Bettmann. **Chapter 12** p. 308, © Davis Barber/PhotoEdit; p. 327, © Tom McCarthy/PhotoEdit

Name Index

Subject Index